The Two Faces of Liberalism

How the Hoover-Roosevelt Debate Shapes the 21st Century

Original Material Selected and Edited by
Gordon Lloyd

M&M Scrivener Press

Published by   M & M Scrivener Press
3 Winter Street, Suite 3, Salem, MA 01970

www.scrivenerpublishing.com

Copyright © 2007 M & M Scrivener Press
First published 2006, reprinted 2010

Conflicts and Trends™in Business Ethics
Series Editor, Nicholas Capaldi

Library of Congress Cataloging-In-Publication Data

The two faces of liberalism : how the Hoover-Roosevelt debate shapes
the 21st century / original material selected and edited by Gordon
Lloyd.
    p. cm. -- (Conflicts and trends in business ethics)
  Includes bibliographical references and index.

  ISBN-10: 0-9764041-2-5 (hardcover : alk. paper)
  ISBN-13: 978-0-9764041-2-5 (hardcover : alk. paper)

  1. New Deal, 1933-1939--Sources. 2. United States--Politics and govern-
ment--1929-1933--Sources. 3. United States--Politics and government--
1933-1945--Sources. 4. Liberalism--United States--History--20th century--
Sources. 5. Liberty--History--20th century--Sources. 6. Hoover, Herbert,
1874-1964--Political and social views. 7. Roosevelt, Franklin D. (Franklin
Delano), 1882-1945--Political and social views. 8. Hoover, Herbert, 1874-
1964--Influence. 9. Roosevelt, Franklin D. (Franklin Delano), 1882-1945--
Influence. I. Lloyd, Gordon, 1942- II. Hoover, Herbert, 1874-1964. III.
Roosevelt, Franklin D. (Franklin Delano), 1882-1945.

E806.T88 2007
973.917--dc22
2006025950

Front cover: photo from the Franklin D. Roosevelt Library
Cover design by Hannus Design

Printed in the United States on acid-free paper.

Contents

Foreword by George H. Nash

Acknowledgements

Introduction   1

Chapter 1: The Nature of "Our American System"   25
1928-1931

I	Herbert Hoover: Presidential Nomination Address August 11, 1928	25
II	Herbert Hoover: Campaign Speech, New York, October 22, 1928	35
III	Herbert Hoover: Campaign Speech, St. Louis, November 2, 1928	39
IV	Herbert Hoover: Annual Message to Congress, December 2, 1930	47
V	Franklin D. Roosevelt: Address to Conference of Governors, June 2, 1931	53
VI	Herbert Hoover: Annual Message to Congress, December 8, 1931	54

Chapter 2: The Need for "Bold, Persistent Experimentation"   66
1932

VII	Franklin D. Roosevelt: Radio Address, *The Forgotten Man*, April 7, 1932	66
VIII	Franklin D. Roosevelt: Oglethorpe University Address, May 22, 1932	69
IX	Democratic Party Platform, June 30, 1932	75
X	Republican Party Platform, Summer 1932	79
XI	Franklin D. Roosevelt: Presidential Nomination Address, July 2, 1932	95
XII	Herbert Hoover: Presidential Nomination Address, August 11, 1932	104
XIII	Franklin D. Roosevelt: Commonwealth Club Address, September 23, 1932	114
XIV	Herbert Hoover: Campaign Speech, New York, October 31, 1932	123
XV	Franklin D. Roosevelt: Address on Long-Range Planning, October 31, 1932	139

XVI   Herbert Hoover: Annual Message to Congress,
           December 6, 1932   148
XVII   Herbert Hoover: Letter to Franklin D. Roosevelt,
           December 20, 1932   154
XVIII   Franklin D. Roosevelt: Letter to Herbert Hoover,
           December 21, 1932   155

Chapter 3: "The Only Thing We Have to Fear is Fear Itself"   157
                               1933-1935
XIX   Herbert Hoover: Letter to Franklin D. Roosevelt,
           February 18, 1933   157
XX   Herbert Hoover: Letter to Franklin D. Roosevelt,
           February 28, 1933   159
XXI   Franklin D. Roosevelt: Letter to Herbert Hoover,
           March 1, 1933   160
XXII   Franklin D. Roosevelt: First Inaugural Address,
           March 4, 1933   160
XXIII   Franklin D. Roosevelt: Fireside Chat, *Banking Crisis,*
           March 12, 1933   165
XXIV   Franklin D. Roosevelt: Fireside Chat, *The New Deal
           Program,* May 7, 1933   169
XXV   The Agricultural Adjustment Act, May 12, 1933   174
XXVI   The National Industrial Recovery Act, June 16, 1933   181
XXVII   Franklin D. Roosevelt: Executive Order NLRB,
           June 29, 1934   189
XXVIII   Franklin D. Roosevelt: Annual Message to Congress,
           January 4, 1935   193
XXIX   A.L.A. Schechter Poultry Corp. v. United States,
           May 27, 1935   201
XXX   The National Labor Relations Act, July 5, 1935   211
XXXI   The Social Security Act, August 14, 1935   216
XXXII   Herbert Hoover: *Spending, Deficits, Debts,* October 5, 1935   229
XXXIII   Franklin D. Roosevelt: *The Meaning of Progress,*
           November 29, 1935   238

Chapter 4: "The Confused State of the Union"   242
                               1936
XXXIV   United States v. Butler, January 6, 1936   242
XXXV   Franklin D. Roosevelt: Annual Message to Congress,
           January 3, 1936   257
XXXVI   Herbert Hoover: *The Confused State of the Union,*
           February 12, 1936   261
XXXVII   Herbert Hoover: *Crisis to Free Men,* June 10, 1936   271

XXXVIII Republican Party Platform, June 11, 1936   280
XXXIX   Democratic Party Platform, June 25, 1936   287
XL   Franklin D. Roosevelt: Re-Nomination Address,
        June 27, 1936   292
XLI   Franklin D. Roosevelt: Fireside Chat, *Dignity of
        Labor,* September 6, 1936   297
XLII   Franklin D. Roosevelt: Address on Private Enterprise,
        October 23, 1936   303

Chapter 5: "Layman's Document or Lawyer's Contract?"   **307**
                              1937
XLIII   Franklin D. Roosevelt: Second Inaugural Address,
        January 20, 1937   307
XLIV   Herbert Hoover: *Hands off the Supreme Court,*
        February 20, 1937   312
XLV   Franklin D. Roosevelt: Fireside Chat, *Reorganization Plan,*
        March 9, 1937   318
XLVI   West Coast Hotel Co. v. Parrish, March 29, 1937   327
XLVII   N.L.R.B. v. Jones & Laughlin Steel Corporation,
        April 12, 1937   332
XLVIII Franklin D. Roosevelt: *A Fair Day's Pay,* May 24, 1937   340
XLIX   Steward Machine Co. v. Davis, May 24, 1937   342
L   Helvering, et. al. v. Davis, May 24, 1937   347
LI   Senate Judiciary Committee Adverse Report, June 7, 1937   350
LII   Franklin D. Roosevelt: Address on Constitution Day,
        September 17, 1937   357
LIII   Herbert Hoover: *Economic Security,* December 16, 1937   365

Chapter 6: The Fate of "Our American System"   **375**
                           1938-1941
LIV   Herbert Hoover: *Challenge to Liberty,* April 8, 1938   375
LV   Franklin D. Roosevelt: Message on Economic
        Concentration, April 29, 1938   379
LVI   Herbert Hoover: *The Dangerous Road for Democracy,*
        May 5, 1938   387
LVII   Franklin D. Roosevelt: Annual Message to Congress,
        January 4, 1939   392
LVIII   Herbert Hoover: *The Real State of the Union,*
        February 13, 1939   402
LVIX   Herbert Hoover: Radio Address, October 24, 1940   411
LX   Franklin D. Roosevelt: Third Inaugural Address,
        January 20, 1941   412

Index   415

Foreword

American politics has often been marked by great rivalries: Thomas Jefferson and Alexander Hamilton, Daniel Webster and John C. Calhoun, Abraham Lincoln and Steven A. Douglas, Woodrow Wilson and Henry Cabot Lodge. In more recent times, presidential elections have frequently pivoted on feuds and quarrels between ambitious men: Lyndon Johnson and John F. Kennedy, Kennedy and Richard Nixon, George W. Bush and John McCain.

In the volume before you, we are introduced to another notable (though less celebrated) presidential rivalry, expressed in the form of a decade-long "conversation" over some of the deepest issues in American public life. Herbert Hoover and Franklin Roosevelt were not always adversaries. Their acquaintance began in 1917 in Washington, D. C., where each was serving in the wartime administration of President Wilson: Hoover as United States Food Administrator and Roosevelt as Assistant Secretary of the Navy. Although never intimates, they had good friends in common, socialized from time to time, and appeared to share a Progressive, Wilsonian outlook—to the extent that an admiring Roosevelt came to see in Hoover a worthy heir to Woodrow Wilson's mantle.

Early in January 1920, Roosevelt wrote to a friend about Hoover: "He is certainly a wonder, and I wish we could make him President of the United States. There could not be a better one." In the next few weeks, Roosevelt quietly encouraged efforts by Democratic and progressive activists to draft Hoover for President on the Democratic party ticket. It is likely that Roosevelt hoped to be Hoover's running mate.

Hoover seemed receptive if ambivalent, at first declaring himself an "independent progressive," repelled by Republican "reactionaries" and democratic "radicals" alike. Eventually the Food Administrator and humanitarian hero, who had been a Bull Moose Progressive in 1912, affirmed a Republican affiliation and maneuvered unsuccessfully for the Republican presidential nomination won by Warren G. Harding. Meanwhile Roosevelt got the Democratic vice presidential nomination he coveted, on a losing ticket headed by James M. Cox.

Although Hoover and Roosevelt's political paths now diverged decisively, the two men remained outwardly friendly during most of the 1920s. As Secretary of Commerce under Presidents Harding and Coolidge, Hoover became one of the three or four most influential men in Washington, a man-on-the-move who hoped to land in the White House. Roosevelt, nearly eight years younger, was an-out-of-office Democrat, soon afflicted with polio and struggling to maintain his political viability. As president of a new trade association called the American Construction Council, he attempted with Hoover's blessing to reform the nation's troubled construction industry. The project brought him into contact with the powerful Secretary of Commerce and provided an opportunity to bask in the reflected glory of his "old friend," Herbert Hoover.

All this changed in 1928, when Hoover was elected President and Roosevelt the governor of New York. Their lingering friendship quickly curdled into a rivalry. At the heart of it was colliding ambition— Hoover was President and Roosevelt wanted to be—exacerbated by a number of unpleasant encounters, misunderstandings, and consequent mistrust. Although personal factors frayed and helped to destroy their friendship, their differences transcended personality and became expressed in ideological terms.

Which brings us to the book of documents in your hands. In 1932, when they battled each other for the presidency, Hoover and Roosevelt both insisted that this was no ordinary campaign. For Roosevelt it was "a call to arms"—a crusade—for a "New Deal" and "a new order of competence and courage" in which the "forgotten man" would finally receive his due. Hoover was equally dramatic. "This contest is more than a contest between two men," he declared in October 1932. "It is more than a contest between two parties. It is a contest between two philosophies of government." The election, he warned—in words he later deemed prophetic—would determine the nation's course for "over a century to come."

Both men meant what they said. In the speeches and related documents assembled in this volume, they articulated a fundamental clash of visions over the American economy, over the "American system of life" (as Hoover called it), and over the essence of American self-understanding—all against the backdrop of a frightening national emergency, the worst since the Civil War.

Hoover and Roosevelt—once friends, now enemies—never met again after March 4, 1933, the day of Roosevelt's presidential inauguration. Yet as Gordon Lloyd's collection of documents abundantly discloses, their frank, long-distance "conversation" did not end. As Roosevelt's New Deal unfolded, the rivalry between himself and his predecessor flared anew, with the roles reversed: now it was Hoover's turn to be the critic and accuser.

Once again, personal ambition and mutual distrust helped to goad the two combatants. Hoover, especially, yearned for an election rematch and vindication. But the argument between them dwarfed such particularities. Both knew that they were engaged in a contest for the American mind and political soul. What had gone wrong since 1929? Was the Great Depression a crisis of capitalism, a product of Hooverian mismanagement, or a catastrophe brought on by uncontrollable happenings abroad? Was the New Deal a humane and pragmatic reform movement or a muddled and meddlesome experiment in collectivism? Did the traditional "American System" of limited government, private initiative, and volunteerism fail disastrously in 1929-1932, or did its successor launch America on a dangerous spiral into socialism? Did the New Deal save American capitalism, or did it delay recovery and poison the wellsprings of prosperity? The political winds blew fiercely in the 1930s. Both Hoover and Roosevelt helped to sustain their intensity.

The two protagonists whose words are reproduced in these pages are long gone from the national scene. Yet it is noteworthy how fresh and resonant their claims and counterclaims continue to be. Ever since the Gilded Age (as someone has observed) the Free Market and Governmental Regulation have defined a polarity in our discourse on public policy: Which is the problem? Which is the solution? In 1981, for instance, in his first inaugural address, President Ronald Reagan boldly proclaimed his intention to "curb the size and influence" of the federal government and to make it "stand by our side, not ride on our back." "We are a nation that has a government," he asserted—"not the other way around."

Herbert Hoover was not a pure Reaganite; there was in him too much of the social engineer and temperamental activist for such a label to be affixed to his name. It has been said of Hoover that he was too progressive for the conservatives and too conservative for the radicals. In the 1920s, as a highly energetic Secretary of Commerce, he often chafed under the constraints of his conservative boss, President Calvin Coolidge." But in the larger sweep of the twentieth century, as Professor Lloyd's fine collection illustrates, Hoover the anti New-Dealer clearly contributed to the critique of ever-aggrandizing statism which has long been integral to American conservatism.

In one sense the Hoover-Roosevelt conversation is over: Franklin Roosevelt won his "revolution." His New Deal liberal welfare state is in place (and then some), and no frontal assault upon it stands much chance of success at the polls. Yet philosophically, rhetorically, and at times programmatically, the Roosevelt/New Dealish approach to public policy remains problematic, thanks in part to Herbert Hoover and the experience of the American people since the Great Depression. Where in American politics should one draw the line between individual liberty and public obligation, between self-reliance and state-mandated security, between entrepreneurial freedom and regulatory government, between self-government and bureaucratic administration? Today, in ever-changing contexts, we grapple with these perennial problems of political philosophy.

For edification on these questions, I urge readers to turn to the pages that follow and to ponder the answers that Herbert Hoover and Franklin Roosevelt gave. You may be surprised by the light their words cast upon our present concerns.

GEORGE H. NASH
Historian and author of
The Life of Herbert Hoover, in three volumes

Acknowledgments

I acknowledge the vast scholarship of others on the New Deal debate and I encourage readers who are interested in exploring the decade-long exchange between Roosevelt and Hoover to consult the following: J. B. S. Hudson, editor, Rendezvous With Destiny (Garden City, NY: Doubleday, 1974), Samuel I. Rosenan, editor, The Public Papers and Addresses of Franklin D. Roosevelt (New York: Random House, Inc., 1938); Rexford Tugwell, FDR: Architect of an Era (New York: Macmillan Co., 1967); Arthur Ekirch, Jr., Ideologies and Utopias: The Impact of the New Deal on American Thought (Chicago: Quadrangle Books, 1969); Herbert Hoover, The New Day: Campaign Speeches of Herbert Hoover, 1928 (Garden City, New York: Doubleday, Inc., 1933); Herbert Hoover, American Ideals versus the New Deal (New York, The Scribner Press, 1936); William Starr Myers, editor, The State Papers and Other Public Writings of Herbert Hoover (Garden City, New York: Doubleday, Inc., 1934); Arthur M. Schlesinger Jr., The Age of Roosevelt (Boston: Houghton Mifflin, 3vols., 1956-1960); Howard Zinn, New Deal Thought (Indianapolis: Bobbs-Merrill Company, Inc., 1965).

I thank Gary Best, Nick Capaldi, Sara Carmack, Susie Cho, David Davenport, Lenore Ealy, Steve Ealy, Angela Edwards, Hans Eicholz, Roberta Herzberg, Ted McAllister, George H. Nash, Lindsey Poulin, John Stark, Anthony Scardino, Marie Ann Thaler, Almis Udrys, and Amina Zeghar for their support, criticism, suggestions, encouragement and conversation over this decade long project. I also thank The Huntington Library in San Marino, California for providing access to most of the original sources used in this collection. Thanks also to the Library of Congress and the National Archives and Records Administration. And finally to Lynnae Pattison-Merget, thank you once again.

Introduction

I. Editor's Purpose

The Hoover-Roosevelt debate in the 1930s—what I have called the Two Faces of Liberalism—not only shapes, but defines, the debates we are having in public policy in the twenty first century. The very questions that concerned Hoover and Roosevelt—what should the public sector and the private sector do to "secure the blessings of liberty"—are the very same questions that inform contemporary public policy. Are we secure because we are free or are we free because we are secure? And if government should do something about solving "the problem" at hand, which level and which branch, should do it? Interestingly, Hoover and Roosevelt also looked to the past at the very moment they confronted the future. Just as we frame our conversation by their debate, they conducted their own exchange with the one hundred and fiftieth anniversary of the American Founding as their backdrop.

I want to encourage the current generation to take a fresh look at the material surrounding the New Deal controversy. To that end, I have reproduced speeches and addresses by the main actors, Franklin D. Roosevelt and Herbert Hoover, sample Acts of Congress that translated the New Deal vision into public policy, as well as critical Supreme Court decisions that first declared the core legislation to be unconstitutional and then constitutionalized the New Deal. Finally, I have included the Democratic and Republican Party platforms from the 1930s.

Thus, I have organized the material in a chronological fashion, all the better I hope to encourage the reader to focus on the evolutionary and developmental character of the New Deal conversation. I want us to reflect on what the Hoover and FDR exchange has to teach us, the current generation, about 1) the interrelationship between "the three liberties": political liberty, civil liberty, and economic liberty, 2) how these "three liberties" compete or cooperate with "the three securities": governmental action, collective responsibility, and economic guarantees, and 3) how undergirding these twin concerns of liberty and security is an even deeper question: has the traditional American institutional system of the separation of powers, local government, and a robust private sector been permanently replaced by the Administrative State run by experts and whose reach knows few bounds?

And this conversation goes all the way back to the American Founding itself. The American Founders claimed that the system they created was an "experiment," and a bold one at that: never had any form of government been established by "reflection and choice." Never before had any "people" deliberated about the form of government under which they would live or the religious and economic relations they would endorse. They did not fear what they were doing: they were replacing the confused state of the union under the Articles of Confederation with "a more perfect union" whose fate would attract the attention of laymen and lawyers into "remote futurity." The Founders relied on what they called institutional "improvements" and public spirit to accomplish this momentous feat. They suggested that liberty depended on careful attention to the separation of powers between the Congress, Executive, and Judiciary as well as the clear distinction between state and local governmental matters and those of a more general nature. And they urged the promotion of what we today call social capital and spiritual capital in order to build the right kind of community support and moral infrastructure without which, they argued, representative democracy would perish.

All this American optimism, and caution, seemed to come crashing down between 1929 and 1933. Hoover and Roosevelt scrambled to make sense of the political, economic, and personal depression. Had liberalism, with its attachment to the private sector in economics and its suspicion of the paternalistic inclinations of government officials, come to an end? Were the liberal ideas of the American Founders part of an old and archaic order that ought to be discarded? Was there a new and improved liberalism that could take its place? One that views the government, especially the federal government, as a friend rather than an enemy of liberty. Or is this "new liberalism" actually new without being either improved or liberal at all?

The Hoover-FDR conversation about liberty and security is *the* American conversation.

I believe it is urgent to reconnect the contemporary student of public policy with an ongoing debate in American history through a careful reading of documents, and examination of speeches, that form the foundation of our current understanding of the American system. The Great Depression and the New Deal have had a profound impact on how Americans engage in a conversation about public policy. The Great Depression is arguably one of the most important economic events in American history and the New Deal ushered in a new kind of politics. And both the economic and political conversations occurred within a larger ethical framework.

My hope is that the reader will find the various arguments of both sides provocative and stimulating, casting new light on an era about which we frequently have predisposed opinions, passions, and interests. I encourage the reader to come to grips with the compelling intricacies of each argument, and recognize the shades of a debate that now dominates the American political landscape: liberty versus security, freedom versus regulation, and representative government versus the Administrative State. These themes have a way of adapting themselves, albeit under various forms, shapes and guises, to every subsequent era of American history. We have seen them in the past; we will, no doubt, see them again in the future. In this spirit, I invite the reader to join in the enduring American political and economic conversation.

II. Hoover-Roosevelt Questions

What can Hoover and Roosevelt do for us, the current generation, as we deal with the new public policy debate they inaugurated in the 1930s? Why did Hoover see the New Deal as "a challenge to liberty," and the American System of limited federal government and robust individual responsibility? He compared it to the European model of statism and warned that we were on the road to socialism. Why did FDR, by contrast, see the New Deal as the opportunity to establish "freedom from fear?" And save democratic capitalism from destruction. These are the questions which undergird the selection of the material in this collection. I have attempted to illuminate the similarities and differences between Hoover and Roosevelt in the selection of readings and I invite the reader to consider their responses to the following specific questions when reading the original material.

What caused the depression, according to Hoover and FDR, and what made it great? Which argument do you find more convincing and why? What was at stake in the elections of 1932 and 1936? What is the relationship between political liberty, civil liberty, and economic liberty in their rhetoric and actions? Is it simply, "the economy, stupid?" Does the specter of class struggle and revolution haunt the Hoover-FDR exchange? Would it be fair to say that Hoover didn't see class struggle to be a central part of the American system, but FDR did?

Do they agree in their understanding of "equality of opportunity" and the role the federal government must play in securing this goal? Or did FDR change the idea of equality from opportunity to outcome? Is it fair to portray Hoover as simply an inept speaker and "muddled" thinker? Can one have limited government in principle and in peacetime, but then yield to extensive government in an emergency? And, more importantly, expect to "muddle" our way back to politics and business as usual once the war or emergency is over? Is FDR clearly redefining America, or is he also "muddled" and inept in a pragmatic, let's try anything and everything manner?

Did they think that the souls of individuals were, so to speak, in a depressed state? Do they agree that there is a moral and spiritual dimension to the conversation? To what extent is the crisis a loss of confidence in political and economic leadership? How, and with what consequences to the conversation, is the image of "war" incorporated in their approaches? What do they mean by liberalism? Did they both think they were saving capitalism and democracy? Did they think that "emergencies" justified an expanded role for government in the economy? Did they agree on the meaning of the general welfare? Were they both enamored with the Progressives program of national reform?

Is the main difference between FDR and Hoover this: FDR was a leader who inspired the forgotten man to action and Hoover was the out of touch incumbent politician who tried to reason with the electorate, failed, and became the forgotten man? Put differently, can we say that FDR was simply better at campaigning and rhetoric than Hoover and did everything in a calculated way to obtain votes?

Or are they in fact offering two different and competing narratives about what it means to be an American? A sort of contest and contrast of philosophies of government? Has the rugged individual been replaced by the forgotten man? And has the language of individual rights and limited government been replaced by the language of collective security and social justice?

III. Sixty Readings on the New Deal

Chapter One consists of five selections drawn from the years 1928-1931. The initial entry is Hoover's Presidential Nomination Address where he states: "We in America today are nearer to the final triumph over poverty than ever before in the history of any land. The poorhouse is vanishing from among us. We have not yet reached the goal, but, given a chance to go forward with the policies of the last eight years, we shall soon with the help of God be in sight of the day when poverty will be banished from this nation." The next two entries are excerpts from Hoover's 1928 campaign speeches: one in New York where he contrasts "the American system of rugged individualism" with the European "doctrines of paternalism and state socialism" and the other in St. Louis where he discusses the "constructive side of government" aimed at providing individuals with equal opportunity through "co-operation with the forces of business." Hoover was swept into office: he received 21,349,993 votes to Alfred Smith's 15,016,169 votes. In the Electoral College, the margin was 444-87. The Gross Domestic Product was $104 billion and unemployment stood at roughly 3%. The Dow rose from 100 in 1924 to 300 by the end of 1928, and made its way up to 381 by July 1929.

This optimism and confidence that swept Hoover into office was, however, short-lived. From October 24—Black Thursday—to October 29—Black Tuesday, the Dow lost 96 points or approximately 30% of its value and stood at just under 300. A record 12.9 million shares and 16.4 million shares changed hands on these two days respectively. Historians typically refer to Black Tuesday as "the moment" that marks the end of the Roaring Twenties, with an unemployment rate of 2% to 4%, and the start of the Great Depression.

By November 13, 1929, the Dow "crashed" even lower to 250. But the market bounced back to 300 in the winter of 1930. Thus, despite the increase in unemployment from 3% in 1929 to 9% in 1930, optimism was still in the air because the economy had, apparently, turned around. "We have passed the worst," declared Hoover. His 1930 Annual Address anticipates the "passing of this depression."

But this was not to be: instead of continuing its expected swing back to normalcy, the Dow went into a free fall and hit a low of 41 in June 1932. And by 1933, unemployment hit a high of 25%, or thirteen million people, Gross Domestic Product had fallen to $56 billion, National Income had fallen from $87 billion in 1929 to $40 billion, 5,000 banks had closed and were closing at a rate of two per day, millions of farmers had lost their land, and nearly one hundred thousand businesses went bankrupt.

The political mood of the country was also changing: in the 1930 mid-term elections, Hoover Republicans lost control of both the House and the Senate. And the time seemed appropriate to launch a new approach to the relationship between government and business. Governor Roosevelt of New York, for example, endorsed government support of unemployment insurance, old-aged pensions, and welfare relief. And in June 1931, FDR addressed the Conference of Governors on the Great Depression. In this address, we see the outlines of "a new economic and social balance" that calls for "positive leadership and definite experiments which have not hitherto been tried." By contrast, Hoover's Second and Third Annual Address to Congress, given in 1930 and 1931 in the midst of the Great Depression, cautions the country against "the entry of the Government into competition with private business." Instead, he suggests that "recovery can be expedited and its effects mitigated by cooperative action." Moreover, "if our economic system does not match our highest expectations at all times, it does not require revolutionary action to bring it into accord with any necessity that experience may prove. It has successfully adjusted itself to changing conditions in the past. It will do so again." Anticipating the punch line of FDR's First Inaugural, Hoover urges Americans to overcome fear itself: "The mobility of our institutions, the richness of our resources, and the abilities of our people enable us to meet them [changing conditions] unafraid."

Chapter Two contains twelve selections from 1932. It begins with two addresses by Roosevelt early in the 1932 campaign. Prior to his nomination, on the fourth ballot, as the Democratic Party candidate for president, FDR spoke over the radio on behalf of "the

forgotten man at the bottom of the economic pyramid." He
accuses Hoover of thinking that a "huge expenditure of public
funds" will solve unemployment. But such a policy continues to
forget "the forgotten man" at the bottom of the pyramid. What
was needed was a comprehensive plan, similar to the one launched
in 1917 to overcome the "great national emergency" of war, to
"restore purchasing power" to the vast majority of Americans. In
May, he expanded the need for conscious planning in an address to
the graduating class at Oglethorpe University. He appealed to the
"courage, the faith and the vision" of the young on behalf of "bold,
persistent experimentation." He suggested that the contemporary
economic crisis could only be overcome "by a larger measure of
social planning," and he welcomed the "fundamental change in our
popular economic thought" that was taking place.

The Democratic Party Platform of 1932 proposed a "drastic
change in economic policies" and demanded a new "covenant with
the people" calling for "advanced planning of public works" and
the regulation of security exchanges. Yet it also called for a
"drastic reduction of government expenditures" by eliminating
bureaucratic waste and "the removal of government from all fields
of private enterprise except where necessary to develop public
works and natural resources in the common interest." The phrase,
"New Deal," is clearly articulated in Roosevelt's Convention Speech
of 1932: "I pledge you, I pledge myself," said FDR, "to a new deal
for the American people." He called for "a new order of
competence and courage," one that would "restore America to its
own people." Much was at stake: "This is more than a political
campaign; it is a call to arms. Give me your help...to win the
crusade." This was the last chance, he said, to save liberalism from
radicalism.

The Republican Platform of 1932 lauded the accomplishments
of the Hoover Administration and pledged to institute policies that
would overcome the "fear and apprehension" caused by the Great
Depression. The plan—unabashedly stated in terms of the
Progressivist agenda—was to "enlist in a war [individually and
collectively] which will not end until the promise of American life is
once more fulfilled." The platform attacks FDR's beliefs by saying
that "this is no time to experiment upon the body politic or
financial." Republicans promised tax relief, a flexible tariff, high
wages, guaranteed collective bargaining, and "vindication of the
rights of the Negro citizen." Herbert Hoover accentuates these

Progressive ideas in his Convention Speech of 1932 where he also
champions individual responsibility and moral foundations. He
has "but one desire...to see [his] country again on the road to
prosperity...to see the principles and ideals of the American people
perpetuated."

On September 23, 1932, FDR delivered a "most daring,"
campaign speech to the Commonwealth Club in San Francisco.
According to the presumed author, Adolf A. Berle, FDR "never saw
that speech until he opened it on the lectern." In the speech, FDR
identified the presence of a serious moral problem: "equality of
opportunity as we have known it no longer exists." The "task of
government in its relation to business" is to develop and implement
"an economic declaration of rights, an economic constitutional
order.   This   is   the   common   task   of   statesmen   and
businessmen...Everyman has a right to life...Everyman has a right
to his property." And "everyman" has a right to "liberty and the
pursuit of happiness." Although Hoover is not mentioned by
name, FDR is, in effect, criticizing Hoover's understanding of
individualism, equality of opportunity, and the purpose of the
"American system." In his Memoirs, Hoover considers this speech
to be more pessimistic than "daring." Drawing on the language of
the 1932 Republican platform and the title of the Progressive
historian Herbert Croly's famous book, he says FDR's speech is
contrary to "the promise of American life."

On October 31, 1932, both Hoover and FDR gave addresses,
Hoover at Madison Square Garden, and FDR in Boston. Hoover,
responding to the Commonwealth speech, opposes the adoption of
"a new deal." He cautions the public that the New Deal threatens
to "undermine and destroy our American system." FDR tells his
Boston audience that he had just listened "to the first part of the
speech of the President in New York tonight." He inserts the
following into his prepared remarks: "My New Deal does not aim
to change [the fundamental principles of America]. It does aim to
bring those principles into effect." Hoover attacks five Democratic
proposals, while FDR proposes five steps toward economic
recovery.

In November 1932, Roosevelt was elected President by a wide
margin: 22,809,638 popular votes to Hoover's 15,758,901. The
Electoral College margin was even wider: 472-59. Interestingly, this
is a virtual replication of the margins by which Hoover beat Smith
in 1928. Also interestingly, despite all the news about potential left

wing gains at the polls, the Socialists and Communists did poorly. Importantly, the Socialist Party, led by Norman Thomas, received its lowest vote since 1900: 881,000. The electorate on whom the Socialists relied—the newly arrived immigrants and the traditional American "lower classes"—voted overwhelmingly for FDR. The Communist Party received even fewer votes: 103,000. Even more telling was the margin of victory for the Democrats over the Republicans in the Congress: 313-117 in the House and 59-36 in the Senate.

Hoover's Final Annual Message to Congress warned that the federal government must not act "as a participant in economic and social life" or "it becomes at once a tyranny in whatever it may touch." And he reminds his audience that the true cause of the Depression in America lies abroad in Europe. He offers words of advice regarding federal expenditures, a balanced budget, bank reorganization, and international cooperation, concluding with a call that federal solutions must not ignore the American experience of self-government, "rooted in religion and fed from purely spiritual springs." The final two selections in Chapter Two are letters between Hoover and FDR concerning the period of transition.

Chapter Three contains fifteen entries covering the New Deal from 1933-1935. [This period is often referred to by Historians as New Deal I[1]] The first selection replicates Hoover's warning that the public has "a steadily degenerating confidence in the future which has reached the height of general alarm." The next selection contains Hoover's warning that the "financial situation has become even more grave." He urges FDR to take "expeditious action." Roosevelt responds in his First Inaugural Address: "The only thing we have to fear is fear itself." He promises to lead "a disciplined attack upon our common problems" and, if necessary, to request "broad executive power to wage a war against the emergency." This is followed by the first and second of Roosevelt's Sunday "Fireside Chats" with the American people for which he became famous. There, he outlines his plan to remove "the phantom of fear" from the banking crisis and then he explains the "well-grounded plan" of the New Deal, describing it as a "partnership" between government and business to save "modern civilization."

I have reproduced excerpts from one of the earliest and most important pieces of New Deal legislation: The National Industrial Recovery Act. [The letters in square parenthesis in the body of the text have been added to assist the reader.] It was introduced to

Congress on June 16, the hundredth day of the special session of Congress. The purpose of the N.I.R.A. was to "encourage national industrial recovery, to foster fair competition, and to provide for the construction of certain useful public works, and for other purposes." Did Roosevelt follow Hoover's approach which was to build a cooperative framework, a "concert of interests" between government and business? Other significant legislation was passed in the first few years of the New Deal, such as the Agricultural Adjustment Act, the National Labor Relations Act, the Executive Order creating the National Labor Relations Board, and the Social Security Act. I have included the essential parts of these documents.

In his Third Annual Message to Congress, FDR identifies a "new order" of "social justice" as the supreme ideal, or promise, of American life. As if responding to Hoover, FDR declares that his New Deal is advancing "under the framework and in the spirit and intent of the American Constitution." He proposes an ambitious plan to provide for "security of a livelihood...security against the major hazards and vicissitudes of life...security of decent homes." He proposes a type of welfare-to-work program, recognizing that dole dependency is a drug that eats away the moral fiber of an individual. Furthermore, FDR advances his belief that the federal government must act where local institutions fail, most specifically in the area of unemployment.

Although the electorate was supportive of this early phase of the New Deal, Roosevelt was not without his critics. Some thought that the New Deal had gone too far while others thought that it had not gone far enough. Among the former was the American Liberty League, established in August 1934, by disgruntled Democrats! Their members attacked the New Deal as a dangerous departure from constitutional practice and actively opposed, for example, the NLRA and the 1935 Wagner Act. Although invited to join the organization, Hoover respectfully declined. On the other hand, Father Charles E. Coughlin, who until 1934 was a supporter of FDR—he is reported to have said: "the New Deal is Christ's Deal"—used his highly popular radio broadcasts to criticize the FDR Administration for not doing enough on behalf of "social justice." And then there was the former Governor of Louisiana and Democratic Party Senator Huey P. Long of Louisiana who formed clubs throughout the south to support his campaign for a guaranteed minimum, and maximum, annual income. His Share

Our Wealth Movement, initially a potential electoral problem for the Democrats, was unable to sustain its appeal after Long's assassination in September 1935. Finally, there was considerable opposition from writers on the left in the Upton Sinclair, Edward Bellamy, and Thorstein Veblen tradition, and on the right in the Southern Agrarian Movement. The latter were particularly vociferous in their objection to the TVA for undermining Southern culture. They also criticized FDR for appropriating Jeffersonian agrarian rhetoric while supporting policies that actually created a dependent farming class.

As important as these people and movements were, however, they are not central to the New Deal conversation. This disaffection on the extreme right and the extreme left did not have an impact on the mid-term election of 1934. Accordingly, I have decided to not include specific writings in this anthology. What is important to note about this election, is that the electorate responded with an overwhelming "yes" to FDR's New Deal electoral theme: "are you better off than you were last year?" The Democrats were now in control of two-thirds of both the House and the Senate. The margin between the Democrats and Republicans was 322-103 in the House and 69-25 in the Senate.

The year 1935 also saw the entry of the Supreme Court into the New Deal debate. In <u>Schecter Poultry Corp. v. United States</u>, the Court declared the National Industrial Recovery Act to be unconstitutional. The Court was particularly troubled by the delegation of legislative power to the President and the interpretation of the interstate commerce clause undergirding the Act. Thus began a two-year conflict between the Supreme Court, the Congress, and the President over the role of the branches of government in the implementation of public policy. In response to the Court decision, Congress passed the NLRA.

On October 5, 1935, Hoover campaigned against the New Deal. He accuses FDR of deliberately "cooking the books" when it comes to explaining government revenue and public spending. But trying to fool the taxpayer is trumped by another New Deal activity: it traps Americans in "meshes of the gigantic spending bureaucracy." What, he asks, have we got in exchange? A reduction in unemployment by "only 700,000." He doubts that the New Deal will make "America a happier, a better place in which to live."

The final selection of this chapter is FDR's brief explanation of the "Meaning of Progress." He decries the 1920s and its "orgy of 'prosperity'" when "Mammon ruled America." He praises the coming together of Americans to raise the level of prices for farm crops, reform banking policy, help home owners, establish "fair regulation of the stock exchanges," and "provide the aged against distressing want" in the form of Social Security.

Chapter Four covers the campaign year of 1936. One of the least appreciated aspects of the New Deal conversation was the extent to which Hoover continued to argue against the public policy of the New Deal long after his defeat by Roosevelt in the 1932 election. During 1936 he made the New Deal the issue of the campaign. I have included Hoover's Lincoln Birthday Dinner Address in Portland, Oregon, as well as his keynote address to the Republican National Convention. In the first, Hoover attacks the New Deal's agenda, policies, and programs calling them "assaults on the spirit of American liberty." He outlines a number of "confusions" among New Deal proponents that have led America to the brink of servitude rather than the promised "finer, better, happier life for the average man and woman." There was, however, one hopeful sign: the Supreme Court has restored "some degree of confidence." This address comes one month after FDR's Annual Message to Congress, also included in this chapter, where FDR gives a positive assessment of the New Deal. In the second entry by Hoover, he declares "the New Deal is a definite attempt to replace the American System of freedom with some sort of European planned existence...there are some principles that cannot be compromised." According to Hoover, "man's vigil and his quest have been to be free;" checks and balances must limit both economic and political concentration of power. Hoover portrays the crisis of the New Deal as "the crisis to free men" in his speech to the Republican Convention: "for the first time in the history of America we have the gospel of class hatred preached from the White House. That is human poison far more deadly than fear."

The public policy positions of the Republicans and Democrats are clearly revealed in the 1936 Platforms, excerpts from which comprise the fourth and fifth selections of this chapter. The Republican Platform states that "America is in peril": political liberty and individual liberty "for the first time are threatened by Government itself." The Republicans condemn the New Deal, accusing Roosevelt of taking over the powers of Congress, of passing unconstitutional laws and of reckless "deficit" spending. The platform calls for the return of relief administration to local nonpolitical agencies, a balanced budget, no more devaluation of the dollar, a revision of personal and corporate taxes, and the right of labor to bargain collectively. The Democratic Platform reaffirms the New Deal, and declares certain self-evident truths, among which are the role of government in the promotion of safety and happiness of its citizens, "protection of the family and the home, establishment of a democracy of opportunity for all the people, [and] aid to those overtaken by disaster." The next selection is FDR's Re-Nomination Address in which he proclaims that "we have conquered fear." The challenge now is to "restore to the people a wider freedom...an American way of life." He declares "war" on the ideas and practices of "economic royalists," and announces, "this generation of Americans have a rendezvous with destiny." The challenge of the current generation is to declare independence from "economic autocracy."

The seventh and eighth entries are Roosevelt's "Fireside Chat" on the Dignity of Labor and his Address on the Survival of Private Enterprise. In the "Fireside Chat," FDR praises the American farmers' "self-reliance" and calls upon the citizens to support emergency spending because "in a physical and a property sense, as well as in a spiritual sense, we are members one of another." FDR takes pride in the assertion that "we have been making fewer and fewer mistakes." In his "Address on the Survival of Private Enterprise," he declares that no one "believes more firmly than I in the system of private business, private property and private profit" lauding that, under the New Deal, coercion and monopoly of business has been prohibited, yet the conditions for private enterprise have been encouraged. In effect, if it weren't for the New Deal, there would be no private enterprise at all.

In January 1936, the Supreme Court, in United States v. Butler, declared the Agricultural Adjustment Act unconstitutional. The Court said that the Act violated the tax clause, the interstate commerce clause, and the Tenth Amendment. And in Morehead v New York, the Supreme Court ruled that the minimum wage law in New York was unconstitutional. Once again, the New Deal programs had been declared constitutional. The Supreme Court itself became an issue in the Presidential election of 1936.

The Republican nominee, Governor Alf Landon of Kansas, the only Republican to win a governor's race in the 1934 elections, had the endorsement of many conservative Democrats, for example Alfred E. Smith, and the overwhelming majority of the nation's newspapers during the 1936 Presidential election. Nevertheless, Roosevelt received 27,752,869 popular and 523 electoral votes to Landon's 16,674,665 popular and 8 electoral votes. Only Maine and Vermont voted for Landon. More importantly for Roosevelt's New Deal program, the Democrats carried over 2/3 of both Houses of Congress: Senate 76-16, House 331-89. This was a "critical election" in American politics for it led to the control of the Congress by the Democratic Party for the next several decades.

Chapter Five marks the climax of the decade of deliberation over the constitutionality of the new political economy. We open with FDR's Second Inaugural. There he declares, "our progress out of the depression is obvious. But that is not all that you and I mean by the new order of things. Our pledge was not merely to do a patchwork job with second-hand materials. By using the new materials of social justice we have undertaken to erect on the old foundations a more enduring structure for the better use of future generations." He identifies the judiciary as the main obstacle to "the new order of things." He identifies this New Order as one that is driven by moral outrage; one that will not tolerate "one-third of a nation ill-housed, ill-clad, ill-nourished."

Roosevelt recommended a reorganization of the judiciary, popularly known as the court-stacking plan. He considered this proposal to be one of the most important of his entire presidency. Eventually the Democratic controlled Congress rebuffed the plan after two months of acrimonious debate, issuing the "Senate Judiciary Committee Adverse Report on the Judicial Reorganization Plan." Even though Congress rejected his proposal, Roosevelt claimed that the Court got the message: the Court switched and declared the New Deal programs constitutional. I have reproduced the essential record of this "switch in time that saved nine."

The second entry is Hoover's "Hands off the Supreme Court" speech where he questions "whether the president by the appointment of additional judges upon the Supreme Court shall revise the Constitution—or whether changes in the Constitution shall be submitted to the people as the Constitution provides." Roosevelt's "Fireside Chat" regarding the Judicial Reorganization Plan is the third entry. He outlines his plan to infuse the Court with young blood and with minds that have a "present-day sense of the Constitution." The Reorganization Plan proposed that Justices of the Supreme Court should retire upon reaching age 70. If a Justice refused to retire, then the President and the Senate could add an additional judge; this process of adding Justices could continue up to a maximum of six, thus potentially increasing the court to 15 members. What kind of Justice would FDR choose? "I will appoint Justices who will act as justices and not as legislators."

Between March and May 1937, the Supreme Court (5-4) reversed itself and constitutionalized the New Deal programs. In West Coast Hotel v Parrish, it upheld the minimum wage law in Washington State, thus overturning the Morehead decision. N.L.R.B. v. Jones & Laughlin Steel Corporation, which overturned Schechter (Chapter Three), is an important example of the Court's Reversal. In May, the Court concurrently decided Steward Machine Co. v. Davis (5-4) and Helvering v. Davis (7-2). In Steward, the Court attempted to "draw the line intelligently between duress and inducement." This decision upheld the constitutionality of the Social Security Act. Similarly, in Helvering, the Court upheld the constitutionality of the federally funded old-age pension program.

There are two additional selections in Chapter Five: Roosevelt's "Fair Day's Pay" speech and his "Address on Constitution Day." In "A Fair Day's Pay," Roosevelt's contribution to the pending deliberations regarding a federal wage-hour law, he describes how "the overwhelming majority of this Nation has little patience with the small minority which vociferates today that prosperity has returned." He now praises the Supreme Court and demands "fair" treatment for the American worker. The Fair Labor Standards Act passed, marking an important new function of American government. FDR's "Address on Constitution Day" solidifies his understanding of the Constitution as a living document, written as a "layman's instrument," not a "lawyer's contract." He calls for "flexible statesmanship of the future" in interpreting what he believes the Founders intentionally left vague: language regarding "commerce between the States, the taxing power and the general welfare."

Also in 1937, Associate Justice Willis Van Devanter, an opponent of the New Deal, retired and was replaced by Hugo Black, a supporter of the New Deal. Over the subsequent four years, Roosevelt had the opportunity to secure the constitutionality of the New Deal with additional appointments. FDR appointed New Deal supporters Hugo Black, Stanley Reed, Felix Frankfurter, and William Douglas. But the immediate impact of FDR's victory over the Court was less than he had anticipated: the issue of increasing the number of Justices left deep scars of division within the Democratic Party and bolstered the electoral performance of the Republicans. Despite the best efforts of Roosevelt himself—he took to the airwaves urging "the election of liberals" in the 1938 Congressional elections—Republicans gained seats for the first time since 1928. They gained 81 seats in the House to narrow the margin to 260-170 and 8 in the Senate and, with the assistance of conservative Democrats, were able to retard the progress of further New Deal legislation. There is much merit to David Kennedy's suggestion that "that this anti-New Deal blast" is the foundation "for modern American Conservatism."

I conclude the collection of New Deal material with three pieces by Roosevelt and four by Hoover. The first selection of **Chapter Six** is Hoover's The Challenge to Liberty speech. Hoover repeats his decade long theme: "In the United States today everybody has lost some confidence and everybody has some fear." There is widespread "fear at home," and the "Planned Economy" is making things worse. The theme that the New Deal is a challenge to liberty is also the title of a collection of essays that he published in 1934 that was endorsed by the Book of the Month Club. There he argued that "government dictation," and the "national regimentation" of industry, commerce, and agriculture was the greatest challenge facing "the American heritage."

This entry is followed by FDR's 1938 "Message to Congress on the Concentration of Economic Power." He decries extensive private influence, whether individual or corporate, over government. His plan to restrain abuses of labor consists of controls on price, production, and wages. He believes his program has as its basic thesis "not that the system of free private enterprise for profit has failed in this generation, but that it has not yet been tried." In the "The Dangerous Road" speech, Hoover accuses the New Deal of weakening "the judgment of men. It sickens initiative and enterprise. It knocks the confidence out of men. It substitutes fear. It destroys millions of jobs." He reminds his audience that there are now 12,000,000 Americans unemployed.

In his Annual Message, the following year, FDR states that "storms from abroad directly challenge three institutions indispensable to Americans": religion, democracy, and international good faith. Hoover, by contrast, in his "The Real State of the Union," argues that the "high purposes of this nation are being undermined by the policies being pursued at home by alien theories from abroad." The threat to liberty comes from home rather than abroad. Hoover's Radio Address is concerned with the President's building of personal power and his intention to break the self-imposed two term tradition. Hoover's point also is that after six years of New Deal public policy, there were still ten million unemployed and there were more regulations in place than had ever been before. Using the Dow stock market index as a measure of improvement, the Dow, with the exception of 1934, rose an average of 38 points a year through 1936. By 1938, however, the Dow had slipped below 100 and was at 139 at the end of 1939. America was no longer in the Hoover Depression; it was in the Roosevelt Recession.

Finally, I reproduce Roosevelt's Third Inaugural Address, following the relative "nail-biter" of an election, in which FDR defeated the Republican nominee Wendell Willkie 27,307,819 to 22,321,018 popular votes, and 449 to 82 Electoral College votes. But this does not tell the full story. The Republican victories in the House and the Senate effectively brought an end to the New Deal era. In 1941, with War spreading throughout Europe, FDR declared the success of his New Deal program and declined to introduce any new proposals. Perhaps foreshadowing his future mobilization of the American people, FDR confirms that the American nation has a body, a mind, and "something more permanent, something larger than the sum of all its parts." Take away the body and the mind, and the spirit will remain and prevail. This spirit is that of democracy, and FDR claimed that with his New Deal program, he saved the democratic system in America. Hoover, by contrast, declared the New Deal to be a failure and continued to warn of the dangers to the American system from the concentration of power in the executive branch.

IV. Interpreting the New Deal

I conclude this Introduction with an overview of the more prominent concerns that have dominated the literature on the New Deal and invite the reader to also bear these interpretations in mind while reading the original sources. Both proponents and antagonists have raised a number of important questions about the nature, scope, and consequences of the New Deal. An exhaustive treatment of the multitudinous reflections on, and interpretations of, the success or failure of the New Deal is beyond the purpose of this Introduction. Rather my purpose is to give the reader a taste of what certain statesmen and scholars have to say about Hoover and FDR.

Winston Churchill admired FDR and his New Deal, once writing the following inscription in a book: "With earnest and best wishes for the success of the greatest crusade of modern times."[2] In public opinion polls, Franklin D. Roosevelt is consistently judged to be one of America's greatest Presidents. They say he was an inspiring leader. They say his policies brought us out of the Great Depression. They say he won the War against Fascism and prevented Socialism from developing in our country. They say his overwhelming Electoral College victories are a testament to his enduring popularity. On the other hand, there are those who believe he was a tyrant who attempted to subvert the Constitution at every move, installing the fear, that he warned everyone against, into the hearts and minds of the citizenry. They say his ad hoc policies caused and prolonged the Great Depression. They say he constructed the path toward Fascism and Socialism in the United States. They say he manipulated the people, and even geared all of the New Deal programs toward the states that would deliver him the presidency.

Was the New Deal a comprehensive program intent on solving America's economic woes? Yes, says Arthur Ekirch, Jr. He explains: "the President and his advisers from the Cabinet and the Brains Trust assumed responsibility for giving direction and focus to the stream of legislation and ideas that characterized the early New Deal. Likening himself in a press conference to the quarterback of the team who calls the plays but who cannot predict the outcome or direction of the game, Roosevelt was the prime mover and catalyst, as well as institutional embodiment and beneficiary, of the changing psychology of the American people."[3] However, according to Raymond Moley, another of FDR's Brain Trusters, "the New Deal was not of one piece. Nor was it the product of a single integrated plan. It was...a loose collection of many ideas—some new, most borrowed from the past—with plenty of improvisations and compromises. Those of us who participated were too busy for mature reflections or to create a system or an over-all pattern."[4] Moley recounts two specific items that the Roosevelt administration was dealing with: "to keep the machinery of government in motion, to help individuals and businesses to stay alive; and at the same time to revive the confidence of the people in their capacity to recover from the depths of the depression. The people of the nation didn't understand what we were doing. But they were convinced that a lot of things were being done. And that alone gave them the spirit to carry on."[5]

What was the balance between equality and liberty under the New Deal? FDR believed that too much of the nation was ill clad, ill housed, and ill fed. Rexford Tugwell notes that during the Roosevelt administration "the government of the United States began making sure that no one would go hungry or cold, and that everyone would have a decent place to live. This undertaking gave 'ordinary' people a sense of security they never had before...This one endeavor was the furthest advance toward equality ever made in this country, and equality had always been a very proud claim among Americans."[6] Ekirch, on the other hand, points out that in order to obtain greater security, individual liberty would suffer: "The emphasis of the New Deal was on a type of liberty that minimized individual freedom in favor of a greater social security and economic equality of the whole."[7] As the readings demonstrate, Herbert Hoover certainly made the loss of liberty his central theme.

How different were Hoover's ideas from Roosevelt's? Could Hoover be the actual "father" of the New Deal? Walter Lippman, for example, stated that: "It was Mr. Hoover who abandoned the principles of laissez-faire in relation to the business cycle, established the conviction that prosperity and depression can be publicly controlled by political action, and drove out of the public consciousness the old idea that depressions must be overcome by private adjustment."[8] Murray Rothbard, operating within the Austrian School of Economics, is also a warm supporter of the view that Hoover paved the way for Roosevelt. The Hoover Administration, says Rothbard, for the first time boldly overthrew laissez-faire and unleashed a continuous barrage of governmental weapons against the Depression[9]. Rothbard challenges the argument that capitalism, free enterprise, or laissez-faire caused the Great Depression and only decisive and extensive action by the federal government brought the country back to prosperity. On the contrary, argues Rothbard, it was the actions of the federal government that both caused and prolonged the depression into a twelve-year "economic holocaust." Edward Guerrant, however, suggests that, "their understanding of the causes of the depression and their policies for restoring prosperity necessarily differed in many respects."[10]

In addition to the explanation for the cause and duration of the Great Depression provided by the Austrian school of Economics, inspired by the work of Ludwig von Mises, there are three other explanations that need to be borne in mind and placed next to the actual explanations offered by Hoover and Roosevelt. The Austrians suggested that excessive credit creation by the new Federal Reserve System in the 1920s caused all sectors of the economy to misread economic signals and inappropriate government interference by government with the market system prolonged the Depression. The Chicago School, led by Milton Friedman, also sees the Federal Reserve System as the cause of the problem but with a twist: the Fed braked when it should have accelerated the money supply and vice versa. The third approach is the Keynesian explanation: the cause of the Depression was market failure due to lack of consumer spending and business investment and the solution is government stimulation of aggregate demand. FDR didn't completely endorse this approach seeing the Depression more the result of anarchistic than failed markets, mal-distribution of income, and over-speculation. The fourth approach is the Hoover explanation: the persistent attachment to the gold standard by monetary authorities, the Smoot-Tawley tariff, and the failure of Europe to emerge out of the Depression.

One of the enduring questions raised by scholars is "Did Keynes influence Roosevelt?" Some argue that Roosevelt's policies are Keynesian. Lord Keynes' contribution to economics is his theory that fiscal policy (government spending and taxation) can affect the strength of the economy by means of direct public investment and by influencing consumer spending. Looking at the New Deal programs, some have argued that Keynes's approach undergird the programs; it is common in academic and political circles to equate Keynesianism with the New Deal.

Keynes wrote Roosevelt in 1933 indicating what was at stake: "You have made yourself the trustee for those in every country who seek to mend the evils of our condition by reasoned experiment within the framework of the existing social system. If you fail, rational choice will be gravely prejudiced throughout the world, leaving orthodoxy and revolution to fight it out. But, if you succeed, new and bolder methods will be tried everywhere, and we may date the first chapter of a new economic era from your accession to office."[11] And in 1934 Roosevelt met with Keynes at the White House. Moreover, in 1936, Keynes again visited the

White House and urged FDR to "alter the mind of the Supreme Court."[12]   And in 1937, Keynes was deeply concerned about the ramifications of the 1937 recession. Was the 1937 recession due to FDR following or not following Keynes's suggestions? And did he follow Keynes in proposing the first deficit in 1938?   Arthur Schlesinger says: "no doubt Keynes strengthened the President's inclination to do what he was going to do anyway, and no doubt he showed the younger men lower down in the administration how to convert an expedient into a policy. But it cannot be said either that spending would not have taken place without his intervention or that it did take place for his reasons."[13]

Was there anything "new" about the New Deal? Henry Steele Commager suggests that there was not: "The New Deal was in fact pretty much what the phrase implied: not a new game with new rules, but a reshuffle of cards that had too long been stacked against the workingman and the farmer and the small shopkeeper. To be sure, there was no guarantee that these players would now hold the winning cards, but at least they had as good a chance as any of the others."[14]   Dexter Perkins, on the other hand, believes that the New Deal did bring something new. "It was new because, in the first place, it emphasized, as never before, the dynamic role of the federal government…[The Roosevelt years] introduced a positive conception of responsibility never emphasized before, responsibility…to relieve want and unemployment through the federal agencies, etc…The economic orthodoxies of an earlier period were severely shaken…In previous depressions it had been supposed that the thing to do was to cut expenses and balance the budget. In the Roosevelt years…the unbalancing of the budget in difficult times became not only current practice but defensible in theory."[15]   William Leuchtenberg confirms the novelty of the New Deal.   Under the New Deal, Washington D.C. took on a more prominent role: "For the first time for many Americans, the federal government became an institution that was directly experienced… Roosevelt gave people a sense of membership in the national community."[16]

Was Roosevelt a fascist, a radical, or simply a new breed of American? Was he, on the contrary, simply an opportunist and an incompetent one at that? One scholar suggests that FDR went very far towards centralization and socialism, but, contrary to contemporary wisdom, prevented a revolution as a result: "The New Deal did not revolutionize American politics, but it changed them significantly...If the New Deal had not changed the economy and the society, the story of American politics in the 1930s surely would have been different. It seems certain that forces of discontent would have grown. Revolutionaries would have stepped up their struggle to giver their direction to these forces, and it seems likely that a form of authoritarianism would have trumped as people of property, anxious about their holding, turned to a strong man who was willing and able to use military and police power to stabilize American politics. But the New Deal, continuing an American tradition of pragmatic reform, promoted social and economic changes, which helped to avoid revolution."[17] Indeed, the Socialist Party dropped out of the electoral picture following 1932.

Was the New Deal a third way? Ekirch portrays the New Deal as a deliberate plan to forge a third alternative to the then dominant ideologies of capitalism and socialism. "Yet the radical appeal of the New Deal's collectivism hardly indicated victory for creeping socialism or the demise of capitalism. Clearly Roosevelt, in pursuing a middle way, was able at once to preserve capitalism and at the same time disarm both is revolutionary and reactionary critics. Thus the new political economy which emerged in the thirties was apparently destined to be an interesting mixture, an amalgam of private enterprise and government controls, an American version of state capitalism and social democracy."[18] Similarly, Morton J. Frisch thinks that FDR's "sobriety and restraint" were as much a part of the action of the New Deal as were the major pieces of legislation. Frisch portrays Roosevelt as a statesman who preserved the continuity of the democratic character of the American regime in a time of unprecedented crisis and class struggle. Thus, FDR actually enriched the American order and preserved the roots of the system.[19]

Was FDR that much of a statesman? "No," say several scholars. He was a demagogue who was inspired by European communists and fascists. Some maintain that FDR indeed assumed dictatorial powers. "In America, not in form but in spirit, the same has come to pass as in ancient Rome when power was transferred to a dictator, but only for a limited period in order to save the Republic. The Romans renounced temporarily democratic rights in order to save Democracy itself."[20] And, let us not forget, that, Stalin referred to FDR, in 1933, as "a decided and courageous leader."[21] Not to be outdone, "the German press envisaged

America as a companion in social adventure and assumed 'that Roosevelt like the New Germany has recognized that liberal capitalism is discredited and finished. Roosevelt is prepared to hasten the advent of the new era of nationalized economy.'"[22]

I invite the reader to consider whether or not the New Deal is a fundamental, or qualitative, departure from the principles of the American polity. In particular, did it involve a new understanding of the relationship between political and economic rights and responsibilities? Did it, for example, change the role of government from securing the conditions for the pursuit of happiness to securing happiness itself?

Notes

[1] Paul K.Conkin argues that this conventional distinction between New Deal I and New Deal II is arbitrary and incorrect. See his New Deal (New York: Crowell, 1967). For the conventional view see Alonzo L. Hamby who distinguishes between the Two New Deals in terms of the "two souls" of America. In effect, New Deal I appealed to the security of the forgotten individual man and New Deal II addressed the security of the small businessman. Others portray New Deal I as a concern with recovery rather than security and New Deal II as more concerned with security than recovery.

[2] Gilbert, Martin. *Churchill, A Life.* Henry Holt & Co, New York: 1991, 552.

[3] Ekirch, Jr., A. *Ideologies and Utopias: The Impact of the New Deal on American Thought.* Quadrangle Books, Chicago: 1969, 97.

[4] Moley, R. *The First New Deal.* Harcourt, Brace & World, Inc. New York: 1966, xvii.

[5] Ibid, xviii. That the New Deal amounted to a series of ad hoc proposals rather than a coherent conceptual approach is widespread in the literature. See for example, Byron W. Doynes et al, ed., *The New Deal and Public Policy,* St. Martins Press, New York, 1998.

[6] Tugwell, R. *FDR: Architect of an Era.* Macmillan Co., New York: 1967, vii.

[7] Ekirch, 101.

[8] Lippman, W. "The Permanent New Deal," *Yale Review,* xxiv. (June 1935), 652.

[9] Rothbard, Murray, "America's Great Depression," Mises Institute, Auburn, Alabama, 2000. Rothbard challenges the following conventional wisdom expressed by Michael C. Sears: "Hoover's philosophy of laissez-faire economics did not meet the needs of Americans in 1932." One of the difficulties with the Rothbard thesis is that it downplays the deep political nature of the Great Depression. But, as the readings in this volume emphasize, the Great Depression was also a political and moral crisis. See Michael C. Sears's comment in Byron W. Daynes et al. eds., 272, where he points out that "The Chicago School" also contends that the cause of the depression was due to government monetary policies, yet there are important differences in interpretation between the Austrian and the Chicago schools. Recently, Jim Powell has reiterated Rothbard's claim that the

New Deal policies exacerbated the Great Depression. But like Rothbard, Powell plays down the political and moral dimensions of the era.

[10] Guerrant, E. *Herbert Hoover and Franklin Roosevelt: Comparison and Contrasts*. Howard Allen, Inc., nd, 19.

[11] Ibid, 656.

[12] A. P. Chew, "Abstract of a Conversation with Mr. John Maynard Keynes," May 8, 1936, http//newdeal.feri.org/misc/keynes1.htm. David M. Kennedy claims that FDR and Keynes had a lack of respect for each other. See his *Freedom From Fear*. Oxford University Press, New York: 1999, 197ff.

[13] Schlesinger, Jr., A. *The Age of Roosevelt: The Politics of Upheaval*. Houghton Mifflin, Boston: 1960, 407.

[14] Leuchtenber, W. *Franklin D. Roosevelt and the New Deal*. Harper & Row, New York: 1963, x. He argues that FDR changed rather than continued the policies of the earlier Progressives. As an aside, the term "New Deal" wasn't new; Mark Twain refers to a new deal in *A Connecticut Yankee*.

[15] Perkins, Dexter. *The New Age of Franklin Roosevelt*. University of Chicago Press, Chicago: 1957, 2. See also Paul K. Conkin's observation that the New Deal established a national fiscal program and added more land to the National Park System than had ever previously been added. By 1938, however, Conkin claims that "the New Deal was over."

[16] Leuchtenber, 331. See also David Kennedy, *Freedom From Fear: The American people in Depression and War, 1929-1945*. Kennedy argues that after the ninth year of the Great Depression and the sixth year of the New Deal policies, there were still 10 million people out of work. Thus the New Deal petered out in 1938 with a whimper rather than a bang. Nevertheless, Kennedy states that the legacy of the New Deal is that it saved capitalism from itself and created the foundation for a new era of prosperity.

[17] Kirkendall, R. "The New Deal and American Politics," in *The New Deal*, eds. Melvyn Dubofsky and Stephen Burwood (New York: Garland Publishing, 1990), 329.

[18] Ekirch, 104.

[19] Morton J.Frisch and Richard G. Stevens, eds., *American Political Thought: The Philosophical Dimensions of American Statesmanship*. Charles Scribner's Sons, New York: 1971, 219-235. To Frisch, FDR was a profound reinterpreter of the American regime who, like Alexander Hamilton, preserved the continuity of the democratic character of the regime in a time of profound unprecedented crisis and potential class struggle. Jordan A. Schwarz in *The New Dealers: Power Politics in the Age of Roosevelt* also portrays the New Dealers as innovative, insightful, responsible, and certainly not socialist. They adopted policies that attempted to overcome the disasters of the Hoover Administration.

[20] *Neue Zurcher Zeiting* (Zurich), Nov. 28, 1932.

[21] *New York Times*, Dec. 22, 1933.

[22] *New York Times*, Jan. 21, 1934 in Halasz, N. *Roosevelt Through Foreign Eyes*. D. Van Nostrand Co., Princeton, NJ: 1961. See also Robert E. Sherwood, *Roosevelt and Hopkins* (New York, 1948) who sees the New Deal as the prologue to the arrival of communism in America.

1

The Nature of "Our American System" (1928 – 1931)

I
Herbert Hoover:
Presidential Nomination Address
August 11, 1928

Nature of Problems Ahead

Our problems of the past seven years have been problems of reconstruction; our problems of the future are problems of construction. They are problems of progress. New and gigantic forces have come into our national life. The Great War released ideas of government in conflict with our principles. We have grown to financial and physical power which compels us into a new setting among nations. Science has given us new tools and a thousand nations. Through them have come to each of us wider relationships, more neighbors, more leisure, broader vision, higher ambitions, greater problems. To insure that these tools shall not be used to limit liberty has brought a vast array of questions in government.

The points of contact between the government and the people are constantly multiplying. Every year wise governmental policies become more vital in ordinary life. As our problems grow so do our temptations grow to venture away from those principles upon which our republic was founded and upon which it has grown to greatness. Moreover we must direct economic progress in support of moral and spiritual progress.

Our party platform deals mainly with economic problems, but our nation is not an agglomeration of railroads, of ships, of factories, of dynamos, or statistics. It is a nation of homes, a nation of men, of women, of children. Every man has a right to ask of us whether the United States is a better place for him, his wife, and his children to live in, because the Republican Party has conducted the government for nearly eight years. Every woman has a right to ask whether her life, her home, her man's job, her hopes, her happiness will be better assured by the continuance of the Republican Party in power. I propose to discuss the questions before me in that light.

Recent Record of the Party

The Republican Party came into authority nearly eight years ago. Discontent and agitation against our democracy were rampant. Fear for the future haunted every heart.

No party ever accepted a more difficult task of reconstruction than did the Republican Party in 1921. The record of these seven and one-half years constitutes a period of rare courage in leadership and constructive action. Never has a political party been able to look back upon a similar period with more satisfaction. Never could it look forward with more confidence that its record would be approved by the electorate.

Commerce and industry have revived. Although the agricultural, coal, and textile industries still lag in their recovery and still require our solicitude and assistance, yet they have made substantial progress. While other countries engaged in the war are only now regaining their pre-war level in foreign trade, our exports, even if we allow for the depreciated dollar, are fifty-eight percent greater than before the war. Constructive leadership and co-operation by the government have released and stimulated the energies of our people. Faith in the future has been restored. Confidence in our form of government has never been greater.

People's Widening Opportunity

But it is not through the recitation of wise policies in government alone that we demonstrate our progress under Republican guidance. To me the test is the security, comfort, and opportunity that have been brought to the average American family. During this less than eight years our population has increased by eight

percent.   Yet our national income has increased by over thirty
billions of dollars per year or more than forty-five percent.   Our
production—and   therefore   our   consumption—of   goods   has
increased by over twenty-five percent.   It is easily demonstrated
that these increases have been widely spread among our whole
people.   Home ownership has grown.   While during this period the
number of families has increased by about 2,300,000, we have built
more than 3,500,000 new and better homes.   In this short time we
have equipped nearly nine million more homes with electricity, and
through it drudgery has been lifted from the lives of women.   The
barriers of time and distance have been swept away and life made
freer and larger by the installation of six million more telephones,
seven million radio sets, and the service of an additional fourteen
million automobiles.   Our cities are growing magnificent with
beautiful buildings, parks, and playgrounds.   Our countryside has
been knit together with splendid roads.

     We have doubled the use of electrical power and with it we have
taken sweat from the backs of men.   The purchasing power of
wages has steadily increased.   The hours of labor have decreased.
The twelve-hour day has been abolished.   Great progress has been
made in stabilization of commerce and industry.   The job of every
man has thus been made more secure.   Unemployment in the sense
of distress is widely disappearing.

Our Prosperity Wisely Enjoyed

     One of the oldest and perhaps the noblest of human aspirations
have been the abolition of poverty.   By poverty I mean the grinding
by undernourishment, cold, and ignorance, and fear of old age of
those who have the will to work.   We in America today are nearer to
the final triumph over poverty than ever before in the history of any
land.   The poorhouse is vanishing from among us.   We have not yet
reached the goal, but, given a chance to go forward with the policies
of the last eight years, we shall soon with the help of God be in sight
of the day when poverty will be banished from this nation.   There is
no guarantee against poverty equal to a job for every man.   That is
the primary purpose of the economic policies we advocate.

     I especially rejoice in the effect of our increased national
efficiency upon the improvement of the American home.   That is
the sanctuary of our loftiest ideals, the source of the spiritual
energy of our people.   The bettered home surroundings, the
expanded schools and playgrounds, and the enlarged leisure which

have come with our economic progress have brought to the average family a fuller life, a wider outlook, a stirred imagination, and a lift in aspirations.

Economic advancement is not an end in itself. Successful democracy rests wholly upon the moral and spiritual quality of its people. Our growth in spiritual achievements must keep pace with our growth in physical accomplishments. Material prosperity and moral progress must march together if we would make the United States that commonwealth so grandly conceived by its founders. Our government, to match the expectations of our people, must have constant regard for those human values that give dignity and nobility to life. Generosity of impulse, cultivation of mind, willingness to sacrifice, spaciousness of spirit—those are the qualities whereby America, growing bigger and richer and more powerful, may become America great and noble. A people or government, to whom these values are not real, because they are not tangible, is in peril. Size, wealth, and power alone cannot fulfill the promise of America's opportunity.

Urgent Need of Farm Relief

The most urgent economic problem in our nation today is in agriculture. It must be solved if we are to bring prosperity and contentment to one-third of our people directly and to all have or people indirectly. We have pledged ourselves to find a solution.

There are many causes for failure of agriculture to win its full share of national prosperity. The after-war deflation of prices not only brought great direct losses to the farmer, but he was often left indebted in inflated dollars to be paid in deflated dollars. Prices are often demoralized through gluts in our markets during the harvest season. Local taxes have been increased to provide the improved roads and schools. The tariff on some products is proving inadequate to protect him from imports from abroad. The increases in transportation rates since the war have greatly affected the price, which he receives for his products. Over six million farmers in times of surplus engage in destructive competition with one another in the sale of their product, often depressing prices below those levels that could be maintained.

Differences of opinion as to both causes and remedy have retarded the completion of a constructive program of relief. It is our plain duty to search out the common ground on which we may mobilize the sound forces of agricultural reconstruction. Our platform lays a solid basis upon which we can build. It offers an affirmative program.

Bearing of Tariff, Waterways, and Marketing

An adequate tariff is the foundation of farm relief. Our consumers increase faster than our producers do. The domestic market must be protected. Foreign products raised under lower standards of living are today competing in our home markets. I would use my office and influence to give the farmer the full benefit of our historic tariff policy....

An outstanding proposal of the party program is the whole-hearted pledge to undertake the reorganization of the marketing system upon sounder and more economical lines. We have already contributed greatly to this purpose by the acts supporting farm co-operatives, the establishment of intermediate credit banks, the regulation of stockyards and public exchanges, and the expansion of the Department of Agriculture. The platform proposes to go much farther. It pledges the creation of a Federal Farm Board of representative farmers to be clothed with authority and resources with which not only to still further aid farmers' co-operatives and pools and to assist generally in solution of farm problems but especially to build up, with federal finance, farmer-owned and farmer-controlled stabilization corporations which will protect the farmer from the depressions and demoralization of seasonal gluts and periodical surpluses.

Expense No Obstacle

Objection has been made that this program, as laid down by the party platform, may require that several hundred millions of dollars of capital be advanced by the Federal Government without obligation upon the individual farmer. With that objection I have little patience. A nation which is spending ninety billions a year can well afford an expenditure of a few hundred millions for a workable program that will give to one-third of its population their fair share of the nation's prosperity. Nor does this proposal put the government into business except so far as it is called upon to furnish capital with which to build up the farmer to the control of his own destinies....

During my term as Secretary of Commerce I have steadily endeavored to build up a system of co-operation between the government and business. Under these co-operative actions all elements interested in the problems of a particular industry such as manufacturer, distributor, worker, and consumer have been called into council together, not for a single occasion but for continuous work. These efforts have been successful beyond any expectation. They have been accomplished without interference or regulation by the government. They have secured progress in the industries, remedy for abuses, elimination of waste, reduction of cost in production and distribution, lower prices to the consumer, and more sable employment and profit. While the problem varies with every different commodity and with every different part of our great country, I should wish to apply the same method to agriculture so that the leaders of every phase of each group can advise and organize on policies and constructive measures. I am convinced that this form of action, as it has done in other industries, can greatly benefit farmer, distributor, and consumer.

The working out of agricultural relief constitutes the most important obligation of the next administration. I stand pledged to these proposals. The object of our policies is to establish for our farmers an income equal to those of other occupations; for the farmer's wife the same comforts in her home as women in other groups; for the farm boys and girls the same opportunity in life as other boys and girls. So far as my own abilities may be of service, I dedicate them to help secure prosperity and contentment in the industry where I and my forefathers were born and nearly all my family still obtain their livelihood.

The Interests of Labor

Having earned my living with my own hands, I cannot have other than the greatest sympathy with the aspirations of those who toil. It has been my good fortune during the past twelve years to have received the co-operation of labor in many directions, and in promotion of many public purposes.

The trade union movement in our country has maintained two departures from such movements in all other countries. They have been staunch supporters of American individualism and American institutions. They have steadfastly opposed subversive doctrines from abroad. Our freedom from foreign social and economic diseases is in large degree due to this resistance by our own labor. Our trade unions, with few exceptions, have welcomed all basic improvement in industrial methods. This largeness of mind has contributed to the advancing standards of living of the whole of our people. They properly have sought to participate—by additions to wages—in the result of improvements and savings which they have helped to make.

During these past years we have grown greatly in the mutual understanding between employer and employee. We have seen a growing realization by the employer that the highest practicable wage is the road to increased consumption and prosperity, and we have seen a growing realization by labor that the maximum use of machines, of effort, and of skill is the road to lower production costs and in the end to higher real wages. Under these impulses and the Republican protective system our industrial output has increased as never before and our wages have grown steadily in buying power. Our workers with their average weekly wages can today buy two and often three times more bread and butter than any wage earner of Europe. At one time we demanded for our workers a "full dinner pail." We have now gone far beyond that conception. Today we demand larger comfort and greater participation in life and leisure.

The Republican platform gives the pledge of the party to the support of labor. It endorses the principle of collective bargaining and freedom in labor negotiations. We stand also pledged to the curtailment of excessive use of the injunction in labor disputes.

The Congress has authorized and has in process of legislation great programs of public works. In addition to the works in development of water resources, we have in progress large undertakings in public roads and the construction of public buildings.

All these projects will probably require an expenditure of upward of one billion dollars within the next four years. It comprises the largest engineering construction ever undertaken by any government. It involves three times the expenditure laid out upon the Panama Canal. It is justified by the growth, need, and wealth of our country. The organization and administration of this construction is a responsibility of the first order. For it we must secure the utmost economy, honesty, and skill. These works, which will provide jobs for an army of men, should so far as practicable be adjusted to take up the slack of unemployment elsewhere.

The Government and Business

With impressive proof on all sides of magnificent progress, no one can rightly deny the fundamental correctness of our economic system. Our pre-eminent advance over nations in the last eight years has been due to distinctively American accomplishments. We do not owe these accomplishments to our vast natural resources. These we have always had. They have not increased. What has changed is our ability to utilize these resources more effectively. It is our human resources that have changed. Man for man and woman for woman, we are today more capable, whether in the work of farm, factory, or business, than ever before. It lies in our magnificent educational system, in the hard-working character of our people, in the capacity of far-sighted leadership in industry, the ingenuity, the daring of the pioneers of new inventions, in the abolition of the saloon, and the wisdom of our national policies.

With the growth and increasing complexity of our economic life the relations of government and business are multiplying daily. They are yearly more dependent upon each other. Where it is helpful and necessary, this relation should be encouraged. Beyond this it should not go. It is the duty of government to avoid regulation as long as equal opportunity to all citizens is not invaded and public rights violated. Government should not engage in business in competition with its citizens. Such actions extinguish the enterprise and initiative which has been the glory of America and which has been the root of its pre-eminence among the nations of the earth. On the other hand, it is the duty of business to conduct itself so that government regulation or government competition is unnecessary.

Business is practical, but it is founded upon faith—faith among our people in the integrity of businessmen, and faith that it will receive fair play from the government. It is the duty of government to maintain that faith. Our whole business system would break down in a day if there was not a high sense of moral responsibility in our business world. The whole practice and ethics of business has made great strides of improvement in the last quarter of a century, largely due to the effort of business and the professions themselves. One of the most helpful signs of recent years is the stronger growth of associations of workers, farmers, business men, and professional men with a desire to cure their own abuses and a purpose to serve public interest. Many problems can be solved through co-operation between government and these self-governing associations to improve methods and practices. When business cures its own abuses it is true self-government, which comprises more than political institutions.

Proper Promotion of Business a Government Function

The government can be of invaluable aid in the promotion of business. The ideal state of business is freedom from those fluctuations from boom to slump which bring on one hand the periods of unemployment and bankruptcy and, on the other, speculation and waste. Both are destructive to progress and fraught with great hardship to every home. By economy in expenditures, wise taxation, and sound fiscal finance it can relieve the burdens upon sound business and promote financial stability. By sound tariff policies it can protect our workmen, our farmers, and our manufacturers from lower standards of living abroad. By scientific research it can promote invention and improvement in methods. By economic research and statistical service it can promote the elimination of waste and contribute to stability in production and distribution. By promotion of foreign trade it can expand the markets for our manufacturers and farmers and thereby contribute greatly to stability and employment.

Our people know that the production and distribution of goods on a large scale is not wrong. Many of the most important comforts of our people are only possible by mass production and distribution. Both small and big business have their full place. The test of business is not its size—the test is whether there is honest competition, whether there is freedom from domination, whether there is integrity and usefulness of purpose. As secretary of commerce I have been greatly impressed by the fact that the foundation of American business is the independent businessman. The Department by encouragement of these associations and by provision of special services has endeavored to place him in a position of equality in information and skill with larger operations. Alike with our farmers his is the stronghold of American individuality. It is here that our local communities receive their leadership. It is here that we refresh our leadership for larger enterprise. We must maintain his opportunity and his individual service. He and the public must be protected from any domination or from predatory business.

The Ideal of Equality

There is one of the ideals of America upon which I wish at this time to lay especial emphasis. For we should constantly test our economic, social, and governmental system by certain ideals which must control them. The founders of our republic propounded the revolutionary doctrine that all men are created equal and all should have equality before the law. This was the emancipation of the individual. And since these beginnings, slowly, surely, and almost imperceptibly, this nation has added a third ideal almost unique to America—the ideal of equal opportunity. This is the safeguard of the individual. The simple life of early days in our republic found but few limitations upon equal opportunity. By the crowding of our people and the intensity and complexity of their activities it takes today a new importance.

Equality of opportunity is the right of every American—rich or poor, foreign or native-born, irrespective of faith or color. It is the right of every individual to attain that position in life to which his ability and character entitle him. By its maintenance we will alone hold open the door of opportunity to every new generation, to every boy and girl. It tolerates no privileged classes or castes or groups who would hold opportunity as their prerogative. Only from confidence that this right will be upheld can flow that unbounded courage and hope which stimulate each individual man and woman to endeavor and to achievement. The sum of their achievement is the gigantic harvest of national progress.

Not Socialism

This ideal of individualism based upon equal opportunity to every citizen is the negation of socialism. It is the negation of anarchy. It is the negation of despotism. It is as if we set a race. We, through free and universal education, provide the training of the runners; we give to them an equal start; we provide in the government the umpire of fairness in the race. The winner is he who shows the most conscientious training, the greatest ability, and the greatest character. Socialism bids all to end the race equally. It holds back the speedy to the pace of the slowest. Anarchy would provide neither training nor umpire. Despotism picks those who should run and those who should win.

Equality of opportunity is a fundamental principle of our nation. With it we must test all our policies. The success or failure of this principle is the test of our government.

Our purpose is to build in this nation a human society, not an economic system. We wish to increase the efficiency and productivity of our country, but its final purpose is happier homes. We shall succeed through the faith, the loyalty, the self-sacrifice, and the devotion to eternal ideals, which live today in every American.

II
Herbert Hoover:
Campaign Speech
New York, October 22, 1928

This campaign now draws near a close. The platforms of the two parties defining principles and offering solutions of various national problems have been presented and are being earnestly considered by our people.

In my acceptance speech I endeavored to outline the spirit and ideals by which I would be guided in carrying that platform into administration. Tonight I will not deal with the multitude of issues which have been already well canvassed. I intend rather to discuss some of those more fundamental principles and ideals upon which I believe the government of the United States should be conducted.

After the war, when the Republican Party assumed administration of the country, we were faced with the problem of determination of the very nature of our national life. During one hundred and fifty years we have builded up a form of self-government and a social system which is peculiarly our own. It differs essentially from all others in the world. It is the American system. It is just as definite and positive a political and social system as has ever been developed on earth. It is founded upon a particular conception of self-government in which decentralized local responsibility is the very base. Further than this, it is founded upon the conception that only through ordered liberty, freedom, and equal opportunity to the individual will his initiative and enterprise spur on the march of progress. And in our insistence upon equality of opportunity has our system advanced beyond all the world.

During the war we necessarily turned to the government to solve every difficult economic problem. The government having absorbed every energy of our people for war, there was no other solution. For the preservation of the state the Federal Government became a centralized despotism which undertook unprecedented responsibilities, assumed autocratic powers, and took over the business of citizens. To a large degree we regimented our whole people temporarily into a socialistic state. However justified in time of war if continued in peace-time it would destroy not only our American system but with it our progress and freedom as well.

When the war closed, the most vital of all issues both in our own country and throughout the world was whether governments should continue their wartime ownership and operation of many instrumentalities of production and distribution. We were challenged with a peace-time choice between the American system of rugged individualism and a European philosophy of diametrically opposed doctrines—doctrines of paternalism and state socialism. The acceptance of these ideas would have meant the destruction of self-government through centralization of government. It would have meant the undermining of the individual initiative and enterprise through which our people have grown to unparalleled greatness.

When the Republican Party came into full power it went at once resolutely back to our fundamental conception of the state and the rights and responsibilities of the individual. Thereby it restored confidence and hope in the American people, it freed and stimulated enterprise; it restored the government to its position as an umpire instead of a player in the economic game. For these reasons the American people have gone forward in progress while the rest of the world has halted and some countries have even gone backwards. If anyone will study the causes of retarded recuperation in Europe, he will find much of it due to stifling of private initiative on one hand, and overloading of the government with business on the other.

There has been revived in this campaign, however, a series of proposals which, if adopted, would be a long step toward the abandonment of our American system and a surrender to the destructive operation of governmental conduct of commercial business. Because the country is faced with difficulty and doubt over certain national problems—that is prohibition, farm relief, and electrical power—our opponents propose that we must thrust government a long way into the businesses which give rise to these problems. In effect, they abandon the tenets of their own party and turn to state socialism as a solution for the difficulties presented by all three. It is proposed that we shall change from prohibition to the state purchase and sale of liquor. If their agriculture relief program means anything, it means the government shall directly or indirectly buy and sell and fix prices of agriculture products. And we are to go into the hydroelectric power business. In other words, we are confronted with a huge program of government in business.

There is, therefore, submitted to the American people a question of fundamental principle. That is: shall we depart from the principles of our American political and economic system, upon which we have advanced beyond all the rest of the world, in order to adopt methods based on principles destructive of its very foundations? And I wish to emphasize the seriousness of these proposals. I wish to make my position clear, for this goes to the very roots of American life and progress.

I should like to state to you the effect that this projection of government in business would have upon our system of self-government and our economic system. That effect would reach to the daily life of every man and woman. It would impair the very basis of liberty and freedom not only for those left outside the fold of expanded bureaucracy but for those embraced within it.

Let us first see the effect upon self-government. When the Federal Government undertakes to go into commercial business it must at once set up the organization and administration of that business, and it immediately finds itself in a labyrinth, every alley of which leads to the destruction of self-government.

Commercial business requires a concentration of responsibility. Self-government requires decentralization and many checks and balances to safeguard liberty. Our government to succeed in business would need to become in effect a despotism. There at once begins the destruction of self-government.

It is a false liberalism that interprets itself into the government operation of commercial business. Every step of bureaucratizing of the business of our country poisons the very roots of liberalism— that is, political equality, free speech, free assembly, free press, and equality of opportunity. It is the road not to more liberty, but to less liberty. Liberalism should be found not striving to spread bureaucracy but striving to set bounds to it. True liberalism seeks all legitimate freedom first in the confident belief that without such freedom the pursuit of all other blessings and benefits is vain. That belief is the foundation of all American progress, political as well as economic.

Liberalism is a force truly of the spirit, a force proceeding from the deep realization that economic freedom cannot be sacrificed if political freedom is to be preserved. Even if governmental conduct of business could give us more efficiency instead of less efficiency, the fundamental objection to it would remain unaltered and unabated. It would destroy political equality. It would increase rather than decrease abuse and corruption. It would stifle initiative and invention. It would undermine the development of leadership. It would cramp and cripple the mental and spiritual energies of our people. It would extinguish equality and opportunity. It would dry up the spirit of liberty and progress. For these reasons primarily it must be resisted. For a hundred and fifty years liberalism has found its true spirit in the American system, not in the European systems.

I do not wish to be misunderstood in this statement. I am defining a general policy. It does not mean that our government is to part with one iota of its national resources without complete protection to the public interest. I have already stated that where the government is engaged in public works for purposes of flood control, of navigation, of irrigation, of scientific research or national defense, or in pioneering a new art, it will at times necessarily produce power or commodities as a by-product. But they must be a by-product of the major purpose, not the major purpose itself.

Nor do I wish to be misinterpreted as believing that the United States is free-for-all and devil-take-the-hindmost. The very essence of equality of opportunity and of American individualism is that there shall be no domination by any group or combination in this republic, whether it be business or political. On the contrary, it demands economic justice as well as political and social justice. It is no system of laissez faire.

I feel deeply on this subject because during the war I had some practical experience with governmental operation and control. I have witnessed not only at home but abroad the many failures of government in business. I have seen its tyrannies, its injustices, its destructions of self-government, its undermining of the very instincts which carry our people forward to progress. I have witnessed the lack of advance, the lowered standards of living, the depressed spirits of people working under such a system. My objection is based not upon theory or upon a failure to recognize wrong or abuse, but I know the adoption of such methods would strike at the very roots of American life and would destroy the very basis of American progress.

Our people have the right to know whether we can continue to solve our great problems without abandonment of our American system. I know we can.

And what have been the results of the American system? Our country has become the land of opportunity to those born without inheritance, not merely because of the wealth of its resources and industry but because of this freedom of initiative and enterprise. Russia has natural resources equal to ours. Her people are equally industrious, but she has not had the blessings of one hundred and fifty years of our form of government and our social system.

By adherence to the principles of decentralized self-government, ordered liberty, equal opportunity, and freedom to the individual, our American experiment in human welfare has yielded a degree of well-being unparalleled in all the world. It has come nearer to the abolition of poverty, to the abolition of fear of want, than humanity has ever reached before. Progress of the past seven years is the proof of it. This alone furnishes the answer to our opponents, who ask us to introduce destructive elements into the system by which this has been accomplished.

I have endeavored to present to you that the greatness of America has grown out of a political and social system and a method of control of economic forces distinctly its own—our American system—which has carried this great experiment in human welfare farther than ever before in all history. We are nearer today to the ideal of the abolition of poverty and fear from the lives of men and women than ever before in any land. And I again repeat that the departure from our American system by injecting principles destructive to it which our opponents propose, will jeopardize the very liberty and freedom of our people, and will destroy equality of opportunity not alone to ourselves but to our children.

III
Herbert Hoover:
Campaign Speech
St. Louis, November 2, 1928

I propose tonight to discuss the constructive side of government. I propose to outline something of the principles which must underlie the relation of government to the constructive tasks which confront us. A few nights ago in New York I had occasion to discuss these principles in application to matters which the government should not undertake. Tonight I discuss them in connection with matters which the government should and must undertake. Government is only in part a negative function. Its purpose is not merely to stand as a watchman over what is forbidden; government must be a constructive force.

The Unique American System

Our country has a political, social, and economic system that is peculiarly our own. It is the American system. It grew out of our revolt from European systems and has ripened with our experience and our ideals. We have seldom tried to express it or define it. It has been the moving force of our progress. It has brought us into the leadership of the world.

The founders of our republic under Divine inspiration set up not alone a great political system of self-government, but they set up also a revolutionary social system in the relation of men toward men.

Our political system is unique in the world. It is unique because of its decentralization of self-government and its checks and balances which safeguard ordered liberty and freedom to each individual. Our social system is unique in the world. It is unique because it is founded not only upon the ideal that all men are created equal and are equal before the law, but also upon the ideal that there shall be equal opportunity among men. We have no frozen classes or stratification of caste in our country. We allow nothing to prevent the rise of every boy and girl to the position to which their initiative and talents will carry them. We have no titles except the descriptions of our jobs.

From our unique political and social ideals we are evolving a unique economic system. We have discarded the original European theory that there is a class struggle between the capital of the few and the labor of the many. Under that theory it was held that labor was a commodity and the laborer in general could never rise far above bare existence, for if he did so the supply of labor would increase and thus constantly pull him back into the cesspool of inevitable poverty.

We Americans have proved this conception wrong. By what amounts to a revolution in ideas and methods, we have developed a new economic system. The dominating idea of that system is that labor on the one hand and capital, which in America means the savings of the people, on the other hand, by joint effort can steadily increase the efficiency of production and distribution. In other words, we find that by joint effort we can steadily increase the production of goods by each individual and we can at the same time decrease the cost of goods. As we increase the volume of goods, we have more to divide, and we thereby steadily lift the standard of living of the whole people. We have proved this to be true, and by this proof we have laid away the old theory of inevitable poverty alongside the theory of human slavery.

These three revolutionary American ideas, political, social, and economic, are interlocked and intermeshed. They are dominated and cemented by the ideal and practice of equal opportunity. They constitute one great system protecting our individualism and stimulating initiative and enterprise in our people. This is the American system. One part of it cannot be destroyed without undermining the whole. For us to adopt other social conceptions, such as federal or state government entry into commercial business in competition with its citizens, would undermine initiative and enterprise and destroy the very foundations of freedom and progress upon which the American system is built....

Constructive Government

There are three potential fields in which the principles and impulses of our American system require that government take constructive action. They comprise those activities which no local community can itself assume and which the individual initiative and enterprise of our people cannot wholly compass. They comprise leadership of the government to solve many difficult problems.

The first of these fields includes the great under-takings in public works such as inland waterways, flood control, reclamation, highways, and public buildings.

The second of these is necessary interest and activity of the Federal Government in fostering education, public health, scientific research, public parks, conservation of national resources, agriculture, industry, and foreign commerce.

The third great field lies in broadening the assistance of the government to the growing efforts of our people to co-operation among themselves to useful social and economic ends.

Federal Highways

This administration has recognized the public necessity of Federal Government contribution to the creation of a definitive system of modern interstate highways. This program is far from completion, and I stand for its continuance. Congress has lately authorized a large program of much-needed public buildings. And

there are other important public works of less immediate interest to
the Midwest to which I have referred upon other occasions. The
whole comprises the largest engineering construction ever
undertaken by any government. It means an expenditure of nearly
a billion of dollars in the next four years, or nearly four times the
outlay on the Panama Canal. As I have said before, these
undertakings are justified by the growth, the need, and the wealth
of our country. The organization and administration of this
construction is a responsibility of the first order. For it we must
secure the utmost economy, honesty, and skill. These works, which
will provide jobs for an army of men, should, so far as practical, be
adjusted to take up the slack of unemployment if it should occur.

A Federal Farm Board

In addition to the tariff and cheaper waterway transportation in
assistance to agriculture, the Republican Party proposes to go
farther. It proposes to set up an institution which will be one of the
most important institutions in our government, designed to meet
not only the varied problems which confront us today but those
which may arise in the future. We propose to create a Federal Farm
Board composed of men of understanding and sympathy for the
problems of agriculture; we propose that this board should have
power to determine the facts, the causes, the remedies which
should be applied to each and every one of the multitude of
problems which we mass under the general term "the agricultural
problem."

This program further provides that the board shall have a broad
authority to act and be authorized to assist in the further
development of co-operative marketing; that it shall assist in the
development of clearing-houses for agricultural products, in the
development of adequate warehousing facilities, in the elimination
of wastes in distribution, and in the solution of other problems as
they arise. But in particular the board is to build up, with initial
advances of capital from the government, farmer-owned and
farmer-controlled stabilization corporations which will protect the
farmer from depressions and the demoralization of summer and
periodic surpluses.

It is proposed that this board should have placed at its disposal
such resources as are necessary to make its action effective.

Thus we give to the Federal Farm Board every arm with which to
deal with the multitude of problems. This is an entirely different

method of approach to solution from that of a general formula; it is flexible and adaptable. No such far-reaching and specific proposal has ever been made by a political party on behalf of any industry in our history. It is a direct business proposition. It marks our desire for establishment of the farmer's stability and at the same time maintains his independence and individuality.

This plan is consonant with our American ideals to avoid the government operation of commercial business, for it places the operation upon the farmer himself, not upon a bureaucracy. It puts the government in its real relation to the citizen—that of co-operation. Its object is to give equality of opportunity to the farmer. I would consider it the greatest honor I could have if it should become my privilege to aid in finally solving this, the most difficult of economic problems presented to our people, and the one in which by inheritance and through long contact I have my deepest interest....

The Principle of Co-operation
...We have in the past quarter of a century evolved a higher sense of organized co-operation than has ever been known before. We have ten thousand examples of this conscious co-operative development in the enormous growth of associational activities. Civic associations, chambers of commerce, trade associations, professional associations, labor unions, trade councils, farm organizations, farm co-operatives, welfare associations—these are so all-embracing that there is scarcely an individual in our country who does not now belong to one or more of them. They represent every phase of our national life both on the economic and on the welfare side. They constitute a vast ferment toward conscious co-operation. They have become a part of the very fabric of American life. While some of them engage in highly objectionable attempts to wrongly influence public opinion and the action of government, the majority of them recognize a responsibility to the public as well as to themselves; and a large part of them are founded solely on public interest.

Wherever these associations undertake high public purposes I wish to see active co-operation by the government with them. Without intrusion the government can serve to bring together discordant elements and to secure co-operation between different industries and groups. It gives great hope of a new basis of solution for many of our problems and progressive action in our

people.   It should be the response of government to our new
economic conceptions.   It is consonant with the American system.
It is a method that reinforces our individualism by reducing, and
not increasing, government interference in business and the life of
our citizens.

Such co-operation strengthens the whole foundations of self-
government and serves to maintain equality of opportunity and
constructive leadership.

This co-operation can take two distinct directions.   It can assist
in the promotion of constructive projects of public interest on one
hand, and it can assist in the cure of abuses by the voluntary
establishment of a higher code of ethics and a stricter standard in
the conduct of business....

Illustrative Examples

First, I may review a case of assistance to labor and business.   In
1923, under my chairmanship, there was organized a series of
committees representing the manufacturers, contractors, engineers,
real estate men, and labor in the building trades.   Its purpose was
to reduce the loss of time due to the seasonal character of these
industries.   As a result of the organization set up, the average
winter unemployment in these trades has been reduced from about
one hundred days to about half that number.   There has been no
decrease in daily wages.   The annual income of the workers in these
trades has been substantially increased by the decrease in idle days,
and the business given greater stability.

Another instance of action of fundamental importance to the
farmer, the businessman, and the worker consists of the measures
taken in co-operation between the government and business
agencies to mitigate the violence of the so-called business cycle.
Booms and slumps have occurred periodically for one hundred
years.   No one suffers more from these periodic hard times, with
their hideous unemployment, decrease in wages, and bankruptcy in
business, than both labor and the farmers.   Time forbids a
discussion of the intricate problems involved and the remedies
which have been inaugurated.   The proof of the effectiveness lies in
the fact that we have had a far longer period of stability in industry
and commerce, far greater security in employment, and larger
buying power for farm products than ever before in our history.
The solution of this question was just as intricate as those which we
face in agriculture....

Avoidance of Unnecessary Regulation

An illustration of another direction of these activities has been in eliminating abuses in a particular industry without resort to legislation and regulation. For a great many years legislation had been debated in Congress providing for the regulation of the lumber industry somewhat on the lines of the pure food laws, in order to protect the honest manufacturers and dealers and the public. In 1923, however, we created a series of committees amongst associations in the lumber industry at their request. In the course of a gradual extension over five years we finally perfected a system for the grading of lumber and for the guaranteeing of those grades to the public, which is now carried out wholly within and by the lumber industry itself. Consequently during these last few years there has been no suggestion of such legislation from Congress. The savings to the public in the elimination of waste and fraud have been estimated by the industry as upwards of two hundred and fifty million dollars a year. This is a clear case where by co-operative methods we have avoided the necessity of regulation with the bureaucracy and interference that flow from it. It is also a clear case of building up of self-government....

In this broad field of co-operation by government lie potentialities which have been barely touched. The government can give leadership and co-operation. It can furnish scientific research. It can give prestige and influence. All of these call for but trivial expenditures. They require no increased bureaucracy. They are of first importance to every branch of American life.

It is by these means of co-operation by the government that we contribute mightily toward business stability and greater productivity in industry. And it is stability that every business man needs that he may thus work out for himself his own destiny without those ill tides over which he has no control.

It is by means of the sort of co-operation from the government that we may contribute greatly to the very foundations of economic progress, that is, to provide continuous and full employment. General employment comes not only with sound policies of government but equally from vigorous co-operation by the government to promote economic welfare. It is by these means that we build such organization of our economic system as to provide a job for all who have the will to work.

Equality of Opportunity

Government has the definite and manifest obligation of giving constructive leadership to the people. In doing so it must not lessen their initiative and enterprise, upon which we must rely for the progress of the race and of the nation. Our system has been built upon the ideal of equality of opportunity. For perhaps a hundred years after the foundation of the Republic, the opportunities of a moving frontier preserved that equality of opportunity. Now with the settlement of the country and with the astonishing speed and intricate complexity of industrial life, the preservation of equality of opportunity becomes yearly and yearly more difficult, and for that very reason is of higher and higher importance. If we would maintain America as the land of opportunity, where every boy and girl may have the chance to climb to that position to which his ability and character entitle him, we shall need to be on increasing guard. If I could drive the full meaning and importance of maintained equality of opportunity into the very consciousness of the American people, I would feel I had made some contribution to American life. It is the most precious of our possessions that the windows of every home shall look out upon unlimited hope. Equality of opportunity is the right of every American, rich or poor, foreign or native born, without respect to race or religion. By its maintenance alone can we hold open the door of full achievement to every new generation and to every boy and girl? Only from confidence that this right will be upheld can flow that unbounded courage and hope which stimulates each individual man and woman to endeavor and to accomplishment. By this principle we should test every act of government, every proposal, whether it be economic or political. I insist upon the most strict regulation of public utilities, because otherwise they would destroy equality of opportunity. I object to the government going into business in competition with its citizens because that would destroy equality of opportunity. And equality of opportunity is the flux with which alone we can melt out full and able leadership to the nation.

The first step to maintained equality of opportunity amongst our people is, as I have said before, that there should be no child in America who has not been born, and who does not live, under sound conditions of health; who does not have full opportunity for education from the kindergarten to the university; who is not free from injurious labor; who does not have stimulation to ambition to the fullest of his or her capacities. It is a matter of concern to our government that we should strengthen the safeguards to health. These activities of helpfulness and of co-operation stretch before us in every direction. A single generation of Americans of such a production would prevent more of crime and of illness, and give more of spirit and of progress than all of the repressive laws and police we can ever invent—and it would cost less.

The American Home

I have said often before in this campaign that we need always to interpret our discussions of economic and material proposals by how they affect the peace, the happiness, and the security and prosperity of every American home. I have tried to interpret to my fellow-countrymen what government means to that home. I stand for a prosperous country because I want good homes. You cannot divide those things that are seen from those that are unseen. The things that we call material are the foundation stones upon which we build the temple of those things that we call spiritual.

Prosperity, security, happiness, and peace rest on sound economic life. Many of the subjects with which we have had to deal are intricate and complex. We must support the maintenance of peace amongst nations, economy in government, the protective tariff, the restriction of immigration, the encouragement of foreign trade, the relief of agriculture, the building of waterways, and a score of other great governmental policies which affect every home in our land. Solution of these questions is not always easy. Only the inexperienced can be positive in offering solutions of great problems. The first necessity in handling of such problems is the assembling of the facts in their proper perspective. The truth must be forged from the metal of facts.

IV
Herbert Hoover:
Annual Message to Congress
December 2, 1930

During the past 12 months we have suffered with other nations from economic depression.

The origins of the depression lie to some extent within our own borders through a speculative period which diverted capital and energy into speculation rather than constructive enterprise. Had over speculation in securities been the only force operating, we should have seen recovery many months ago, as these particular dislocations have generally readjusted themselves.

In the larger view the major forces of the depression now lie outside of the United States, and our recuperation has been retarded by the unwarranted degree of fear and apprehension created by these outside forces.

The extent of the depression is indicated by the following approximate percentages of activity during the past three months as compared with the highly prosperous year of 1928.

Value of department store sales	93% of 1928
Volume of manufacturing production	80% of 1928
Volume of mineral production	90% of 1928
Volume of factory employment	84% of 1928
Total of bank deposits	105% of 1928
Wholesale prices-all commodities	83% of 1928
Cost of living	94% of 1928

Various other indexes indicate a total decrease of activity from 1928 of from 15 to 20 percent.

There are many factors which give encouragement for the future. The fact that we are holding from 80 to 85 percent of our normal activities and incomes; that our major financial and industrial institutions have come through the storm unimpaired; that price levels of major commodities have remained approximately stable for sometime; that a number of industries are showing signs of increasing demand; that the world at large is readjusting itself to the situation; all reflect grounds for confidence. We should remember that these occasions have been met many times before, that they are but temporary, that our country is today stronger and richer in resources, in equipment, in skill, than ever in its history. We are in an extraordinary degree self-sustaining; we will overcome world influences and will lead the march of prosperity as we have always done hitherto.

Economic depression can not be cured by legislative action or executive pronouncement. Economic wounds must be healed by the action of the cells of the economic body—the producers and consumers themselves. Recovery can be expedited and its effects mitigated by cooperative action. That cooperation requires that every individual should sustain faith and courage; that each should maintain his self-reliance; that each and every one should search for methods of improving his business or service; that the vast majority whose income is unimpaired should not hoard out of fear but should pursue their normal living and recreations; that each should seek to assist his neighbors who may be less fortunate; that each industry should assist its own employees; that each community and each state should assume its full responsibilities for organization of employment and relief of distress with that sturdiness and independence which built a great Nation.

The best contribution of government lies in encouragement of this voluntary cooperation in the community. The Government, National, state, and local, can join with the community in such programs and do its part. A year ago I, together with other officers of the Government, initiated extensive cooperative measures throughout the country.

The first of these measures was an agreement of leading employers to maintain the standards of wages and of labor leaders to use their influence against strife. In a large sense these undertakings have been adhered to and we have not witnessed the usual reductions of wages which have always heretofore marked depressions. The index of union wage scales shows them to be today fully up to the level of any of the previous years. In consequence the buying power of the country has been much larger than would otherwise have been the case. Of equal importance the Nation has had unusual peace in industry and freedom from public disorder which has characterized previous depressions.

The second direction of cooperation has been that our governments, National, state, and local, the industries and business so distribute employment as to give work to the maximum number of employees.

The third direction of cooperation has been to maintain and even extend construction work and betterments in anticipation of the future. It has been the universal experience in previous depressions that public works and private construction have fallen off rapidly with the general tide of depression. On this occasion, however, the increased authorization and generous appropriations by the Congress and the action of states and municipalities have resulted in the expansion of public construction to an amount even above that in the most prosperous years. In addition, the cooperation of public utilities, railways, and other large organizations has been generously given in construction and betterment work in

anticipation of future need. The Department of commerce advises
me that as a result, the volume of this type of construction work,
which amounted to roughly $6,300,000,000 in 1929, instead of
decreasing will show a total of abut $7,000,000,000 for 1930. There
has, of course, been a substantial decrease in the types of
construction which could not be undertaken in advance of need.

The fourth direction of cooperation was the organization in such
states and municipalities, as was deemed necessary, of committees
to organize local employment, to provide for employment agencies,
and to effect relief of distress.

The result of magnificent cooperation throughout the country
has been the actual suffering has been kept to a minimum during
the past 12 months, and our unemployment has been far less in
proportion than in other large industrial countries. Some time ago
it became evident that unemployment would continue over the
winter and would necessarily be added to from seasonal causes
and that the savings of workpeople would be more largely
depleted. We have as a nation a definite duty to see that no
deserving person in our country suffers from hunger or cold. I
therefore set up a more extensive organization to stimulate more
intensive cooperation throughout the country. There has been a
most gratifying degree of response, from governors, mayors, and
other public officials, from welfare organizations, and from
employers in concerns both large and small. The local communities
through their voluntary agencies have assumed the duty of
relieving individual distress and are being generously supported by
the public.

As a contribution to the situation the Federal Government is
engaged upon the greatest program of waterway, harbor, flood
control, public building, highway, and airway improvement in all
our history. This, together with loans to merchant shipbuilders,
improvement of the Navy and in military aviation, and other
construction work of the Government will exceed $520,000,000 for
this fiscal year. This compares with $253,000,000 in the fiscal year
1928. The construction works already authorized and the
continuation of policies in Government aid will require a continual
expenditure upwards of half a billion dollars annually.

I favor still further temporary expansion of these activities in aid
to unemployment during this winter. The Congress will, however,
have presented to it numbers of projects, some of them under the
guise of, rather than the reality of, their usefulness in the increase of

employment during the depression. There are certain common-sense limitations upon any expansions of construction work. The Government must not undertake works that are not of sound economic purpose and that have not been subject to searching technical investigation, and which have not been given adequate consideration by the Congress. The volume of construction work in the Government is already at the maximum limit warranted by financial prudence as a continuing policy. To increase taxation for purposes of construction work defeats its own purpose, as such taxes directly diminish employment in private industry. Again any kind of construction requires, after its authorization, a considerable time before labor can be employed in which to make engineering, architectural, and legal preparations. Our immediate problem is the increase of employment for the next six months, and new plans which do not produce such immediate result or which extend commitments beyond this period are not warranted.

The enlarged rivers and harbors, public building, and highway plans authorized by the Congress last session, however, offer an opportunity for assistance by the temporary acceleration of construction of these programs even faster than originally planned especially if the technical requirements of the laws which entail great delays could be amended in such fashion as to speed up acquirements of land and the letting of contracts.

With view, however, to the possible need for acceleration, we, immediately upon receiving those authorities from the Congress five months ago, began the necessary technical work in preparation for such possible eventuality. I have canvassed the departments of the Government as to the maximum amount that can be properly added to our present expenditure to accelerate all construction during the next six months, and I feel warranted in asking the Congress for an appropriation of from $100,000,000 to $150,000,000 to provide such further employment in this emergency. In connection therewith we need some authority to make enlarged temporary advances of Federal highway aid to the states.

I recommend that this appropriation be made distributable to the different departments upon recommendation of a committee of the Cabinet and approval by the President. Its application to works already authorized by the Congress assures its use in directions of economic importance and to public welfare. Such action will imply an expenditure upon construction of all kinds of over $650,000,000 during the next twelve months.

Agriculture

The worldwide depression has affected agriculture in common with all other industries. The average price of farm produce has fallen to about 80 percent of the levels of 1928. This average is, however, greatly affected by wheat and cotton, which have participated in worldwide overproduction and have fallen to about 60 percent of the average price of the year 1928. Excluding these commodities, the prices of all other agricultural products are about 84 percent of those of 1928. The average Wholesale prices of other primary goods, such as nonferrous metals, have fallen to 76 percent of 1928.

In order that the Government may meet its full obligation toward our countrymen in distress through no fault of their own, I recommend that an appropriation should be made to the Department of Agriculture to be loaned for the purpose of seed and feed for animals. Its application should as hitherto in such loans be limited to a gross amount to any one individual, and secured upon the crop.

Legislation

We have determined upon a national policy of consolidation of the railways as a necessity of more stable, and more economically operated transportation. Further legislation is necessary to facilitate such consolidation. In the public interest we should strengthen the railways that they may meet our future needs.

I recommend that the Congress institute an inquiry into some aspects of the economic working of thee laws. I do not favor repeal of the Sherman Act. The prevention of monopolies is of most vital public importance. Competition is not only the basis of protection to the consumer but is the incentive to progress.

It is urged by many thoughtful citizens that the peculiar economic effect of the income tax on so-called capital gains at the present rate is to enhance speculative inflation and likewise impede business recovery. I believe this to be the case and I recommend that a study be made of the economic effects of this tax and of its relation to the general structure of our income tax law.

I urge further consideration by the Congress of the recommendations I made a year ago looking to the development through temporary Federal aid of adequate state and local services for health of children and the further stamping out of communicable disease, particularly in the rural sections. The advance of scientific discovery, methods, and social thought imposes a new vision in these matters. The drain upon the Federal Treasury is comparatively small. The results both economic and moral are of the utmost importance.

It is my belief that after passing of this depression, when we can examine it in retrospect, we shall need to consider a number of other questions as to what action may be taken by the Government to remove possible governmental influences which make for instability and to better organize mitigation of the effect of depression. It is as yet too soon to constructively formulate such measures.

V
Franklin D. Roosevelt:
Address to Conference of Governors
Indiana, June 2, 1931

At a time when our country, in common with most of the rest of the world, is suffering from a severe dislocation of economic progress, all of the people are naturally and properly asking questions about state and national navigation. It seems strange to them that with capacities of production developed to the highest degree the world has ever seen, there should come this severe depression, when many who are anxious to work cannot find food for their families while at the same time there is such a surplus of food supplies and other necessities that those who are growing crops and manufacturing can find no markets.

This situation has suggested to many that some new factor is needed to our economic life and this new factor must come from utilizing our experience and our ingenuity to draft and to organize concerted plans for the better use of our resources and the better planning of our social and economic life in general.

It is not enough to talk about being of good cheer. Frankly, I cannot take the Pollyanna attitude as a solution to our problems. It is not enough to apply old remedies. A new economic and social balance calls for positive leadership and definite experiments which have not hitherto been tried.

More and more, those who are the victims of dislocations and defects of our social and economic life are beginning to ask respectfully, but insistently of us who are in positions of public responsibility why government can not and should not act to protect its citizens from disaster. I believe the question demands an answer and that the ultimate answer is that government, both state and national, must accept the responsibility of doing what it can do—soundly with considered forethought, and along definitely constructive, not passive lines.

VI
Herbert Hoover:
Annual Message to Congress
December 8, 1931

The chief influence affecting the state of the Union during the past year has been continued worldwide economic disturbance. Our national concern has been to meet the emergencies it has created for us and to lay the foundations for recovery.

If we lift our vision beyond these immediate emergencies we find fundamental national gains even amid depression. In meeting the problems of this difficult period, we have witnessed a remarkable development of the sense of cooperation in the community. For the first time in the history of our major economic depressions there has been a notable absence of public disorders and industrial conflict. Above all there is an enlargement of social and spiritual responsibility among the people. The strains and stresses upon business have resulted in closer application in saner policies, and in better methods. Public improvements have been carried out on a larger scale than even in normal times. The country is richer in physical property, in newly discovered resources, and in productive capacity than ever before. There has been constant gain in knowledge and education; there has been continuous advance in science and invention; there has been distinct gain in public health. Business depressions have been recurrent in the life of our country and are but transitory. The nation has emerged from each of them with increased strength and virility because of the enlightenment they have brought, the readjustments and the larger understanding of the realities and obligations of life and work which come from them.

Foreign Affairs
We are at peace with the world. We have cooperated with other nations to preserve peace. The rights of our citizens abroad have been protected.

The economic depression has continued and deepened in every part of the world during the past year. In many countries political instability, excessive armaments, debts, governmental expenditures, and taxes have resulted in revolutions, in unbalanced budgets and monetary collapse and financial panics, in dumping of goods upon world markets, and in diminished consumption of commodities.

Within two years there have been revolutions or acute social disorders in 19 countries, embracing more than half the population of the world. Ten countries have been unable to meet their external obligations. In 14 countries, embracing a quarter of the world's population, former monetary standards have been temporarily abandoned. In a number of countries there have been acute financial panics or compulsory restraints upon banking. These disturbances have many roots in the dislocations from the World War. Every one of them has reacted upon us. They have sharply affected the markets and prices of our agricultural and industrial products. They have increased unemployment and greatly embarrassed our financial and credit system.

As our difficulties during the past year have plainly originated in large degree from these sources, any effort to bring about our own recuperation has dictated the necessity of cooperation by us with other nations in reasonable effort to restore world confidence and economic stability.

Cooperation of our Federal Reserve System and our banks with the central banks in foreign countries has contributed to localize and ameliorate a number of serious financial crises or moderate the pressures upon us and thus avert disasters which would have affected us....

The Domestic Situation

Many undertakings have been organized and forwarded during the past year to meet the new and changing emergencies which have constantly confronted us.

Broadly the community has cooperated to meet the needs of honest distress, and to take such emergency measures as would sustain confidence in our financial system and would cushion the violence of liquidation in industry and commerce, thus giving time for orderly readjustment of costs, inventories, and credits without panic and widespread bankruptcy. These measures have served those purposes and will promote recovery.

In these measures we have striven to mobilize and stimulate private initiative and local and community responsibility. There has been the least possible government entry into the economic field, and that only in temporary and emergency form. Our citizens and our local governments have given a magnificent display of unity and action, initiative and patriotism in solving a multitude of difficulties and in cooperating with the Federal Government.

For a proper understanding of my recommendations to the Congress it is desirable very briefly to review such activities during the past year.

The emergencies of unemployment have been met by action in many directions. The appropriations for the continued speeding up of the great Federal construction program have provided direct and indirect aid to unemployment upon a large scale. By organized unity of action, the states and municipalities have also maintained large programs of public improvement. Many industries have been prevailed upon to anticipate and intensify construction. Industrial concerns and other employers have been organized to spread available work amongst all their employees instead of discharging a portion of them. A large majority have maintained wages at as high levels as the safe conduct of their business would permit. This course has saved us from industrial conflict and disorder which have characterized all previous depressions. Immigration has been curtailed by administrative action. Upon the basis of normal immigration the decrease amounts to about 300,000 individuals who otherwise would have been added to our unemployment. The expansion of Federal employment agencies under appropriations by the Congress has proved most effective. Through the President's organization for unemployment relief, public and private agencies were successfully mobilized last winter to provide employment and other measures against distress. Similar organization gives assurance against suffering during the coming winter. Committees of leading citizens are now active at practically every point of unemployment. In the large majority they have been assured the funds necessary which, together with local government aids, will meet the situation. A few exceptional localities will be further organized. The evidence of the Public Health Service shows an actual decrease of sickness and infant and general mortality below normal years. No greater proof could be adduced that our people have been protected from hunger and cold and that the sense of social responsibility in the nation has responded to the need of the unfortunate....

Further Measures

The major economic forces and weaknesses at home and abroad have now been exposed and can be appraised, and the time is ripe for forward action to expedite our recovery.

Although some of the causes of our depression are due to speculation, inflation of securities and real estate, unsound foreign investments, and mismanagement of financial institutions, yet our self-contained national economy, with its matchless strength and resources, would have enabled us to recover long since but for the continued dislocations, shocks and setbacks from abroad....

The situation largely arises from an unjustified lack of confidence. We have enormous volumes of idle money in the banks and in hoarding. We do not require more money or working capital—we need to put what we have to work.

The fundamental difficulties which have brought about financial strains in foreign countries do not exist in the United States. No external drain on our resources can threaten our position, because the balance of international payments is in our favor; we owe less to foreign countries than they owe to us; our industries are efficiently organized; our currency and bank deposits are protected by the greatest gold reserve in history.

Our first step toward recovery is to reestablish confidence and thus restore the flow of credit which is the very basis of our economic life. We must put some steel beams in the foundations of our credit structure. It is our duty to apply the full strength of our government not only to the immediate phases, but to provide security against shocks and the repetition of the weaknesses which have been proven.

The recommendations which I here lay before the Congress are designed to met these needs by strengthening financial, industrial, and agricultural life through the medium of our existing institutions, and thus to avoid the entry of the government into competition with private business.

Federal Government Finance

The first requirement of confidence and of economic recovery is financial stability of the United States Government. I shall deal with fiscal questions at greater length in the Budget message. But I must at this time call attention to the magnitude of the deficits which have developed and the resulting necessity for determined and courageous policies. These deficits arise in the main from the heavy decrease in tax receipts due to the depression and to the increase in expenditure on construction in aid to unemployment, aids to agriculture, and upon services to veterans....

We must have insistent and determined reduction in government expenses. We must face a temporary increase in taxes. Such increase should not cover the whole of these deficits or it will retard recovery. We must partially finance the deficit by borrowing. It is my view that the amount of taxation should be fixed so as to balance the Budget for 1933 except for the statutory debt retirement. Such government receipts would assure the balance of the following year's budget including debt retirement. It is my further view that the additional taxation should be imposed solely as an emergency measure terminating definitely two years from July 1 next. Such a basis will give confidence in the determination of the government to stabilize its finance and will assure taxpayers of its temporary character. Even with increased taxation, the government will reach the utmost safe limit of its borrowing capacity by the expenditures for which we are already obligated and the recommendations here proposed. To go further than these limits in either expenditures, taxes, or borrowing will destroy confidence, denude commerce and industry of their resources, jeopardize the financial system, and actually extend unemployment and demoralize agriculture rather than relieve it.

Federal Land Banks

I recommend that the Congress authorize the subscription by the Treasury of further capital to the Federal Land Banks to be retired as provided in the original act, or when funds are available, and that repayments of such capital be treated as a fund available for further subscriptions in the same manner. It is urgent that the banks be supported so as to stabilize the market values of their bonds and thus secure capital for the farmers at low rates, that they may continue their services to agriculture and that they may meet the present situation with consideration to the farmers.

Deposits in Closed Banks

A method should be devised to make available quickly to depositors some portion of their deposits in closed banks as the assets of such banks may warrant. Such provision would go far to relieve distress in a multitude of families, would stabilize values in many communities, and would liberate working capital to thousands of concerns. I recommend that measures be enacted promptly to accomplish these results and I suggest that the Congress should consider the development of such a plan through the Federal Reserve Banks.

Home Loan Discount Banks

I recommend the establishment of a system of home-loan discount banks as the necessary companion in our financial structure of the Federal Reserve Banks and our Federal Land Banks. Such action will relieve present distressing pressures against home and farm property owners. It will relieve pressures upon and give added strength to building and loan associations, savings banks, and deposit banks, engaged in extending such credits. Such action would further decentralize our credit structure. It would revive residential construction and employment. It would enable such loaning institutions more effectually to promote home ownership. I discussed this plan at some length in a statement made public November 14, last. This plan has been warmly endorsed by the recent National Conference upon Home Ownership and Housing, whose members were designated by the governors of the states and the groups interested.

Reconstruction Finance Corporation

In order that the public may be absolutely assured and that the government may be in position to meet any public necessity, I recommend that an emergency Reconstruction Corporation of the nature of the former War Finance Corporation should be established. It may not be necessary to use such an instrumentality very extensively. The very existence of such a bulwark will strengthen confidence. The Treasury should be authorized to subscribe a reasonable capital to it, and it should be placed in liquidation at the end of two years. Its purpose is by strengthening the weak spots to thus liberate the full strength of the nation's resources. It should be in position to facilitate exports by American agencies; make advances to agricultural credit agencies where necessary to protect and aid the agricultural industry; to make temporary advances upon proper securities to established industries, railways, and financial institutions which can not otherwise secure credit, and where such advances will protect the credit structure and stimulate employment. Its functions would not overlap who's of the National Credit Corporation.

Federal Reserve Eligibility

On October 6th I issued a statement that I should recommend to the Congress an extension during emergencies of the eligibility provisions in the Federal Reserve Act. This statement was approved by a representative gathering of the members of both Houses of the Congress, including members of the appropriate committees. It was approved by the officials of the Treasury Department, and I understand such an extension has been approved by a majority of the governors of the Federal Reserve banks. Nothing should be done which would lower the safeguards of the system.

The establishment of the mortgage-discount banks herein referred to will also contribute to further reserve strength in the banks without inflation.

Banking Laws

Our people have a right to a banking system in which their deposits shall be safeguarded and the flow of credit less subject to storms. The need of a sounder system is plainly shown by the extent of bank failures. I recommend the prompt improvement of the banking laws. Changed financial conditions and commercial practices must me met. The Congress should investigate the need for separation between different kinds of banking; an enlargement of branch banking under proper restrictions; and the methods by which enlarged membership in the Federal Reserve System may be brought about....

Railways

The railways present one of our immediate and pressing problems. They are and must remain the backbone of our transportation system. Their prosperity is interrelated with the prosperity of all industries. Their fundamental service in transportation, the volume of the employment, their buying power for supplies from other industries, the enormous investment in their securities, particularly their bonds, by insurance companies, savings banks, benevolent and other trusts, all reflect their partnership in the whole economic fabric. Through these institutions the railway bonds are in a large sense the investment of every family. The well-maintained and successful operation and the stability of railway finances are of primary importance to economic recovery. They should have more effective opportunity to reduce operating costs by proper consolidation. As their rates must be regulated in public interest, so also approximate regulation should be applied to competing services by the authority. The methods of the regulation should be revised. The Interstate Commerce Commission has made important and far-reaching recommendations upon the whole subject, which I commend to the early consideration of the Congress.

Antitrust Laws

In my message of a year ago I commented on the necessity of congressional inquiry into the economic action of the antitrust laws. There is wide conviction that some change should be made especially in the procedure under thee laws. I do not favor their repeal. Such action would open wide the door to price fixing, monopoly, and destruction of healthy competition. Particular attention should be given to the industries founded upon natural resources, especially where destructive competition produces great wastes of these resources and brings great hardships upon operators, employees, and the public. In recent years there has been continued demoralization in the bituminous coal, oil, and lumber industries. I again commend the matter to the consideration of the Congress.

Unemployment

As an aid to unemployment the Federal Government is engaged in the greatest program of public building, harbor, flood control, highway, waterway, aviation, merchant and naval ship construction in all history... .

We must avoid burdens upon the government which will create more unemployment in private industry than can be gained by further expansion of employment by the Federal Government. We can now stimulate employment and agriculture more effectually and speedily through the voluntary measures in progress, through the thawing out of credit, through the building up of stability abroad, through the home loan discount banks, through an emergency finance corporation and the rehabilitation of the railways and other such directions.

I am opposed to any direct or indirect government role. The breakdown and increased unemployment in Europe is due in part to such practices. Our people are providing against distress from unemployment in true American fashion by a magnificent response to public appeal and by action of the local governments.

Electrical-Power Regulation

I have recommended in previous messages the effective regulation of interstate electrical power as the essential function of the reorganized Federal Power Commission. I renew the recommendation. It is urgently needed in public protection.

Muscle Shoals

At my suggestion, the Governors and Legislatures of Alabama and Tennessee selected three members each for service on a committee to which I appointed a representative of farm organizations and two representatives of the War Department for the purpose of recommending a plan for disposal of these properties which would be in the interest of the people of those states and the agricultural industry throughout the country. I shall transmit the recommendations to the Congress.

Reorganization of Federal Departments

I have referred in previous messages to the profound need of further reorganization and consolidation of Federal administrative functions to eliminate overlap and waste, and to enable coordination and definition of government policies now wholly impossible in scattered and conflicting agencies which deal with parts of the same major function. I shall lay before the Congress further recommendations upon this subject, particularly in relation to the Department of the Interior. There are two directions of such reorganization, however, which have an important bearing upon the emergency problems with which we are confronted.

Shipping Board

At present the Shipping Board exercises large administrative functions independent of the executive. These administrative functions should be transferred to the Department of Commerce, in keeping with that single responsibility which has been the basis of our governmental structure since its foundation. There should be created in that department a position of Assistant Secretary for Merchant Marine, under whom this work and the several bureaus having to do with merchant marine may be grouped.

The Shipping Board should be made a regulatory body active also in advisory capacity on loans and policies, in keeping with its original conception. Its regulatory powers should be amended to include regulation of coastwise shipping so as to assure stability and better service. It is also worthy of consideration that the regulation of rates and services upon the inland waterways should be assigned to such a reorganized board.

Reorganization of Public Works Administration

I recommend that all building and construction activities of the government now carried on by many departments be consolidated into an independent establishment under the President to be known as the "Public Works Administration" directed by a Public Works Administrator. This agency should undertake all construction work in service to the different departments of the government (except naval and military work). The services of the Corps of Army Engineers should be delegated in rotation for military duty to this administration in continuation of the supervision of river and harbor work. Great economies, sounder policies, more effective coordination to employment, and expedition in all construction work would result from this consolidation.

Inland Waterway and Harbor Improvement

These improvements are now proceeding upon an unprecedented scale. Some indication of the volume of work in progress is conveyed by the fact that during the current year over 380,000,000 cubic yards of material have been moved—an amount equal to the entire removal in the construction of the Panama Canal. The Mississippi waterway system, connecting Chicago, Kansas City, Pittsburgh, and New Orleans, will be in full operation during 1933. Substantial progress is being made upon the projects of the upper Missouri, upper Mississippi, etc. Negotiations are now in progress with Canada for the construction of the St. Lawrence Waterway.

The Tariff

Wages and standards of living abroad have been materially lowered during the past year. The temporary abandonment of the gold standard by certain countries has also reduced their production costs compared to ours. Fortunately any increases in the tariff which may be necessary to protect agriculture and industry from these lowered foreign costs, or decreases in items which may prove to be excessive, may be undertaken at any time by the Tariff Commission under authority which it possesses by virtue of the tariff act of 1930. The commission during the past year has reviewed the rates upon over 254 items subject to tariff. As a result of vigorous and industrious action, it is up to date in the consideration of pending references and is prepared to give prompt attention to any further applications. This procedure presents an orderly method for correcting inequalities. I am opposed to any general congressional revision of the tariff. Such action would disturb industry, business, and agriculture. It would prolong the depression.

Public Health

I again call attention to my previous recommendations upon this subject, particularly in its relation to children. The moral results are of the utmost importance.

Conclusion

It is inevitable that in these times much of the legislation proposed to the Congress and many of the recommendations of the executive must be designed to meet emergencies. In reaching solutions we must not jeopardize those principles which we have found to be the basis of the growth of the nation. The Federal Government must not encroach upon nor permit local communities to abandon that precious possession of local initiative and responsibility. Again, just as the largest measure of responsibility in the government of the nation rests upon local self-government, so does the largest measure of social responsibility in our country rest upon the individual. If the individual surrenders his own initiative and responsibilities, he is surrendering his own freedom and his own liberty. It is the duty of the national government to insist that both the local governments and the individual shall assume and bear these responsibilities as a fundamental of preserving the very basis of our freedom.

Many vital changes and movements of vast proportions are taking place in the economic world. The effect of these changes upon the future can not be seen clearly as yet. Of this, however, we are sure: Our system, based upon the ideals of individual initiative and of equality of opportunity, is not an artificial thing. Rather it is the outgrowth of the experience of America, and expresses the faith and spirit of our people. It has carried us in a century and a half to leadership of the economic world. If our economic system does not match our highest expectations at all times, it does not require revolutionary action to bring it into accord with any necessity that experience may prove. It has successfully adjusted itself to changing conditions in the past. It will do so again. The mobility of our institutions, the richness of our resources, and the abilities of our people enable us to meet them unafraid. It is a distressful time for many of our people, but they have shown qualities as high in fortitude, courage, and resourcefulness as ever in our history. With that spirit, I have faith that out of it will come a sounder life, a truer standard of values, a greater recognition of the results of honest effort, and a healthier atmosphere in which to rear our children. Ours must be a country of such stability and security as can not fail to carry forward and enlarge among all the people that abundant life of material and spiritual opportunity which it has represented among all nations since its beginning.

2

The Need for "Bold, Persistent Experimentation" (1932)

VII
Franklin D. Roosevelt:
Radio Address, *The Forgotten Man*
April 7, 1932

Although I understand that I am talking under the auspices of the Democratic National Committee, I do not want to limit myself to politics. I do not want to feel that I am addressing an audience of Democrats or that I speak merely as a Democrat myself. The present condition of our national affairs is too serious to be viewed through partisan eyes for partisan purposes.

Fifteen years ago my public duty called me to an active part in a great national emergency, the World War. Success then was due to a leadership whose vision carried beyond the timorous and futile gesture of sending a tiny army of 150,000 trained soldiers and the regular navy to the aid of our allies. The generalship of that moment conceived of a whole nation mobilized for war, economic, industrial, social and military resources gathered into a vast unit capable of and actually in the process of throwing into the scales ten million men equipped with physical needs and sustained by the realization that behind them were the united efforts of 110,000,000 human beings. It was a great plan because it was built from bottom to top and not from top to bottom.

In my calm judgment, the nation faces today a more grave emergency than in 1917.

It is said that Napoleon lost the battle of Waterloo because he forgot his infantry—he staked too much upon the more spectacular but less substantial cavalry. The present administration in Washington provides a close parallel. It has either forgotten or it does not want to remember the infantry of our economic army.

These unhappy times call for the building of plans that rest upon the forgotten, the unorganized but the indispensable units of economic power, for plans like those of 1917 that build from the bottom up and not from the top down, that put their faith once more in the forgotten man at the bottom of the economic pyramid.

Obviously, these few minutes tonight permit no opportunity to lay down the ten or a dozen closely related objectives of a plan to meet our present emergency, but I can draw a few essentials, a beginning in fact, of a planned program.

It is the habit of the unthinking to turn in times like this to the illusions of economic magic. People suggest that a huge expenditure of public funds by the Federal Government and by State and local governments will completely solve the unemployment problem. But it is clear that even if we could raise many billions of dollars and find definitely useful public works to spend these billions on, even all that money would not give employment to the seven million or ten million people who are out of work. Let us admit frankly that it would be only a stopgap. A real economic cure must go to the killing of the bacteria in the system rather than to the treatment of external symptoms.

How much do the shallow thinkers realize, for example, that approximately one-half of our whole population, fifty or sixty million people, earn their living by farming or in small towns whose existence immediately depends on farms. They have today lost their purchasing power. Why? They are receiving for farm products less than the cost to them of growing these farm products. The result of this loss of purchasing power is that many other millions of people engaged in industry in the cities cannot sell industrial products to the farming half of the nation. This brings home to every city worker that his own employment is directly tied up with the farmer's dollar. No nation can long endure half bankrupt. Main Street, Broadway, the mills, the mines will close if half the buyers are broke.

I cannot escape the conclusion that one of the essential parts of a national program of restoration must be to restore purchasing power to the farming half of the country. Without this the wheels of railroads and of factories will not turn.

Closely associated with this first objective is the problem of keeping the home-owner and the farm-owner where he is, without being dispossessed through the foreclosure of his mortgage. His relationship to the great banks of Chicago and New York is pretty remote. The two billion dollar fund which President Hoover and the Congress have put at the disposal of the big banks, the railroads and the corporations of the nation is not for him.

His is a relationship to his little local bank or local loan company. It is a sad fact that even though the local lender in many cases does not want to evict the farmer or home-owner by foreclosure proceedings, he is forced to do so in order to keep his bank or company solvent. Here should be an objective of government itself, to provide at least as much assistance to the little fellow as it is now giving to the large banks and corporations. That is another example of building from the bottom up.

One other objective closely related to the problem of selling American products is to provide a tariff policy based upon economic common sense rather than upon politics, hot air, and pull. This country during the past few years, culminating with the Hawley-Smoot Tariff in 1929, has compelled the world to build tariff fences so high that world trade is decreasing to the vanishing point. The value of goods internationally exchanged is today less than half of what it was three or four years ago.

Every man and woman who gives any thought to the subject knows that if our factories run even 80 percent of capacity, they will turn out more products than we as a nation can possibly use ourselves. The answer is that if they run on 80 percent of capacity, we must sell some goods abroad. How can we do that if the outside nations cannot pay us in cash? And we know by sad experience that they cannot do that. The only way they can pay us is in their own goods or raw materials, but this foolish tariff of ours makes that impossible.

What we must do is this: revise our tariff on the basis of a reciprocal exchange of goods, allowing other nations to buy and to pay for our goods by sending us such of their goods as will not seriously throw any of our industries out of balance, and incidentally making impossible in this country the continuance of pure monopolies which cause us to pay excessive prices for many of the necessities of life.

Such objectives as these three, restoring farmers' buying power, relief to the small banks and homeowners and a reconstructed tariff policy, are only a part of ten or a dozen vital factors. But they seem to be beyond the concern of a national administration which can think in terms only of the top of the social and economic structure. It has sought temporary relief from the top down rather than permanent relief from the bottom up. It has totally failed to plan ahead in a comprehensive way. It has waited until something has cracked and then at the last moment has sought to prevent total collapse.

It is high time to get back to fundamentals. It is high time to admit with courage that we are in the midst of an emergency at least equal to that of war. Let us mobilize to meet it.

VIII
Franklin D. Roosevelt:
Oglethorpe University Address
May 22, 1932

For me, as for you, this is a day of honorable attainment. For the honor conferred upon me I am deeply grateful, and I felicitate you upon yours, even though I cannot share with you that greater satisfaction which comes from a laurel worked for and won. For many of you, doubtless, this mark of distinction which you have received today has meant greater sacrifice by your parents or by yourselves, than you anticipated when you matriculated almost four years ago. The year 1928 does not seem far in the past, but since that time, as all of us are aware, the world about us has experienced significant changes. Four years ago, if you heard and believed the tidings of the time, you could expect to take your place in a society well supplied with material things and could look forward to the not too distant time when you would be living in your own homes, each (if you believed the politicians) with a two-car garage; and, without great effort, would be providing yourselves and your families with all the necessities and amenities of life, and perhaps in addition, assure by your savings their security and your own in the future. Indeed, if you were observant, you would have seen that many of your elders had discovered a still easier road to material success. They had found that once they had accumulated a few dollars they needed only to put them in the proper place and then sit back and read in comfort the hieroglyphics called stock quotations which proclaimed that their wealth was mounting miraculously without any work or effort on their part. Many who were called and who are still pleased to call themselves the leaders of finance celebrated and assured us of an eternal future for this easy-chair mode of living. And to the stimulation of belief in this dazzling chimera were lent not only the voices of some of our public men in high office, but their influence and the material aid of the very instruments of government which they controlled.

How sadly different is the picture which we see around us today! If only the mirage had vanished, we should not complain, for we should all be better off. But with it have vanished, not only the easy gains of speculation, but much of the savings of thrifty and prudent men and women, put by for their old age and for the education of their children. With these savings has gone, among millions of our fellow citizens, that sense of security to which they have rightly felt they are entitled in a land abundantly endowed with natural resources and with productive facilities to convert them into the necessities of life for all of our population. More calamitous still, there has vanished with the expectation of future security the certainty of today's bread and clothing.

Some of you—I hope not many—are wondering today how and where you will be able to earn your living a few weeks or a few months hence. Much has been written about the hope of youth. I prefer to emphasize another quality. I hope that you, who have spent four years in an institution whose fundamental purpose, I take it, is to train us to pursue truths relentlessly and to look at them courageously, will face the unfortunate state of the world about you with greater clarity of vision than many of your elders.

As you have viewed this world of which you are about to become a more active part, I have no doubt that you have been impressed by its chaos, its lack of plan. Perhaps some of you have used stronger language. And stronger language is justified. Even had you been graduating, instead of matriculating, in these rose-colored days of 1928, you would, I believe, have perceived this condition. For beneath all the happy optimism of those days there existed a lack of plan and a great waste.

This failure to measure true values and to look ahead extended to almost every industry, every profession, every walk of life. Take, for example, the vocation of higher education itself.

If you had been intending to enter the profession of teaching, you would have found that the universities, the colleges, the normal schools of our country were turning out annually far more trained teachers than the schools of the country could possibly use or absorb. You and I know that the number of teachers needed in the nation is a relatively stable figure, little affected by the depression and capable of fairly accurate estimate in advance with due consideration for our increase in population. And yet, we have continued to add teaching courses, to accept every young man or young woman in those courses without any thought or regard for the law of supply and demand. In the State of New York alone, for example, there are at least seven thousand qualified teachers who are out of work, unable to earn a livelihood in their chosen profession just because nobody had the wit or the forethought to tell them in their younger days that the profession of teaching was gravely oversupplied.

Take, again, the profession of the law. Our common sense tells us that we have too many lawyers and that thousands of them, thoroughly trained, are either eking out a bare existence or being compelled to work with their hands, or are turning to some other business in order to keep themselves from becoming objects of charity. The universities, the bar, the courts themselves have done little to bring this situation to the knowledge of young men who are considering entering any one of our multitude of law schools. Here again foresight and planning have been notable for their complete absence.

In the same way we cannot review carefully the history of our industrial advance without being struck with its haphazardness, the gigantic waste with which it has been accomplished, the superfluous duplication of productive facilities, the continual scrapping of still useful equipment, the tremendous mortality in industrial and commercial undertakings, the thousands of dead-end trails into which enterprise has been lured, the profligate waste of natural resources. Much of this waste is the inevitable by-product of progress in a society which values individual endeavor and which is susceptible to the changing tastes and customs of the people of which it is composed. But much of it, I believe, could have been prevented by greater foresight and by a larger measure of social planning. Such controlling and directive forces as have been developed in recent years reside to a dangerous degree in groups having special interests in our economic order, interests which do not coincide with the interests of the nation as a whole. I believe that the recent course of our history has demonstrated that, while we may utilize their expert knowledge of certain problems and the special facilities with which they are familiar, we cannot allow our economic life to be controlled by that small group of men whose chief outlook upon the social welfare is tinctured by the fact that they can make huge profits from the lending of money and the marketing of securities—an outlook which deserves the adjectives "selfish" and "opportunist."

You have been struck, I know, by the tragic irony of our economic situation today. We have not been brought to our present state by any natural calamity—by drought or floods or earthquakes or by the destruction of our productive machine or our manpower. Indeed, we have a superabundance of raw materials, a more than ample supply of equipment for manufacturing these materials into the goods which we need, and transportation and commercial facilities for making them available to all who need them. But raw materials stand unused, factories stand idle, railroad traffic continues to dwindle, merchants sell less and less, while millions of able-bodied men and women, in dire need, are clamoring for the opportunity to work. This is the awful paradox with which we are confronted, a stinging rebuke that challenges our power to operate the economic machine which we have created.

We are presented with a multitude of views as to how we may again set into motion that economic machine. Some hold to the theory that the periodic slowing down of our economic machine is one of its inherent peculiarities—a peculiarity which we must grin, if we can, and bear because if we attempt to tamper with it we shall cause even worse ailments. According to this theory, as I see it, if we grin and bear long enough, the economic machine will eventually begin to pick up speed and in the course of an indefinite number of years will again attain that maximum number of revolutions which signifies what we have been wont to miscall prosperity, but which, alas, is but a last ostentatious twirl of the economic machine before it again succumbs to that mysterious impulse to slow down again. This attitude toward our economic machine requires not only greater stoicism, but greater faith in immutable economic law and less faith in the ability of man to control what he has created than I, for one, have. Whatever elements of truth lie in it, it is an invitation to sit back and do nothing; and all of us are suffering today, I believe, because this comfortable theory was too thoroughly implanted in the minds of some of our leaders, both in finance and in public affairs.

Other students of economics trace our present difficulties to the ravages of the World War and its bequest of unsolved political and economic and financial problems. Still others trace our difficulties to defects in the world's monetary systems. Whether it be an original cause, an accentuating cause, or an effect, the drastic change in the value of our monetary unit in terms of the commodities is a problem which we must meet straightforwardly. It is self-evident that we must either restore commodities to a level approximating their dollar value of several years ago or else that we must continue the destructive process of reducing, through defaults or through deliberate writing down, obligations assumed at a higher price level.

Possibly because of the urgency and complexity of this phase of our problem some of our economic thinkers have been occupied with it to the exclusion of other phases of as great importance.

Of these other phases, that which seems most important to me in the long run is the problem of controlling by adequate planning the creation and distribution of those products which our vast economic machine is capable of yielding. It is true that capital, whether public or private, is needed in the creation of new enterprise and that such capital gives employment.

But think carefully of the vast sums of capital or credit which in the past decade have been devoted to unjustified enterprises—to the development of unessentials and to the multiplying of many products far beyond the capacity of the nation to absorb. It is the same story as the thoughtless turning out of too many school teachers and too many lawyers.

Here again, in the field of industry and business, many of those whose primary solicitude is confined to the welfare of what they call capital have failed to read the lessons of the past few years and have been moved less by calm analysis of the needs of the nation as a whole than by a blind determination to preserve their own special stakes in the economic order. I do not mean to intimate that we have come to the end of this period of expansion. We shall continue to need capital for the production of newly-invented devices, for the replacement of equipment worn out or rendered obsolete by our technical progress; we need better housing in many of our cities and we still need in many parts of the country more good roads, canals, parks and other improvements.

But it seems to me probable that our physical economic plant will not expand in the future at the same rate at which it has expanded in the past. We may build more factories, but the fact remains that we have enough now to supply all of our domestic needs, and more, if they are used. With these factories we can now make more shoes, more textiles, more steel, more radios, more automobiles, more of almost everything than we can use.

No, our basic trouble was not an insufficiency of capital. It was an insufficient distribution of buying power coupled with an over-sufficient speculation in production. While wages rose in many of our industries, they did not as a whole rise proportionately to the reward to capital, and at the same time the purchasing power of other great groups of our population was permitted to shrink. We accumulated such a superabundance of capital that our great bankers were vying with each other, some of them employing questionable methods, in their efforts to lend this capital at home and abroad.

I believe that we are at the threshold of a fundamental change in our popular economic thought, that in the future we are going to think less about the producer and more about the consumer. Do what we may have to do to inject life into our ailing economic order; we cannot make it endure for long unless we can bring about a wiser, more equitable distribution of the national income.

It is well within the inventive capacity of man, who has built up this great social and economic machine capable of satisfying the wants of all, to insure that all who are willing and able to work receive from it at least the necessities of life. In such a system, the reward for a day's work will have to be greater, on the average, than it has been, and the reward to capital, especially capital which is speculative, will have to be less. But I believe that after the experience of the last three years, the average citizen would rather receive a smaller return upon his savings in return for greater security for the principal, than experience for a moment the thrill or the prospect of being a millionaire only to find the next moment that his fortune, actual or expected, has withered in his hand because the economic machine has again broken down.

It is toward that objective that we must move if we are to profit by our recent experiences. Probably few will disagree that the goal is desirable. Yet many, of faint heart, fearful of change, sitting tightly on the roof-tops in the flood, will sternly resist striking out for it, lest they fail to attain it. Even among those who are ready to attempt the journey there will be violent differences of opinion as to how it should be made. So complex, so widely distributed over our whole society are the problems which confront us that men and women of common aim do not agree upon the method of attacking them. Such disagreement leads to doing nothing, to drifting. Agreement may come too late.

The country needs and, unless I mistake its temper, the country demands bold, persistent experimentation. It is common sense to take a method and try it: If it fails, admit it frankly and try another. But above all, try something. The millions who are in want will not stand by silently forever while the things to satisfy their needs are within easy reach.

We need enthusiasm, imagination and the ability to face facts, even unpleasant ones, bravely. We need to correct, by drastic means if necessary, the faults in our economic system from which we now suffer. We need the courage of the young. Yours is not the task of making your way in the world, but the task of remaking the world which you will find before you. May every one of us be granted the courage, the faith and the vision to give the best that is in us to that remaking!

IX
Democratic Party Platform
June 30, 1932

In this time of unprecedented economic and social distress the Democratic Party declares its conviction that the chief causes of this condition were the disastrous policies pursued by our government since the World War, of economic isolation, fostering the merger of competitive businesses into monopolies and encouraging the indefensible expansion and contraction of credit for private profit at the expense of the public.

Those who were responsible for these policies have abandoned the ideals on which the war was won and thrown away the fruits of victory, thus rejecting the greatest opportunity in history to bring peace, prosperity, and happiness to our people and to the world.

They have ruined our foreign trade, destroyed the values of our commodities and products, crippled our banking system, robbed millions of our people of their life savings, and thrown millions more out of work, produced wide-spread poverty and brought the government to a state of financial distress unprecedented in time of peace.

The only hope for improving present conditions, restoring employment, affording permanent relief to the people, and bringing the nation back to the proud position of domestic happiness and of financial, industrial, agricultural and commercial leadership in the world lies in a drastic change in economic governmental policies.

We believe that a party platform is a covenant with the people to be faithfully kept by the party when entrusted with power, and that the people are entitled to know in plain words the terms of the contract to which they are asked to subscribe. We hereby declare this to be the platform of the Democratic Party:

The Democratic Party solemnly promises by appropriate action to put into effect the principles, policies and reforms herein advocated, and to eradicate the policies, methods, and practices herein condemned. We advocate an immediate and drastic reduction of governmental expenditures by abolishing useless commissions and offices, consolidating departments and bureaus, and eliminating extravagance, to accomplish a saving of not less than twenty-five percent in the cost of federal government, and we call upon the Democratic Party in the States to make a zealous effort to achieve a proportionate result.

We favor maintenance of the national credit by a federal budget annually balanced on the basis of accurate executive estimates within revenues, raised by a system of taxation levied on the principle of ability to pay.

We advocate a sound currency to be preserved at all hazards and an international monetary conference called on the invitation of our government to consider the rehabilitation of silver and related questions.

We advocate a competitive tariff for revenue, with a fact-finding tariff commission free from executive interference, reciprocal tariff agreements with other nations, and an international economic conference designed to restore international trade and facilitate exchange.

We advocate the extension of federal credit to the states to provide unemployment relief wherever the diminishing resources of the states make it impossible for them to provide for the needy; expansion of the federal program of necessary and useful construction affected with a public interest, such as adequate flood control and waterways.

We advocate the spread of employment by a substantial reduction in the hours of labor, the encouragement of the shorter week by applying that principle in government service. We advocate advance planning of public works.

We advocate unemployment and old age insurance under state laws.

We favor the restoration of agriculture, the nation's basic industry; better financing of farm mortgages through recognized farm bank agencies at low rates of interest on an amortization plan, giving preference to credits for the redemption of farms and homes sold under foreclosure.

Extension and development of Farm Cooperative movements and effective control of crop surpluses so that our farmers may have the full benefit of the domestic market.

The enactment of every constitutional measure that will aid the farmers to receive for their basic farm commodities prices in excess of cost.

We advocate a Navy and an Army adequate for national defense, based on a survey of all facts affecting the existing establishments, that the people in time of peace may not be burdened by an expenditure fast approaching a billion dollars annually.

We advocate strengthening and impartial enforcement of the anti-trust laws, to prevent monopoly and unfair trade practices, and revision thereof for the better protection of labor and the small producer and distributor.

The conservation, development, and use of the nation's water power in the public interest.

The removal of government from all fields of private enterprise except where necessary to develop public works and natural resources in the common interest.

We advocate protection of the investing public by requiring to be filed with the government and carried in advertisements of all offerings of foreign and domestic stocks and bonds true information as to bonuses, commissions, principal invested, and interests by the sellers.

Regulation to the full extent of federal power of: (a) holding companies which sell securities in interstate commerce, (b) rates of utility companies operating across state lines, (c) exchanges in securities and commodities.

We advocate quicker methods of realizing on assets for the relief of depositors of suspended banks, and a more rigid supervision of national banks for the protection of depositors and the prevention of the use of their moneys in speculation to the detriment of local credits.

The severance of affiliated security companies from, and the divorce of the investment banking business from, commercial banks, and further restriction of federal reserve banks in permitting the use of federal reserve facilities for speculative purposes.

We advocate the full measure of justice and generosity for all war veterans who have suffered disability or disease caused by or resulting from actual service in time of war and for their dependents.

Simplification of legal procedure and reorganization of the judicial system to make the attainment of justice speedy, certain, and at less cost.

Continuous publicity of political contributions and expenditures; strengthening of the Corrupt Practices Act and severe penalties for misappropriation of campaign funds.

We advocate the repeal of the Eighteenth Amendment. To affect such repeal we demand that the Congress immediately propose a Constitutional Amendment to truly representative conventions in the states called to act solely on that proposal. We urge the enactment of such measures by the several states as will actually promote temperance, effectively prevent the return of the saloon and bring the liquor traffic into the open under complete supervision and control by the states.

We demand that the Federal Government effectively exercise its power to enable the states to protect themselves against importation of intoxicating liquors in violation of their laws.

Pending repeal, we favor immediate modification of the Volstead Act to legalize the manufacture and sale of beer and other beverages of such alcoholic content as is permissible under the Constitution and to provide there from a proper and needed revenue.

We advocate continuous responsibility of government for human welfare, especially for the protection of children.

We condemn the improper and excessive use of money in political activities.

We condemn paid lobbies of special interests to influence members of Congress and other public servants by personal contact.

We condemn action and utterances of high public officials designed to influence stock exchange prices.

We condemn the open and covert resistance of administration officials to every effort made by Congressional committees to curtail the extravagant expenditures of the government and to revoke improvident subsidies granted to favorite interests.

We condemn the extravagance of the Farm Board, its disastrous action which made the Government a speculator of farm products and the unsound policy of restricting agricultural products to the demands of domestic markets.

We condemn the usurpation of power by the State Department in assuming to pass upon foreign securities offered by international bankers as a result of which billions of dollars in questionable bonds have been sold to the public upon the implied approval of the Federal Government.

We condemn the Hawley-Smoot Tariff Law, the prohibitive rates of which have resulted in retaliatory action by more than forty countries, created international economic hostilities, destroyed international trade, driven our factories into foreign countries, robbed the American farmer of his foreign markets, and increased the cost of production.

In conclusion, to accomplish these purposes and to recover economic liberty we pledge the nominees of this convention the best efforts of a great party whose founder announced the doctrine which guides us now in the hour of our country's need:

Equal rights to all; special privileges to none.

X
Republican Party Platform
Summer 1932

We, the representatives of the Republican Party, in convention assembled, renew our pledge to the principles and traditions of our party and dedicate it anew to the service of the nation.

We meet in a period of widespread distress and of an economic depression that has swept the world. The emergency is second only to that of a great war. The human suffering occasioned may well exceed that of a period of actual conflict.

The supremely important problem that challenges our citizens and government alike is to break the back of the depression, to restore the economic life of the nation and to bring encouragement and relief to the thousands of American families that are sorely afflicted.

The people themselves, by their own courage, their own patient and resolute effort in the readjustments of their own affairs, can and will work out the cure. It is our task as a party, by leadership and a wise determination of policy, to assist that recovery.

To that task we pledge all that our party possesses in capacity, leadership, resourcefulness and ability. Republicans, collectively and individually, in nation and State, hereby enlist in a war which will not end until the promise of American life is once more fulfilled.

Leadership

For nearly three years the world has endured an economic depression of unparalleled extent and severity. The patience and courage of our people have been severely tested, but their faith in themselves, in their institutions and in their future remains unshaken. When victory comes, as it will, this generation will hand on to the next a great heritage unimpaired.

This will be due in large measure to the quality of the leadership that this country has had in the White House a leader—wise, courageous, patient, understanding, resourceful, ever present at his post of duty, tireless in his efforts and unswervingly faithful to American principles and ideals.

At the outset of the depression, when no man could foresee its depth and extent, the President succeeded in averting much distress by securing agreement between industry and labor to maintain wages and by stimulating programs of private and governmental construction. Throughout the depression unemployment has been limited by the systematic use of part-time employment as a substitute for the general discharge of employees. Wage scales have not been reduced except under compelling necessity. As a result there have been fewer strikes and less social disturbance than during any similar period of hard times.

The suffering and want occasioned by the great drought of 1930 were mitigated by the prompt mobilization of the resources of the Red Cross and of the government. During the trying winters of 1930-31 and 1931-32 a nation-wide organization to relieve distress was brought into being under the leadership of the President. By the spring of 1931 the possibility of a business upturn in the United States was clearly discernible when, suddenly, a train of events was set in motion in Central Europe which moved forward with extraordinary rapidity and violence, threatening the credit structure of the world and eventually dealing a serious blow to this country.

The President foresaw the danger. He sought to avert it by proposing a suspension of inter-governmental debt payments for one year, with the purpose of relieving the pressure at the point of greatest intensity. But the credit machinery of the nations of Central Europe could not withstand the strain, and the forces of disintegration continued to gain momentum until in September Great Britain was forced to depart from the gold standard. This momentous event, followed by a tremendous raid on the dollar, resulted in a series of bank suspensions in this country, and the hoarding of currency on a large scale.

Again the President acted. Under his leadership the National Credit Association came into being. It mobilized our banking resources, saved scores of banks from failure, helped restore confidence and proved of inestimable value in strengthening the credit structure.

By the time the Congress met the character of our problems was clearer than ever. In his message to Congress the President outlined a constructive and definite program which in the main has been carried out; other portions may yet be carried out.

The Railroad Credit Corporation was created. The capital of the Federal Land Banks was increased. The Reconstruction Finance Corporation came into being and brought protection to millions of depositors, policyholders and others.

Legislation was enacted enlarging the discount facilities of the Federal Reserve System, and, without reducing the legal reserves of the Federal Reserve Banks, releasing a billion dollars of gold; a formidable protection against raids on the dollar and a greatly enlarged basis for an expansion of credit.

An earlier distribution to depositors in closed banks has been brought about through the action of the Reconstruction Finance Corporation. Above all, the national credit has been placed in an impregnable position by provision for adequate revenue and a program of drastic curtailment of expenditures. All of these measures were designed to lay a foundation for the resumption of business and increased employment.

But delay and the constant introduction and consideration of new and unsound measures has kept the country in a state of uncertainty and fear, and offset much of the good otherwise accomplished.

The President has recently supplemented his original program to provide for distress, to stimulate the revival of business and employment, and to improve the agricultural situation, he recommended extending the authority of the Reconstruction Finance Corporation to enable it: (a) To make loans to political subdivisions of public bodies or private corporations for the purpose of starting construction of income-producing or self-liquidating projects which will at once increase employment; (b) To make loans upon security of agricultural commodities so as to insure the carrying of normal stocks of those commodities, and thus stabilize their loan value and price levels; (c) To make loans to the Federal Farm Board to enable extension of loans to farm cooperatives and loans for export of agricultural commodities to quarters unable to purchase them; (d) To loan up to $300,000,000 to such States as are unable to meet the calls made on them by their citizens for distress relief.

The President's program contemplates an attack on a broad front, with far-reaching objectives, but entailing no danger to the budget. The Democratic program, on the other hand, contemplates a heavy expenditure of public funds, a budget unbalanced on a large scale, with a doubtful attainment of at best a strictly limited objective.

We strongly endorse the President's program.

Unemployment and Relief

True to American traditions and principles of government, the administration has regarded the relief problem as one of State and local responsibility. The work of local agencies, public and private has been coordinated and enlarged on a nation-wide scale under the leadership of the President.

Sudden and unforeseen emergencies such as the drought have been met by the Red Cross and the Government. The United States Public Health Service has been of inestimable benefit to stricken areas.

There has been magnificent response and action to relieve distress by citizens, organizations and agencies, public and private throughout the country.

Public Economy

Constructive plans for financial stabilization cannot be completely organized until our national, State and municipal governments not only balance their budgets but curtail their current expenses as well to a level which can be steadily and economically maintained for some years to come.

We urge prompt and drastic reduction of public expenditure and resistance to every appropriation not demonstrably necessary to the performance of government, national or local.

The Republican Party established and will continue to uphold the gold standard and will oppose any measure which will undermine the government's credit or impair the integrity of our national currency. Relief by currency inflation is unsound in principle and dishonest in results. The dollar is impregnable in the marts of the world today and must remain so. An ailing body cannot be cured by quack remedies. This is no time to experiment upon the body politic or financial.

Banks and the Banking System

The efficient functioning of our economic machinery depends in no small measure on the aid rendered to trade and industry by our banking system. There is need of revising the banking laws so as to place our banking structure on a sounder basis generally for all concerned, and for the better protection of the depositing public there should be more stringent supervision and broader powers vested in the supervising authorities. We advocate such a revision.

One of the serious problems affecting our banking system has arisen from the practice of organizing separate corporations by the same interests as banks, but participating in operations which the banks themselves are not permitted legally to undertake. We favor requiring reports of and subjecting to thorough and periodic examination all such affiliates of member banks until adequate information has been acquired on the basis of which this problem may definitely be solved in a permanent manner.

International Conference

We favor the participation by the United States in an international conference to consider matters relating to monetary questions, including the position of silver, exchange problems, and commodity prices, and possible cooperative action concerning them.

Home Loan Discount Bank System

The present Republican administration has initiated legislation for the creation of a system of federally supervised home loan discount banks, designed to serve the home owners of all parts of the country and to encourage home ownership by making possible long term credits for homes on more stable and more favorable terms.

There has arisen in the last few years a disturbing trend away from home ownership. We believe that everything should be done by Governmental agencies, national State and local, to reverse this tendency, to aid home owners by encouraging better methods of home financing; and to relieve the present inequitable tax burden on the home. In the field of national legislation we pledge that the measures creating a home loan discount system will be pressed in Congress until adopted.

Agriculture

Farm distress in America has its root in the enormous expansion of agricultural production during the war, the deflation of 1919, 1920 and the dislocation of markets after the war. There followed, under Republican Administrations, a long record of legislation in aid of the cooperative organization of farmers and in providing farm credit. The position of agriculture was gradually improved. In 1928 the Republican Party pledged further measures in aid of agriculture, principally tariff protection for agricultural products and the creation of a Federal Farm Board "clothed with the necessary power to promote the establishment of a farm marketing system of farmer-owned and controlled stabilization corporations."

Almost the first official act of President Hoover was the calling of a special session of Congress to redeem these party pledges. They have been redeemed.

The 1930 tariff act increased the rates on agricultural products by 30 percent, upon industrial products only 12 percent. That act equalized, so far as legislation can do so, the protection afforded the farmer with the protection afforded industry, and prevented a vast flood of cheap wool, grain, livestock, dairy and other products for entering the American market.

By the Agricultural Marketing Act, the Federal Farm Board was created and armed with broad powers and ample funds.

The Federal Farm Board, created by the Agricultural Marketing Act, has been compelled to conduct its operations during a period in which all commodity prices, industrial as well as agricultural, have fallen to disastrous levels. A period of decreasing demand and of national calamities such as drought and flood has intensified the problem of agriculture.

Nevertheless, after only a little more than two years' efforts, the Federal Farm Board has many achievements of merit to its credit. It has increased the membership of the cooperative farms marketing associations to coordinate efforts of the local associations. By cooperation with other Federal agencies, it has made available to farm marketing associations a large value of credit, which, in the emergency, would not have otherwise been available.

Due to the 1930 tariff act and the agricultural marketing act, it can truthfully be stated that the prices received by the American farmer for his wheat, corn, rye, barley, oats, flaxseed, cattle, butter and many other products, cruelly low though they are, are higher than the prices received by the farmers of any competing nation for the same products.

The Republican Party has also aided the American farmer by relief of the sufferers in the drought-stricken areas, through loans for rehabilitation and through road building to provide employment, by the development of the inland waterway system, by the perishable product act, by the strengthening of the extension system, and by the appropriation of $125,000,000 to recapitalize the Federal land banks and enable them to extend time to worthy borrowers.

The Republican Party pledges itself to the principle of assistance to cooperative marketing associations, owned and controlled by the farmers themselves, through the provisions of the agricultural marketing act, which will be promptly amended or modified as experience shows to be necessary to accomplish the objects set forth in the preamble of that act.

Tariff and the Marketing Act

The party pledges itself to make such revision of tariff schedules as economic changes require to maintain the parity of protection to agriculture with other industry.

The American farmer is entitled not only to tariff schedules on his products but to protection from substitutes therefore.

We will support any plan which will help to balance production against demand, and thereby raise agricultural prices, provided it is economically sound and administratively workable without burdensome bureaucracy.

The burden of taxation borne by the owners of farmland constitutes one of the major problems of agriculture.

President Hoover has aptly and truly said, "Taxes upon real property are easiest to enforce and are the least flexible of all taxes. The tendency under pressure of need is to continue these taxes unchanged in times of depression, despite the decrease in the owner's income. Decreasing price and decreasing income results in an increasing burden upon property owners...the tax burden upon real estate is wholly out of proportion to that upon other forms of property and income. There is no farm relief more needed today than tax relief."

The time has come for a reconsideration of our tax systems, Federal, State and local, with a view to developing a better coordination, reducing duplication and relieving unjust burdens. The Republican Party pledges itself to this end.

More than all else, we point to the fact that, in the administration of executive departments, and in every plan of the President for the coordination of national effort and for strengthening our financial structure, for expanding credit, for rebuilding the rural credit system and laying the foundations for better prices, the President has insisted upon the interest of the American farmer.

The fundamental problem of American agriculture is the control of production to such volume as will balance supply with demand. In the solution of this problem the cooperative organization of farmers to plan production, and the tariff, to hold the home market for American farmers, are vital elements. A third element equally as vital is the control of the acreage of land under cultivation, as an aid to the efforts of the farmer to balance production.

We favor a national policy of land utilization which looks to national needs, such as the administration has already begun to formulate. Such a policy must foster reorganization of taxing units in areas beset by tax delinquency and divert lands that are submarginal for crop production to other uses. The national welfare plainly can be served by the acquisition of submarginal lands for watershed protection, grazing, forestry, public parks and game preserves. We favor such acquisition.

The Tariff

The Republican Party has always been the staunch supporter of the American system of a protective tariff. It believes that the home market, built up under that policy, the greatest and richest market in the world, belongs first to American agriculture, industry and labor. No pretext can justify the surrender of that market to such competition as would destroy our farms, mines and factories, and lower the standard of living which we have established for our workers.

Because many foreign countries have recently abandoned the gold standard, as a result of which the costs of many commodities produced in such countries have, at least for the time being, fallen materially in terms of American currency, adequate tariff protection is today particularly essential to the welfare of the American people.

The Tariff Commission should promptly investigate individual commodities so affected by currency depreciation and report to the President any increase in duties found necessary to equalize domestic with foreign costs of production.

To fix the duties on some thousands of commodities, subject to highly complex conditions, is necessarily a difficult technical task. It is unavoidable that some of the rates established by legislation should, even at the time of their enactment, to be too low or too high. Moreover, a subsequent change in costs or other conditions may render obsolete a rate that was before appropriate. The Republican Party has, therefore, long supported the policy of a flexible tariff, giving power to the President, after investigation by an impartial commission and in accordance with prescribed principles, to modify the rates named by the Congress.

We commend the President's veto of the measure, sponsored by Democratic Congressmen, which would have transferred from the President to Congress the authority to put into effect the findings of the Tariff Commission. Approval of the measure would have returned tariff making to politics and destroyed the progress made during ten years of effort to lift it out of log-rolling methods. We pledge the Republican Party to a policy which will retain the gains made and enlarge the present scope of greater progress.

Veterans

Our country is honored whenever it bestows relief on those who have faithfully served its flag. The Republican Party, appreciative of this solemn obligation and honor, has made its sentiments evident in Congress.

Increased hospital facilities have been provided, payments in compensation have more than doubled and in the matters of rehabilitation, pensions and insurance, generous provision has been made.

The administration of laws dealing with the relief of the veterans and their dependents has been a difficult task, but every effort has been made to carry service to the veterans and bring about not only a better and generous interpretation of the law but a sympathetic consideration of the many problems of the veteran.

We believe that every veteran incapacitated in any degree by reason of illness should be cared for and compensated, so far as compensation is possible, by a grateful nation, and that the dependents of those who lost their lives in war or whose death since the war in which service was rendered in traceable to service causes, should be provided for adequately. Legislation should be in accord with this principle.

Disability from causes subsequent and not attributable to war and the support of dependents of decreased veterans whose death is unconnected with war have been to some measure accepted obligations of the nation as a part of the debt due.

A careful study should be made of existing veterans' legislation with a view to elimination of inequalities and injustices and effecting all possible economies, but without departing from our purpose to provide on a sound basis full and adequate relief for our service disabled men, their widows and orphans.

Wages and Work

We believe in the principle of high wages.

We favor the principle of the shorter working week and shorter work day with its application to government as well as to private employment, as rapidly and as constructively as conditions will warrant.

We favor legislation designed to stimulate, encourage and assist in home building.

Labor

Collective bargaining by responsible representatives of employers and employees of their own choice, without the interference of any one, is recognized and approved.

Legislation, such as laws, prohibiting alien contract labor, peonage labor and the shanghaiing of sailors; the eight-hour law on government contracts and in government employment; provision for railroad safety devices, of methods of conciliation, mediation and arbitration in industrial labor disputes, including the adjustment of railroad disputes; the providing of compensation for injury to government employees (the forerunner of Federal workers' compensation acts), and other laws to aid and protect labor are of Republican origin, and have had and will continue to have the unswerving support of the party.

Employment

We commend the constructive work of the United States Employment Service in the Department of Labor. This service was enlarged and its activities extended through an appropriation made possible by the President with the cooperation of the Congress. It has done high service for the unemployed in the ranks of civil life and in the ranks of the former soldiers of the World War.

Freedom of Speech

Freedom of speech, press and assemblages are fundamental principles upon which our form of government rests. These vital principles should be preserved and protected.

Public Utilities

Supervision, regulation and control of inter-state public utilities in the interest of the public is a established policy of the Republican Party, to the credit of which stands the creation of the Interstate Commerce Commission, with its authority to assure reasonable transportation rates, sound railway finance and adequate service.

As proof of the progress made by the Republican Party in government control of public utilities, we cite the reorganization under this administration of the Federal Power Commission, with authority to administer the Federal Water Power Act. We urge legislation to authorize this commission to regulate the charges for electric current when transmitted across State lines.

Transportation

The promotion of agriculture, commerce and industry requires coordination of transportation by rail, highway, air and water. All should be subjected to appropriate and constructive regulation.

The public will, of course, select the form of transportation best fitted to its particular service, but the terms of competition fixed by public authority should operate without discrimination, so that all common carriers by rail, highway, air and water shall operate under conditions of equality.

Inland Waterways

The Republican Party recognizes that low cost transportation for bulk commodities will enable industry to develop in the midst of agriculture in the Mississippi Valley, thereby creating a home market for farm products in that section. With a view to aiding agriculture in the middle west the present administration has pushed forward as rapidly as possible the improvement of the Mississippi waterway system, and we favor the continued vigorous prosecution of these works to the end that agriculture and industry in that great area may enjoy the benefits of these improvements at the earliest possible date.

The railroads constitute the backbone of our transportation system and perform an essential service for the country. The railroad industry is our largest employer of labor and the greatest consumer of goods. The restoration of their credit and the maintenance of their ability to render adequate service are of paramount importance to the public, to their many thousands of employees and to savings banks, insurance companies and other similar institutions, to which the savings of the people have been entrusted.

We should continue to encourage the further development of the merchant marine under American registry and ownership.

Under the present administration the American merchant fleet has been enlarged and strengthened until it now occupies second place among the merchant marines of the world.

By the gradual retirement of the government from the field of ship operations and marked economies in costs, the United States Shipping Board will require no appropriation for the fiscal year 1933 for ship operations.

St. Lawrence Seaway

The Republican Party stands committed to the development of the Great Lakes-St. Lawrence seaway. Under the direction of President Hoover negotiation of a treaty with Canada for this development is now at a favorable point. Recognizing the inestimable benefits which will accrue to the nation from placing the ports of the Great Lakes on an ocean base, the party reaffirms allegiance to this great project and pledges its best efforts to secure its early completion.

Highways

The Federal policy to cooperate with the States in the building of roads was thoroughly established when the Federal Highway Act of 1921 was adopted under a Republican Congress. Each year since that time appropriations have been made which have greatly increased the economic value of highway transportation and helped to raise the standards and opportunities of rural life.

We pledge our support to the continuation of this policy in accordance with our needs and resources.

Civil Service

The merit system has been amply justified since the organization of the Civil Service by the Republican Party. As a part of our governmental system it is now unassailable. We believe it should remain so.

The Eighteenth Amendment

A nation-wide controversy over the Eighteenth Amendment now distracts attention from the constructive solution of many pressing national problems. The principle of national prohibition as embodied in the amendment was supported and opposed by members of both great political parties. It was submitted to the States by members of Congress of different political faith and ratified by State Legislatures of different political majorities. It was not then and is not now a partisan political question.

We do not favor a submission limited to the issue of retention or repeal, for the American nation never in its history has gone backward, and in this case the progress which has been thus far made must be preserved, while the evils must be eliminated.

We therefore believe that the people should have an opportunity to pass upon a proposed amendment the provision of which, while retaining in the Federal Government power to preserve the gains already made in dealing with the evils inherent in the liquor traffic, shall allow the States to deal with the problem as their citizens may determine, but subject always to the power of the Federal Government to protect those States where prohibition may exist and safeguard our citizens everywhere from the return of the saloon and attendant abuses.

Such an amendment should be promptly submitted to the States by Congress, to be acted upon by State conventions called for the sole purpose in accordance with the provisions of Article V of the Constitution and adequately safeguarded so as to be truly representative.

Conservation

The wise use of all natural resources freed from monopolistic control is a Republican policy, initiated by Theodore Roosevelt. The Roosevelt, Coolidge and Hoover reclamation projects bear witness to the continuation of that policy. Forestry and all other conservation activities have been supported and enlarged.

The conservation of oil is a major problem to the industry and the nation. The administration has sought to bring coordination of effort through the States, the producers and the Federal Government. Progress has been made and the effort will continue.

The Negro

For seventy years the Republican Party has been the friend of the American Negro. Vindication of the rights of the Negro citizen to enjoy the full benefits of life, liberty and the pursuit of happiness is traditional in the Republican Party, and our party stands pledged to maintain equal opportunity and rights for Negro citizens. We do not propose to depart from that tradition nor to alter the spirit or letter of that pledge.

Welfare, Work and Children

The children of our nation, our future citizens, have had the most solicitous thought of our President. Child welfare and protection has been a major effort of this administration. The organization of the White House Conference on Child Health and Protection is regarded as one of the outstanding accomplishments of this administration.

Welfare work in all its phases has had the support of the President and aid of the administration. The work of organized agencies—local, State and Federal—has been advanced and an increased impetus given by the recognition and help. We approve and pledge a continuation of that policy.

Indians

We favor the fullest protection of the property rights of the American Indians and the provision for them of adequate educational facilities.

Reorganization of Government Bureaus

Efficiency and economy demand reorganization of government bureaus. The problem is non-partisan and must be so treated if it is to be solved. As a result of years of study and personal contact with conflicting activities and wasteful duplication of effort, the President is particularly fitted to direct measures to correct the situation. We favor legislation by Congress which will give him the required authority.

Democratic Failure

The vagaries of the present Democratic House of Representatives offer characteristic and appalling proof of the existing incapacity of that party for leadership in a national crisis. Individualism running amuck has displaced party discipline and has trampled under foot party leadership. A bewildered electorate has viewed the spectacle with profound dismay and deep misgivings.

Goaded to desperation by their confessed failure, the party leaders have resorted to "pork barrel" legislation to obtain a unity of action which could not otherwise be achieved. A Republican President stands resolutely between the helpless citizen and the disaster threatened by such measures; and the people, regardless of party, will demand his continued service.

Many times during his useful life has Herbert Hoover responded to such a call, and his response has never disappointed. He will not disappoint us now.

Party Government

The delays and differences which recently hampered efforts to obtain legislation imperatively demanded by prevailing critical conditions strikingly illustrate the menace to self-government brought about by the weakening of party ties and party fealty.

Experience has demonstrated that coherent political parties are indispensable agencies for the prompt and effective operation of the functions of our government under the Constitution.

Only by united party action can consistent, well-planned and wholesome legislative programs be enacted. We believe that the majority of the Congressmen elected in the name of a party have the right and duty to determine the general policies of that party and are, in general, bound to adhere to such policies. Any other course inevitably makes of Congress a body of detached delegates which, instead of representing the collective wisdom of our people, become the confused voices of a heterogeneous group of unrelated local prejudices.

We believe that the time has come when Senators and Representatives of the United States should be impressed with the inflexible truth that their first concern should be the welfare of the United States and the well-being of all of its people, and that stubborn pride of individual opinion is not a virtue, but an obstacle to the orderly and successful achievement of the objects of representative government.

Only by cooperation can self-government succeed. Without it election under a party aegis becomes a false pretense.

We earnestly request that Republicans throughout the Union demand that their representatives in the Congress pledge themselves to these principles, to the end that the insidious influences of party disintegration may not undermine the very foundations of the Republic.

Conclusion

Generally on economic matters we pledge the Republican Party:

1. To maintain unimpaired the national credit.
2. Instructions to the Federal Reserve Board and the Secretary of the Treasury to attempt to manipulate commodity prices.
3. The guarantee of bank deposits.
4. The squandering of the public resources and the unbalancing of the budget through pork-barrel appropriations which bear little relation to distress and would tend through delayed business revival to decrease rather than increase employment.

Recognizing that real relief to unemployment must come through a revival of industrial activity and agriculture, to the promotion of which our every effort must be directed, our party in State and nation undertakes to do all in its power that is humanly possible to see that distress is fully relieved in accordance with American principles and traditions.

No successful solution of the problems before the country today can be expected from a Congress and a President separated by partisan lines or opposed in purposes and principles. Responsibility cannot be placed unless a clear mandate is given by returning to Washington a Congress and a Chief Executive united in principles and program.

The return to power of the Republican Party with that mandate is the duty of every voter who believes in the doctrines of the party and its program as herein stated. Nothing else, we believe, will insure the orderly recovery of the country and that return to prosperous days which every American so ardently desires.

The Republican Party faces the future unafraid!

With courage and confidence in ultimate success, we will strive against the forces that strike at our social and economic ideals, and our political institutions.

XI
Franklin D. Roosevelt:
Presidential Nomination Address
Democratic National Convention, July 2, 1932

Chairman Walsh, my friends of the Democratic National Convention of 1932:

I appreciate your willingness after these six arduous days to remain here, for I know well the sleepless hours which you and I have had. I regret that I am late, but I have no control over the winds of Heaven and could only be thankful for my Navy training.

The appearance before a National Convention of its nominee for President, to be formally notified of his selection, is unprecedented and unusual, but these are unprecedented and unusual times. I have started out on the tasks that lie ahead by breaking the absurd traditions that the candidate should remain in professed ignorance of what has happened for weeks until he is formally notified of that event many weeks later.

My friends, may this be the symbol of my intention to be honest and to avoid all hypocrisy or sham, to avoid all silly shutting of the eyes to the truth in this campaign. You have nominated me and I know it, and I am here to thank you for the honor.

Let it also be symbolic that in so doing I broke traditions. Let it be from now on the task of our Party to break foolish traditions. We will break foolish traditions and leave it to the Republican leadership, far more skilled in that art, to break promises.

Let us now and here highly resolve to resume the country's interrupted march along the path of real progress, of real justice, of real equality for all of our citizens, great and small. Our indomitable leader in the interrupted march is no longer with us, but there still survives today his spirit. Many of his captains, thank God, are still with us, to give us wise counsel. Let us feel that in everything we do there still lives with us, if not the body, the great indomitable unquenchable, progressive soul of our Commander-in-Chief, Woodrow Wilson.

I have many things on which I want to make my position clear at the earliest possible moment in this campaign. That admirable document, the platform which you have adopted, is clear. I accept it 100 percent.

And you can accept my pledge that I will leave no doubt or ambiguity on where I stand on any question of moment in this campaign.

As we enter this new battle, let us keep always present with us some of the ideals of the Party: The fact that the Democratic Party by tradition and by the continuing logic of history, past and present, is the bearer of liberalism. And of progress and at the same time of safety to our institutions. And if this appeal fails, remember well, my friends, that a resentment against the failure of Republican leadership—and note well that in this campaign I shall not use the word "Republican Party," but shall use, day in and day out, the words, "Republican leadership"—the failure of Republican leaders to solve our troubles may degenerate into unreasoning radicalism.

The great social phenomenon of the depression, unlike others before it, is that it has produced but a few of the disorderly manifestations that too often attend upon such times.

Wild radicalism has made few converts, and the greatest tribute that I can pay to my countrymen is that in these days of crushing want, there persists an orderly and hopeful spirit on the part of millions of our people who have suffered so much. To fail to offer them a new chance is not only to betray their hopes but to misunderstand their patience.

To meet by reaction that danger of radicalism is to invite disaster. Reaction is no barrier to the radical. It is a challenge, a provocation. The way to meet that danger is to offer a workable program of reconstruction, and the party to offer it is the party with clean hands.

This, and this only, is a proper protection against blind reaction on the one hand and an improvised, hit-or-miss, irresponsible opportunism on the other.

There are two ways of viewing the government's duty in matters affecting economic and social life. The first sees to it that a favored few are helped and hopes that some of their prosperity will leak through, sift through, to labor, to the farmer, to the small businessman. That theory belongs to the party of Toryism, and I had hoped that most of the Tories left this country in 1776.

But it is not and never will be the theory of the Democratic Party. This is no time for fear, for reaction or for timidity. Here and now I invite those nominal Republicans who find that their conscience cannot be squared with the groping and the failure of their party leaders to join hands with us; here and now, in equal measure, I warn those nominal Democrats who squint at the future with their faces turned toward the past, and who feel no responsibility to the demands of the new time, that they are out of step with their Party.

Yet, the people of this country want a genuine choice this year, not a choice between two names for the same reactionary doctrine. Ours must be a party of liberal thought, of planned action, of enlightened international outlook, and of the greatest good to the greatest number of our citizens.

Now it is inevitable—and the choice is that of the times—it is inevitable that the main issue of this campaign should revolve about the clear fact of our economic condition, a depression so deep that it is without precedent in modern history. It will not do merely to state, as do Republican leaders to explain their broken promises of continued inaction, that the depression is worldwide. That was not their explanation of the apparent prosperity of 1928. The people will not forget the claim made by them then that prosperity was only a domestic product manufactured by a Republican President and a Republican Congress. If they claim paternity for the one they cannot deny paternity for the other.

I cannot take up all the problems today. I want to touch on a few that are vital. Let us look a little at the recent history and simple economics, the kind of economics that you and I and the average man and woman talk.

In the years before 1929 we know that this country had completed a vast cycle of building and inflation; for ten years we expanded on the theory of repairing the wastes of the War, but actually expanding far beyond that, and also beyond our natural and normal growth. Now it is worth remembering, and the cold figures of finance prove it, that during that time there was little or no drop in the prices that the consumer had to pay, although those same figures proved that the cost of production fell very greatly; corporate profit resulting from this period was enormous; at the same time little of that profit was devoted to the reduction of prices. The consumer was forgotten. Very little of it went into increased wages; the worker was forgotten, and by no means an adequate proportion was even paid out in dividends—the stockholder was forgotten.

And, incidentally, very little of it was taken by taxation to the beneficent government of those years.

What was the result? Enormous corporate surpluses piled up—the most stupendous in history. Where, under the spell of delirious speculation, did those surpluses go? Let us talk economics that the figures prove and that we can understand. Why, they went chiefly in two directions: first, into new and unnecessary plants which now stand stark and idle; and second, into the call-money market of Wall Street, either directly by the corporations, or indirectly through the banks. Those are the facts. Why blink at them?

Then came the crash. You know the story. Surpluses invested in unnecessary plants became idle. Men lost their jobs; purchasing power dried up; banks became frightened and started calling loans. Those who had money were afraid to part with it. Credit contracted. Industry stopped. Commerce declined, and unemployment mounted.

And here we are today.

Translate that into human terms. See how the events of the past three years have come home to specific groups of people: first, the group dependent on industry; second, the group dependent on agriculture; third, and made up in large part of members of the first two groups, the people who are called "small investors and depositors." In fact, the strongest possible tie between the first two groups, agriculture and industry, is the fact that the savings and to a degree the security of both are tied together in that third group—the credit structure of the nation.

Never in history have the interests of all people been so united in a single economic problem. Picture to yourself, for instance, the great groups of property owned by millions of our citizens, represented by credits issued in the form of bonds and mortgages—government bonds of all kinds, Federal, State, county, municipal; bonds of industrial companies, of utility companies; mortgages on real estate in farms and cities, and finally the vast investments of the nation in the railroads. What is the measure of the security of each of those groups? We know well that in our complicated, interrelated credit structure if any one of these credit groups collapses they may all collapse. Danger to one is danger to all.

How, I ask, has the present administration in Washington treated the interrelationship of these credit groups: The answer is clear: It has not recognized that interrelationship existed at all. Why, the nation asks, has Washington failed to understand that all of these groups, each and every one, the top of the pyramid and the bottom of the pyramid, must be considered together, that each and every one of them is dependent on every other; each and every one of them affecting the whole financial fabric?

Statesmanship and vision, my friends, require relief to all at the same time.

Just one word or two on taxes, the taxes that all of us pay toward the cost of government of all kinds.

I know something of taxes. For three long years I have been going up and down this country preaching that government—Federal and State and local—costs too much. I shall not stop that preaching. As an immediate program of action we must abolish useless offices. We must eliminate unnecessary functions of government—functions, in fact, that are not definitely essential to the continuance of government. We must merge; we must consolidate subdivisions of government, and, like the private citizen, give up luxuries which we can no longer afford.

And now one word about unemployment, and incidentally about agriculture. I have favored the use of certain types of public works as a further emergency means of stimulating employment and the issuance of bonds to pay for such public works, but I have pointed out that no economic end is served if we merely build without building for a necessary purpose. Such works, of course, should insofar as possible be self-sustaining if they are to be financed by the issuing of bonds. So as to spread the points of all kinds as widely as possible, we must take definite steps to shorten the working day and the working week.

Let us use common sense and business sense. Just as one example, we know that a very hopeful and immediate means of relief, both for the unemployed and for agriculture, will come from a wide plan of converting many millions of acres of marginal and unused land into timberland through reforestation. There are tens of millions of acres east of the Mississippi River alone in abandoned farms, in cut-over land, now growing up in worthless brush. Why, every European Nation has a definite land policy, and has had one for generations. We have none. Having none, we face a future of soil erosion and timber famine. It is clear that economic foresight and immediate employment march hand in hand in the call for the reforestation of these vast areas.

In so doing, employment can be given to a million men. That is the kind of public work that is self-sustaining, and therefore capable of being financed by the issuance of bonds which are made secure by the fact that the growth of tremendous crops will provide adequate security for the investment.

Yes, I have a very definite program for providing employment by that means. I have done it, and I am doing it today in the State of New York. I know that the Democratic Party can do it successfully in the nation. That will put men to work, and that is an example of the action that we are going to have.

Now as a further aid to agriculture, we know perfectly well—but have we come out and said so clearly and distinctly? We should repeal immediately those provisions of law that compel the Federal Government to go into the market to purchase, to sell, to speculate in farm products in a futile attempt to reduce farm surpluses. And they are the people who are talking of keeping government out of business. The practical way to help the farmer is by an arrangement that will, in addition to lightening some of the impoverishing burdens from his back, do something toward the reduction of the surpluses of staple commodities that hang on the market. It should be our aim to add to the world prices of staple products that amount of a reasonable tariff protection, to give agriculture the same protection that industry has today.

And in exchange for this immediately increased return I am sure that the farmers of this nation would agree ultimately to such planning of their production as would reduce the surpluses and make it unnecessary in later years to depend on dumping those surpluses abroad in order to support domestic prices. That result has been accomplished in other nations—why not America too?

Farm leaders and farm economists, generally, agree that a plan based on that principle is a desirable first step in the reconstruction of agriculture. It does not in itself furnish a complete program, but it will serve in great measure in the long run to remove the pall of a surplus without the continued perpetual threat of world dumping. Final voluntary reduction of surplus is a part of our objective, but the long continuance and the present burden of existing surpluses make it necessary to repair great damage of the present by immediate emergency measures.

Such a plan as that, my friends, does not cost the government any money, nor does it keep the government in business or in speculation.

As to the actual wording of a bill, I believe that the Democratic Party stands ready to be guided by whatever the responsible farm groups themselves agree on. That is a principle that is sound; and again I ask for action.

One more word about the farmer, and I know that every delegate in the hall who lives in the city knows why I lay emphasis on the farmer. It is because one-half of our population, over 50,000,000 people, are dependent on agriculture; and, my friends, if those 50,000,000 people have no money, no cash, to buy what is produced in the city, the city suffers to an equal or greater extent.

That is why we are gong to make the voters understand this year that this nation is not merely a nation of independence, but it is, if we are to survive, bound to be a nation of interdependence—town and city, and North and South, East and West. That is our goal, and that goal will be understood by the people of this country no matter where they live.

Yes, the purchasing power of that half of our population dependent on agriculture is gone. Farm mortgages reach nearly ten billions of dollars today and interest charges on that alone are $560,000,000 a year. But that is not all. The tax burden caused by extravagant and inefficient local government is an additional factor. Our most immediate concern should be to reduce the interest burden on these mortgages.

Rediscounting of farm mortgages under salutary restrictions must be expanded and should, in the future, be conditioned on the reduction of interest rates. Amortization payments, maturities should likewise in this crisis be extended before rediscount is permitted where the mortgagor is sorely pressed. That, my friends is another example of practical, immediate relief: Action.

I aim to do the same things, and it can be done, for the small homeowner in our cities and villages. We can lighten his burden and develop his purchasing power. Take away, my friends, that spectre of too high an interest rate. Take away that spectre of the due date just a short time away. Save homes—save homes for the thousands of self-respecting families, and drive out that spectre of insecurity from our midst.

Out of all the tons of printed paper, out of all the hours of oratory, the recriminations, the defenses, the happy-thought plans in Washington and in every State, there emerges one great, simple, crystal-pure fact that during the past ten years: a nation of 120,000,000 people has been led by the Republican leaders to erect an impregnable barbed wire entanglement around its borders through the instrumentality of tariffs which have isolated us from all other human beings in all the rest of the round world. I accept that admirable tariff statement in the platform of this convention. It would protect American business and American labor. By our acts of the past we have invited and received the retaliation of other nations. I propose an invitation to them to forget the past, to sit at the table with us, as friends, and to plan with us for the restoration of the trade of the world. Go into the home of the businessman. He knows what the tariff has done for him. Go into the home of the factory worker. He knows why goods do not move. Go into the home of the farmer. He knows how the tariff has helped to ruin him.

At last our eyes are open. At last the American people are ready to acknowledge that Republican leadership was wrong and that the Democracy is right.

My program, of which I can only touch on these points, is based upon the simple moral principle: the welfare and the soundness of a nation depend first upon what the great mass of the people wish and need; and second, whether or not they are getting it.

What do the people of America want more than anything else? To my mind, they want two things: work, with all the moral and spiritual values that go with it; and with work, a reasonable measure of security—security for themselves and for their wives and children. Work and security—these are more than words. They are more than facts. They are the spiritual values, the true goal toward which our efforts of reconstruction should lead.

There are the values that this program in intended to gain; these are the values we have failed to achieve by the leadership we now have.

Our Republican leaders tell us economic laws—sacred, inviolable, unchangeable—cause panics which no one could prevent. But while they prate of economic laws, men and women are starving. We must lay hold of the fact that economic laws are not made by nature. They are made by human beings.

Yes, when—not if—when we get the chance, the Federal Government will assume bold leadership in distress relief. For years Washington has alternated between putting its head in the sand and saying there is no large number of destitute people in our midst who need food and clothing, and then saying the states should take care of them, if there are. Instead of planning two and a half years ago to do what they are now trying to do, they kept putting it off from day to day, week to week, and month to month, until the conscience of America demanded action.

I say that while primary responsibility for relief rests with localities now, as ever, yet the Federal Government has always had and still has a continuing responsibility for the broader public welfare. It will soon fulfill that responsibility.

And now, just a few words about our plans for the next four months. By coming here instead of waiting for a formal notification, I have made it clear that I believe we should eliminate expensive ceremonies and that we should set in motion at once, tonight, my friends, the necessary machinery for an adequate presentation of the issues to the electorate of the nation.

I myself have important duties as Governor of a great State, duties which in these times are more arduous and more grave than at any previous period. Yet I feel confident that I shall be able to make a number of short visits to several parts of the nation. My trips will have as their first objective the study at first hand, from the lips of men and women of all parties and all occupations, of the actual conditions and needs of every part of an interdependent country.

One word more: Out of every crisis, every tribulation, every disaster, mankind rises with some share of greater knowledge, of higher decency, or purer purpose. Today we shall have come through a period of loose thinking, descending morals, an era of selfishness, among individual men and women and among nations. Blame not governments alone for this. Blame ourselves in equal share. Let us be frank in acknowledgement of the truth that many amongst us have made obeisance to Mammon, that the profits of speculation, the easy road without toil, have lured us from the old barricades. To return to higher standards we must abandon the false prophets and seek new leaders of our own choosing.

Never before in modern history have the essential differences between the two major American parties stood out in such striking contrast as they do today. Republican leaders not only have failed in material things, they have failed in national vision, because in disaster they have held out no hope, they have pointed out no path for the people below to climb back to places of security and of safety in our American life.

Throughout the nation, men and women, forgotten in the political philosophy of the government of the last years look to us here for guidance and for more equitable opportunity to share in the distribution of national wealth.

On the farms, in the large metropolitan areas, in the smaller cities and in the villages, millions of our citizens cherish the hope that their old standards of living and of thought have not gone forever. Those millions cannot and shall not hope in vain.

I pledge you, I pledge myself, to a new deal for the American people. Let us all here assembled constitute ourselves prophets of a new order of competence and of courage. This is more than a political campaign; it is a call to arms. Give me your help, not to win votes alone, but to win in the crusade to restore America to its own people.

XII
Herbert Hoover:
Presidential Nomination Address
Sent to the Republican National Convention
Washington, D.C., August 11, 1932

Mr. Chairman and My Fellow Citizens:

In accepting the great honor you have brought me, I desire to speak so simply and so plainly that every man and woman in the United States who may hear or read my words cannot misunderstand.

The last three years have been a time of unparalleled economic calamity. They have been years of greater suffering and hardship than any which have come to the American people since the aftermath of the Civil War. As we look back over these troubled years we realize that we have passed through two stages of dislocation and stress.

Before the storm broke we were steadily gaining in prosperity. Our wounds from the war were rapidly healing. Advances in science and invention had opened vast vistas of new progress. Being prosperous, we became optimistic—all of us. From optimism some of us went to over expansion in anticipation of the future, and from over expansion to reckless speculation. In the soil poisoned by speculation grew those ugly weeds of waste,

exploitation, and abuse of financial power. In this overproduction
and speculative mania we marched with the rest of the world.
Then three years ago came retribution by the inevitable worldwide
slump in consumption of goods, in prices, and employment. At
that juncture it was the normal penalty for a reckless boom such as
we have witnessed a score of times in our history. Through such
depressions we have always passed safely after a relatively short
period of losses, of hardship and adjustment. We adopted policies
in the government, which were fitting to the situation. Gradually
the country began to right itself. Eighteen months ago there was
solid basis for hope that recovery was in sight.

Then there came to us a new calamity, a blow from abroad of
such dangerous character as to strike at the very safety of the
Republic. The countries of Europe proved unable to withstand the
stress of the depression. The memories of the world had ignored
the fact that the insidious diseases left by the Great War had not
been cured. The skill and intelligence of millions in Europe had
been blotted out by battle, disease and starvation. Stupendous
burdens of national debts had been built up. Poisoned springs of
political instability lay in the treaties which closed the war. Fears
and hates held armaments to double those before the war.
Governments were fallaciously seeking to build back by enlarged
borrowing, by subsidizing industry and employment with taxes
that slowly sapped the savings upon which industry must be
rejuvenated and commerce solidly built. Under these strains the
financial systems of many foreign countries crashed one by one.

New blows from decreasing world consumption of goods and
from failing financial systems rained upon us. We are part of a
world the disturbance of whose remotest populations affects our
financial system, our employment, our markets, and prices of our
farm products. Thus beginning eighteen months ago, the
worldwide storm rapidly grew to hurricane force and the greatest
economic emergency in all history. Unexpected, unforeseen, and
violent shocks with every month brought new dangers and new
emergencies. Fear and apprehension gripped the heart of our
people in every village and city.

If we look back over the disasters of these three years, we find
that three-quarters of the population of the globe has suffered from
the flames of revolution. Many nations have been subject to
constant change and vacillation of government. Others have

resorted to dictatorship or tyranny in desperate attempts to preserve some sort of social order....

Two courses were open. We might have done nothing. That would have been utter ruin. Instead, we met the situation with proposals to private business and the Congress of the most gigantic program of economic defense and counter attack ever evolved in the history of the Republic. We put it into action.

Our measures have repelled these attacks of fear and panic. We have maintained the financial integrity of our government. We have cooperated to restore and stabilize the situation abroad. As a nation we have paid every dollar demanded of us. We have used the credit of the government to aid and protect our institutions, public and private. We have provided methods and assurances that there shall be none to suffer from hunger and cold. We have instituted measures to assist farmers and homeowners. We have created vast agencies for employment. Above all, we have maintained the sanctity of the principles upon which this Republic has grown great.

In a large sense the test of success of our program is simple. Our people, while suffering great hardships have been and will be cared for. In the long view our institutions have been sustained intact and are now functioning with increasing confidence of the future. As a nation we are undefeated and unafraid. Government by the people has not been defiled.

With the humility of one who by necessity has stood in the midst of this storm I can say with pride that the distinction for these accomplishments belongs not to the government or to any individual. It is due to the intrepid soul of our people. It is to their character, their fortitude, their initiative, and their courage that we owe these results. We of this generation did not build the great Ship of State. But the policies I have inaugurated have protected and aided its navigation in this storm. These policies and programs have not been partisan. I gladly give tribute to those members of the Democratic Party in Congress whose patriotic cooperation against factional and demagogic opposition has assisted in a score of great undertakings. I likewise give credit to Democratic as well as Republican leaders among our citizens for the cooperation and help.

A record of these dangers and these policies in the last three years will be set down in books. Much of it is interest only to history. Our interest now is the future. I dwell upon these policies and problems only where they illustrate the questions of the day and our course in the future. As a government and as a people we still have much to do. We must continue the building of our measures of restoration. We must profit by the lessons of this experience.

Before I enter upon a discussion of these policies I wish to say something of my conception of the relation of our government to the people and of the responsibilities of both, particularly as applied to these times. The spirit and devising of this government by the people was to sustain a dual purpose—on the one hand to protect our people among nations and in domestic emergencies by great national power, and on the other to preserve individual liberty and freedom through local government.

The function of the Federal Government in these times is to use its reserve powers and its strength for the protection of citizens and local governments by supporting our institutions against forces beyond their control. It is not the function of the government to relieve individuals of the responsibilities to their neighbors, or to relieve private institutions of their responsibilities to the public, or of local government to the States, or of State governments to the Federal Government. In giving that protection and that aid the Federal Government must insist that all of them exert their responsibilities in full. It is vital that the programs of the government shall not compete with or replace any of them but shall add to their initiative and their strength. It is vital that by the use of public avenues and public credit in emergency the nation shall be strengthened and not weakened.

And in all these emergencies and crises, and in all our future policies, we must also preserve the fundamental principles of our social and economic system. That system is founded upon a conception of ordered freedom. The test of that freedom is that there should be maintained equality of opportunity to every individual so that he may achieve for himself the best to which his character, ability, and ambition entitle him. It is only by this release of initiative, this insistence upon individual responsibility, that we accrue the great sums of individual accomplishment which carry this nation forward. This is not an individualism which permits men to run riot in selfishness or to over-ride equality of opportunity for others. It permits no violation of ordered liberty. In the race after the false gods of materialism, men and groups have forgotten their country. Equality of opportunity contains no conception of exploitation by any selfish, ruthless, class-minded men or groups. They have no place in the American system. As against these stand the guiding ideals and concepts of our nation. I propose to maintain them.

The solution of our many problems which arise from the shifting scene of national life is not to be found in haphazard experimentation or by revolution. It must be through organic development of our national life under these ideals. It must secure that cooperative action which builds initiative and strength outside of government. It does not follow, because our difficulties are stupendous, because there are some souls timorous enough to doubt the validity and effectiveness of our ideals and our system, that we must turn to a State-controlled or State-directed social or economic system in order to cure our troubles. That is not liberalism; it is tyranny. It is the regimentation of men under autocratic bureaucracy with all its extinction of liberty, or hope, and of opportunity. Of course, no man of understanding says that our system works perfectly. It does not. The human race is not perfect. Nevertheless, the movement of a true civilization is toward freedom rather than regimentation. This is our ideal.

Ofttimes the tendency of democracy in presence of national danger is to strike blindly, to listen to demagogues and slogans, all of which would destroy and would not save. We have refused to be stampeded into such courses. Ofttimes democracy elsewhere in the world has been unable to move fast enough to save itself in emergency. There have been disheartening delays and failures in legislation and private action which have added to the losses of our people, yet this democracy of ours has proved its ability to act.

Our emergency measures of the last three years form a definite strategy dominated in the background by these American principles and ideals, forming a continuous campaign waged against the forces of destruction on an ever widening or constantly shifting front.

Thus we have held that the Federal Government should in the presence of great national danger use its powers to give leadership to the initiative, the courage, and the fortitude of the people themselves; but it must insist upon individual, community, and state responsibility. That it should furnish leadership to assure the coordination and unity of all existing agencies, governmental and private, for economic and humanitarian action. That where it becomes necessary to meet emergencies beyond the power of these agencies by the creation of new government instrumentalities, they should be of such character as not to supplant or weaken, but rather to supplement and strengthen, the initiative and enterprise of the people. That they must, directly, or indirectly, serve all the people. Above all, that they should be set up in such form that once the emergency is passed then can and must be demobilized and withdrawn leaving our governmental, economic, and social structure strong and whole.

We have not feared boldly to adopt unprecedented measures to meet the unprecedented violence of the storm. But, because we have kept ever before us these eternal principles of our nation, The American Government in its ideals is the same as it was when the people gave the Presidency into my trust. We shall keep it so. We have resolutely rejected the temptation under pressure of immediate events, to resort to those panaceas and short cuts which, even if temporarily successful, would ultimately undermine and weaken what has slowly been built and molded by experience and effort throughout these hundred and fifty years.

There are national policies wider than the emergency, wider than the economic horizon. They are set forth in our platform. Having the responsibility of this office, my views upon them are clearly and often set out in the public record. I may, however, summarize some of them.

I am squarely for a protective tariff. I am against the proposal of "a competitive tariff for revenue" as advocated by our opponents. That would place our farmers and our workers in competition with peasant and sweated labor products.

I am against their proposals to destroy the usefulness of the bipartisan Tariff Commission, the establishment of whole effective powers we secured during this administration twenty-five years after it was first advocated by President Theodore Roosevelt. That instrumentality enables us to correct any injustice and to readjust the rates of duty to shifting economic change, without constant tinkering and orgies of logrolling in Congress. If our opponents will descend from vague generalizations to any particular schedule, if it be higher than necessary to protect our people or insufficient for their protection, it can be remedied by this bipartisan commission.

I favor rigidly restricted immigration. I have by executive direction, in order to relieve us of added unemployment, already reduced the inward movement to less than the outward movement. I shall adhere to that policy.

I have repeatedly recommended to the Congress a revision of the railway transportation laws, in order that we may create greater stability and greater assurance of vital service in all our transportation. I shall persist in it.

I have repeatedly recommended the Federal regulation of interstate power. I shall persist in that. I have opposed the Federal Government undertaking the operation of the power business. I shall continue that opposition.

I have for years supported the conservation of national resources. I have made frequent recommendations to the Congress in respect thereto, including legislation to correct the waste and destruction of these resources through the present interpretations of the antitrust laws. I shall continue to urge such action.

This depression has exposed many weaknesses in our economic system. There have been exploitation and abuse of financial power. We will fearlessly and unremittingly reform such abuses. I have recommended to the Congress the reform of our banking laws. Unfortunately this legislation has not yet been enacted. The American people must have protection from insecure banking through a stronger system. They must be relieved from conditions which permit the credit machinery of the country to be made available without adequate check for wholesale speculation in securities with ruinous consequences to millions of our citizens and to national economy. I recommended to the Congress emergency relief for depositors in closed banks. For seven years I have repeatedly warned against private loans abroad for nonproductive purposes. I shall persist in those matters.

I have insisted upon a balanced budget as the foundation of all public and private financial stability and of all public confidence. I shall insist on the maintenance of that policy. Recent increases in revenues, while temporary, should be again examined, and if they tend to sap the vitality of industry, and thus retard employment, they must be revised....

I have repeatedly for seven years urged the Congress either themselves to abolish obsolete bureaus and commissions and to reorganize the whole government structure in the interest of the economy, or to give someone the authority to do so. I have succeeded partially in securing authority, but I regret that no substantial act under it is to be effective until approved by the next Congress.

With the collapse in world prices and depreciated currencies the farmer was never so dependent upon his tariff protection for recovery as he is at the present time. We shall hold to that. We have enacted many measures of emergency relief to agriculture. They are having effect. I shall keep them functioning until the strain is past. The original purpose of the Farm Board was to strengthen the efforts of the farmer to establish his own farmer-owned, farmer-controlled marketing agencies. It has greatly succeeded in this purpose, even in these times of adversity. The departure of the Farm Board from its original purpose by making loans to farmers' cooperatives to preserve prices from panic served the emergency, but such action in normal times is absolutely destructive to the farmers' interests.

We still have vast problems to solve in agriculture. No power on earth can restore prices except by restoration of general recovery and markets. Every measure we have taken looking to general recovery is of benefit to the farmer. There is no relief to the farmer by extending government bureaucracy to control his production and thus curtail his liberties, nor by subsidies that bring only more bureaucracy and ultimate collapse. I shall oppose them.

The most practicable relief to the farmer today aside from the general economic recovery is a definite program of readjustment and coordination of national, state, and local taxation which will relieve real property, especially the farms, from unfair burdens of taxation which the current readjustment in values has brought about. To that purpose I propose to devote myself.

I have always favored the development of rivers and harbors and highways. These improvements have been greatly expedited. We shall continue that work to completion. After twenty years of discussion between the United States and the great nation to the north, I have signed a treaty for the construction of the Great Lakes-St. Lawrence seaway. That treaty does not injure the Chicago to the Gulf waterway, the work upon which, together with the whole Mississippi system I have expedited, and in which I am equally interested. We shall undertake this great seaway, the greatest pubic improvement upon our continent, with its consequent employment of many men as quickly as the treaty is ratified.

There are many other important subjects fully set forth in the platform and in my public statements in the past.

The leadership of the Federal Government is not to be confined to economic and international questions. There are problems of the home, of education of children, of citizenship, the most vital of all to the future of the nation. Except in the case of aid to States which I have recommended for stimulation of the protection and health of children, they are not matters of legislation. We have given leadership to the initiative of our people for social advancement through organization against illiteracy, through the White House conferences on protection and health of children, through the National Conference on Home Ownership, through stimulation to social and recreational agencies. There are the visible evidences of spiritual leadership by government. They will be continued and constantly invigorated.

My fellow citizens, the discussion of great problems of economic life and of government often seems abstract and cold. But within their right solution lie the happiness and hope of a great people. Without such solution all else is mere verbal sympathy.

Today millions of our fellow countrymen are out of work. Prices of the farmers' products are below a living standard. Many millions more who are in business or hold employment are haunted by fears for the future. No man with a spark of humanity can sit in my place without suffering from the picture of their anxieties and hardships before him day and night. They would be more than human if they were not led to blame their condition upon the government in power. I have understood their sufferings and have worked to the limits of my strength to produce action that would really help them.

Much remains to be done to attain recovery. The emergency measures now in action represent an unparalleled use of national power to relieve distress, to provide employment, to serve agriculture, the preserve the stability of the government, to maintain the integrity of our institutions. Our policies prevent unemployment caused by floods of imported goods and laborers. Our policies preserve peace. They embrace cooperation with other nations in those fields in which we can serve. With patience and perseverance these measures will succeed.

Despite the dislocation of economic life our great tools of production and distribution are more efficient than ever before; our fabulous natural resources, our farms, our homes, our skill are unimpaired. From the hard-won experience of this depression we shall build stronger methods of prevention and stronger methods of protection to our people from the abuses which have become evident. We shall march to far greater accomplishment.

With united effort we can and will turn the tide toward the restoration of business, employment, and agriculture. It will call for the utmost devotion and wisdom. Every reserve of American courage and vision must be called upon to sustain us and to plan wisely for the future.

Through it all our first duty is to preserve unfettered that dominant American spirit which has produced our enterprise and individual character. That is the bedrock of the past, and that is the guaranty of the future. Not regimented mechanisms but free men is our goal. Herein is the fundamental issue. A representative democracy, progressive and unafraid to meet its problems, but meeting them upon the foundations of experience and not upon the wave of emotion or the insensate demands of a radicalism which grasps at every opportunity to exploit the sufferings of a people.

With these courses we shall emerge from this great national strain with our American system of life and government strengthened. Our people will be free to reassert their energy and enterprise in a society eager to reward in full measure those whose industry serves its well being. Our youth will find the doors of equal opportunity still open.

The problems of the next few years are not only economic. They are also moral and spiritual. The present check to our material success must deeply stir our national conscience upon the purposes of life itself. It must cause us to revalue and reshape our drift from materialism to a higher note of individual and national ideals.

Underlying every purpose is the spiritual application of moral ideals which are the fundamental basis of happiness in a people. This is a land of homes, churches, schoolhouses dedicated to the sober and enduring satisfactions of family life and the rearing of children in an atmosphere of ideals and religious faith. Only with these high standards can we hold society together, and only from them can government survive or business prosper. They are the sole insurance to the safety of our children and the continuity of the nation.

If it shall appear that while I have had the honor of the Presidency I have contributed the part required from this high office to bringing the Republic through this dark night, and if in my administration we shall see the break of dawn to a better day, I shall have done my part in the world. No man can have a greater honor than that.

I have but one desire: that is, to see my country again on the road to prosperity which shall be more sane and lasting through the lesson of experience, to see the principles and ideals of the American people perpetuated.

I rest the case of the Republican Party on the intelligence and the just discernment of the American people. Should my countrymen again place upon me the responsibilities of this high office, I shall carry forward the work of reconstruction. I shall hope long before another four years have passed to see the world prosperous and at peace and every American home again in the sunshine of genuine progress and genuine prosperity. I shall seek to maintain untarnished and unweakened those fundamental traditions and principles upon which our nation was founded and upon which it has grown. I shall invite and welcome the help of every man and woman in the preservation of the United States for the happiness of its people. This is my pledge to the nation and to Almighty God.

XIII
Franklin D. Roosevelt:
Commonwealth Club Address
San Francisco, California, September 23, 1932

My friends:

I count it a privilege to be invited to address the Commonwealth Club. It has stood in the life of this city and State, and it is perhaps accurate to add, the nation, as a group of citizen leaders interested in fundamental problems of government, and chiefly concerned with achievement of progress in government through non-partisan means. The privilege of addressing you, therefore, in the heat of a political campaign, is great. I want to respond to your courtesy in terms consistent with your policy.

I want to speak not of politics but of government. I want to speak not of parties, but of universal principles. They are not political, except in that larger sense in which a great American once expressed a definition of politics, that nothing in all of human life is foreign to the science of politics.

I do want to give you, however, a recollection of a long life spent for a large part in public office. Some of my conclusions and observations have been deeply accentuated in these past few weeks. I have traveled far—from Albany to the Golden Gate. I have seen many people, and heard many things, and today, when in a sense my journey has reached the half-way mark, I am glad of the opportunity to discuss with you what it all means to me.

Sometimes, my friends, particularly in years such as these, the hand of discouragement falls upon us. It seems that things are in a rut, fixed, settled, that the world has grown old and tired and very much out of joint. This is the mood of depression, of dire and weary depression.

But then we look around us in America, and everything tells us that we are wrong. America is new. It is the process of change and development. It has the great potentialities of youth and particularly is this true of the great west, and of this coast, and of California.

I would not have you feel that I regard this as in any sense a new community. I have traveled in many parts of the world, but never have I felt the arresting thought of the change and development more that here, where the old, mystic East would seem to be near to us, where the currents of life and thought and commerce of the whole world meet us. This factor alone is sufficient to cause man to stop and think of the deeper meaning of things, when he stands in this community.

But more than that, I appreciate that the membership of this club consists of men who are thinking in terms beyond the immediate present, beyond their own immediate tasks, beyond their own individual interests. I want to invite you, therefore, to consider with me in the large, some of the relationships of government and economic life that go deeply into our daily lives, our happiness, our future and our security.

The issue of government has always been whether individual men and women will have to serve some system of government or economics, or whether a system of government and economics exists to serve individual men and women. This question has persistently dominated the discussion of government for many generations. On questions relating to these things men have differed, and for time immemorial it is probable that honest men will continue to differ.

The final word belongs to no man; yet we can still believe in change and in progress. Democracy, as a dear old friend of mine in Indiana, Meredith Nicholson, has called it, is a quest, a never ending seeking for better things, and in the seeking for these things and the striving for them, there are many roads to follow. But, if we map the course of these roads, we find that there are only two general directions.

When we look about us, we are likely to forget how hard people have worked to win the privilege of government. The growth of the national governments of Europe was a struggle for the development of a centralized force in the nation, strong enough to impose peace upon ruling barons. In many instances the victory of the central government, the creation of a strong central government, was a haven of refuge to the individual. The people preferred the master far away to the exploitation and cruelty of the smaller master near at hand.

But the creators of national government were perforce-ruthless men. They were often cruel in their methods, but they did strive steadily toward something that society needed and very much wanted, a strong central State able to keep the peace, to stamp out civil war, to put the unruly nobleman in his place, and to permit the bulk of individuals to live safely. The man of ruthless force had his place in developing a pioneer country, just as he did in fixing the power of the central government in the development of the nations. Society paid him well for his services and its development. When the development among the nations of Europe, however, had been completed, ambition and ruthlessness, having served their term, tended to overstep their mark.

There came a growing feeling that government was conducted for the benefit of a few who thrived unduly at the expense of all. The people sought a balancing—a limiting force. There came gradually, through town councils, trade guilds, national parliaments by constitution and by popular participation and control, limitations on arbitrary power.

Another factor that tended to limit the power of those who ruled, was the rise of the ethical conception that a ruler bore a responsibility for the welfare of his subjects.

The American colonies were born in this struggle. The American Revolution was a turning point in it. After the Revolution the struggle continued and shaped itself in the public life of the country. There were those who because they had seen the confusion which attended the years of war for American independence surrendered to the belief that popular government was essentially dangerous and essentially unworkable. They were honest people, my friends, and we cannot deny that their experience had warranted some measure of fear. The most brilliant, honest and able exponent of this point of view was Hamilton. He was too impatient of slow-moving methods. Fundamentally he believed that the safety of the republic lay in the autocratic strength of its government, that the destiny of individuals was to serve that government, and that fundamentally a great and strong group of central institutions, guided by a small group of able and public spirited citizens, could best direct all government.

But Mr. Jefferson, in the summer of 1776, after drafting the Declaration of Independence turned his mind to the same problem and took a different view. He did not deceive himself with outward forms. Government to him was a means to an end, not an end in itself; it might be either a refuge and a help or a threat and a danger, depending on the circumstances. We find him carefully analyzing the society for which he was to organize a government. "We have no paupers. The great mass of our population is of laborers, our rich who cannot live without labor, either manual or professional, being few and of moderate wealth. Most of the laboring class possess property, cultivate their own lands, have families and from the demand for their labor, are enabled to exact from the rich and the competent such prices as enable them to feed abundantly, clothe above mere decency, to labor moderately and raise their families."

These people, he considered, had two sets of rights, those of "personal competency" and those involved in acquiring and possessing property. By "personal competency" he meant the right of free thinking, freedom of forming and expressing opinions, and freedom of personal living, each man according to his own rights. To insure the first set of rights, a government must so order its functions as not to interfere with the individual. But even Jefferson realized that the exercise of property rights might so interfere with the rights of the individual that the government, without whose assistance the property rights could not exist, must intervene, not to destroy individualism, but to protect it.

You are familiar with the great political duel which followed; and how Hamilton, and his friends, building toward a dominant centralized power were at length defeated in the great election of 1800, by Mr. Jefferson's party. Out of that duel came the two parties, Republican and Democratic, as we know them today.

So began, in American political life, the new day, the day of the individual against the system, the day in which individualism was made the great watchword of American life. The happiest of economic conditions made that day long and splendid. On the Western frontier, land was substantially free. No one, who did not shirk the task of earning a living, was entirely without opportunity to do so. Depressions could, and did, come and go; but they could not alter the fundamental fact that most of the people lived partly by selling their labor and partly by extracting their livelihood from the soil, so that starvation and dislocation were practically impossible. At the very worst there was always the possibility of climbing into a covered wagon and moving west where the untilled prairies afforded a haven for men to whom the East did not provide a place. So great were our natural resources that we could offer this relief not only to our own people, but to the distressed of all the world; we could invite immigration from Europe, and welcome it with open arms. Traditionally, when a depression came, a new section of land was opened in the west and even our temporary misfortune served our manifest destiny.

It was in the middle of the nineteenth century that a new force was released and a new dream created. The force was what is called the industrial revolution, the advance of steam and machinery and the rise of the forerunners of the modern industrial plant. The dream was the dream of an economic machine, able to raise the standard of living for everyone; to bring luxury within the reach of the humblest; to annihilate distance by steam power and later by electricity, and to release everyone from the drudgery of the heaviest manual toil. It was to be expected that this would necessarily affect government. Heretofore, government had merely been called upon to produce conditions within which people could live happily, labor peacefully, and rest secure. Now it was called upon to aid in the consummation of this new dream. There was, however, a shadow over the dream. To be made real, it required use of the talents of men of tremendous will and tremendous ambition, since by no other force could the problems of financing and engineering and new developments be brought to a consummation.

So manifest were the advantages of the machine age, however, that the United States fearlessly, cheerfully, and, I think, rightly, accepted the bitter with the sweet. It was thought that no price was too high to pay for the advantages which we could draw from a finished industrial system. This history of the last half century is accordingly in large measure a history of a group of financial Titans, whose methods were not scrutinized with too much care, and who were honored in proportion as they produced the results, irrespective of the means they used. The financiers who pushed the railroads to the Pacific were always ruthless, often wasteful, and frequently corrupt; but they did build railroads, and we have them today. It has been estimated that the American investor paid the American railway system more than three times over in the process, but despite this fact the net advantage was to the United States. As long as we had free land; as long as population was growing by leaps and bounds; as long as our industrial plants were insufficient to supply our own needs, society chose to give the ambitious man free play and unlimited reward provided only that he produced the economic plant so much desired. During this period of expansion, there was equal opportunity for all and the business of government was not to interfere but to assist in the development of industry. This was done at the request of businessmen themselves. The tariff was originally imposed for the purpose of "fostering our infant industry," a phrase I think the older among you will remember as a political issue not so long ago. The railroads were subsidized, sometimes by grants of money, oftener by grants of land; some of the most valuable oil lands in the United States were granted to assist the financing of the railroad which pushed through the Southwest. A nascent merchant marine was assisted by grants of money, or by mail subsidies, so that our stream shipping might ply the seven seas. Some of my friends tell me that they do not want the government in business. With this I agree; but I wonder whether they realize the implications of the past. For while it has been American doctrine that the government must not go into business in competition with private enterprises, still it has been traditional particularly in Republican Administrations for business urgently to ask the government to put at private disposal all kinds of government assistance. The same man who tells you that he does not want to see the government interfere in business—and he means it, and has plenty of good reasons for saying so—is the first to go to Washington and ask the government for a prohibitory tariff on his product. When things get just bad enough—as they did two years ago—he will go with equal speed to the United States government and ask for a loan; and the Reconstruction Finance Corporation is the outcome of it. Each group has sought protection from the government for its own special interests, without realizing that the function of government must be to favor no small group at the expense of its duty to protect the rights of personal freedom and of private property of all its citizens....

A glance at the situation today only too clearly indicates that equality of opportunity as we have known it no longer exists. Our industrial plant is built; the problem just now is whether under existing conditions it is not overbuilt. Our last frontier has long since been reached, and there is practically no more free land. More than half of our people do not live on the farms or on lands and cannot derive a living by cultivating their own property. There is no safety valve in the form of a Western prairie to which those thrown out of work by the Eastern economic machines can go for a new start. We are not able to invite the immigration from Europe to share our endless plenty. We are now providing a drab living for our own people.

Our system of constantly rising tariffs has at last reacted against us to the point of closing our Canadian frontier on the north, our European markets on the east, many of our Latin American markets to the south, and a goodly proportion of our Pacific markets on the west, through the retaliatory tariffs of those countries. It has forced many of our great industrial institutions who exported their surplus production to such countries, to establish plants in such countries, within the tariff walls. This has resulted in the reduction of the operation of their American plants, and opportunity for employment.

Just as freedom to farm has ceased, so also the opportunity in business has narrowed. It still is true that men can start small enterprises, trusting to native shrewdness and ability to keep abreast of competitors; but area after area has been pre-empted altogether by the great corporations, and even in the fields which still have no great concerns, the small man starts under a handicap. The unfeeling statistics of the past three decades show that the independent businessman is running a losing race. Perhaps he is forced to the wall; perhaps he cannot command credit; perhaps he is "squeezed out," in Mr. Wilson's words, by highly organized corporate competitors, as your corner grocery man can tell you. Recently a careful study was made of the concentration of business in the United States. It showed that our economic life was dominated by some six hundred odd corporations who controlled two-thirds of American industry. Ten million small businessmen divided the other third. More striking still, it appeared that if the process of concentration goes on at the same rate, at the end of another century we shall have all American industry controlled by a dozen corporations, and run by perhaps a hundred men. But plainly, we are steering a steady course toward economic oligarchy, if we are not there already.

Clearly, all this calls for a re-appraisal of values. A mere builder of more industrial plants, a creator of more railroad systems, an organizer of more corporations, is as likely to be a danger as a help. The day of the great promoter or the financial Titan, to whom we granted everything if only he would build, or develop, is over. Our task now is not discovery, or exploitation of natural resources, or necessarily producing more goods. It is the soberer, less dramatic business of administering resources and plants already in hand, of seeking to reestablish foreign markets for our surplus production, of meeting the problem of under consumption, of adjusting production to consumption, of distributing wealth and products more equitably of adapting existing economic organizations to the service of the people. The day of enlightened administration has come.

Just as in older times the central government was first a haven of refuge, and then a threat, so now in a closer economic system the central and ambitious financial unit is no longer a servant of national desire, but a danger. I would draw the parallel one step farther. We did not think because national government had become a threat in the 18th century that therefore we should abandon the principle of national government. Nor today should we abandon the principle of strong economic units called corporations, merely because their power is susceptible of easy abuse. In other times we dealt with the problem of an unduly ambitious central government. So today we are modifying and controlling our economic units.

As I see it, the task of government in its relation to business is to assist the development of an economic declaration of rights, an economic constitutional order. This is the common task of statesman and businessman. It is the minimum requirement of a more permanently safe order of things.

Every man has a right to life; and this means that he has also a right to make a comfortable living. He may by sloth or crime decline to exercise that right; but it may not be denied him. We have no actual famine or dearth; our industrial and agricultural mechanism can produce enough and to spare. Our government, formal and informal, political and economic, owes to every one an avenue to possess himself of a portion of that plenty sufficient for his needs, through his own work.

Every man has a right to his own property, which means a right to be assured, to the fullest extent attainable, in the safety of his savings. By no other means can men carry the burdens of those parts of life which, in the nature of things, afford no chance of labor, childhood, sickness, old age. In all thought of property, this right is paramount; all other property rights must yield to it. If, in accord with this principle, we must restrict the operations of the speculator, the manipulator, even the financier, I believe we must accept the restriction as needful, not to hamper individualism but to protect it.

These two requirements must be satisfied, in the main, by the individuals who claim and hold control of the great industrial and financial combinations, which dominate so large a part of our industrial life. They have undertaken to be not businessmen, but princes—princes of property. I am not prepared to say that the system which produces them is wrong. I am very clear that they must fearlessly and competently assume the responsibility which goes with the power. So many enlightened businessmen know this that the statement would be little more than a platitude, were it not for an added implication.

This implication is, briefly, that the responsible heads of finance and industry instead of acting each for himself, must work together to achieve the common end. They must, where necessary, sacrifice this or that private advantage; and in reciprocal self-denial must seek a general advantage. It is here that formal government—political government, if you choose, comes in. Whenever in the pursuit of this objective the lone wolf, the unethical competitor, the reckless promoter, the Ishmael or Insull whose hand is against every man's, declines to join in achieving an end recognized as being for the public welfare, and threatens to drag the industry back to a state of anarchy, the government may properly be asked to apply restraint. Likewise, should the group ever use its collective power contrary to the public welfare, the government must be swift to enter and protect the public interest.

The government should assume the function of economic regulation only as a last resort, to be tried only when private initiative, inspired by high responsibility, with such assistance and balance as government can give, has finally failed. As yet there has been no final failure, because there has been no attempt; and I decline to assume that this nation is unable to meet the situation.

The final term of the high contract was for liberty and the pursuit of happiness. We have learnt a great deal of both in the past century. We know that individual liberty and individual happiness mean nothing unless both are ordered in the sense that one man's meat is not another man's poison. We know that the old "rights of personal competency"—the right to read, to think, to speak, to choose and live a mode of life, must be respected at all hazards. We know that liberty to do anything which deprives others of those elemental rights is outside the protection of any compact; and that government in this regard is the maintenance of a balance, within which every individual may have a place if he will take it; in which every individual may find safety if he wishes it; in which every individual may attain such power as his ability permits, consistent with his assuming the accompanying responsibility.

Faith in America, faith in our tradition of personal responsibilities, faith in our institutions, faith in ourselves demands that we recognize the new terms of the old social contract. We shall fulfill them, as we fulfilled the obligation of the apparent Utopia which Jefferson imagined for us in 1776, and which Jefferson, Roosevelt and Wilson sought to bring to realization. We must do so, lest a rising tide of misery engendered by our common failure, engulf us all. But failure is not an American habit; and in the strength of great hope we must all shoulder our common load.

XIV
Herbert Hoover:
Campaign Speech
Madison Square Garden, New York,
October 31, 1932

This campaign is more than a contest between two men. It is more than a contest between two parties. It is a contest between two philosophies of government.

We are told by the opposition that we must have a change, that we must have a new deal. It is not the change that comes from normal development of national life to which I object, but the proposal to alter the whole foundations of our national life which have been builded through generations of testing and struggle, and of the principles upon which we have builded the nation. The expressions our opponents use must refer to important changes in our economic and social system and our system of government, otherwise they are nothing but vacuous words. And I realize that in this time of distress many of our people are asking whether our social and economic system is incapable of the great primary function of providing security and comfort of life to all of the firesides of our 25,000,000 homes in America, whether our social system provides for the fundamental development and progress of our people, whether our form of government is capable of originating and sustaining that security and progress.

This question is the basis upon which our opponents are appealing to the people in their fears and distress. They are proposing changes and so-called new deals which would destroy the very foundations of our American system.

Our people should consider the primary facts before they come to the judgment—not merely through political agitation, the glitter of promise, and the discouragement of temporary hardships—whether they will support changes which radically affect the whole system which has been builded up by a hundred and fifty years of the toil of our fathers. They should not approach the question in the despair with which our opponents would clothe it.

Our economic system has received abnormal shocks during the last three years, which temporarily dislocated its normal functioning. These shocks have in a large sense come from without our borders, but I say to you that our system of government has enabled us to take such strong action as to prevent the disaster which would otherwise have come to our nation. It has enabled us further to develop measures and programs which are now demonstrating their ability to bring about restoration and progress.

We must go deeper than platitudes and emotional appeals of the public platform in the campaign, if we will penetrate to the full significance of the changes which our opponents are attempting to float upon the wave of distress and discontent from the difficulties we are passing through. We can find what our opponents would do after searching the record of their appeals to discontent, group and sectional interest. We must search for them in the legislative acts which they sponsored and passed in the Democratic-controlled House of Representatives in the last session of Congress. We must look into measures for which they voted and which were defeated. We must inquire whether or not the Presidential and Vice-

Presidential candidates have disavowed these acts. If they have not, we must conclude that they form a portion and are a substantial indication of the profound changes proposed.

And we must look still further than this as to what revolutionary changes have been proposed by the candidates themselves.

We must look into the type of leaders who are campaigning for the Democratic ticket, whose philosophies have been well known all their lives, whose demands for a change in the American system are frank and forceful. I can respect the sincerity of these men in their desire to change our form of government and our social and economic system, though I shall do my best tonight to prove they are wrong. I refer particularly to Senator Norris, Senator LaFollette, Senator Cutting, Senator Huey Long, Senator Wheeler, William R. Hearst, and other exponents of a social philosophy different from the traditional American one. Unless these men feel assurance of support to their ideas they certainly would not be supporting these candidates and the Democratic Party. The seal of these men indicates that they have sure confidence that they will have voice in the administration of our government.

I may say at once that the changes proposed from all these Democratic principals and allies are of the most profound and penetrating character. If they are brought about, this will not be the America which we have known in the past.

Let us pause for a moment and examine the American system of government, of social and economic life, which it is now proposed that we should alter. Our system is the product of our race and of our experience in building a nation to heights unparalleled in the whole history of the world. It is system peculiar to the American people. It differs essentially from all others in the world. It is an American system.

It is founded on the conception that only through ordered liberty, through freedom to the individual, and equal opportunity to the individual will his initiative and enterprise be summoned to spur that march of progress.

It is by the maintenance of equality of opportunity and therefore of a society absolutely fluid in freedom of the movement of its human particles that our individualism departs from the individualism of Europe. We resent class distinction because there can be no rise for the individual through the frozen strata of classes, and no stratification of classes can take place in a mass livened by the free rise of its particles. Thus in our ideals the able and ambitious are able to rise constantly from the bottom to leadership in the community.

This freedom of the individual creates of itself the necessity and the cheerful willingness of men to act cooperatively in a thousand ways and for every purpose as occasion arises; and it permits such voluntary cooperations to be dissolved as soon as they have served their purpose, to be replaced by new voluntary associations for new purposes.

There has thus grown within us, to gigantic importance, a new conception. That is, this voluntary cooperation within the community. Cooperation to perfect the social organizations; cooperation for the care of this in distress; cooperation for the advancement of knowledge, of scientific research, of education; for cooperative action in the advancement of many phases of economic life. This is self-government by the people outside of government; it is the most powerful development of individual freedom and equal opportunity that has taken place in the century and a half since our fundamental institutions were founded.

It is in the further development of this cooperation and a sense of its responsibility that we should find solutions for many of our complex problems, and not by the extension of government into our economic and social life. The greatest function of government is to build up that cooperation, and its most resolute action should be to deny the extension of bureaucracy. We have developed great agencies of cooperation by the assistance of the government which promote and protect the interests of individuals and the smaller units of business. The Federal Reserve System, in its strengthening and support of the smaller banks; the Farm Board, in its strengthening and support of the farm cooperatives; the Home Loan banks, in the mobilizing of building and loan associations and saving banks; the Federal land banks, in giving independence and strength to land mortgage associations; the great mobilization of relief to distress, the mobilization of business and industry in measures of recovery, and a score of other activities are not socialism—they are the essence of protection to the development of free men.

The primary conception of this whole American system is not the regimentation of men but the cooperation of free men. It is founded upon the conception of responsibility of the individual to the community, of the responsibility of local government to the State, of the State to the national government.

It is founded on a peculiar conception of self-government designed to maintain this equal opportunity to the individual, and through decentralization it brings about and maintains these responsibilities. The centralization of government will undermine responsibilities and will destroy the system.

Our government differs from all previous conceptions, not only in this decentralization, but also in the separation of functions between the legislative, executive, and judicial arms of government, in which the independence of the judicial arm is the keystone of the whole structure.

It is founded on a conception that in times of emergency, when forces are running beyond the control of local communities and of States, then the great reserve powers of the Federal Government shall be brought into action to protect the community. But when these forces have ceased there must be a return of State, local, and individual responsibility.

The implacable march of scientific discovery with its train of new inventions presents every year new problems to government and new problems to the social order. Questions often arise whether, in the face of the growth of these new and gigantic tools, democracy can remain master in its own house, can preserve the fundamentals of our American system. I contend that it can; and I contend that this American system of ours has demonstrated its validity and superiority over any system yet invented by human minds.

It has demonstrated it in the face of the greatest test of our history—that is the emergency which we have faced in the last three years.

When the political and economic weakness of many nations of Europe, the result of the World War and its aftermath, finally culminated in collapse of their institutions, the delicate adjustments of our economic and social life received a shock unparalleled in our history. No one knows that better than you of New York. No one knows its causes better than you. That the crisis was so great that many of the leading banks sought directly or indirectly to convert their assets into gold or its equivalent with the result that they practically ceased to function as credit institutions; that many of our citizens sought flight for their capital to other countries; that many of them attempted to hoard gold in

large amounts.   These were but indications of the flight of
confidence and of the belief that our government could not
overcome these forces.

Yet these forces were overcome—perhaps by narrow margins—
and this action demonstrates what the courage of a nation can
accomplish under the resolute leadership in the Republican Party.
And I say the Republican Party because our opponents, before and
during the crisis, proposed no constructive program; though some
of their members patriotically supported ours.   Later on the
Democratic House of Representatives did develop the real thought
and ideas of the Democratic Party, but it was so destructive that it
had to be defeated, for it would have destroyed, not healed.

In spite of all these obstructions we did succeed.   Our form of
government did prove itself equal to the task. We saved this nation
from a quarter of a century of chaos and degeneration, and we
preserved the savings, the insurance policies, gave a fighting chance
to men to hold their homes.   We saved the integrity of our
government and the honesty of the American dollar.   And we
installed measurers which today are bringing back recovery.
Employment, agriculture, business—all of these show the steady, if
slow, healing of our enormous wound.

I therefore contend that the problem of today is to continue these
measures and policies to restore this American system to its normal
functioning, to repair the wounds it has received, to correct the
weaknesses and evils which would defeat that system.   To enter
upon a series of deep changes to embark upon this inchoate new
deal which has been propounded in this campaign would be to
undermine and destroy our American system.

Before we enter upon such courses, I would like you to consider
what the results of this American system have been during the last
thirty years—that is, one single generation.   For if it can be
demonstrated, that by means of this, our unequaled political,
social, and economic system, we have secured a lift in the
standards of living and a diffusion of comfort and hope to men
and women, the growth of equal opportunity, the widening of all
opportunity, such as had never been seen in the history of the
world, then we should not tamper with it or destroy it; but on the
contrary we should restore it and, by its gradual improvement and
perfection, foster it into new performance for our country and for
our children....

Our people in these thirty years grew in the sense of social responsibility. There is profound progress in the relation of the employer and employed. We have more nearly met with a full hand the most sacred obligation of man, that is, the responsibility of a man to his neighbor. Support to our schools, hospitals, and institutions for the care of the afflicted surpassed in totals of billions the proportionate service in any period of history in any nation in the world....

But I ask you what has happened. These thirty years of incomparable improvement in the scale of living, the advance of comfort and intellectual life, inspiration, and ideals did not arise without right principles animating the American system which produced them. Shall that system be discarded because vote-seeking men appeal to distress and say that the machinery is all wrong and that it must be abandoned or tampered with? Is it not more sensible to realize the simple fact that some extraordinary force has been thrown into the mechanism, temporarily deranging its operation? Is it not wiser to believe that the difficulty is not with the principles upon which our American system is founded and designed through all these generations of inheritance? Should not our purpose be to restore the normal working of that system which has brought to us such immeasurable benefits, and not destroy it?

And in order to indicate to you that the proposals of our opponents will endanger or destroy our system, I propose to analyze a few of the proposals of our opponents in their relation to these fundamentals.

First Proposal

A proposal of our opponents which would break down the American system is the expansion of government expenditure by yielding to sectional and group raids on the Public Treasury. The extension of government expenditures beyond the minimum limit necessary to conduct the proper functions of the government enslaves men to work for the government. If we combine the whole governmental expenditures—national, State, and municipal—we will find that before the World War each citizen worked, theoretically, twenty-five days out of each year for the government. In 1924 he worked forty-six days a year for the government. Today he works for the support of all forms of government sixty-one days out of the year.

No nation can conscript its citizens for this proportion of men's time without national impoverishment and destruction of their liberties. Our nation cannot do it without destruction to our whole conception of the American system. The Federal Government has been forced in this emergency to unusual expenditure, but in partial alleviation of these extraordinary and unusual expenditures the Republican Administration has made a successful effort to reduce the ordinary running expenses of the government. Our opponents have persistently interfered with such policies. I only need recall to you that the Democratic House of Representatives passed bills in the last session that would have increased our expenditures by $3,500,000,000 or 87 percent. Expressed in day's labor, this would have meant the conscription of sixteen days' additional work from every citizen for the government. This I stopped.

These expenditures proposed by the Democratic House of Representatives for the benefit of special groups and special sections of our country directly undermine the American system. Those who pay are in the last analysis, the man who works at the bench, the desk, and on the farm. They take away his comfort, stifle his leisure, and destroy his equal opportunity.

Second Proposal

Another proposal of our opponents which would destroy the American system is that of inflation of the currency. The bill which passed the last session of the Democratic House called upon the Treasury of the United States to issue $2,300,000,000 in paper currency that would be unconvertible into solid values. Call it what you will, greenbacks or fiat money. It was that nightmare which overhung our own country for years after the Civil War.

In our special situation today the issuance of greenbacks means the immediate departure of this country from the gold standard, as there could be no provision for the redemption of such currency in gold. The new currency must obviously go to immediate and constantly fluctuating discount when associated with currency convertible in gold. The oldest law of currency is that bad money drives out the good, for a population—every individual—will hoard good currency from circulation, and at once the government is forced to print more and more bad paper currency. No candidate and no speaker in this campaign has disavowed this action of the Democratic House. In spite of this visible experience within recollection of this generation, with all its pitiable results, fiat money is proposed by the Democratic Party as a potent measure for relief from this depression.

Third Proposal

In the last session the Congress, under the personal leadership of the Democratic Vice-Presidential candidate, and their allies in the Senate, enacted a law to extend the Government into personal banking business. This I was compelled to veto, out of fidelity to the whole American system of life and government. I may repeat a part of that veto message—and it remains unchallenged by any Democratic leader. I said: It would mean loans against security for any conceivable purpose on any conceivable security to anybody who wants money. It would place the government in private business in such fashion as to violate the very principle of public relations upon which we have builded our nation, and renders insecure its very foundations. Such action would make the Reconstruction Corporation the greatest banking and money-lending institution of all history. It would constitute a gigantic centralization of banking and finance to which the American people have been properly opposed over a hundred years. The purpose of the expansion is no longer in the spirit of solving a great major emergency but to establish a privilege whether it serves a great national end or not.

Fourth Proposal

Another proposal of our opponents which would wholly alter our American system of life is to reduce the protective tariff and its results upon our economic structure has become gradually embedded into our economic life since the first protective tariff act passed by the American Congress under the administration of George Washington. There have been gaps at times of Democratic control when this protection has been taken away. But it has been so embedded that its removal has never failed to bring disaster. Whole towns, communities, and forms of agriculture with their homes, schools, and churches have been built up under this system of protection. The grass will grow in streets of a hundred cities, a thousand towns; the weeds will overrun the fields of millions of farms if that protection be taken away. Their churches and schoolhouses will decay.

Fifth Proposal

Another proposal is that the government go into the power business. Three years ago, in view of the extension of the use of transmission of power over State boards and the difficulties of State regulatory bodies in the face of this interstate action, I recommended to the Congress that such interstate power should be placed under regulation by the Federal Government in cooperation with the State authorities.

That recommendation was in accord with the principles of the Republican Party over the last fifty years, to provide regulation where public interest had developed in tools of industry which was beyond control and regulation of the States.

I succeeded in creating an independent Power Commission to handle such matters, but the Democratic House declined to approve the further powers to this commission necessary for such regulation.

I have stated unceasingly that I am opposed to the Federal Government going into the power business. I have insisted upon rigid regulation. The Democratic candidate has declared that under the same conditions which may make local action of this character desirable, he is prepared to put the Federal Government into the power business. He is being actively supported by a score of Senators in this campaign, many of whose expenses are being paid by the Democratic National Committee, who are pledged to Federal Government development and operation of electrical power....

There are national emergencies which require that the government should temporarily enter the field of business but that they must be emergency actions and in matters where the cost of the project is secondary to much higher consideration. There are many localities where the Federal Government is justified in the construction of great dams and reservoirs, where navigation, flood control, reclamation, or stream regulation are of dominant importance, and where they are beyond the capacity or purpose of private or local government capital to construct. In these cases, power is often a by-product and should be disposed of by contract or lease. But for the Federal Government to deliberately go out to build up and expand such an occasion to the major purpose of a power and manufacturing business is to break down the initiative and enterprise of the American people; it is destruction of equality of opportunity among our people; it is the negation of the ideals upon which our civilization has been based.

This bill raises one of the important issues confronting our people. That is squarely the issue of Federal Government ownership and operation of power and manufacturing business not as a minor by-product but as a major purpose. Involved in this question is the agitation against the conduct of the power industry. The power problem is not to be solved by the Federal Government going into the power business, nor is it to be solved by the project in this bill. The remedy for abuses in the conduct of that industry lies in regulation and not by the Federal Government entering upon the business itself. I have recommended to the Congress on various occasions that action should be taken to establish Federal regulation of interstate power in cooperation with State authorities. This bill would launch the Federal Government upon a policy of ownership of power utilities upon a basis of competition instead of by the proper government function of regulation for the protection of all the people. I hesitate to contemplate the future of our institutions, of our government, and of our country, if the preoccupation of its officials is to be no longer the promotion of justice and equal opportunity but is to be devoted to barter in the markets. That is not liberalism; it is degeneration.

From their utterances in this campaign and elsewhere we are justified in the conclusion that our opponents propose to put the Federal Government in the power business with all its additions to Federal bureaucracy, its tyranny over State and local governments, its undermining of State and local responsibilities and initiative.

Sixth Proposal

I may cite another instance of absolutely destructive proposals to our American system by our opponents.

Recently there was circulated through the unemployed in the country a letter from the Democratic candidate in which he stated that he would support measures for the inauguration of self-liquidating public works such as the utilization of water resources, flood control, land reclamation, to provide employment for all surplus labor at all times....

Incidentally, the Democratic candidate has said on several occasions that we must reduce surplus production of agricultural products, and yet he proposes to extend this production on a gigantic scale through expansion of reclamation and new agricultural areas to the ruin of the farmer.

I have said before, and I want to repeat on this occasion, that the only method by which we can stop the suffering and unemployment is by returning our people to their normal jobs in their normal homes, carrying on their normal functions of living. This can be done only by sound processes of protecting and stimulating recovery of the existing economic system upon which we have builded our progress thus far—preventing distress and giving such sound employment as we can find in the meantime.

Seventh Proposal

Recently at Indianapolis, I called attention to the statement made by Governor Roosevelt in his address on October 25th with respect to the Supreme Court of the United States. He said: "After March 4, 1929, the Republican Party was in complete control of all branches of the government—Executive, Senate, and House, and I may add, for good measure, in order to make it complete, the Supreme Court as well."

I am not called upon to defend the Supreme Court of the United States from this slurring reflection. Fortunately that court has jealously maintained over the years its high standard of integrity, impartiality, and freedom from influence of either the Executive or Congress, so that the confidence of the people is sound and unshaken.

But is the Democratic candidate really proposing his conception of the relation of the Executive and the Supreme Court? If that is his idea, he is proposing the most revolutionary new deal, the most stupendous breaking of precedent, the most destructive undermining of the very safeguard of our form of government yet proposed by a Presidential candidate.

Eighth Proposal

In order that we may get at the philosophical background of the mind which pronounces the necessity for profound change in our American system and a new deal, I would call your attention the address delivered by the Democratic candidate in San Francisco, early in October. He said: "Our industrial plant is built. The problem just now is whether under existing conditions it is not overbuilt. Our last frontier has long since been reached. There is practically no more free land. There is no safety valve in the Western prairies where we can go for a new start...The mere building of more industrial plants, the organization of more corporations is as likely to be as much a danger as a help...Our task now is not the discovery of natural resources or necessarily the production of more goods, it is the sober, less dramatic business of administering the resources and plants already in hand...establishing markets for surplus production, of meeting the problem of under-consumption, distributing the wealth and products more equitably and adopting the economic organization to the service of the people."

There are many of these expressions with which no one would quarrel. But I do challenge the whole idea that we have ended the advance of America, that this country has reached the zenith of its power, the height of its development. That is the counsel of despair for the future of America. That is not the spirit by which we shall emerge from this depression. That is not the spirit that made this country. If it is true, every American must abandon the road of countless progress and unlimited opportunity. I deny that the promise of American life has been fulfilled, for that means we have begun the decline and fall. No nation can cease to move forward without degeneration of spirit.

I would quote from gentlemen who have emitted this same note of pessimism in economic depressions going back for one hundred years. What Governor Roosevelt has overlooked is the fact that we are yet but on the frontiers of development of science and of invention. I have only to remind you that discoveries in electricity, the internal-combustion engine, the radio—all of which have spring into being since our land was settled—have in themselves represented the greatest advances in America. This philosophy upon which the Governor of New York proposes to conduct the Presidency of the United States is the philosophy of stagnation, of despair. It is the end of hope. The destinies of this country should not be dominated by that spirit in action. It would be the end of the American system.

I have recited to you the progress of this last generation. Progress in that generation was not due to the opening up of new agricultural land; it was due to the scientific research, the opening of new invention, new flashes of light from the intelligence of our people. These brought the improvements in agriculture and in industry. There are a thousand inventions for comfort in lockers of science and invention which have not yet come to light; all are but on their frontiers. As for myself, I am confident that if we do not destroy this American system, if we continue to stimulate scientific research, if we continue to give it the impulse of initiative and enterprise, if we continue to build voluntary cooperative action instead of financial concentration, if we continue to build it into a system of free men, my children will enjoy the same opportunity that has come to me and to the whole 120,000,000 of my countrymen. I wish to see American Government conducted in this faith and in this hope.

If these measures, these promises, which I have discussed; or there failures to disavow these projects; this attitude of mind, mean anything, they mean the enormous expansion of the Federal Government; they mean the growth of bureaucracy such as we have never seen in our history. No man who has not occupied my position in Washington can fully realize the constant battle which must be carried on against incompetence, corruption, tyranny of government expanded into business activities. If we first examine the effect on our form of government of such a program, we come at once to the effect of the most gigantic increase in expenditure ever known in history. That alone would break down the savings, the wages, the equality of opportunity among our people. These measures would transfer vast responsibilities to the Federal Government from the States, the local governments, and the individuals. But that is not all; they would break down our form of government. Our legislative bodies cannot delegate their authority to any dictator, but without such delegation every member of these bodies is impelled in representation of the interest of his constituents constantly to seek privilege and demand service in the use of such agencies. Every time the Federal Government extends its arm, 531 Senators and Congressmen become actual boards of directors of that business.

We have heard a great deal in this campaign about reactionaries, conservatives, progressives, liberals, and radicals. I have not yet heard an attempt by any one of the orators who mouth these phrases to define the principles upon which they base these classifications. There is one thing I can say without any question of doubt—that is, that the spirit of liberalism is to create free men; it is not the regimentation of men. It is not the extension of bureaucracy. I have said in this city before now that you cannot extend the mastery of government over the daily life of a people without somewhere making it master of people's souls and thoughts. Expansion of government in business means that the government, in order to protect itself from the political consequences of its errors, is driven irresistibly without peace to greater and greater control of the nation's press and platform. Free speech does not live many hours after free industry and free commerce die. It is a false liberalism that interprets itself into government operation of business. Every step in that direction poisons the very roots of liberalism. It poisons political equality, free speech, free press, and equality of opportunity. It is the road not to liberty but to less liberty. True liberalism is found not in striving to spread bureaucracy, but in striving to set bounds to it. True liberalism seeks all legitimate freedom first in the confident belief that without such freedom the pursuit of other blessings is in vain. Liberalism is a force truly of the spirit proceeding from the deep realization that economic freedom cannot be sacrificed if political freedom is to be preserved.

Even if the government conduct of business could give us the maximum of efficiency instead of least efficiency, it would be purchased at the cost of freedom. It would increase rather than decrease abuse and corruption, stifle initiative and invention, under-mine development of leadership, cripple mental and spiritual energies of our people, extinguish equality of opportunity, and dry up the spirit of liberty and progress. Men who are going about this country announcing that they are liberals because of their promises to extend the government in business are not liberals; they are reactionaries of the United States.

And I do not wish to be misquoted or misunderstood. I do not mean that our government is to part with one iota of its national resources without complete protection to the public interest. I have already stated that democracy must remain master in its own house. I have stated that abuse and wrongdoing must be punished and controlled. Nor do I wish to be misinterpreted as stating that the United States is a free-for-all and devil-take-the-hindermost society.

The very essence of equality of opportunity of our American system is that there shall be no monopoly or domination by any group or section in this country, whether it be business, sectional, or a group interest. On the contrary, our American system demands economic justice as well as political and social justice; it is not a system of laissez faire.

I am not setting up the contention that our American system is perfect. No human ideal has ever been perfectly attained, since humanity itself is not perfect. But the wisdom of our forefathers and the wisdom of the thirty men who have preceded me in this office hold to the conception that progress can be attained only as the sum of accomplishments of free individuals, and they have held unalterably to these principles.

In the ebb and flow of economic life our people in times of prosperity and ease naturally tend to neglect the vigilance over their rights. Moreover, wrongdoing is obscured by apparent success in enterprise. Then insidious diseases and wrongdoings grow apace. But we have in the past seen in times of distress and difficulty that wrongdoing and weakness come to the surface, and our people, in their endeavors to correct these wrongs, are tempted to extremes which may destroy rather than build.

It is men who do wrong, not our institutions. It is men who violate the laws and public rights. It is men, not institutions, who must be punished.

In my acceptance speech four years ago at Palo Alto I stated that: "One of the oldest aspirations of the human race was the abolition of poverty. By poverty I mean the grinding by under-nourishment, cold, ignorance, fear of old age to those who have the will to work."

I stated that: "In America today we are nearer a final triumph over poverty than in any land. The poorhouse has vanished from among us; we have not reached that goal, but given a chance to go forward, we shall, with the help of God, be in sight of the day when poverty will be banished from this nation."

Our Democratic friends have quoted this passage many times in this campaign. I do not withdraw a word of it. When I look about the world even in these times of trouble and distress I find it more true in this land than anywhere else under the traveling sun. I am not ashamed of it, because I am not ashamed of holding ideals and purposes for the progress of the American people. Are my Democratic opponents prepared to state that they do not stand for this ideal or this hope? For my part, I propose to continue to strive for it, and I hope to live to see it accomplished.

My countrymen, the proposals of our opponents represent a profound change in American life—less in concrete proposals, bad as that many be, than by implication and by evasion. Dominantly in their spirit they represent a radical departure from the foundations of 150 years which have made this the greatest nation in the world. This election is not a mere shift from the ins to the outs. It means deciding the direction our nation will take over a century to come.

My conception of America is a land where men and women may walk in ordered liberty, where they may enjoy the advantages of wealth not concentrated in the hands of a few but diffused through the lives of all, where they build and safeguard their homes, give to their children full opportunities of American life, where every man shall be respected in the faith that his conscience and his heart direct him to follow, where people secure in their liberty shall have leisure and impulse to seek a fuller life. That leads to the release of the energies of men and women, to the wider vision and higher hope; it leads to opportunity for greater and greater service not alone of man to man in our country but from country to the world. It leads to health in body and a spirit unfettered, youthful, eager with a vision stretching beyond the farthest horizons with an open mind, sympathetic and generous. But that must be builded upon our experience with the past, upon the foundations which have made our country great. It must be the product of our truly American system.

XV
Franklin D. Roosevelt:
Address on Long-Range Planning
Boston, Massachusetts, October 31, 1932

I hope I have learned the lesson that reason and tolerance have their place in all things; and I want to say frankly that they are never so appropriate as when they prevail in a political campaign.

I say this with some feeling because I express widespread opinion when I note that the dignity of the office of President of the United States has suffered during the past week. The President began this campaign with the same attitude with which he has approached so many of the serious problems of the past three years. He sought to create the impression that there was no campaign going on at all, just as he had sought to create the impression that all was well with the United States, and that there was no depression.

But, my friends, the people of this country spoiled these plans. They demanded that the administration which they placed in power four years ago, and which has cost them so much, give an accounting. They demanded this accounting in no uncertain terms.

This demand of the people has continued until it has become an overwhelming, irresistible drift of public opinion. It is more than a drift. It is a tempest.

As that storm of approval for the Democratic policies has grown, several moods have come over the utterances of the Republican leader.

First, they were plaintively apologetic. Then the next move was indignation at the Congress of the United States. Finally, they have in desperation resorted to the breeding of panic and fear.

At first the President refused to recognize that he was in a contest. But as the people with each succeeding week have responded to our program with enthusiasm, he recognized that we were both candidates. And then, dignity died.

At Indianapolis he spoke of my arguments, misquoting them. But at Indianapolis he went further. He abandoned argument for personalities.

In the presence of a situation like this, I am tempted to reply in kind. But I shall not yield to the temptation to which the President yielded. On the contrary, I reiterate my respect for his person and for his office. But I shall not be deterred even by the President of the United States from the discussion of grave national issues and from submitting to the voters the truth about their national affairs, however unpleasant that truth may be.

The ballot is the indispensable instrument of a free people. It should be the true expression of their will; and it is intolerable that the ballot should be coerced—whatever the form of coercion, political or economic.

The autocratic will of no man—be he President, or general, or captain of industry—shall ever destroy the sacred right of the people themselves to determine for themselves who shall govern them.

An hour ago, before I came to the Arena, I listened in for a few minutes to the first part of the speech of the President in New York tonight. Once more he warned the people against changing— against a new deal—stating that it would mean changing the fundamental principles of America, what he called the sound principles that have been so long believed in this country. My friends, my New Deal does not aim to change those principles. It does aim to bring those principles into effect.

Secure in their undying belief in their great tradition and in the sanctity of a free ballot, the people of this country—the employed, the partially employed and the unemployed, those who are fortunate enough to retain some of the means of economic well-being, and those from whom these cruel conditions have taken everything—have stood with patience and fortitude in the face of adversity.

There they stand. And they stand peacefully, even when they stand in the breadline. Their complaints are not mingled with threats. They are willing to listen to reason at all times. Throughout this great crisis the stricken army of the unemployed has been patient, law-abiding, orderly, because it is hopeful.

But, the party that claims as its guiding tradition the patient and generous spirit of the immortal Abraham Lincoln, when confronted by an opposition which has given to this nation an orderly and constructive campaign for the past four months, has descended to an outpouring of misstatements, threats and intimidation.

The administration attempts to undermine reason through fear by telling us that the world will come to an end on November 8th if it is not returned to power for four years more. Once more it is a leadership that is bankrupt, not only in ideals but in ideas. It sadly misconceives the good sense and the self-reliance of our people.

These leaders tell us further that, in the event of change, the present administration will be unable to hold in check the economic forces that threaten us in the period between Election Day and Inauguration Day. They threaten American business and American workers with dire destruction from November to March.

They crack the "whip of fear" over the backs of American voters, not only here but across the seas as well.

There is another means of spreading fear—through certain Republican industrial leaders. I have said, without being controverted, that 5,000 men in effect control American industry. These men, possessed of such great power, carry likewise a great responsibility. It is their duty to use every precaution to see that this power is never used to destroy or to limit the sound public policy of the free and untrammeled exercise of the power of the ballot.

In violation of that duty, some of these 5,000 men who control industry are today invading the sacred political rights of those over whom they have economic power. They are joining in the chorus of fear initiated by the President, by the Ambassador, by the Secretary of the Treasury, and by the Republican National Committee.

They are telling their employees that if they fail to support the administration of President Hoover, such jobs as these employees have will be in danger. Such conduct is un-American and worthy of censure at the ballot box. I wonder how some of those industrial leaders would feel if somebody else's "baby had the measles." In other words, would they agree that it would be equally reprehensible if any political leader were to seek reprisal against them—against any coercing employer who used such means against political leaders? Let us fight our political battles with political arguments, and not prey upon men's economic necessities.

After all, their threats are empty gestures. You and I know that their industries have been sliding downhill. You know, and I know, that the whole program of the present administration has been directed only to prevent a further slipping downhill. You know, and I know, that therein lies the difference between the leaderships of the two parties.

You know, and I know, that the Democratic Party is not satisfied merely with arresting the present decline. Of course we will do that to the best of our ability; but we are equally interested in seeking to build up and improve, and to put these industries in a position where their wheels will turn once more, and where opportunity will be given to them to reemploy the millions of workers that they have laid off under the administration of President Hoover.

It is not enough merely to stabilize, to lend money! It is essential to increase purchasing power in order that goods may be sold. There must be people capable of buying goods in order that goods may be manufactured and sold. When that time comes, under our new leadership, these same gentlemen who now make their threats will be found doing business at the old stand as usual.

The American voter, the American working-man and working woman, the mill-worker of New England, the miner of the West, the railroad worker, the farmer, and the white-collar man will answer these silly, spiteful threats with their ballots on November 8th.

The present leadership in Washington stands convicted, not because it did not have the means to plan, but fundamentally because it did not have the will to do. That is why the American people on November 8th will register their firm conviction that this administration has utterly and entirely failed to meet the great emergency.

The American people are heart-sick people for "hope deferred maketh the heart sick."

Now, my friends, we are considering unemployment tonight, and I am going to start by setting forth the positive policy which the President's Commission under the leadership of the Secretary of Commerce urged should be done. There is a lot of it which is still good.

It was a 5-point program. And as a program it was good.

First, it urged that government should reduce expenditures for public works during periods of prosperity, and that, during those periods, government should build up reserves with which to increase expenditures during periods of unemployment and industrial depression. But was that done? Not one penny's worth. No reserves were built up for the rainy day.

Second, the report said that the Federal Government should work with the railroads in the preparation of a long-time constructive program. Was that done? No. The Republican Administration did not give effect to this proposal. Instead of working with the railroads, to consolidate their lines and put them on a sound economical basis, the administration waited until the depression had laid them low, and then had nothing for them except to loan them more money, when they were already heavily in debt.

Third, the report proposed the setting up of safeguards against too rapid inflation, and consequently too rapid deflation of bank credit. As I have shown, the President and his Secretary of the Treasury went to the other extreme and encouraged speculation.

Fourth, the report recommended an adequate system of unemployment insurance. No one in the administration in Washington has assumed any leadership in order to bring about positive action by the States to make this unemployment insurance a reality. Someday, in our leadership, we are going to get it.

Fifth, it suggested an adequate system of public employment offices. But when Senator Wagner introduced a bill to establish Federal employment offices, President Hoover vetoed the measure that Secretary Herbert Hoover had sponsored. It seems to me, speaking in this great section of the country where there are so many business men, that business men who believe in sound planning and action, must feel that there is danger to the country in the continuance of a leadership that has shown such incapacity, such ineptitude, such heedlessness of common sense and of sound business principles. What we need in Washington is less fact finding and more thinking.

Immediate relief of the unemployed is the immediate need of the hour. No mere emergency measures of relief are adequate. We must do all we can. We have emergency measures but we know that our goal, our unremitting objective, must be to secure not temporary employment but the permanence of employment to the workers of America. Without long-range stability of employment for our workers, without a balanced economy between agriculture and industry, there can be no healthy national life.

We have two problems: first, to meet the immediate distress, second, to build up a basis of permanent employment.

As to "immediate relief," the first principle is that this nation, this national government, if you like, owes a positive duty that no citizen shall be permitted to starve. That means that while the immediate responsibility for relief rests, or course, with local, public and private charity, in so far as these are inadequate the States must carry on the burden, and whenever the States themselves are unable adequately to do so the Federal Government owes the positive duty of stepping into the breach.

It is worth while noting that from that disastrous time of 1929 on the present Republican Administration took a definite position against the recognition of that principle. It was only because of the insistence of the Congress of the United States and the unmistakable voice of the people of the United States that the President yielded and approved the National Relief Bill this summer.

In addition to providing emergency relief, the Federal Government should and must provide temporary work wherever that is possible. You and I know that in the national forests, on flood prevention, and on the development of waterway projects that have already been authorized and planned but not yet executed, tens of thousands, and even hundreds of thousands of our unemployed citizens can be given at least temporary employment.

Third, the Federal Government should expedite the actual construction of public works already authorized. The country would be horrified if it knew how little construction work authorized by the last Congress and approved by the President has actually been undertaken on this date, the 31st of October. And I state to you the simple fact that much of the work for which Congress has given authority will not be under way and giving employment to people until sometime next summer.

Finally, in that larger field that looks further ahead, we call for a coordinated system of employment exchanges, the advance planning of public works, and unemployment reserves. Who, then, is to carry on these measures and see them through? The first, employment exchanges, is clearly and inescapably a task of the Federal Government, although it will require the loyal and intelligent cooperation of State and local agencies throughout the land. To that Federal action I pledge my administration. The second, the advance planning of public works, again calls for a strong lead on the part of the government at Washington. I pledge my administration to the adoption of that principle, both as to enterprises of the Federal Government itself and as to construction within the several States which is made possible by Federal aid; and I shall urge upon State and local authorities throughout the nation that they follow this example in Washington. The third, unemployment reserves, must under our system of government be primarily the responsibility of the several States. That, the Democratic platform, on which I stand, makes entirely clear.

In addition to all this, there has been long overdue a reduction of the hours of work and a reduction of the number of working days per week. After all, the greatest justification of modern industry is the lessening of the toil of men and women. These fruits will be dead fruits unless men earn enough so that they can buy the things that are produced, so that they can have the leisure for the cultivation of body, mind and spirit, which the great inventions are supposed to make possible. That means that government itself must set an example in the case of its own employees. It means also that government must exert its persuasive leadership to induce industry to do likewise.

Here then is a program of long-range planning which requires prompt and definite action and the cooperation of Federal and State and local governments, as well as of forward-looking citizens of both parties throughout the land. The proposals are specific, they are far-reaching. To advocate a less drastic program would be to misread the lessons of the depression and to express indifference to the country's future welfare.

There is one final objective of my policy which is more vital and more basic than all else. I seek to restore the purchasing power of the American people. The return of that purchasing power, and only that, will put America back to work.

We need to restore our trade with the world. Under Republican leadership we have lost it, and the President of the United States seems to be indifferent about finding it again.

And now I am going to talk to a city audience about farming. I do not make one kind of speech to a farm audience and another kind of speech to a city audience. We need to give to fifty million people, who live directly or indirectly on agriculture, a price for their products in excess of the cost of production. You know how and why that affects us in the cities. To give them an adequate price for their products means to give them the buying power necessary to start your mills and mines to work to supply their needs. Fifty million people cannot buy your goods, because they cannot get a fair price for their products. You are poor because they are poor.

I favor—and do not let the false statements of my opponents deceive you—continued protection for American agriculture as well as American industry. I favor more than that. I advocate, and will continue to advocate, measures to give the farmer an added benefit, called a tariff benefit, to make the tariff effective on his products. What good does a 42-cent tariff on wheat mean to the farmer when he is getting 30 cents a bushel on his farm? That is a joke. The most enlightened of modern American businessmen likewise favor such a tariff benefit for agriculture. An excellent example is your own fellow Bostonian, Mr. Harriman, President of the Chamber of Commerce of the United States, who has recently proclaimed a plan for the restoration of agriculture not unlike my own.

The President of the United States does not favor a program of that kind, or, so far as I can make out, of any practical kind. He has closed the door of hope to American agriculture, and when he did that, he closed the door of hope to you also.

He says proudly that he has effectively restricted immigration in order to protect American labor. I favor that; but I might add that in the enforcement of the immigration laws too many abuses against individual families have been revealed time and time again.

But when the President speaks to you, he does not tell you that by permitting agriculture to fall into ruin millions of workers from the farms have crowded into our cities. These men have added to unemployment. They are here because agriculture is prostrate. A restored agriculture will check this migration from the farm. It will keep these farmers happily, successfully, at home; and it will leave more jobs for you. It will provide a market for your products, and that is the key to national economic restoration.

One word more. I have spoken of getting things done. The way we get things done under our form of government is through joint action by the President and the Congress. The two branches of government must cooperate if we are to move forward. That is necessary under our constitution, and I believe in our constitutional form of government.

But the President of the United States cannot get action from the Congress. He seems unable to cooperate. He quarreled with a Republican Congress and he quarreled with a half Republican Congress. He will quarrel with any kind of Congress, and he cannot get things done.

That is something that the voters have considered and are considering and are going to remember one week from tomorrow. You and I know, and it is certainly a fact, that the next Congress will be Democratic. I look forward to cooperating with it. I am confident that I can get things done through cooperation because for four years I have had to work with a Republican Legislature in New York.

I have been able to get things done in Albany by treating the Republican members of the Legislature like human beings and as my associates in government. I have said that I look forward to the most pleasant relations with the next Democratic Congress, but in addition to that let me make it clear that on that great majority of national problems which ought not to be handled in any partisan manner, I confidently expect to have pleasant relations with Republicans in the Senate and the House of Representatives as well as with Democrats.

After the fourth of March, we—meaning thereby the President and the members of both parties in the Halls of Congress—will, I am confident, work together effectively for the restoration of American economic life.

I decline to accept present conditions as inevitable or beyond control. I decline to stop at saying, "It might have been worse." I shall do all that I can to prevent it from being worse but—and here is the clear difference between the President and myself—I go on to pledge action to make things better.

The United States of America has the capacity to make things better. The nation wants to make things better. The nation prays for the leadership of action that will make things better. That will be shown in every State in the Union—all 48 of them—a week from tomorrow. We are through with "Delay" we are through with "Despair"; we are ready, and waiting for better things.

XVI
Herbert Hoover:
Annual Message to Congress
December 6, 1932

In accord with my constitutional duty, I transmit herewith to the Congress information upon the state of the Union together with recommendation of measures for its consideration.

Our country is at peace. Our national defense has been maintained at a high state of effectiveness. All of the executive departments of the government have been conducted during the year with a high devotion to public interest. There has been a far larger degree of freedom from industrial conflict than hitherto known. Education and science have made further advances. The public health is today at its highest known level. While we have recently engaged in the aggressive contest of a national election, its very tranquility and the acceptance of its results furnish abundant proof of the strength of our institutions.

In the face of widespread hardship our people have demonstrated daily a magnificent sense of humanity, of individual and community responsibility for the welfare of the less fortunate. They have grown in their conceptions and organization for cooperative action for the common welfare.

In the provision against distress during this winter, the great private agencies of the country have been mobilized again; the generosity of our people has again come into evidence to a degree in which all America may take great pride. Likewise the local authorities and the states are engaged everywhere in supplemental measures of relief. The provisions made for loans from the Reconstruction Finance Corporation, to states that have exhausted their own resources, guarantee that there should be no hunger or suffering from cold in the country. The large majority of states are showing a sturdy cooperation in the spirit of the Federal aid....

Economic Situation

The unparalleled worldwide economic depression has continued through the year. Due to the European collapse, the situation developed during last fall and winter into a series of most acute crises. The unprecedented emergency measures enacted and policies adopted undoubtedly saved the country from economic disaster.   After serving to defend the national security, these measurers began in July to show their weight and influence toward improvement of conditions in many parts of the country....

The measures and policies which have procured this turn toward recovery should be continued until the depression is passed, and then the emergency agencies should be promptly liquidated. The expansion of credit facilities by the Federal Reserve System and the Reconstruction Finance Corporation has been of incalculable value. The loans of the latter for reproductive works, and to railways for the creation of employment; its support of the credit structure through loans to banks, insurance companies, railways, building and loan associations, and to agriculture has protected the savings and insurance policies of millions of our citizens and had relieved millions of borrowers from duress; they have enabled industry and business to function and expand. The assistance given to Farm Loan Banks, the establishment of the Home Loan Banks and Agricultural Credit Associations—all in their various ramifications have placed large sums of money at the disposal of the people in protection and aid. Beyond this, the extensive organization of the country in voluntary action has produced profound results....

Continued constructive policies promoting the economic recovery of the country must be the paramount duty of the government. The result of the agencies we have created and the policies we have pursued has been to buttress our whole domestic financial structure and greatly to restore credit facilities.   But progress in recovery requires another element as well—that is fully restored confidence in the future. Institutions and men may have resources and credit but unless they have confidence progress is halting and insecure.

There are three definite directions in which action by the government at once can contribute to strengthen further the forces of recovery by strengthening of confidence. They are the necessary foundations to any other action, and their accomplishment would at once promote employment and increase prices.

The first of these directions of action is the continuing reduction of all government expenditures, whether national, state, or local. The difficulties of the country demand undiminished efforts toward economy in government in every direction. Embraced in this problem is the unquestioned balancing of the Federal Budget.

That is the first necessity of national stability and is the foundation of further recovery. It must be balanced in an absolutely safe and sure manner if full confidence is to be inspired.

The second direction for action is the complete reorganization at once of our banking system. The shocks to our economic life have undoubtedly been multiplied by the weakness of this system, and until they are remedied recovery will be greatly hampered.

The third direction for immediate action is vigorous and whole-souled cooperation with other governments in the economic field. That our major difficulties find their origins in the economic weakness of foreign nations requires no demonstration. The first need today is strengthening of commodity prices. That can not be permanently accomplished without expansion in consumption of goods through the return of stability and confidence in the world at large and that in turn can not be fully accomplished without cooperation with other nations.

At the last session the Congress responded to my request for authority to reorganize the government departments. The act provides for the grouping and consolidation of executive and administrative agencies according to major purpose, and thereby reducing the number and overlap and duplication of effort. Executive orders issued for these purposes are required to be transmitted to the Congress while in session and do not become effective until after the expiration of 60 calendar days after such transmission, unless the Congress shall sooner approve.

I shall issue such executive orders within a few days grouping or consolidating over fifty executive and administrative agencies including a large number of commissions and "independent" agencies.

The second step, of course, remains that after these various bureaus and agencies are placed cheek by jowl into such groups, the administrative officers in charge of the groups shall eliminate their overlap and still further consolidate these activities. Therein lie large economies.

The Congress must be warned that a host of interested persons inside and outside the government whose vision is concentrated on some particular function will at once protest against these proposals. These same sorts of activities have prevented reorganization of the government for over a quarter of a century. They must be disregarded if the task is to be accomplished.

Banking

The basis of every other and every further effort toward recovery is to reorganize at once our banking system. The shocks to our economic system have undoubtedly multiplied by the weakness of our financial system. I first called attention of the Congress in 1929 to this condition, and I have unceasingly recommended remedy since that time. The subject has been exhaustively investigated both by the committees of the Congress and the officers of the Federal Reserve System.

The banking and financial system is presumed to serve in furnishing the essential lubricant to the wheels of industry, agriculture, and commerce, that is, credit. Its diversion from proper use, its improper use, or its insufficiency instantly brings hardship and dislocation in economic life. As a system our banking has failed to meet this great emergency. It can be said without question of doubt that our losses and distress have been greatly augmented by its wholly inadequate organization. Its inability as a system to respond to our needs is today a constant drain upon progress toward recovery. In this statement I am not referring to individual banks or bankers. Thousands of them have shown distinguished courage and ability. On the contrary, I am referring to the system itself, which is so organized, or so lacking in organization, that in an emergency its very mechanism jeopardizes or paralyzes the action of sound banks and its instability is responsible for periodic dangers to our whole economic system.

It is today a matter of satisfaction that the rate of bank failures, of hoarding, and the demands upon Reconstruction Corporation have greatly lessened. The acute phases of the crisis have obviously passed and the time has now come when this national danger and this failure to respond to national necessities must be ended and the measures to end them can be safely undertaken. Methods of reform have been exhaustively examined. There is no reason now why solution should not be found at the present session of the Congress. Inflation of currency or governmental conduct of banking can have no part in these reforms. The government must abide within the field of constructive organization, regulation, and the enforcement of safe practices only.

Parallel with reform in the banking laws must be changes in the Federal Farm Loan Banking system and in the Joint Stock Land Banks. Some of these changes should be directed to permanent improvement and some to emergency aid to our people where they wish to fight to save their farms and homes.

I wish again to emphasize this view—that these widespread banking reforms are a national necessity and are the first requisites for further recovery in agriculture and business. They should have immediate consideration as steps greatly needed to further recovery.

I have placed various legislative needs before the Congress in previous messages, and these views require no amplification on this occasion. I have urged the need for reform in our transportation and power regulation, in the antitrust laws as applied to our national resource industries, western range conservation, extension of Federal aid to the child-health services, membership in the World Court, the ratification of the Great Lakes-St. Lawrence Seaway Treaty, revision of the bankruptcy acts, revision of Federal court procedure. And many other pressing problems.

These and other special subjects I shall where necessary deal with by special communications to the Congress.

The activities of our government are so great, when combined with the emergency activities which have arisen out of the world crisis, that even the briefest review of them would render the annual message unduly long. I shall therefore avail myself of the fact that every detail of the government is covered in the reports to the Congress by each of the departments and agencies of the government.

Conclusion

It seems to me appropriate upon this occasion to make certain general observations upon the principles which must dominate the solution of problems now pressing upon the nation. Legislation in response to national needs will be effective only if every such act conforms to a complete philosophy of the people's purposes and destiny. Ours is a distinctive government with a unique history and background, consciously dedicated to specific ideals of liberty and to a faith in the inviolable sanctity of the individual human spirit. Furthermore, the continued existence and adequate functioning of our government is preservation of ordered liberty and stimulation of progress depends upon the maintenance of state, local, institutional, and individual sense of responsibility. We have builded a system of individualism peculiarly our own which must not be forgotten in any governmental acts, for from it have grown greater accomplishments than those of any other nation.

On the social and economic sides, the background of our American system and the motivation of progress is essentially that we should allow free play of social and economic forces as far as will not limit equality of opportunity and as will at the same time stimulate the initiative and enterprise of our people. In the maintenance of this balance the Federal Government can permit of no privilege to any person or group. It should act as a regulatory agent and not as a participant in economic and social life. The moment the government participates, it becomes at once a tyranny in whatever direction it may touch. We have around us numerous such experiences, no one of which can be found to have justified itself except in cases where the people as a whole have met forces beyond their control, such as those of the Great War and this great depression, where the full powers of the Federal Government must be exerted to protect the people. But even these must be limited to an emergency sense and must be promptly ended when these dangers are overcome.

With the free development of science and the consequent multitude of inventions, some of which are absolutely revolutionary in our national life, the government must not only stimulate the social and economic responsibility of individuals and private institutions but it must also give leadership to cooperative action amongst the people which will soften the effect of these revolutions and thus secure social transformations in an orderly manner. The highest form of self-government is the voluntary cooperation within our people for such purposes.

But I would emphasize again that social and economic solutions, as such, will not avail to satisfy the aspirations of the people unless they conform with the traditions of our race, deeply grooved in their sentiments through a century and a half of struggle for ideals of life that are rooted in religion and fed from purely spiritual springs.

XVII
Herbert Hoover:
Letter to Franklin D. Roosevelt
December 20, 1932

I have your telegram expressing the difficulties which you find in cooperation at the present time. In the face of foreign conditions which are continually degenerating agricultural prices, increasing unemployment and creating economic difficulties for our people, I am unwilling to admit that cooperation cannot be established between the outgoing and incoming administrations which will give earlier solution and recovery from these difficulties.

If you will review my previous communications and conversations I think you will agree that while outlining the nature of the problems my proposals to you have been directed to the setting up not of solutions but of the machinery through which by preparedness the ultimate solution of these questions can be expedited and coordinated to the end that many months of delay and increasing losses to our people may be avoided.

I fully recognize that your solution of these questions of debt, the world economic problems and disarmament might vary from my own. These conclusions obviously cannot be attained in my administration and will lie entirely within your administration. I wish especially to avoid any embarrassment to your work and thus have no intention of committing the incoming administration to any particular policy prior to March 4. Even the exploratory work you suggest should be participated in by men in whom you have confidence, and I wish to facilitate it. What I deem of the utmost importance is that when you assume responsibility on March 4 machinery of your approval will be here, fully informed and ready to function according to the policies you may determine.

My frequent statements indicate agreement with you that debts, world economic problems and disarmament require selective treatment, but you will agree with me that they also require coordination and preparation either in the individual hands of the president or in the hands of men selected to deal with them and advise them. There is thus no thought of submerging the World Economic Conference with other questions, but rather to remove the barriers from successful issue of that conference.

With view to again making an effort to secure cooperation and that solidarity of national action which the situation needs, I would be glad if you could designate Mr. Owen D. Young, Colonel House, or any other men of your party possessed of your views and your confidence and at the same time familiar with these problems, to sit with the principal officers of this administration in endeavor to see what steps can be taken to avoid delays of precious time and inevitable losses that will ensue from such delays.

XVIII
Franklin D. Roosevelt:
Letter to Herbert Hoover
December 21, 1932

Dear Mr. President:

I think perhaps the difficulties to which you refer are not in finding the means or the willingness for cooperation but, rather, in defining clearly those things concerning which cooperation between us is possible.

We are agreed that commitments to any particular policy prior to March fourth are for many reasons inadvisable and indeed impossible.   There remains therefore before that date only the possibility of exploratory work and preliminary surveys.

Please let me reiterate not only that I am glad to avoid the loss of precious time through delay in starting these preliminaries but also that I shall gladly receive such information and expression of opinion concerning all of those international questions which because of existing economic and other conditions must and will be among the first concerns of my administration.

However, for me to accept any joint responsibility in the work of exploration might well be construed by the debtor or other nations, collectively or individually, as a commitment—moral even though not legal, as to policies and courses of action.

The designation of a man or men of such eminence as your telegram suggests would not imply mere fact-finding; it would suggest the presumption that such representatives were empowered to exchange views on matters of large and binding policy.

Current press dispatches from abroad already indicate that the joint action which you propose would most certainly be interpreted there as much more of a policy commitment than either you or I actually contemplate.

May I respectfully suggest that your proceed with the selection of your representatives to conduct the preliminary exploration necessary with individual debtor nations and representatives to discuss the agenda of the World Economic conference, making it clear that none of these representatives is authorized to bind this government as to any ultimate policy.

If this be done, let me repeat that I shall be happy to receive their information and their expressions of opinion.

To that I add the thought that between now and March fourth I shall be very glad if you will keep me advised as to the progress of the preliminary discussions, and I also shall be happy to consult with you freely during this period.

3

"The Only Thing We Have to Fear is Fear Itself" (1933 – 1935)

XIX
Herbert Hoover:
Letter to Franklin D. Roosevelt
February 18, 1933

A most critical situation has arisen in the country of which I feel it my duty to advise you confidentially. I am therefore taking this course of writing you myself and sending it to you through the Secret Service for your hand direct as obviously its misplacement would only feed the fire and increase the dangers.

The major difficulty is the state of the public mind, for there is a steadily degenerating confidence in the future which has reached the height of general alarm. I am convinced that a very early statement by you upon two or three policies of your administration would serve greatly to restore confidence and cause a resumption of the march of recovery.

The large part which fear and apprehension play in the situation can be well demonstrated by repeated experience in the past few years and the tremendous lift which has come at times by the removal of fear can be easily demonstrated.

One of the major underlying elements in the broad problem of recovery is the re-expansion of credit so critically and abruptly deflated by the shocks from Europe during the last half of 1931. The visible results were public fear, hoarding, bank failures, withdrawal of gold, flight of capital, falling prices, increased unemployment, etc. Early in 1932 we created the agencies which have steadily expanded available credit ever since that time and continue to expand it today. But confidence must run parallel with expanding credit and the instances where confidence has been injured run precisely with the lagging or halting of recovery.

With the election, there came the natural and inevitable hesitation all along the economic line pending the demonstration of the policies of the new administration. But a number of very discouraging things have happened on top of this natural hesitation. The breakdown in balancing the budget by the House of Representatives; the proposals for inflation of the currency and the wide spread discussion of it; the publication of R.F.C. loans and the bank runs, hoarding and bank failures from this cause; increase in unemployment due to imports from depreciated currency countries; failure of the Congress to enact banking, bankruptcy and other vital legislation; unwillingness of the Congress to face reduction in expenditures; proposals to abrogate constitutional responsibility by the Congress with all the chatter about dictatorship, and other discouraging effects upon the public mind. They have now culminated to a state of alarm which is rapidly reaching the dimensions of a crisis. Hoarding has risen to a new high level; the bank structure is weakened as witness Detroit and increased failures in other localities. There are evidences of flight of capital and foreign withdrawals of gold. In other words we are confronted with precisely the same phenomena we experienced late in 1931 and again in the spring of 1932. The whole has its final expression in the increase of unemployment, suffering and general alarm.

I therefore return to my suggestion at the beginning as to the desirability of clarifying the public mind on certain essentials which will give renewed confidence. It is obvious that as you will shortly be in position to make whatever policies you wish effective, you are the only one who can give these assurances. Both the nature of the cause of public alarm and experience give such an action the prospect of success in turning the tide. I do not refer to action on all the causes of alarm but it would steady the country greatly if there could be prompt assurance that there will be no tampering or inflation of the currency; that the budget will be unquestionably balanced even if further taxation is necessary; that the government credit will be maintained by refusal to exhaust it in issue of securities. The course you have adopted in inquiring into the problems of world stabilization are already known and helpful. It would be of further help if the leaders were advised to cease publication of R.F.C. business.

I am taking the liberty of addressing you because both of my anxiety over the situation and my confidence that from four years of experience that such tides as are now running can be moderated and the processes of regeneration which are always running can be released.

XX
Herbert Hoover:
Letter to Franklin D. Roosevelt
February 28, 1933

It is my duty to inform you that the financial situation has become even more grave and the lack of confidence extended further than when I wrote to you on February 18th. I am confident that a declaration even now on the line I suggested at that time would contribute greatly to restore confidence and would save losses and hardships to millions of people.

My purpose however is to urge you—upon the basis of evident facts—that the gravity of the situation is such that it is desirable that the co-ordinate arm of the government should be in session quickly after March 4th. There is much legislation urgently needed but will not be completed by the present session. The new Congress being in majority with the administration is capable of expeditious action.

But beyond that, it would make for stability in the public mind and there are contingencies in which immediate action may be absolutely essential in the next few days.

I am at your disposal to discuss the situation upon your arrival here or otherwise. I wish to assure you of the deep desire of my colleagues and myself to co-operate with you in every way.

XXI
Franklin D. Roosevelt:
Letter to Herbert Hoover
March 1, 1933

I am dismayed to find that the enclosed which I wrote in N.Y. a week ago did not go to you, through an assumption by my secretary that it was only a draft of a letter.

Now I have yours of yesterday and can only tell you that I appreciate your fine spirit of co-operation and that I am in constant touch with the situation through Mr. Woodin, who is conferring with Ogden and with various people in N.Y. I am inclined to agree that a very early special session will be necessary—and by tonight or tomorrow I hope to settle on a definite time—I will let you know—you doubtless know of the proposal to give authority to the Treasury to deposit funds directly in any bank.

I get to Washington late tomorrow night and will look forward to seeing you on Friday.

XXII
Franklin D. Roosevelt:
First Inaugural Address
March 4, 1933

I am certain that my fellow Americans expect that on my induction into the Presidency I will address them with a candor and a decision which the present situation of our nation impels. This is preeminently the time to speak the truth, the whole truth, frankly and boldly. Nor need we shrink from honestly facing conditions in our country today. This great nation will endure as it has endured, will revive and will prosper. So, first of all, let me assert my firm belief that the only thing we have to fear is fear itself—nameless, unreasoning unjustified terror which paralyzes needed efforts to convert retreat into advance. In every dark hour of our national life a leadership of frankness and vigor has met with that understanding and support of the people themselves, which is essential to victory. I am convinced that you will again give that support to leadership in these critical days.

In such a spirit on my part and on yours we face our common difficulties. They concern, thank God, only material things. Values have shrunken to fantastic levels; taxes have risen; our ability to pay has fallen; government of all kinds is faced by serious curtailment of income; the means of exchange are frozen in the currents of trade; the withered leaves of industrial enterprise lie on every side; farmers find no markets for their produce; the savings of many years in thousands of families are gone.

More important, a host of unemployed citizens face the grim problem of existence, and an equally great number toil with little return. Only a foolish optimist can deny the dark realities of the moment.

Yet our distress comes from no failure of substance. We are stricken by no plague of locusts. Compared with the perils, which our forefathers conquered because they believed and were not afraid, we have still much to be thankful for. Nature still offers her bounty and human efforts have multiplied it. Plenty is at our doorstep, but a generous use of it languishes in the very sight of the supply. Primarily this is because the rulers of the exchange of mankind's goods have failed, through their own stubbornness and their own incompetence, have admitted their failure, and abdicated. Practices of the unscrupulous money changers' stand indicted in the court of public opinion, rejected by the hearts and minds of men. True they have tried, but their efforts have been cast in the pattern of an outworn tradition. Faced by failure of credit they have proposed only the lending of more money. Stripped of the lure of profit by which to induce our people to follow their false leadership, they have resorted to exhortations, pleading tearfully for restored confidence. They know only the rules of a generation of self-seekers. They have no vision, and when there is no vision the people perish.

The money changers have fled from their high seats in the temple of our civilization. We may now restore that temple to the ancient truths. The measure of the restoration lies in the extent to which we apply social values more noble than mere monetary profit.

Happiness lies not in the mere possession of money; it lies in the joy of achievement, in the thrill of creative effort. The joy and moral stimulation of work no longer must be forgotten in the mad chase of evanescent profits. These dark days will be worth all they cost us if they teach us that our true destiny is not to be ministered unto but to minister to ourselves and to our fellow men.

Recognition of the falsity of material wealth as the standard of success goes hand in hand with the abandonment of the false belief that public office and high political position are to be valued only by the standards of pride of place and personal profit; and there must be an end to a conduct in banking and in business which too often has given to a sacred trust the likeness of callous and selfish wrongdoing. Small wonder that confidence languishes, for it thrives only on honesty, on honor, on the sacredness of obligations, on faithful protection, on unselfish performance; without them it can not live.

Restoration calls, however, not for changes in ethics alone. This nation asks for action, and action now.

Our greatest primary task is to put people to work. This is no unsolvable problem if we face it wisely and courageously. It can be accomplished in part by direct recruiting by the government itself, treating the task as we would treat the emergency of a war, but at the same time, through this employment, accomplishing greatly needed projects to stimulate and reorganize the use of our natural resources.

Hand in hand with this we must frankly recognize the overbalance of population in our industrial centers and, by engaging on a national scale in a redistribution, endeavor to provide a better use of the land for those best fitted for the land. The task can be helped by definite efforts to raise the values of agricultural products and with this the power to purchase the output of our cities. It can be helped by preventing realistically the tragedy of the growing loss through foreclosure of our small homes and our farms. It can be helped by insistence that the Federal, State and local governments act forthwith on the demand that their cost be drastically reduced. It can be helped by the unifying of relief activities, which today are often scattered, uneconomical, and unequal. It can be helped by national planning for and supervision of all forms of transportation and of communications and other utilities which have a definitely public character. There are many ways in which it can be helped, but it can never be helped merely by talking about it. We must act and act quickly.

Finally, in our progress toward a resumption of work we require two safeguards against a return of the evils of the old order; there must be a strict supervision of all banking and credits and investments; there must be an end to speculation with other people's money, and there must be provision for an adequate but sound currency.

These are the lines of attack. I shall presently urge upon a new Congress in special session detailed measures for their fulfillment, and I shall seek the immediate assistance of the several States.

Through this program of action we address ourselves to putting our own national house in order and making income balance outgo. Our international trade relations, though vastly important, are in point of time and necessity secondary to the establishment of a sound national economy. I favor as a practical policy the putting of first things first. I shall spare no effort to restore world trade by international economic readjustment, but the emergency at home can not wait on that accomplishment.

The basic thought that guides these specific means of national recovery is not narrowly nationalistic. It is the insistence, as a first consideration, upon the interdependence of the various elements in all parts of the United States: a recognition of the old and permanently important manifestation of the American spirit of the pioneer. It is the way to recovery. It is the immediate way. It is the strongest assurance that the recovery will endure.

In the field of world policy I would dedicate this nation to the policy of the good neighbor; the neighbor who resolutely respects himself and, because he does so, respects the rights of others; the neighbor who respects his obligations and respects the sanctity of his agreements in and with a world of neighbors.

If I read the temper of our people correctly, we now realize as we have never realized before our interdependence on each other; that we can not merely take but we must give as well; that if we are to go forward, we must move as a trained and loyal army willing to sacrifice for the good of a common discipline, because without such discipline no progress is made, no leadership becomes effective. We are, I know, ready and willing to submit our lives and property to such discipline, because it makes possible a leadership, which aims at a larger good. This I propose to offer, pledging that the larger purposes will bind upon us all as a sacred obligation with a unity of duty hitherto evoked only in time of armed strife.

With this pledge taken, I assume unhesitatingly the leadership of this great army of our people dedicated to a disciplined attack upon our common problems. Action in this image and to this end is feasible under the form of government, which we have inherited from our ancestors. Our Constitution is so simple and practical that it is possible always to meet extraordinary needs by changes in emphasis and arrangement without loss of essential form. That is why our constitutional system has proved itself the most superbly enduring political mechanism the modern world has produced. It has met every stress of vast expansion of territory, of foreign wars, of bitter internal strife, of world relations. It is to be hoped that the normal balance of executive and legislative authority may be wholly adequate to meet the unprecedented task before us. But it may be that an unprecedented demand and need for undelayed action may call for temporary departure from that normal balance of public procedure.

I am prepared under my constitutional duty to recommend the measures that a stricken nation in the midst of a stricken world may require. These measures, or such other measures as the Congress may build out of its experience and wisdom, I shall seek, within my constitutional authority, to bring to speedy adoption. But in the event that the Congress shall fail to take one of these two courses and in the event that the national emergency is still critical, I shall not evade the clear course of duty that will then confront me. I shall ask the Congress for the one remaining instrument to meet the crisis: broad executive power to wage a war against the emergency, as great as the power that would be given to me if we were in fact invaded by a foreign foe.

For the trust reposed in me I will return the courage and the devotion that befit the time. I can do no less.

We face the arduous days that lie before us in the warm courage of the national unity; with the clear consciousness of seeking old and precious moral values; with the clear satisfaction that comes from the stern performance of duty by old and young alike. We aim at the assurance of a rounded and permanent national life. We do not distrust the future of essential democracy. The people of the United States have not failed. In their need they have registered a mandate that they want direct, vigorous action. They have asked for discipline and direction under leadership. They have made me the present instrument of their wishes. In the spirit of the gift I take it.

In this dedication of a nation we humbly ask the blessing of God. May He protect each and every one of us. May He guide me in the days to come.

XXIII
Franklin D. Roosevelt:
Fireside Chat, *On the Banking Crisis*
March 12, 1933

I want to talk for a few minutes with the people of the United States about banking—with the comparatively few who understand the mechanics of banking but more particularly with the overwhelming majority who use banks for the making of deposits and the drawing of checks. I want to tell you what has been done in the last few days, why it was done, and what the next steps are going to be. I recognize that the many proclamations from State Capitols and from Washington, the legislation, the Treasury regulations, etc., couched for the most part in banking and legal terms should be explained for the benefit of the average citizen. I owe this in particular because of the fortitude and good temper with which everybody has accepted the inconvenience and hardships of the banking holiday. I know that when you understand what we in Washington have been about I shall continue to have your cooperation as fully as I have had your sympathy and help during the past week.

First of all let me state the simple fact that when you deposit money in a bank the bank does not put the money into a safe deposit vault. It invests your money in many different forms of credit—bonds, commercial paper, mortgages and many other kinds of loans. In other words, the bank puts your money to work to keep the wheels of industry and of agriculture turning around. A comparatively small part of the money you put into the bank is kept in currency—an amount which in normal times is wholly sufficient to cover the cash needs of the average citizen. In other words the total amount of all the currency in the country is only a small fraction of the total deposits in all of the banks.

What, then, happened during the last few days of February and the first few days of March? Because of undermined confidence on the part of the public, there was a general rush by a large portion of our population to turn bank deposits into currency or gold. A rush so great that the soundest banks could not get enough currency to meet the demand. The reason for this was that on the spur of the moment it was, of course, impossible to sell perfectly sound assets of a bank and convert them into cash except at panic prices far below their real value.

By the afternoon of March 3 scarcely a bank in the country was open to do business. Proclamations temporarily closing them in whole or in part had been issued by the Governors in almost all the states.

It was then that I issued the proclamation providing for the nation-wide bank holiday, and this was the first step in the Government's reconstruction of our financial and economic fabric.

The second step was the legislation promptly and patriotically passed by the Congress confirming my proclamation and broadening my powers so that it became possible in view of the requirement of time to intend the holiday and lift the ban of that holiday gradually. This law also gave authority to develop a program of rehabilitation of our banking facilities. I want to tell our citizens in every part of the nation that the national Congress—Republicans and Democrats alike—showed by this action a devotion to public welfare and a realization of the emergency and the necessity for speed that it is difficult to match in our history.

The third stage has been the series of regulations permitting the banks to continue their functions to take care of the distribution of food and household necessities and the payment of payrolls.

This bank holiday while resulting in many cases of great inconvenience is affording us the opportunity to supply the currency necessary to meet the situation. No sound bank is a dollar worse off than it was when it closed its doors last Monday. Neither is any bank which may turn out not to be in a position for immediate opening. The new law allows the twelve Federal Reserve banks to issue additional currency on good assets and thus the banks which reopen will be able to meet every legitimate call. The new currency is being sent out by the Bureau of Engraving and Printing in large volume to every part of the country. It is sound currency because it is backed by actual, good assets.

As a result we start tomorrow, Monday, with the opening of banks in the twelve Federal Reserve Bank cities—those banks which on first examination by the Treasury have already been found to be all right. This will be followed on Tuesday by the resumption of all their functions by banks already found to be sound in cities where there are recognized clearing houses. That means about 250 cities of the United States.

On Wednesday and succeeding days banks in smaller places all through the country will resume business, subject, of course, to the Government's physical ability to complete its survey. It is necessary that the reopening of banks be extended over a period in order to permit the banks to make applications for necessary loans, to obtain currency needed to meet their requirements and to enable the Government to make common sense checkups. Let me make it clear to you that if your bank does not open the first day you are by no means justified in believing that it will not open. A bank that opens on one of the subsequent days is in exactly the same status as the bank that opens tomorrow.

I know that many people are worrying about State banks not members of the Federal Reserve System. These banks can and will receive assistance from members banks and from the Reconstruction Finance Corporation. These state banks are following the same course as the national banks except that they get their licenses to resume business from the state authorities, and these authorities have been asked by the Secretary of the Treasury to permit their good banks to open up on the same schedule as the national banks. I am confident that the state banking departments will be as careful as the national government in the policy relating to the opening of banks and will follow the same broad policy. It is possible that when the banks resume a very few people who have not recovered from their fear may again begin withdrawals. Let me make it clear that the banks will take care of all needs—and it is my belief that hoarding during the past week has become an exceedingly unfashionable pastime. It needs no prophet to tell you that when the people find that they can get their money—that they can get it when they want it for all legitimate purposes—the phantom of fear will soon be laid. People will again be glad to have their money where it will be safely taken care of and where they can use it conveniently at any time. I can assure you that it is safer to keep your money in a reopened bank than under the mattress.

The success of our whole great national program depends, of course, upon the cooperation of the public—on its intelligent support and use of a reliable system.

Remember that the essential accomplishment of the new legislation is that it makes it possible for banks more readily to convert their assets into cash than was the case before. More liberal provision has been made for banks to borrow on these assets at the Reserve Banks and more liberal provision has also been made for issuing currency on the security of those good assets. This currency is not fiat currency. It is issued only on adequate security—and every good bank has an abundance of such security.

One more point before I close. There will be, of course, some banks unable to reopen without being reorganized. The new law allows the Government to assist in making these reorganizations quickly and effectively and even allows the Government to subscribe to at least a part of new capital which may be required.

I hope you can see from this elemental recital of what your government is doing that there is nothing complex, or radical in the process.

We had a bad banking situation. Some of our bankers had shown themselves either incompetent or dishonest in their handling of the people's funds. They had used the money entrusted to them in speculations and unwise loans. This was of course not true in the vast majority of our banks but it was true in enough of them to shock the people for a time into a sense of insecurity and to put them into a frame of mind where they did not differentiate, but seemed to assume that the acts of a comparative few had tainted them all. It was the Government's job to straighten out this situation and do it as quickly as possible—and the job is being performed.

I do not promise you that every bank will be reopened or that individual losses will not be suffered, but there will be no losses that possibly could be avoided; and there would have been more and greater losses had we continued to drift. I can even promise you salvation for some at least of the sorely pressed banks. We shall be engaged not merely in reopening sound banks but in the creation of sound banks through reorganization. It has been wonderful to me to catch the note of confidence from all over the country. I can never be sufficiently grateful to the people for the loyal support they have given me in their acceptance of the judgment that has dictated our course, even though all of our processes may not have seemed clear to them.

After all there is an element in the readjustment of our financial system more important than currency, more important than gold, and that is the confidence of the people. Confidence and courage are the essentials of success in carrying out our plan. You people must have faith; you must not be stampeded by rumors or guesses. Let us unite in banishing fear. We have provided the machinery to restore our financial system; it is up to you to support and make it work.

It is your problem no less than it is mine. Together we cannot fail.

XXIV
Franklin D. Roosevelt:
Fireside Chat, *The New Deal Program*
May 7, 1933

On a Sunday night a week after my Inauguration I used the radio to tell you about the banking crisis and the measures we were taking to meet it. I think that in that way I made clear to the country various facts that might otherwise have been misunderstood and in general provided a means of understanding which did much to restore confidence.

Tonight, eight weeks later, I come for the second time to give you my report—in the same spirit and by the same means to tell you about what we have been doing and what we are planning to do.

Two months ago we were facing serious problems. The country was dying by inches. It was dying because trade and commerce had declined to dangerously low levels; prices for basic commodities were such as to destroy the value of the assets of national institutions such as banks, savings banks, insurance companies, and others. These institutions, because of their great needs, were foreclosing mortgages, calling loans, refusing credit. Thus there was actually in process of destruction the property of millions of people who had borrowed money on that property in terms of dollars which had had an entirely different value from the level of March 1933. That situation in that crisis did not call for any complicated consideration of economic panaceas or fancy plans. We were faced by a condition and not a theory.

There were just two alternatives: The first was to allow the foreclosures to continue, credit to be withheld and money to go into hiding, and thus forcing liquidation and bankruptcy of banks, railroads and insurance companies and a re-capitalizing of all business and all property on a lower level. This alternative meant a continuation of what is loosely called "deflation," the net result of which would be an extraordinary hardship on all property owners and, incidentally, extraordinary hardships on persons working for wages through an increase in unemployment and a further reduction of the scale.

It is easy to see that the result of this course would have not only economic effects of a very serious nature but social results that might bring incalculable harm. Even before I was inaugurated I came to the conclusion that such a policy was too much to ask the American people to bear. It involved not only a further loss of homes, farms, savings and wages but also a loss of spiritual values—the loss of that sense of security for the present and the future so necessary to the peace and contentment of the individual and of his family. When you destroy these things you will find it difficult to establish confidence of any sort in the future. It was clear that mere appeals from Washington for confidence and the mere lending of more money to shaky institutions could not stop this downward course. A prompt program applied as quickly as possible seemed to me not only justified, but imperative to our national security. The Congress, and when I say Congress I mean the members of both political parties, fully understood this and gave me generous and intelligent support. The members of Congress realized that methods of normal times had to be replaced in the emergency by measures, which were suited to the serious and pressing requirements of the moment. There was no actual surrender of power, Congress retained its constitutional authority and no one has the slightest desire to change the balance of powers. The function of Congress is to decide what has to be done and to select the appropriate agency to carry out its will. This policy it has strictly adhered to. The only thing that has been happening has been to designate the President as the agency to carry out certain of the purposes of the Congress. This was constitutional and in keeping with the past American tradition.

The legislation which has been passed or in the process of enactment can properly be considered as part of a well-grounded plan.

First, we are giving opportunity of employment to one-quarter of a million of the unemployed, the young men who have dependents, to go into the forestry and flood prevention work. This is a big task because it means feeding, clothing and caring for nearly twice as many men as we have in the regular army itself. In creating this civilian conservation corps we are killing two birds with one stone. We are clearly enhancing the value of our natural resources and second, we are relieving an amount of actual distress. This great group of men have entered upon their work on a voluntary basis, no military training is involved and we are conserving not only our natural but our human resources. One of the great values to this work is the fact that it is direct and the intervention of very little machinery.

Second, I have requested the Congress and have secured action upon a proposal to put the great properties owned by our government at Muscle Shoals to work after long years of wasteful inaction, and with this a broad plan for the improvement of a vast area in the Tennessee Valley. It will add to the comfort and happiness of hundreds of thousands of people and the incident benefits will reach the entire nation.

Next, the Congress is about to pass legislation that will greatly ease the mortgage distress among the farmers and the home owners of the nation, by providing for the easing of the burden of debt now bearing so heavily upon millions of our people.

Our next step in seeking immediate relief is a grant of half a billion dollars to help the states, counties and municipalities in their duty to care for those who need direct and immediate relief.

In addition to all this, the Congress also passed legislation authorizing the sale of beer in such states as desired. This has already resulted in considerable reemployment and, incidentally, has provided much tax revenue.

Now as to the future:

We are planning to ask the Congress for legislation to enable the government to undertake public works, thus stimulating directly and indirectly the employment of many others in well-considered projects.

Further legislation has been taken up which goes much more fundamentally into our economic problems. The Farm Relief Bill seeks by the use of several methods, alone or together, to bring about an increased return to farmers for their major farm products, seeking at the same time to prevent in the days to come disastrous over-production which so often in the past has kept farm commodity prices far below a reasonable return. This measure provides wide powers for emergencies. The extent of its use will depend entirely upon what the future has in store.

Well-considered and conservative measures will likewise be proposed which will attempt to give to the workers of the country a more fair wage return, prevent cut-throat competition and unduly long hours for labor, and at the same time to encourage each industry to prevent over-production....

I am very certain that the people of this country understand and approve the broad purposes behind new governmental policies relating to agriculture and industry and transportation. We found ourselves faced with more agricultural products than we could possibly consume ourselves and surpluses which other nations did not have the cash to buy from us except at prices ruinously low. We found our factories able to turn out more goods than we could possibly consume, and at the same time have been faced with a falling export demand. We have found ourselves with more facilities to transport goods and crops than there were goods and crops to be transported. All of this has been caused in large part by a complete failure to understand the danger signals that have been flying ever since the close of the World War. The people of this country have been erroneously encouraged to believe that they could keep on increasing the output of farm and factory indefinitely and that some magician would find ways and means for that increased output to be consumed with reasonable profit to the producer.

But today we have reason to believe that things are a little better than they were two months ago. Industry has picked up, railroads are carrying more freight, farm prices are better, but I am not going to indulge in issuing proclamations of over-enthusiastic assurance. We cannot ballyhoo ourselves back to prosperity. I am going to be honest at all times with the people of the country. I do not want the people of this country to take the foolish course of letting this improvement come back on another speculative wave. I do not want the people to believe that because of unjustified optimism we can resume the ruinous practice of increasing our crop output and our factory output in the hope that a kind providence find buyers at high prices. Such a course may bring us immediate and false prosperity but it will be kind of prosperity that will lead us into another tailspin.

It is wholly wrong to call the measures that we have taken government control of farming, control of industry, and control of transportation. It is rather a partnership between government and farming and industry and transportation, not partnership in profits, for the profits would still go to the citizens, but rather a partnership in planning and partnership to see that the plans are carried out.

We are working toward a definite goal, which is to prevent the return of conditions which came very close to destroying what we call modern civilization. The actual accomplishment of our purpose cannot be attained in a day. Our policies are wholly within purposes for which our American Constitutional Government was established 150 years ago.

I know that the people of this country will understand this and will also understand the spirit in which we are undertaking this policy. I do not deny that we may make mistakes of procedure as we carry out the policy. I have no expectation of making a hit every time I come to bat. What I seek is the highest possible batting average, not only for myself but for the team. Theodore Roosevelt once said to me: "If I can be right 75 percent of the time I shall come up to the fullest measure of my hopes."

A series of conditions arose three weeks ago which very readily might have meant, first, a drain on our gold by foreign countries, and secondly, as a result of that, a flight of American capital, in the form of gold, out of our country. It is not exaggerating the possibility to tell you that such an occurrence might well have taken from us the major part of our gold reserve and resulted in such a further weakening of our government and private credit as to bring on actual panic conditions and the complete stoppage of the wheels of industry.

The administration has the definite objective of raising commodity prices to such an extent that those who have borrowed money will, on the average, be able to repay that money in the same kind of dollar which they borrowed. We do not seek to let them get such a cheap dollar that they will be able to pay back a great deal less than they borrowed. In other words, we seek to correct a wrong and not to create another wrong in the opposite direction. That is why powers are being given to the administration to provide, if necessary, for an enlargement of credit, in order to correct the existing wrong. These powers will be used when, as, and if it may be necessary to accomplish the purpose.

Hand in hand with the domestic situation which, of course, is our first concern, is the world situation, and I want to emphasize to you that the domestic situation is inevitably and deeply tied in with the conditions in all of the other nations of the world. In other words, we can get, in all probability, a fair measure of prosperity to return in the United States, but it will not be permanent unless we get a return to prosperity all over the world.

In the conferences which we have held and are holding with the leaders of other nations, we are seeking four great objectives. First, a general reduction of armaments and through this the removal of the fear of invasion and armed attack, and, at the same time, a reduction in armament costs, in order to help in the balancing of government budgets and the reduction of taxation. Secondly, a cutting down of the trade barriers, in order to re-start the flow of exchange of crops and goods between nations. Third, the setting up of a stabilization of currencies, in order that trade can make contracts ahead. Fourth, the reestablishment of friendly relations and greater confidence between all nations.

Our foreign visitors these past three weeks have responded to these purposes in a very helpful way. All of the nations have suffered alike in this great depression. They have all reached the conclusion that each can best be helped by the common action of all. It is in this spirit that our visitors have met with us and discussed our common problems. The international conference that lies before us must succeed. The future of the world demands it and we have each of us pledged ourselves to the best joint efforts to that end.

To you, the people of this country, all of us, the Members of the Congress and the members of this administration owe a profound debt of gratitude. Throughout the depression you have been patient. You have granted us wide powers; you have encouraged us with a widespread approval of our purposes. Every ounce of strength and every resource at our command we have devoted to the end of justifying your confidence. We are encouraged to believe that a wise and sensible beginning has been made. In the present spirit of mutual confidence and mutual encouragement we go forward.

XXV
The Agricultural Adjustment Act
May 12, 1933

TITLE I. AGRICULTURAL ADJUSTMENT
[A] Declaration of Emergency

SEC. 1. That the present acute economic emergency being in pa the consequence of a severe and increasing disparity between prices of agricultural and other commodities, which disparity largely destroyed the purchasing power of farmers for indu

products, has broken down the orderly exchange of commodities, and has seriously impaired the agricultural assets supporting the national credit structure, it is hereby declared that these conditions in the basic industry of agriculture have affected transactions in agricultural commodities with a national public interest, have burdened and obstructed the normal currents of commerce in such commodities, and render imperative the immediate enactment of Title I of this Act.

[B] Declaration of Policy

SEC. 2. It is hereby declared to be the policy of Congress—

(1) To establish and maintain such balance between the production and consumption of agricultural commodities, and such marketing conditions therefor or, as will reestablish prices to farmers at a level that will give agricultural commodities a purchasing power with respect to articles that farmers buy, equivalent to the purchasing power of agricultural commodities in the base period. The base period in the case of all agricultural commodities except tobacco shall be the prewar period, August 1909 - July 1914. In the case of tobacco, the base period shall be the postwar period, August 1919 - July 1929.

(2) To approach such equality of purchasing power by gradual correction of the present inequalities therein at as rapid a rate as is deemed feasible in view of the current consumptive demand in domestic and foreign markets.

(3) To protect the consumers' interest by readjusting farm production at such a level that will not increase the percentage of the consumers' retail expenditures for agriculture commodities, or products derived therefrom which is returned to the farmer, above the percentage which was returned to the farmer in the prewar period, August 1909 - July 1914.

SEC. 6. (a) The Secretary of Agriculture is hereby authorized to enter into option contracts with the producers of cotton to sell to any such producer an amount of cotton to be agreed upon not in excess of the amount of reduction in production of cotton by such producer below the amount produced by him in the preceding crop year, in all cases where such producer agrees in writing to reduce the amount of cotton produced by him in 1933, below his production in the previous year, by not less than 30 per centum, without increase in commercial fertilization per acre.

(b) To any such producer so agreeing to reduce production the Secretary of Agriculture shall deliver a nontransferable-option contract agreeing to sell to said producer an amount, equivalent to the amount of his agreed reduction, of the cotton in the possession and control of the Secretary.

(c) The producer is to have the option to buy said cotton at the average price paid by the Secretary for the cotton procured under section 3, and is to have the right at any time up to January 1, 1934, to exercise his option, upon proof that he has complied with his contract and with all the rules and regulations of the Secretary of Agriculture with respect thereto, by taking said cotton upon payment by him of his option price and all actual carrying charges on such cotton, or the Secretary may sell such cotton for the account of such producer, paying him the excess of the market price at the date of sale over the average price above referred to after deducting all actual and necessary carrying charges: *Provided,* That in no event shall the producer be held responsible or liable for financial loss incurred in the holding of such cotton or on account of the carrying charges therein: *Provided further,* That such agreement to curtail cotton production shall contain a further provision that such cotton producer shall not use the land taken out of cotton production for the production for sale, directly or indirectly, of any other nationally produced agricultural commodity or product....

Commodity Benefits
[C] General Powers

SEC. 8. In order to effectuate the declared policy, the Secretary of Agriculture shall have power—

(1) To provide for reduction in the acreage or reduction in the production for market, or both, of any basic agricultural commodity, through agreements with producers or by other voluntary methods, and to provide for rental or benefit payments in connection therewith or upon that part of the production of any basic agricultural commodity required for domestic consumption, in such amounts as the Secretary deems fair and reasonable, to be paid out of any moneys available for such payments....

(2) To enter into marketing agreements with processors, associations of producers and others engaged in the handling, in the current of interstate or foreign commerce of any agricultural commodity or project thereof, after due notice and opportunity for hearing to interested parties. The making of any such agreement shall not be held to be in violation of any of the antitrust laws of the

United States, and any such agreement shall be deemed to be lawful....

(3) To issue licenses permitting processors, associations of producers and others to engage in the handling, in the current of interstate or foreign commerce, of any agricultural commodity or product thereof, or any competing commodity or product thereof. Such licenses shall be subject to such terms and conditions, not in conflict with existing Acts of Congress or regulations pursuant thereto, as may be necessary to eliminate unfair practices or charges that prevent or tend to prevent the effectuation of the declared policy and the restoration of normal economic conditions in the marketing of such commodities or products and the financing thereof. The Secretary of Agriculture may suspend or revoke any such license, after due notice and opportunity for hearing, for violations of the terms or conditions thereof....

[D] Processing Tax

SEC. 9. (a) To obtain revenue for extraordinary expenses incurred by reason of the national economic emergency, there shall be levied processing taxes as hereinafter provided. When the Secretary of Agriculture determines that rental or benefit payments are to be made with respect to any basic agricultural commodity, he shall proclaim such determination, and a processing tax shall be in effect with respect to such commodity from the beginning of the marketing year therefor next following the date of such proclamation. The processing tax shall be levied, assessed, and collected upon the first domestic processing of the commodity, whether of domestic production or imported, and shall be paid by the processor....

(b) The processing tax shall be at such rate as equals the difference between the current average farm price for the commodity and the fair exchange value of the commodity; except that if the Secretary has reason to believe that the tax at such rate will cause such reduction in the quantity of the commodity or products thereof domestically consumed as to result in the accumulation of surplus stocks of the commodity or products thereof or in the depression of the farm price of the commodity, then he shall cause an appropriate investigation to be made and afford due notice and opportunity for hearing to interested parties. If thereupon the Secretary finds that such result will occur, the processing tax shall be at such rate as will prevent such accumulation of surplus stocks and depression of the farm price the commodity....

(c) For the purposes of part 2 of this title the fair exchange value of a commodity shall be the price therefor that will give the commodity the same purchasing power, with respect to articles farmers buy, as such commodity had during the base period specified in section 2....

(d) As used in part 2 of this title—(1) In case of wheat, rice, and corn, the term "processing" means the milling or other processing (except cleaning and drying) of wheat, rice, or corn for market, including custom milling for toll as well as commercial milling, but shall not include the grinding or cracking thereof not in the form of flour for feed purposes only; (2) In case of cotton, the term "processing" means the spinning, manufacturing, or other processing (except ginning) of cotton and the term "cotton" shall not include cotton linters.

Sec. 12. (a) There is hereby appropriated, out of any money in the Treasury not otherwise appropriated, the sum of $100,000,000 to be available to the Secretary of Agriculture for administrative expenses under this title and for rental and benefit payments made with respect to reduction in acreage or reduction in production for market under part 2 of this title. Such sum shall remain available until expended.

Sec. 15. (d) The Secretary of Agriculture shall ascertain from time to time whether the payment of the processing tax upon any basic agricultural commodity is causing or will cause to the processors thereof disadvantages in competition from competing commodities by reason of excessive shifts in consumption between such commodities or products thereof. If the Secretary of Agriculture finds, after investigation and due notice and opportunity for hearing to interested parties, that such disadvantages in competition exist, or will exist, he shall proclaim such finding. The Secretary shall specify in this proclamation the competing commodity and the compensating rate of tax on the processing thereof necessary to prevent such disadvantages in competition. Thereafter there shall be levied, assessed, and collected upon the first domestic processing of such competing commodity a tax, to be paid by the processor, at the rate specified, until such rate is altered pursuant to a further finding under this section, or the tax or rate thereof on the basic agricultural commodity is altered or terminated. In no case shall the tax imposed upon such competing commodity exceed that imposed per equivalent unit, as determined by the Secretary, upon the basic agricultural commodity.

Sec. 16. (a) Upon the sale or other disposition of any article processed wholly or in chief value from any commodity with respect to which a processing tax is to be levied, that on the date the tax first takes effect or wholly terminated with respect to the commodity, is held for sale or other disposition (including articles in transit) by any person, there shall be made a tax adjustment as follows: (1) Whenever the processing tax first takes effect, there shall be levied, assessed, and collected a tax to be paid by such person equivalent to the amount of the processing tax which would be payable with respect to the commodity from which processed if the processing had occurred on such date; (2) Whenever the processing tax is wholly terminated, there shall be refunded to such person a sum (or if it has not been paid, the tax shall be abated) in an amount equivalent to the processing tax with respect to the commodity from which processed.

(b) The tax imposed by subsection (a) shall not apply to the retail stocks of persons engaged in retail trade, held at the date the processing tax first takes effect; but such retail stocks shall not be deemed to include stocks held in a warehouse on such date, or such portion of other stocks held on such date as are not sold or otherwise disposed of within thirty days thereafter. The tax refund or abatement provided in subsection (a) shall not apply to the retail stocks of persons engaged in retail trade, held on the date the processing tax is wholly terminated.

TITLE III. FINANCING AND EXERCISING

POWER CONFERRED BY SECTION 8 OF ARTICLE I OF THE CONSTITUTION: TO COIN MONEY AND TO REGULATE THE VALUE THEREOF

SEC. 43. Whenever the President finds, upon investigation, that (1) the foreign commerce of the United States is adversely affected by reason of the depreciation in the value of the currency of any other government or governments in relation to the present standard value of gold, or (2) action under this section is necessary in order to regulate and maintain the parity of currency issues of the United States, or (3) an economic emergency requires an expansion of credit, or (4) an expansion of credit is necessary to secure by international agreement a stabilization at proper levels of

180

the currencies of various governments, the President is authorized, in his discretion—

(1) To direct the Secretary of the Treasury to cause to be issued in such amount or amounts as he may from time to time order United States notes, in the same size and of similar color to the Federal Reserve notes heretofore issued and in denominations of $1, $5, $10, $20, $50, $100, $500, $1,000, and $10,000; but notes issued under this subsection shall be issued only for the purpose of meeting maturing Federal obligations to repay sums borrowed by the United States and for purchasing United States bonds and other interest-bearing obligations of the United States: *Provided,* That when any such notes are used for such purpose the bond or other obligation so acquired or taken up shall be retired and canceled. Such notes shall be issued at such times and in such amounts as the President may approve but the aggregate amount of such notes outstanding at any time shall not exceed $3,000,000,000. There is hereby appropriated, out of any money in the Treasury not otherwise appropriated, an amount sufficient to enable the Secretary of the Treasury to retire and cancel 4 per centum annually of such outstanding notes, and the Secretary of the Treasury is hereby directed to retire and cancel annually 4 per centum of such outstanding notes. Such notes and all other coins and currencies heretofore or hereafter coined or issued by or under the authority of the United States shall be legal tender for all debts public and private.

(2) By proclamation to fix the weight of the gold dollar in grains nine tenths fine and also to fix the weight of the silver dollar in grains nine tenths fine at a definite fixed ratio in relation to the gold dollar at such amounts as he finds necessary from his investigation to stabilize domestic prices or to protect the foreign commerce against the adverse effect of depreciated foreign currencies, and to provide for the unlimited coinage of such gold and silver at the ratio so fixed, or in case the government of the United States enters into an agreement with any government or governments under the terms of which the ratio between the value of gold and other currency issued by the United States and by any such government or governments is established, the President may fix the weight of the gold dollar in accordance with the ratio so agreed upon, and such gold dollar, the weight of which is so fixed, shall be the standard unit of value, and all forms of money issued or coined by the United States shall be maintained at a parity with this standard

and it shall be the duty of the Secretary of the Treasury to maintain such parity, but in no event shall the weight of the gold dollar be fixed so as to reduce its present weight by more than 50 per centum....

SEC. 45. (a) The President is authorized for a period of six months from the date of the passage of this Act, to accept silver in payment of the whole or any part of the principal or interest now due, or to become due within six months after such date, from any foreign government or governments on account of any indebtedness to the United States, such silver to be accepted at not to exceed the price of 50 cents an ounce in United States currency. The aggregate value of the silver accepted under this section shall not exceed $200,000,000....

SEC. 46. Section 19 of the Federal Reserve Act, as amended, is amended by inserting immediately after paragraph (c) thereof the following new paragraph:

"Notwithstanding the foregoing provisions of this section, the Federal Reserve Board, upon the affirmative vote of not less than five of its members and with the approval of the President, may declare that an emergency exists by reason of credit expansion, and may by regulation during such emergency increase or decrease from time to time, in its discretion, the reserve balances required to be maintained against either demand or time deposits."

XXVI
The National Industrial Recovery Act
June 16, 1933

TITLE I. INDUSTRIAL RECOVERY
[A] Declaration of Policy

Sec. 1. A national emergency productive of widespread unemployment and disorganization of industry, which burdens interstate and foreign commerce, affects the public welfare, and undermines the standards of living of the American people, is hereby declared to exist. It is hereby declared to be the policy of Congress to remove obstructions to the free flow of interstate and foreign commerce which tend to diminish the amount thereof; and to provide for the general welfare by promoting the organization of industry for the purpose of cooperative action among trade groups, to induce and maintain united action of labor and management under adequate governmental sanctions and supervision, to eliminate unfair competitive practices, to promote the fullest possible utilization of the present productive capacity of industries, to avoid undue restriction of production (except as may be temporarily required), to increase the consumption of industrial and agricultural products by increasing purchasing power, to reduce and relieve unemployment, to improve standards of labor, and otherwise to rehabilitate industry and to conserve natural resources.

[B] Administrative Agencies

Sec. 2.   This title shall cease to be in effect and any agencies established here under shall cease to exist at the expiration of two years after the date of enactment of this Act, or sooner if the President shall by proclamation or the Congress shall by joint resolution declare that the emergency recognized by section 1 has ended.

[C] Codes of Fair Competition

Sec. 3.   (a) Upon the application to the President by one or more trade or industrial associations or groups, the President may approve a code or codes of fair competition for the trade or industry or subdivision thereof, represented by the applicant or applicants, if the President finds (1) that such associations or groups impose no inequitable restrictions on admission to membership therein and are truly representative of such trades or industries or subdivisions thereof and (2) that such code or codes are not designed to promote monopolies or to eliminate or oppress small enterprises and will not operate to discriminate against them, and will tend to effectuate the policy of this title: *Provided,* That such code or codes shall not permit monopolies or monopolistic practices: *Provided further,* That where such code or codes affect the services and welfare of persons engaged in other steps of the economic process, nothing in this section shall deprive such persons of the right to be heard prior to approval by the President of such code or codes.   The President may, as a condition of his approval of any such code, impose such conditions (including requirements for the making of reports and the keeping of accounts) for the protection of consumers, competitors, employees, and others, and in furtherance of the public interest and may provide such exceptions to and exemptions from the provisions of such code, as the President in his discretion deems necessary to effectuate the policy herein declared.

(b) After the President shall have approved any such code, the provisions of such code shall be the standards of fair competition for such trade or industry or subdivision thereof. Any violation of such standards in any transaction in or affecting interstate or foreign commerce shall be deemed an unfair method of competition in commerce within the meaning of the Federal Trade Commission Act, as amended; but nothing in this title shall be construed to impair the powers of the Federal Trade Commission under such Act, as amended.

(d) Upon his own motion, or if complaint is made to the President that abuses inimical to the public interest and contrary to the policy herein declared are prevalent in any trade or industry or subdivision thereof, and if no code of fair competition therefore has theretofore been approved by the President, the President, after such public notice and hearing as he shall specify, may prescribe and approve a code of fair competition for such trade or industry or subdivision thereof, which shall have the same effect as a code of fair competition approved by the President under subsection (a) of this section

[D] Agreements and Licenses

Sec. 4. (a) The President is authorized to enter into agreements with, and to approve voluntary agreements between and among, persons engaged in a trade or industry, labor organizations, and trade or industrial organizations, associations, or groups, relating to any trade or industry, if in his judgment such agreements will aid in effectuating the policy of this title with respect to transactions in or affecting interstate or foreign commerce, and will be consistent with the requirements of clause (2) of subsection (a) of section 3 for a code of fair competition.

(b) Whenever the President shall find that destructive wage or price cutting or other activities contrary to the policy of this title are being practiced in any trade or industry or any subdivision thereof, and, after such public notice and hearing as he shall specify shall find it essential to license business enterprises in order to make effective a code of fair competition or an agreement under this title or otherwise to effectuate the policy of this title, and shall publicly so announce, no person shall, after a date fixed in such an announcement, engage in or carry on any business, in or affecting interstate or foreign commerce, specified in such announcement unless he shall have first obtained a license issued pursuant to such regulations as the President shall prescribe. The President may suspend or revoke any such license, after due notice and opportunity for hearing for violations of the terms or conditions thereof. Any order of the President suspending or revoking any such license shall be final in accordance with law.

Sec. 5. While this title is in effect, and for sixty days thereafter, any code, agreement, or license approved, prescribed, or issued and in effect under this title, and an action complying with the provisions thereof taken during such period, shall be exempt from the provisions of the antitrust laws of the United States.

Nothing in this Act, and no regulation there under, shall prevent an individual from pursuing the vocation of manual labor and selling or trading the products thereof; nor shall anything in this Act, or regulation there under, prevent anyone from marketing or trading the produce of his farm.

[E] Limitations Upon Application of Title

Sec. 6. (a) No trade or industrial association or group shall be eligible to receive the benefit of the provisions of this title until it files with the President a statement containing such information relating to the activities of the association or group as the President shall by regulation prescribe.

Sec. 7. (a) Every code of fair competition, agreement, and license approved, prescribed or issued under this title shall contain the following conditions: (1) That employees shall have the right to organize and bargain collectively through representatives of their own choosing, and shall be free from the interference, restraint, or coercion of employers of labor, or their agents, in the designation of such representatives or in self-organization or in other concerted activities for the purpose of collective bargaining or other mutual aid or protection; (2) that no employee and no one seeking employment shall be required as a condition of employment to join any company union or to refrain from joining, organizing, or assisting a labor organization of his own choosing; and (3) that employers shall comply with the maximum hours of labor, minimum rates of pay, and other conditions of employment, approved or prescribed by the President.

(b) The President shall, so far as practicable, afford every opportunity to employer; and employees in any trade or industry or subdivision thereof with respect to which the conditions referred to in clauses (1) and (2) of subsection (a) prevail, to establish by mutual agreement, the standards as to the maximum hours of labor, minimum rates of pay, and such other conditions of employment as may be necessary in such trade or industry or subdivision thereof to effectuate the policy of this title, and the standards established in such agreements, when approved by the President, shall have the same effect as a code of fair competition.

(c) Where no such mutual agreement has been approved by the President he may investigate the labor practices, policies, wages, hours of labor, and conditions of employment in such trade or industry or subdivision thereof; and upon the basis of such investigations, and after such hearings as the President finds advisable, he is authorized to prescribe a limited code of fair competition fixing such maximum hours of labor, minimum rates of pay, and other conditions of employment in the trade or industry or subdivision thereof investigated as he finds to be necessary to effectuate the policy of this title, which shall have the same effect as a code of fair competition approved by the President under subsection (a) of section 3. The President may differentiate according to experience and skill of the employees affected and according to the locality of employment; but no attempt shall be made to introduce any classification according to the nature of the work involved which might tend to set a maximum as well as a minimum wage.

(d) As used in this title, the term "person" includes any individual, partnership, association, trust, or corporation.

TITLE II. PUBLIC WORKS AND CONSTRUCTION PROJECTS
[F] Federal Emergency Administration of Public Works

Sec. 201.   (a) To effectuate the purposes of this title, the President is hereby authorized to create a Federal Emergency Administration of Public Works, all the powers of which shall be exercised by a Federal Emergency Administrator of Public Works, and to establish such agencies, to accept and utilize such voluntary and uncompensated services, to appoint, without regard to the civil service laws, such officers and employees, and to utilize such Federal officers and employees, and, with the consent of the State, such State and local officers and employees as he may find necessary, to prescribe their authorities, duties, responsibilities, and tenure, and, without regard to the Classification Act of 1923, as amended, to fix the compensation of any officers and employees so appointed.   The President may delegate any of his functions and powers under this title to such officers, agents, and employees as he may designate or appoint.

(b) The Administrator may, without regard to the civil service laws or the Classification Act of 1923, as amended, appoint and fix the compensation of such experts and such other officers and employees as are necessary to carry out the provisions of this title; and may make such expenditures (including expenditures for personal services and rent at the seat of government and elsewhere, for law books and books of reference, and for paper, printing and binding) as are necessary to carry out the provisions of this title.

(d) After the expiration of two years after the date of the enactment of this Act, or sooner if the President shall by proclamation or the Congress shall by joint resolution declare that the emergency recognized by section 1 has ended, the President shall not make any further loans or grants or enter upon any new construction under this title, and any agencies established hereunder shall cease to exist and any of their remaining functions shall be transferred to such departments of the government as the President shall designate.

Sec. 202.   The Administrator, under the direction of the President, shall prepare a comprehensive program of public works, which shall include among other things the following:

(a) Construction, repair, and improvement of public highways and park ways, public buildings, and any publicly owned instrumentalities and facilities; (b) conservation and development of natural resources, including control, utilization, and purification of waters, prevention of soil or coastal erosion, development of water power, transmission of electrical energy, and construction of river and harbor improvements and flood control and also the construction of any river or drainage improvement required to perform or satisfy any obligation incurred by the United States through a treaty with a foreign government heretofore ratified and to restore or develop for the use of any State or its citizens water taken from or denied to them by performance on the part of the United States of treaty obligations heretofore assumed: *Provided,* That no river or harbor improvements shall be carried out unless they shall have heretofore or hereafter been adopted by the Congress or are recommended by the Chief of Engineers of the United States Army; (c) any projects of the character heretofore constructed or carried on either directly by public authority or with public aid to serve the interests of the general public; (d) construction, reconstruction, alteration, or repair under public regulation or control of low-cost housing and slum clearance projects; (e) any project (other than those included in the foregoing classes) of any character heretofore eligible for loans under subsection (a) of section 201 of the Emergency Relief and Construction Act of 1932, as amended, and paragraph (3) of such subsection (a) shall for such purposes be held to include loans for the construction or completion of hospitals the operation of which is partly financed from public funds, and of reservoirs and pumping plants and for the construction of dry docks; and if in the opinion of the President it seems desirable, the construction of naval vessels within the terms and/or limits established by the London Naval Treaty of 1930 and of aircraft required therefor and construction of heavier-than-air aircraft and technical construction for the Army Air Corps and such Army housing projects as the President may approve, and provision of original equipment for the mechanization or motorization of such Army tactical units as he may designate: *Provided, however,* That in the event of an international agreement for the further limitation of armament, to which the United States is signatory, the President is hereby authorized and empowered to suspend, in whole or in part, any such naval or military construction or mechanization and motorization of Army units.

Sec. 203. (a) With a view to increasing employment quickly (while reasonably securing any loans made by the United States) the President is authorized and empowered, through the Administrator or through such other agencies as he may designate or create, (1) to construct, finance, or aid in the construction or financing of any public-works project included in the program prepared pursuant to section 202; (2) upon such terms as the President shall prescribe, to make grants to States, municipalities, or other public bodies for the construction, repair, or improvement of any such project, but no such grant shall be in excess of 30 per centum of the cost of the labor and materials employed upon such project; (3) to acquire by purchase, or by exercise of the power of eminent domain, any real or personal property in connection with the construction of any such project, and to sell any security acquired or any property so constructed or acquired or to lease any such property with or without the privilege of purchase: *Provided,* That all moneys received from any such sale or lease or the repayment of any loan shall be used to retire obligations issued

pursuant to section 209 of this Act, in addition to any other
moneys required to be used for such purpose; (4) to aid in the
financing of such railroad maintenance and equipment as may be
approved by the Interstate Commerce Commission as desirable for
the improvement of transportation facilities; *Provided,* That in
deciding to extend any aid or grant hereunder to any State, county,
or municipality the President may consider whether action is in
process or in good faith assured therein reasonably designed to
bring the ordinary current expenditures thereof within the prudently
estimated revenues thereof.

(d) The President, in his discretion, and under such terms as he
may prescribe, may extend any of the benefits of this title to any
State, county, or municipality notwithstanding any constitutional
or legal restriction or limitation on the right or power of such State,
county, or municipality to borrow money or incur indebtedness.

Sec. 204.   (a) For the purpose of providing for emergency
construction of public high ways and related projects, the President
is authorized to make grants to the highway departments of the
several States in an amount not less than $400,000,000, to be
expended by such departments in accordance with the provisions
of the Federal Highway Act, approved November 9, 1921, as
amended and supplemented.

Sec. 205.   (a) Not less than $50,000,000 of the amount made
available by this Act shall be allotted for (A) national forest
highways, (B) national forest roads, trails, bridges, and related
projects, (C) national park roads and trails in national parks owned
or authorized, (D) roads on Indian reservations, and (E) roads
through public lands, to be expended in the same manner as
provided in paragraph (2) of section 301 of the Emergency Relief
and Construction Act of 1932, in the case of appropriations
allocated for such purposes, respectively, in such section 301, to
remain available until expended.

Sec. 206.   All contracts let for construction projects and all loans
and grants pursuant to this title shall contain such provisions as
are necessary to insure (1) that no convict labor shall be employed
on any such project (2) that (except in executive, administrative,
and supervisory positions), so far as practicable and feasible, no
individual directly employed on any such project shall be permitted
to work more than thirty hours in any one week; (3) that all
employees shall be paid just and reasonable wages which shall be
compensation sufficient to provide, for the hours of labor as

limited, a standard of living in decency and comfort, (4) that in the employment of labor in connection with any such project, preference shall be given, where they are qualified, to ex-service men with dependents, and then in the following order: (A) To citizens of the United States and aliens who have declared their intention of becoming citizens, who are bona fide residents of the political subdivision and/or county in which the work is to be performed and (B) to citizens of the United States and aliens who have declared their intention of becoming citizens, who are bona fide residents of the State, Territory, or district in which the work is to be performed: *Provided,* That these preferences shall apply only where such labor is available and qualified to perform the work to which the employment relates; and (5) that the maximum of human labor shall be used in lieu of machinery wherever practicable and consistent with sound economy and public advantage.

XXVII
Franklin D. Roosevelt:
Executive Order Creating the National Labor Relations Board
June 29, 1934

Publishing Information

By virtue of and pursuant to the authority vested in me under Title I of the National Industrial Recovery Act (ch90, 48 Stat. 195, Tit. 15, U.S.C., sec 701) and under Joint Resolution approved June 19, 1934 (Public Res. 44, 73d Congress), and in order to effectuate the policy of said Title and the purposes of the said Joint Resolution, it is hereby ordered as follows:

Creation of the National Labor Relations Board

SECTION 1. (a) There is hereby created in connection with the Department of Labor a board to be known as the National Labor Relations Board (hereinafter referred to as the Board), which shall be composed of Lloyd Garrison of Wisconsin, Chairman, Henry Alvin Millis of Illinois, and Edwin S. Smith of Massachusetts....

Original Jurisdiction of the Board

SECTION 2. The Board is hereby authorized (a) To investigate issues, facts, practices, and activities of employers or employees in any controversies arising under Section 7(a) of the National Industrial Recovery Act or which are burdening or obstruction, or threatening to burden or obstruct, the free flow of interstate commerce, and (b) To order and conduct elections and on its own initiative to take steps to enforce its orders in the manner provided in Section 2 of Public Resolution 44, 73d Congress, and (c) Whenever it is the public interest, to hold hearings and make findings of fact regarding complaints of discrimination against or discharge of employees or other alleged violations of Section 7(a) of the National Industrial Recovery Act and such parts of any code or agreement as incorporate said Section, and (d) To prescribe, with the approval of the President, such rules and regulations as are authorized by Section 3 of Public Resolution 44, 73d Congress, and to recommend to the President such other rules and regulations relating to collective bargaining, labor representation, and labor elections as the President is authorized to prescribe by Section 10(a) of the National Industrial Recovery Act, and (e) Upon the request of the parties to a labor dispute, to act as a Board of Voluntary Arbitration or to select a person or agency for voluntary arbitration.

Relationship to Other Labor Boards

SECTION 3. (a) The Board is hereby authorized and directed (1) To study the activities of such boards as have been or may hereafter be created to deal with industrial or labor relations, in order to report through the Secretary of Labor to the President whether such boards should be designated as special boards and given the powers that the President is authorized to confer by Public Resolution 44, 73d Congress; and (2) To recommend, through the Secretary of Labor, to the President the establishment, whenever necessary, of "Regional Labor Relations Boards" and special labor boards for particular Industries vested with the powers that the President is authorized to confer by Public Resolution 44, 73d Congress; and (3) To receive from such regional, industrial, and special boards as may be designated or established under the two preceding sub-sections reports of their activities and to review or hear appeals from such boards in cases in which (1) the board recommends review or (2) there is a division of opinion in the board or (3) the National Labor Relations Board deems review will serve the public interest

(b) The National Labor Board created by Executive Order of August 5, 1933, and continued by Executive Order No. 6511 of December 16, 1933, shall cease to exist on July 9, 1934; and each local or regional labor board, established under the authority of section 2(b) of the said Executive Order of December 16, 1933, if it is not designated in accordance with subsection 3(a)(1) of this order, shall crease to exist at such time as the National Labor Relations Board shall determine. The National Labor Relations Board shall have authority to conduct all investigations and proceedings being conducted by boards that are abolished by this subsection; and all records, papers and property of such boards shall become records, papers, and property of the National Labor Relations Board....

Relationship to Other Executive Agencies

(c) The National Labor Relations Board may decline to take cognizance of any labor dispute where there is another means of settlement provided for by agreement, industrial code, or law which has not been utilized.

(d) Whenever the National Labor Relations Board or any board designated or established in accordance with subsections 3(a)(1) or 3(a)(2) of this order has taken, or has announced its intention to take jurisdiction of any case or controversy involving either section 7(a) of the National Industrial Recovery Act or Public Resolution 44, 73d Congress, no other person or agency in the executive branch of the Government, except upon the request of the National Labor Relations Board, or except as otherwise provided in subsection 3(a)(3) of this order, shall take, or continue to entertain, jurisdiction if such case or controversy.

(e) Whenever the National Labor Relations Board or any board designated or established in accordance with subsections 3(a)(1) or 3(a)(2) of this order has made a finding of facts, or issued any order in any case or controversy involving section 7(a) of the National Industrial Recovery Act or Public Resolution 44, 73d Congress such finding of facts and such order shall (except as otherwise provided in subsection 3(a)(3) of this order or except as otherwise recommended by the National Labor Relations Board) be final and not subject to review by any person or agency in the executive branch of the Government.

Statement by the President Accompanying the Foregoing Executive Order, June 30, 1934

The Executive Order that I have just issued carries out the mandate of Congress, as expressed in Public Resolution No. 44, 73d Congress, approved June 19, 1934. It establishes upon a firm statutory basis the additional machinery by which the United

States Government will to take jurisdiction of any case or controversy involving either section 7(a) of the National Industrial Recovery Act or Public Resolution 44, 73d Congress.

For many weeks, but particularly during the last ten days, officials of the Department of Labor, the National Recovery Administration and the National labor Board have been in conference with me and with each other on this subject. It has been our common objective to find an agency or agencies suitable for the disposition of these difficult problems, and after making such selection to make clear to the public how this machinery works and how it can be utilized in the interest of maintaining orderly industrial relations and justice as between employers and employees and the general public, and enforcing the statutes and other provisions of law that relate to collective bargaining and similar labor relations.

The Executive Order creates in connection with the Department of Labor, but not subject to the judicial supervision of the Secretary of Labor, a National Labor Relations Board composed of three impartial persons, each of whom will receive a salary of $10,000 a year this Board is given the power to make investigations to hold labor elections to hear cases of discharge of employees and to act as voluntary arbitrator.   In addition, the Board is authorized to recommend to the President that in such cases as they deem it desirable, existing labor boards such as the industrial boards already created in the cotton textile industry or the petroleum industry, and such as the various Regional Labor Boards, should be reestablished under the authority of the Joint Resolution just passed by Congress and approved by me on June 19, 1934 and also to recommend that additional boards of a similar character should be newly created. Whenever any regional, industrial or special board is established or created under the authority of the Joint Resolution it will report for administrative purposes to the National Labor Relations Board, by the decisions of the regional, industrial or special boards will be subject to review by the National Board only where it is clear that such review will serve the public interest. Furthermore, the Board can utilize and refer cases to suitable State or local tribunals.

The existing National Labor Board is by the Executive Order abolished, effective July 9, 1934, but the new National Labor Relations Board will have the benefit of the expert personnel of the old Board and of such of the subordinate regional labor boards as it may deem necessary. The new Board will have the advantages of the experience of the old Board....

One of the most important features of the new arrangement is that the National Labor Relations Board and all subordinate boards will make regular reports through the Secretary of Labor to the President...Reports furnished regularly in this manner will be invaluable in the event that any permanent legislation is later contemplated and in developing a systematic knowledge of the general character of the labor relations problems in the United States of America which must be justly and expeditiously handled.

The very presence of this Board and any boards it may authorize will have undoubtedly a salutary effect in making it possible for individual conciliators to arrive at settlements of local grievances promptly. Indeed it is my hope that so far as possible adjustment in labor relations and the correction of labor abuses can be effectively made at the source of the dispute without bringing the parties before national authorities located in Washington....

This Executive Order, I believe, marks a great step forward in administrative efficiency and more important in governmental policy in labor matters. It meets the universal demand not only of employers and employees, but of the public that the machinery for adjusting labor relations should be clarified so that every person may know where to turn for the adjustment of grievances.

XXVIII
Franklin D. Roosevelt:
Annual Message to Congress
January 4, 1935

The Constitution wisely provides that the Chief Executive shall report to the Congress on the state of the Union, for through you, the chosen legislative representatives, our citizens everywhere may fairly judge the progress of our governing. I am confident that today, in the light of the events of the past two years, you do not consider it merely a trite phrase when I tell you that I am truly glad to greet you and that I look forward to common counsel, to useful cooperation, and to genuine friendships between us.

We have undertaken a new order of things; yet we progress to it under the framework and in the spirit and intent of the American Constitution. We have proceeded throughout the nation a measurable distance on the road toward this new order. Materially,

I can report to you substantial benefits to our agricultural population, increased industrial activity, and profits to our merchants. Of equal moment, there is evident a restoration of that spirit of confidence and faith which marks the American character. Let him, who, for speculative profit or partisan purpose, without just warrant would seek to disturb or dispel this assurance, take heed before he assumes responsibility for any act which slows our onward steps.

Throughout the world, change is the order of the day. In every nation economic problems, long in the making, have brought crises of many kinds for which the masters of old practice and theory were unprepared. In most nations social justice, no longer a distant ideal, has become a definite goal, and ancient governments are beginning to heed the call.

Thus, the American people do not stand alone in the world in their desire for change. We seek it through tested liberal traditions, through processes which retain all of the deep essentials of that republican form of representative government first given to a troubled world by the United States.

As the various parts in the program begun in the Extraordinary Session of the 73rd Congress shape themselves in practical administration, the unity of our program reveals itself to the nation. The outlines of the new economic order, rising from the disintegration of the old, are apparent. We test what we have done as our measures take root in the living texture of life. We see where we have built wisely and where we can do still better.

The attempt to make a distinction between recovery and reform is a narrowly conceived effort to substitute the appearance of reality for reality itself. When a man is convalescing from illness, wisdom dictates not only cure of the symptoms, but also removal of their cause.

It is important to recognize that while we seek to outlaw specific abuses, the American objective of today has an infinitely deeper, finer and more lasting purpose than mere repression. Thinking people in almost every country of the world have come to realize certain fundamental difficulties with which civilization must reckon. Rapid changes—the machine age, the advent of universal and rapid communication and many other new factors—have brought new problems. Succeeding generations have attempted to keep pace by reforming in piecemeal fashion this or that attendant abuse. As a result, evils overlap and reform becomes confused and frustrated. We lose sight, from time to time, of our ultimate human objectives.

Let us, for a moment, strip from our simple purpose the confusion that results from a multiplicity of detail and from millions of written and spoken words.

We find our population suffering from old inequalities, little changed by past sporadic remedies. In spite of our efforts and in spite of our talk, we have not weeded out the over privileged and we have not effectively lifted up the underprivileged. Both of these manifestations of injustice have retarded happiness. No wise man has any intention of destroying what is known as the profit motive because by the profit motive we mean the right by work to earn a decent livelihood for ourselves and for our families.

We have, however, a clear mandate from the people, that Americans must forswear that conception of the acquisition of wealth which, through excessive profits, creates undue private power over private affairs and, to our misfortune, over public affairs as well. In building toward this end we do not destroy ambition, nor do we seek to divide our wealth into equal shares on stated occasions. We continue to recognize the greater ability of some to earn more than others. But we do assert that the ambition of the individual to obtain for him and his a proper security, a reasonable leisure, and a decent living throughout life, is an ambition to be preferred to the appetite for great wealth and great power.

I recall to your attention my message to the Congress last June in which I said: "among our objectives I place the security of the men, women and children of the nation first." That remains our first and continuing task; and in a very real sense every major legislative enactment of this Congress should be a component part of it.

In defining immediate factors which enter into our quest, I have spoken to the Congress and the people of three great divisions: (1) The security of a livelihood through the better use of the national resources of the land in which we live; (2) The security against the major hazards and vicissitudes of life; (3) The security of decent homes.

I am now ready to submit to the Congress a broad program designed ultimately to establish all three of these factors of security—a program which because of many lost years will take many future years to fulfill.

A study of our national resources, more comprehensive than any previously made, shows the vast amount of necessary and practicable work which needs to be done for the development and preservation of our natural wealth for the enjoyment and advantage of our people in generations to come. The sound use of land and water is far more comprehensive than the mere planting of trees, building of dams, distributing of electricity or retirement of sub-marginal land. It recognizes that stranded populations, either in the country or the city, cannot have security under the conditions that now surround them.

To this end we are ready to begin to meet this problem—the intelligent care of population throughout our nation, in accordance with an intelligent distribution of the means of livelihood for that population. A definite program for putting people to work, of which I shall speak in a moment, is a component part of this greater program of security of livelihood through the better use of our national resources.

Closely related to the broad problem of livelihood is that of security against the major hazards of life. Here also, a comprehensive survey of what has been attempted or accomplished in many nations and in many States proves to me that the time has come for action by the national government. I shall send to you, in a few days, definite recommendations based on these studies. These recommendations will cover the broad subjects of unemployment insurance and old age insurance, of benefits for children, for mothers, for the handicapped, for maternity care and for other aspects of dependency and illness where a beginning can now be made.

The third factor—better homes for our people—has also been the subject of experimentation and study. Here, too, the first practical steps can be made through the proposals which I shall suggest in relation to giving work to the unemployed.

Whatever we plan and whatever we do should be in the light of these three clear objectives of security. We cannot afford to lose valuable time in haphazard public policies which cannot find a place in the broad outlines of these major purposes. In that spirit I come to an immediate issue made for us by hard and inescapable circumstance—the task of putting people to work. In the spring of 1933 the issue of destitution seemed to stand apart; today, in the light of our experience and our new national policy, we find we can put people to work in ways which conform to, initiate and carry forward the broad principles of that policy.

The first objectives of emergency legislation of 1933 were to relieve destitution, to make it possible for industry to operate in a more rational and orderly fashion, and to put behind industrial recovery the impulse of large expenditures in government undertakings. The purpose of the National Industrial Recovery Act to provide work for more people succeeded in a substantial manner within the first few months of its life, and the Act has continued to maintain employment gains and greatly improved working conditions in industry.

The program of public works provided for in the Recovery Act launched the Federal Government into a task for which there was little time to make preparation and little American experience to follow. Great employment has been given and is being given by these works.

More than two billions of dollars have also been expended in direct relief to the destitute. Local agencies of necessity determined the recipients of this form of relief. With inevitable exceptions the funds were spent by them with reasonable efficiency and as a result actual want of food and clothing in the great majority of cases has been overcome.

But the stark fact before us is that great numbers still remain unemployed.

A large proportion of these unemployed and their dependents have been forced on the relief rolls. The burden on the Federal Government has grown with great rapidity. We have here a human as well as an economic problem. When humane considerations are concerned, Americans give them precedence. The lessons of history, confirmed by the evidence immediately before me, show conclusively that continued dependence upon relief induces a spiritual and moral disintegration fundamentally destructive to the national fibre. To dole out relief in this way is to administer a narcotic, a subtle destroyer of the human spirit. It is inimical to the dictates of sound policy. It is in violation of the traditions of America. Work must be found for able-bodied but destitute workers.

The Federal Government must and shall quit this business of relief.

I am not willing that the vitality of our people be further sapped by the giving of cash, of market baskets, of a few hours of weekly work cutting grass, raking leaves or picking up papers in the public parks. We must preserve not only the bodies of the unemployed from destitution but also their self-respect, their self-reliance and courage and determination. This decision brings me to the problem of what the government should do with approximately five million unemployed now on the relief rolls.

About one million and a half of these belong to the group which in the past was dependent upon local welfare efforts. Most of them are unable for one reason or another to maintain themselves independently—for the most part, through no fault of their own. Such people, in the days before the great depression, were cared for by local efforts—by States, by counties, by towns, by cities, by churches and by private welfare agencies. It is my thought that in the future they must be cared for as they were before. I stand ready through my own personal efforts, and through the public influence of the office that I hold, to help these local agencies to get the means necessary to assume this burden.

The security legislation which I shall propose to the Congress will, I am confident, be of assistance to local effort in the care of this type of cases. Local responsibility can and will be resumed, for, after all, common sense tells us that the wealth necessary for this task existed and still exists in the local community, and the dictates of sound administration require that this responsibility be in the first instance a local one.

There are, however, an additional three and one half million employable people who are on relief. With them the problem is different and the responsibility is different. This group was the victim of a nation-wide depression caused by conditions which were not local but national. The Federal Government is the only governmental agency with sufficient power and credit to meet this situation. We have assumed this task and we shall not shrink from it in the future. It is a duty dictated by every intelligent consideration of national policy to ask you to make it possible for the United States to give employment to all of these three and one half million employable people now on relief, pending their absorption in a rising tide of private employment.

It is my thought that with the exception of certain of the normal public building operations of the government, all emergency public works shall be united in a single new and greatly enlarged plan.

With the establishment of this new system we can supersede the Federal Emergency Relief Administration with a coordinated authority which will be charged with the orderly liquidation of our present relief activities and the substitution of a national chart for the giving of work.

This new program of emergency public employment should be governed by a number of practical principles.

1. All work undertaken should be useful—not just for a day, or a year, but useful in the sense that it affords permanent improvement in living conditions or that it creates future new wealth for the nation.

2. Compensation on emergency public projects should be in the form of security payments which should be larger than the amount now received as a relief dole, but at the same time not so large as to encourage the rejection of opportunities for private employment or the leaving of private employment to engage in government work.

3. Projects should be undertaken on which a large percentage of direct labor can be used.

4. Preference should be given to those projects which will be self-liquidating in the sense that there is a reasonable expectation that the government will get its money back at some future time.

5. The projects undertaken should be selected and planned so as to compete as little as possible with private enterprises. This suggests that if it were not for the necessity of giving useful work to the unemployed now on relief, these projects in most instances would not now be undertaken.

6. The planning of projects would seek to assure work during the coming fiscal year to the individuals now on relief, or until such time as private employment is available. In order to make adjustment to increasing private employment, work should be planned with a view to tapering it off in proportion to the speed with which the emergency workers are offered positions with private employers.

7. Effort should be made to locate projects where they will serve the greatest unemployment needs as shown by present relief rolls, and the broad program of the National Resources Board should be freely used for guidance in selection. Our ultimate objective being the enrichment of human lives, the government has the primary duty to use its emergency expenditures as much as possible to serve those who cannot secure the advantages of private capital....

The work itself will cover a wide field including clearance of slums, which for adequate reasons cannot be undertaken by private capital; in rural housing of several kinds, where, again, private capital is unable to function; in rural electrification; in the reforestation of the great watersheds of the nation; in an intensified program to prevent soil erosion and to reclaim blighted areas; in improving existing road systems and in constructing national highways designed to handle modern traffic; in the elimination of grade crossings; in the extension and enlargement of the successful work of the Civilian Conservation Corps; in non-Federal works, mostly self-liquidating and highly useful to local divisions of government; and on many other projects which the nation needs and cannot afford to neglect.

This is the method which I propose to you in order that we may better meet this present-day problem of unemployment. Its greatest advantage is that it fits logically and usefully into the long-range permanent policy of providing the three types of security which constitute as a whole an American plan for the betterment of the future of the American people.

I shall consult with you from time to time concerning other measures of national importance. Among the subjects that lie immediately before us are the consolidation of Federal Regulatory Administration over all forms of transportation, the renewal and clarification of the general purposes of the National Industrial Recovery Act, the strengthening of our facilities for the prevention, detection and treatment of crime and criminals, the restoration of sound conditions in the public utilities field through abolition of the evil features of holding companies, the gradual tapering off of the emergency credit activities of government, and improvement in our taxation forms and methods.

We have already begun to feel the bracing effect upon our economic system of a restored agriculture. The hundreds of millions of additional income that farmers are receiving are finding their way into the channels of trade. The farmers' share of the national income is slowly rising. The economic facts justify the widespread opinion of those engaged in agriculture that our provisions for maintaining a balanced production give at this time the most adequate remedy for an old and vexing problem. For the present, and especially in view of abnormal world conditions, agricultural adjustment with certain necessary improvements in methods should continue....

The ledger of the past year shows many more gains than losses. Let us not forget that, in addition to saving millions from utter destitution, child labor has been for the moment outlawed, thousands of homes saved to their owners and most important of all, the morale of the nation has been restored. Viewing the year 1934 as a whole, you and I can agree that we have a generous measure of reasons for giving thanks.

It is not empty optimism that moves me to a strong hope in the coming year. We can, if we will, make 1935 a genuine period of good feeling, sustained by a sense of purposeful progress. Beyond the material recovery, I sense a spiritual recovery as well. The people of America are turning as never before to those permanent values that are not limited to the physical objectives of life. There are growing signs of this on every hand. In the face of these spiritual impulses we are sensible of the Divine Providence to which nations turn now, as always, for guidance and fostering care.

XXIX
A.L.A. Schechter Poultry Corp. v. United States, 295 U.S. 495, May 27, 1935 (Opinion of the Court)

HUGHES, C. J. Petitioners were convicted in the District Court of the United States for the Eastern District of New York on eighteen counts of an indictment charging violations of what is known as the "Live Poultry Code," and on an additional count for conspiracy to commit such violations. By demurrer to the indictment and appropriate motions on the trial, the defendants contended (1) that the Code had been adopted pursuant to an unconstitutional delegation by Congress of legislative power; (2) that it attempted to regulate intrastate transactions which lay outside the authority of Congress; and (3) that in certain provisions it was repugnant to the due process clause of the Fifth Amendment.

The defendants are slaughterhouse operators...A.L.A. Schechter Poultry Corporation and Schechter Live Poultry Market are corporations conducting wholesale poultry slaughterhouse markets in Brooklyn, New York City.

Defendants ordinarily purchase their live poultry from commission men at the West Washington Market in New York City or at the railroad terminals serving the City, but occasionally they purchase from commission men in Philadelphia. They buy the poultry for slaughter and resale. After the poultry is trucked to their slaughterhouse markets in Brooklyn, it is there sold, usually within twenty-four hours, to retail poultry dealers and butchers who sell directly to consumers. The poultry purchased from defendants is immediately slaughtered, prior to delivery, by shochtim in defendants' employ. Defendants do not sell poultry in interstate commerce.

The "Live Poultry Code" was promulgated under section 3 of the National Industrial Recovery Act. That section authorizes the President to approve "codes of fair competition." Such a code may be approved for a trade or industry, upon application by one or more trade or industrial associations or groups, if the President finds (1) that such associations or groups "impose no inequitable restrictions on admission to membership therein and are truly representative," and (2) that such codes are not designed "to promote monopolies or to eliminate or oppress small enterprises and will not operate to discriminate against them, and will tend to effectuate the policy" of Title I of the act. Such codes "shall not permit monopolies or monopolistic practices." As a condition of his approval, the President may "impose such conditions (including requirements for the making of reports and the keeping of accounts) for the protection of consumers, competitors, employees, and others, and in furtherance of the public interest, and may provide such exceptions to and exemptions from the provisions of such code as the President in his discretion deems necessary to effectuate the policy herein declared." Where such a code has not been approved, the President may prescribe one, either on his own motion or on complaint. Violation of any provision of a code (so approved or prescribed) "in any transaction in or affecting interstate or foreign commerce" is made a misdemeanor punishable by a fine of not more than $500 for each offense, and each day the violation continues is to be deemed a separate offense.

The "Live Poultry Code" was approved by the President on April 13, 1934. Its divisions indicate its nature and scope. The Code has eight articles entitled (1) purposes, (2) definitions, (3) hours, (4) wages, (5) general labor provisions, (6) administration, (7) trade practice provisions, and (8) general.

The declared purpose is "To effect the policies of title I of the National Industrial Recovery Act." The Code is established as "a code for fair competition for the live poultry industry of the metropolitan area in and about the City of New York." That area is described as embracing the five boroughs of New York City, the counties of Rockland, Westchester, Nassau and Suffolk in the State of New York, the counties of Hudson and Bergen in the State of New Jersey, and the county of Fairfield in the State of Connecticut.

The "industry" is defined as including "every person engaged in the business of selling, purchasing for resale, transporting, or handling and/or slaughtering live poultry, from the time such poultry comes into the New York metropolitan area to the time it is first sold in slaughtered form," and such "related branches" as may from time to time be included by amendment. Employers are styled "members of the industry," and the term employee is defined to embrace "any and all persons engaged in the industry, however compensated," except "members."

The Code fixes the number of hours for work-days. It provides that no employee, with certain exceptions, shall be permitted to work in excess of forty (40) hours in any one week, and that no employee, save as stated, "shall be paid in any pay period less than at the rate of fifty (50) cents per hour." The article containing "general labor provisions" prohibits the employment of any person under sixteen years of age, and declares that employees shall have the right of "collective bargaining," and freedom of choice with respect to labor organizations, in the terms of section 7(a) of the Act. The minimum number of employees, who shall be employed by slaughterhouse operators, is fixed, the number being graduated according to the average volume of weekly sales.

The seventh article, containing "trade practice provisions," prohibits various practices which are said to constitute "unfair methods of competition."

Of the eighteen counts of the indictment upon which the defendants were convicted, aside from the count for conspiracy, two counts charged violation of the minimum wage and maximum hour provisions of the Code, and ten counts were for violation of the requirement (found in the "trade practice provisions") of "straight killing." The charges in the ten counts, respectively, were that the defendants in selling to retail dealers and butchers had permitted "selections of individual chickens taken from particular coops and half coops."

Of the other six counts, one charged the sale to a butcher of an unfit chicken; two counts charged the making of sales without having the poultry inspected or approved in accordance with regulations or ordinances of the City of New York; two counts charged the making of false reports or the failure to make reports relating to the range of daily prices and volume of sales for certain periods; and the remaining count was for sales to slaughterers or dealers who were without licenses required by the ordinances and regulations of the City of New York.

Two preliminary points are stressed by the government with respect to the appropriate approach to the important questions presented. We are told that the provision of the statute authorizing the adoption of codes must be viewed in the light of the grave national crisis with which Congress was confronted. Undoubtedly, the conditions to which power is addressed are always to be considered when the exercise of power is challenged. Extraordinary conditions may call for extraordinary remedies. But the argument necessarily stops short of an attempt to justify action which lies outside the sphere of constitutional authority.   Extraordinary conditions do not create or enlarge constitutional power.   The Constitution established a national government with powers deemed to be adequate, as they have proved to be both in war and peace, but these powers of the national government are limited by the constitutional grants. Those who act under these grants are not at liberty to transcend the imposed limits because they believe that more or different power is necessary.   Such assertions of extra-constitutional authority were anticipated and precluded by the explicit terms of the Tenth Amendment—"The powers not delegated to the United States by the Constitution, nor prohibited it to the States, are reserved to the States respectively, or to the people."

The further point is urged that the national crisis demanded a broad and intensive cooperative effort by those engaged in trade and industry, and that this necessary cooperation was sought to be fostered by permitting them to initiate the adoption of codes. But the statutory plan is not simply one for voluntary effort. It does not seek merely to endow voluntary trade or industrial associations or groups with privileges or immunities. It involves the coercive exercise of the lawmaking power. The codes of fair competition, which the statute attempts to authorize, are codes of laws. If valid, they place all persons within their reach under the obligation of positive law, binding equally those who assent and those who do not assent. Violations of the provisions of the codes are punishable as crimes.

[A] The question of the delegation of legislative power

For a statement of the authorized objectives and content of the "codes of fair competition" we are referred repeatedly to the "Declaration of Policy" in section one of Title I of the Recovery Act. Thus, the approval of a code by the President is conditioned on his finding that it "will tend to effectuate the policy of this title." Sec. 3 (a). The President is authorized to impose such conditions "for the protection of consumers, competitors, employees, and others, and in furtherance of the public interest, and may provide such exceptions to and exemptions from the provisions of such code as the President in his discretion deems necessary to effectuate the policy herein declared." *Id.* The "policy herein declared" is manifestly that set forth in section one. That declaration embraces a broad range of objectives. Among them we find the elimination of "unfair competitive practices."

We think the conclusion is inescapable that the authority sought to be conferred by Section 3 was not merely to deal with "unfair competitive practices" which offend against existing law, and could be the subject of judicial condemnation without further legislation, or to create administrative machinery for the application of established principles of law to particular instances of violation. Rather, the purpose is clearly disclosed to authorize new and controlling prohibitions through codes of laws which would embrace what the formulators would propose, and what the President would approve, or prescribe, as wise and beneficent measures for the government of trades and industries in order to bring about their rehabilitation, correction and development, according to the general declaration of policy in section one. Codes of laws of this sort are styled "codes of fair competition."

We find no real controversy upon this point and we must determine the validity of the Code in question in this aspect.

The question, then, turns upon the authority which Section 3 of the Recovery Act vests in the President to approve or prescribe. If the codes have standing as penal statutes, this must be due to the effect of the executive action. But Congress cannot delegate legislative power to the President to exercise an unfettered discretion to make whatever laws he thinks may be needed or advisable for the rehabilitation and expansion of trade or industry.

Accordingly we turn to the Recovery Act to ascertain what limits have been set to the exercise of the President's discretion. *First,* the

President, as a condition of approval, is required to find that the trade or industrial associations or groups which propose a code, "impose no inequitable restrictions on admission to membership" and are "truly representative." That condition, however, relates only to the status of the initiators of the new laws and not to the permissible scope of such laws. *Second,* the President is required to find that the code is not "designed to promote monopolies or to eliminate or oppress small enterprises and will not operate to discriminate against them." And, to this is added a proviso that the code "shall not permit monopolies or monopolistic practices." But these restrictions leave virtually untouched the field of policy envisaged by section one, and, in that wide field of legislative possibilities, the proponents of a code, refraining from monopolistic designs, may roam at will and the President may approve or disapprove their proposals as he may see fit.

Nor is the breadth of the President's discretion left to the necessary implications of this limited requirement as to his findings. As already noted, the President in approving a code may impose his own conditions, adding to or taking from what is proposed, as "in his discretion" he thinks necessary "to effectuate the policy" declared by the Act. Of course, he has no less liberty when he prescribes a code of his own motion or on complaint, and he is free to prescribe one if a code has not been approved. The Act provides for the creation by the President of administrative agencies to assist him, but the action or reports of such agencies, or of his other assistants—their recommendations and findings in relation to the making of codes—have no sanction beyond the will of the President, who may accept, modify or reject them as he pleases. Such recommendations or findings in no way limit the authority which section 3 undertakes to vest in the President with no other conditions than those there specified. And this authority relates to a host of different trades and industries, thus extending the President's discretion to all the varieties of laws which he may deem to be beneficial in dealing with the vast array of commercial and industrial activities throughout the country.

Such a sweeping delegation of legislative power finds no support in the decisions upon which the government especially relies.

To summarize and conclude upon this point: Section 3 of the Recovery Act is without precedent. It supplies no standards for any trade, industry or activity. It does not undertake to prescribe rules of conduct to be applied to particular states of fact determined by appropriate administrative procedure. Instead of prescribing rules of conduct, it authorizes the making of codes to prescribe them. For that legislative undertaking, section 3 sets up no standards, aside from the statement of the general aims of rehabilitation, correction and expansion described in section one. In view of the scope of that broad declaration, and of the nature of the few restrictions that are imposed, the discretion of the President in approving or prescribing codes, and thus enacting laws for the government of trade and industry throughout the country, is virtually unfettered. We think that the code-making authority thus conferred is an unconstitutional delegation of legislative power.

[B] The question of the application of the provisions of the Live Poultry Code to intrastate transactions

This aspect of the case presents the question whether the particular provisions of the Live Poultry Code, which the defendants were convicted for violating and for having conspired to violate, were within the regulating power of Congress.

These provisions relate to the hours and wages of those employed by defendants in their slaughterhouses in Brooklyn and to the sales there made to retail dealers and butchers.

(1) Were these transactions *"in"* interstate commerce? Much is made of the fact that almost all the poultry coming to New York is sent there from other States. But the code provisions, as here applied, do not concern the transportation of the poultry from other States to New York, or the transactions of the commission men or others to whom it is consigned, or the sales made by such consignees to defendants. When defendants had made their purchases, whether at the West Washington Market in New York City or at the railroad terminals serving the City, or elsewhere, the poultry was trucked to their slaughterhouses in Brooklyn for local disposition. The interstate transactions in relation to that poultry then ended. Defendants held the poultry at their slaughterhouse markets for slaughter and local sale to retail dealers and butchers who in turn sold directly to consumers. Neither the slaughtering nor the sales by defendants were transactions in interstate commerce.

The undisputed facts thus afford no warrant for the argument that the poultry handled by defendants at their slaughterhouse markets was in a *"current"* or *"flow"* of interstate commerce and was thus subject to congressional regulation. The mere fact that there may be a constant flow of commodities into a State does not mean that the flow continues after the property has arrived and has become commingled with the mass of property within the State and is there held solely for local disposition and use. So far as the poultry here in question is concerned, the flow in interstate commerce had ceased. The poultry had come to a permanent rest within the State. It was not held, used, or sold by defendants in relation to any further transactions in interstate commerce and was not destined for transportation to other states. Hence, decisions which deal with a stream of interstate commerce—where goods come to rest within a State temporarily and are later to go forward in interstate commerce—and with the regulations of transactions involved in that practical continuity of movement, are not applicable here.

(2) Did the defendants' transactions directly *"affect"* interstate commerce so as to be subject to federal regulation? The power of Congress extends not only to the regulation of transactions which are part of interstate commerce, but to the protection of that commerce from injury.

In determining how far the federal government may go in controlling intrastate transactions upon the ground that they "affect" interstate commerce, there is a necessary and well-established distinction between direct and indirect effects. The precise line can be drawn only as individual cases arise, but the distinction is clear in principle. Direct effects are illustrated by the railroad cases we have cited, as *e. g.*, the effect of failure to use prescribed safety appliances on railroads which are the highways of both interstate and intrastate commerce, injury to an employee engaged in interstate transportation by the negligence of an employee engaged in an intrastate movement, the fixing of rates for intrastate transportation which unjustly discriminate against interstate commerce. But where the effect of intrastate transactions upon interstate commerce is merely indirect, such transactions remain within the domain of state power. If the commerce clause were construed to reach all enterprises and transactions which could be said to have an indirect effect upon interstate commerce, the federal authority would embrace practically all the activities of the people and the authority of the State over its domestic concerns would exist only by sufferance of the federal government. Indeed, on such a theory, even the development of the State's commercial facilities would be subject to federal control.

The distinction between direct and indirect effects has been clearly recognized in the application of the Anti-Trust Act. Where a combination or conspiracy is formed, with the intent to restrain interstate commerce or to monopolize any part of it, the violation of the statute is clear. But where that intent is absent, and the objectives are limited to intrastate activities, the fact that there may be an indirect effect upon interstate commerce does not subject the parties to the federal statute, notwithstanding its broad provisions.

While these decisions related to the application of the federal statute, and not to its constitutional validity, the distinction between direct and indirect effects of intrastate transactions upon interstate commerce must be recognized as a fundamental one, essential to the maintenance of our constitutional system. Otherwise as we have said, there would be virtually no limit to the federal power and for all practical purposes we should have a completely centralized government. We must consider the provisions here in question in the light of this distinction.

The question of chief importance relates to the provisions of the Code as to the hours and wages of those employed in defendants' slaughterhouse markets. It is plain that these requirements are imposed in order to govern the details of defendants' management of their local business. The persons employed in slaughtering and selling in local trade are not employed in interstate commerce. Their hours and wages have no direct relation to interstate commerce. The question of how many hours these employees should work and what they should be paid differs in no essential respect from similar questions in other local businesses which handle commodities brought into a State and there dealt in as a part of its internal commerce. This appears from an examination of the considerations urged by the government with respect to conditions in the poultry trade. Thus, the government argues that hours and wages affect prices; that slaughterhouse men sell at a small margin above operating costs; that labor represents 50 to 60 percent of these costs; that a slaughterhouse operator paying lower wages or reducing his cost by exacting long hours of work, translates his saving into lower prices; that this results in demands for a cheaper grade of goods; and that the cutting of prices brings about demoralization of the price structure. Similar conditions may be adduced in relation to other businesses. The argument of the government proves too much. If the federal government may determine the wages and hours of employees in the internal commerce of a State, because of their relation to cost and prices and their indirect effect upon interstate commerce, it would seem that a similar control might be exerted over other elements of cost, also affecting prices, such as the number of employees, rents, advertising, methods of doing business, etc. All the processes of production and distribution that enter into cost could likewise be controlled. If the cost of doing an intrastate business is in itself the permitted object of federal control, the extent of the regulation of cost would be a question of discretion and not of power.

The government also makes the point that efforts to enact state legislation establishing high labor standards have been impeded by the belief that unless similar action is taken generally, commerce will be diverted from the States adopting such standards, and that this fear of diversion has led to demands for federal legislation on the subject of wages and hours. The apparent implication is that the federal authority under the commerce clause should be deemed to extend to the establishment of rules to govern wages and hours in intrastate trade and industry generally throughout the country, thus overriding the authority of the States to deal with domestic problems arising from labor conditions in their internal commerce.

It is not the province of the Court to consider the economic advantages or disadvantages of such a centralized system. It is sufficient to say that the Federal Constitution does not provide for it. Our growth and development have called for wide use of the commerce power of the federal government in its control over the expanded activities of interstate commerce, and in protecting that commerce from burdens, interferences, and conspiracies to restrain and monopolize it. But the authority of the federal government may not be pushed to such an extreme as to destroy the distinction, which the commerce clause itself establishes, between commerce "among the several States" and the internal concerns of a State. The same answer must be made to the contention that is based upon the serious economic situation which led to the passage of the Recovery Act—the fall in prices, the decline in wages and employment, and the curtailment of the market for commodities. Stress is laid upon the great importance of maintaining wage distributions which would provide the necessary stimulus in starting "the cumulative forces making for expanding commercial activity." Without in any way disparaging this motive, it is enough to say that the recuperative efforts of the federal government must be made in a manner consistent with the authority granted by the Constitution.

We are of the opinion that the attempt through the provisions of the Code to fix the hours and wages of employees of defendants in their intrastate business was not a valid exercise of federal power.

On both the grounds we have discussed, the attempted delegation of legislative power, and the attempted regulation of intrastate transactions which affect interstate commerce only indirectly, we hold the code provisions here in question to be invalid and that the judgment of conviction must be reversed.

XXX
The National Labor Relations Act
July 5, 1935

Findings and Policy

SECTION 1. The denial by employers of the right of employees to organize and the refusal by employers to accept the procedure of collective bargaining lead to strikes and other forms of industrial strife or unrest, which have the intent or the necessary effect of burdening or obstructing commerce by (a) impairing the efficiency, safety, or operation of the instrumentalities of commerce; (b) occurring in the current of commerce; (c) materially affecting, restraining, or controlling the flow of raw materials or manufactured or processed goods from or into the channels of commerce, or the prices of such materials or goods in commerce; or (d) causing diminution of employment and wages in such volume as substantially to impair or disrupt the market for goods flowing from or into the channels of commerce.

The inequality of bargaining power between employees who do not possess full freedom of association or actual liberty of contract, and employers who are organized in the corporate or other forms of ownership association substantially burdens and affects the flow of commerce, and tends to aggravate recurrent business depressions, by depressing wage rates and the purchasing power of wage earners in industry and by preventing the stabilization of competitive wage rates and working conditions within and between industries.

Experience has proved that protection by law of the right of employees to organize and bargain collectively safeguards commerce from injury, impairment, or interruption, and promotes the flow of commerce by removing certain recognized sources of industrial strife and unrest, by encouraging practices fundamental to the friendly adjustment of industrial disputes arising out of differences as to wages, hours, or other working conditions, and by restoring equality of bargaining power between employers and employees.

It is hereby declared to be the policy of the United States to eliminate the causes of certain substantial obstructions to the free flow of commerce and to mitigate and eliminate these obstructions when they have occurred by encouraging the practice and procedure of collective bargaining and by protecting the exercise by workers of full freedom of association, self-organization, and designation of representatives of their own choosing, for the purpose of negotiating the terms and conditions of their employment or other mutual aid or protection.

SEC. 2. When used in this Act—

(3) The term "employee" shall include any employee, and shall not be limited to the employees of a particular employer, unless the Act explicitly states otherwise, and shall include any individual whose work has ceased as a consequence of, or in connection with, any current labor dispute or because of any unfair labor practice, and who has not obtained any other regular and substantially equivalent employment, but shall not include any individual employed as an agricultural laborer, or in the domestic service of any family or person at his home, or any individual employed by his parent or spouse....

(5) The term "labor organization" means any organization of any kind, or any agency or employee representation committee or plan, in which employees participate and which exists for the purpose, in whole or in part, of dealing with employers concerning grievances, labor disputes, wages, rates of pay, hours of employment, or conditions of work.

(6) The term "commerce" means trade, traffic, commerce, transportation, or communication among the several States....

(7) The term "affecting commerce" means in commerce, or burdening or obstructing commerce or the free flow of commerce, or having led or tending to lead to a labor dispute burdening or obstructing commerce or the free flow of commerce....

(9) The term "labor dispute" includes any controversy concerning terms, tenure or conditions of employment, or concerning the association or representation of persons in

negotiating, fixing, maintaining, changing, or seeking to arrange terms or conditions of employment, regardless of whether the disputants stand in the proximate relation of employer and employee....

National Labor Relations Board

SEC. 3. (a) There is hereby created a board, to be known as the "National Labor Relations Board," which shall be composed of three members, who shall be appointed by the President, by and with the advice and consent of the Senate. One of the original members shall be appointed for a term of one year, one for a term of three years, and one for a term of five years, but their successors shall be appointed for terms of five years each, except that any individual chosen to fill a vacancy shall be appointed only for the unexpired term of the member whom he shall succeed. The President shall designate one member to serve as chairman of the Board. Any member of the Board may be removed by the President, upon notice and hearing, for neglect of duty or malfeasance in office, but for no other cause....

SEC. 6. (a) The Board shall have authority from time to time to make, amend, and rescind such rules and regulations as may be necessary to carry out the provisions of this Act. Such rules and regulations shall be effective upon publication in the manner which the Board shall prescribe.

Rights of Employees

SEC. 7. Employees shall have the right of self-organization, to form, join, or assist labor organizations, to bargain collectively through representatives of their own choosing, and to engage in concerted activities, for the purpose of collective bargaining or other mutual aid or protection.

SEC. 8. It shall be an unfair labor practice for an employer—

(1) To interfere with, restrain, or coerce employees in the exercise of the rights guaranteed in section 7....

(3) By discrimination in regard to hire or tenure of employment or any term or condition of employment to encourage or discourage membership in any labor organization: *Provided,* That nothing in this Act, or in the National Industrial Recovery Act (U.S. C., Supp. VII, title 15, sees. 701712), as amended from time to time, or in any code or agreement approved or prescribed thereunder, or in any other statute of the United States, shall preclude an employer from making an agreement with a labor organization (not established,

maintained, or assisted by any action defined in this Act as an unfair labor practice) to require as a condition of employment membership therein, if such labor organization is the representative of the employees as provided in section 9 (a), in the appropriate collective bargaining unit covered by such agreement when made.

(4) To discharge or otherwise discriminate against an employee because he has filed charges or given testimony under this Act.

(5) To refuse to bargain collectively with the representatives of his employees, subject to the provisions of Section 9 (a).

Representatives and Elections

SEC. 9. (a) Representatives designated or selected for the purposes of collective bargaining by the majority of the employees in a unit appropriate for such purposes, shall be the exclusive representatives of all the employees in such unit for the purposes of collective bargaining in respect to rates of pay, wages, hours of employment, or other conditions of employment: *Provided,* That any individual employee or a group of employees shall have the right at any time to present grievances to their employer.

(b) The Board shall decide in each case whether, in order to insure to employees the full benefit of their right to self-organization and to collective bargaining, and otherwise to effectuate the policies of this Act, the unit appropriate for the purposes of collective bargaining shall be the employer unit, craft unit, plant unit, or subdivision thereof.

(c) Whenever a question affecting commerce arises concerning the representation of employees, the Board may investigate such controversy and certify to the parties, in writing, the name or names of the representatives that have been designated or selected. In any such investigation, the Board shall provide for an appropriate hearing upon due notice, either in conjunction with a proceeding under section 10 or otherwise, and may cake a secret ballot of employees, or utilize any other suitable method to ascertain such representatives.

(d) Whenever an order of the Board made pursuant to section 10 (c) is based in whole or in part upon facts certified following an investigation pursuant to subsection (c) of this section, and there is a petition for the enforcement or review of such order, such certification and the record of such investigation shall be included in the transcript of the entire record required to be filed under subsections 10 (e) or 10 (f), and thereupon the decree of the court enforcing, modifying, or setting aside in whole or in part the order of the Board shall be made and entered upon the pleadings, testimony, and proceedings set forth in such transcript.

Prevention of Unfair Labor Practices

SEC. 10. (a) The Board is empowered, as hereinafter provided, to prevent any person from engaging in any unfair labor practice (listed in section 8) affecting commerce. This power shall be exclusive, and shall not be affected by any other means of adjustment or prevention that has been or may be established by agreement, code, law, or other wise.

(c) The testimony taken by such member, agent or agency or the Board shall be reduced to writing and filed with the Board. Thereafter, in its discretion, the Board upon notice may take further testimony or hear argument. If upon all the testimony taken the Board shall be of the opinion that any person named in the complaint has engaged in or is engaging in any such unfair labor practice, then the Board shall state its findings of fact and shall issue and cause to be served on such person an order requiring such person to cease and desist from such unfair labor practice, and to take such affirmative action, including reinstatement of employees with or without back pay, as will effectuate the policies of this Act. Such order may further require such person to make reports from time to time showing the extent to which it has complied with the order. If upon all the testimony taken the Board shall be of the opinion that no person named in the complaint has engaged in or is engaging in any such unfair labor practice, then the Board shall state its findings of fact and shall issue an order dismissing the said complaint....

Investigatory Powers

SEC. 11. For the purpose of all hearings and investigations...

(1) The Board, or its duly authorized agents or agencies, shall at all reasonable times have access to, for the purpose of examination, and the right to copy any evidence of any person being investigated or proceeded against that relates to any matter under investigation or in question. Any member of the Board shall have power to issue subpoenas requiring the attendance and testimony of witnesses and the production of any evidence that relates to any matter under investigation or in question, before the Board, its member, agent, or agency conducting the hearing or investigation....

SEC. 12. Any person who shall willfully resist, prevent, impede, or interfere with any member of the Board or any of its agents or agencies in the performance of duties pursuant to this Act shall be punished by a fine of not more than $5,000 or by imprisonment for not more than one year, or both.

Limitations

SEC. 13. Nothing in this Act shall be construed so as to interfere with or impede or diminish in any way the right to strike....

SEC. 15. If any provision of this Act, or the application of such provision to any person or circumstance, shall be held invalid, the remainder of this Act, or the application of such provision to persons or circumstances other than those as to which it is held invalid, shall not be affected thereby....

XXXI
The Social Security Act
August 14, 1935
(Excerpts)

TITLE I. GRANTS TO STATES FOR OLD AGE ASSISTANCE
[A] Appropriation

SECTION 1. For the purpose of enabling each State to furnish financial assistance, as far as practicable under the conditions in such State, to aged needy individuals, there is hereby authorized to be appropriated for the fiscal year ending June 30, 1936, the sum of $49,750,000, and there is hereby authorized to be appropriated for each fiscal year thereafter a sum sufficient to carry out the purposes of this title. The sums made available under this section shall be used for making payments to States which have submitted, and had approved by the Social Security Board established by Title VII, State plans for old-age assistance.

[B] State Old-age Assistance Plans

SEC. 2. (a) A State plan for old-age assistance must (1) provide that it shall be in effect in all political subdivisions of the State, and, if administered by them, be mandatory upon them; (2) provide for financial participation by the State; (3) either provide for the establishment or designation of a single State agency to administer the plan, or provide for the establishment or designation of a single State agency to supervise the administration of the plan; (4) provide for granting to any individual, whose claim for old-age assistance is denied, an opportunity for a fair hearing before such State agency; (5) provide such methods of administration (other than those relating to selection, tenure of office, and compensation of personnel) as are found by the Board to be necessary for the efficient operation of the plan; (6) provide that the State agency will make such reports, in such form and containing such information, as the Board may from time to time require, and comply with such provisions as the Board may from time to time find necessary to assure the correctness and verification of such reports; and (7) provide that, if the State or any of its political subdivisions collects from the estate of any recipient of old-age assistance any amount with respect to old-age assistance furnished him under the plan, one-half of the net amount so collected shall be promptly paid to the United States. Any payment so made shall be deposited in the Treasury to the credit of the appropriation for the purposes of this title.

(b) The Board shall approve any plan which fulfills the conditions specified in subsection (a), except that it shall not approve any plan which imposes, as a condition of eligibility for old-age assistance under the plan—(1) An age requirement of more than sixty-five years, except that the plan may impose, effective until January 1, 1940, an age requirement of as much as seventy years; or (2) Any residence requirement which excludes any resident of the State who has resided therein five years during the nine years immediately preceding the application for old-age assistance and has resided therein continuously for one year immediately preceding the application; or (3) Any citizenship requirement which excludes any citizen of the United States.

[C] Payment to States

SEC. 3. (a) From the sums appropriated therefore, the Secretary of the Treasury shall pay to each State which has an approved plan for old-age assistance, for each quarter, beginning with the quarter commencing July 1, 1935, (1) an amount, which shall be used exclusively as old-age assistance, equal to one-half of the total of the sums expended during such quarter as old-age assistance under the State plan with respect to each individual who at the time of such expenditure is sixty-five years of age or older and is not an inmate of a public institution, not counting so much of such expenditure with respect to any individual for any month as exceeds $30, and (2) 5 per centum of such amount, which shall be used for paying the costs of administering the State plan or for old-age assistance, or both, and for no other purpose: *Provided,* That the State plan, in order to be approved by the Board, need not provide for financial participation before July 1, 1937 by the State, in the case of any State which the Board, upon application by the State and after reasonable notice and opportunity for hearing to the State, finds is prevented by its constitution from providing such financial participation.

(b) The method of computing and paying such amounts shall be as follows: (1) The Board shall, prior to the beginning of each quarter, estimate the amount to be paid to the State for such quarter under the provisions of clause (1) of subsection (a), such estimate to be based on (A) a report filed by the State containing its estimate of the total sum to be expended in such quarter in accordance with the provisions of such clause, and stating the amount appropriated or made available by the State and its political subdivisions for such expenditures in such quarter, and if such amount is less than one-half of the total sum of such estimated expenditures, the source or sources from which the difference is expected to be derived, (B) records showing the number of aged individuals in the State, and (C) such other investigation as the Board may find necessary....

TITLE II. FEDERAL OLD-AGE BENEFITS
[A] Old-Age Benefit Payments
SEC. 202. (a) Every qualified individual shall be entitled to receive, with respect to the period beginning on the date he attains the age of sixty-five, or on January 1, 1942, whichever is the later, and ending on the date of his death, an old-age benefit (payable as nearly as practicable in equal monthly installments) as follows:

(1) If the total wages determined by the Board to have been paid to him, with respect to employment after December 31, 1936, and before he attained the age of sixty-five, were not more than $3,000, the old-age benefit shall be at a monthly rate of one-half of 1 per centum of such total wages;

(2) If such total wages were more than $3,000, the old-age benefit shall be at a monthly rate equal to the sum of the following: (A) One-half of 1 per centum of $3,000; plus (B) One-twelfth of 1 per centum of the amount by which such total wages exceeded $3,000 and did not exceed $45,000; plus (C) One-twenty-fourth of

1 per centum of the amount by which such total wages exceeded $45,000. (b) In no case shall the monthly rate computed under subsection (a) exceed $85....

[B] Payments upon Death

SEC. 203. (a) If any individual dies before attaining the age of sixty-five, there shall be paid to his estate an amount equal to 3 1/2 per centum of the total wages determined by the Board to have been paid to him, with respect to employment after December 31, 1936....

[C] Payments to Aged Individuals Not Qualified for Benefits

SEC. 204. (a) There shall be paid in a lump sum to any individual who, upon attaining the age of sixty-five, is not a qualified individual, an amount equal to 3 1/2 per centum of the total wages determined by the Board to have been paid to him, with respect to employment after December 31, 1936, and before he attained the age of sixty-five.

(b) After any individual becomes entitled to any payment under subsection (a), no other payment shall be made under this title in any manner measured by wages paid to him, except that any part of any payment under subsection (a) which is not paid to him before his death shall be paid to his estate....

SEC. 210...(b) The term "employment" means any service, of whatever nature, performed within the United States by an employee for his employer, except (1) Agricultural labor; (2) Domestic service in a private home; (3) Casual labor not in the course of the employer's trade or business; (4) Service performed as an officer or member of the crew of a vessel documented under the laws of the United States or of any foreign country; (5) Service performed in the employ of the United States Government or of an instrumentality of the United States; (6) Service performed in the employ of a State, a political subdivision thereof, or an instrumentality of one or more States or political subdivisions; (7) Service performed in the employ of a corporation, community chest, fund, or foundation, organized and operated exclusively for religious, charitable, scientific, literary, or educational purposes, or for the prevention of cruelty to children or animals, no part of the net earnings of which inures to the benefit of any private shareholder or individual.

TITLE III. GRANTS TO STATES FOR UNEMPLOYMENT COMPENSATION ADMINISTRATION

[A] Appropriation

SECTION 301. For the purpose of assisting the States in the administration of their unemployment compensation laws, there is hereby authorized to be appropriated, for the fiscal year ending June 30, 1936, the sum of $4,000,000, and for each fiscal year thereafter the sum of $49,000,000, to be used as hereinafter provided.

[B] Payments to States

SEC. 302. (a) The Board shall from time to time certify to the Secretary of the Treasury for payment to each State which has an unemployment compensation law approved by the Board under Title IX, such amounts as the Board determines to be necessary for the proper administration of such law during the fiscal year in which such payment is to be made. The Board's determination shall be based on (1) the population of the State; (2) an estimate of the number of persons covered by the State law and of the cost of proper administration of such law; and (3) such other factors as the Board finds relevant. The Board shall not certify for payment under this section in any fiscal year a total amount in excess of the amount appropriated therefore for such fiscal year....

[C] Provisions of State Laws

SEC. 303. (a) The Board shall make no certification for payment to any State unless it finds that the law of such State, approved by the Board under Title IX, includes provisions for—(1) Such methods of administration (other than those relating to selection, tenure of office, and compensation of personnel) as are found by the Board to be reasonably calculated to insure full payment of unemployment compensation when due; and (2) Payment of unemployment compensation solely through public employment offices in the State or such other agencies as the Board may approve; and (3) Opportunity for a fair hearing, before an impartial tribunal, for all individuals whose claims for unemployment compensation are denied; and (4) The payment of all money received in the unemployment fund of such State, immediately upon such receipt, to the Secretary of the Treasury to the credit of the Unemployment Trust Fund established by section 904; and (5) Expenditure of all money requisitioned by the State agency from the Unemployment Trust Fund, in the payment of unemployment compensation, exclusive of expenses of administration; and (6) The making of such reports, in such form and containing such information, as the Board may from time to time require, and compliance with such provisions as the Board may from time to time find necessary to assure the correctness and verification of such reports; and (7) Making available upon request to any agency of the United States charged with the administration of public works or assistance through public employment, the name, address, ordinary occupation and employment status of each recipient of unemployment compensation, and a statement of such recipient's rights to further compensation under such law.

(b) Whenever the Board, after reasonable notice and opportunity for hearing to the State agency charged with the administration of the State law, finds that in the administration of the law there is— (1) a denial, in a substantial number of cases, of unemployment compensation to individuals entitled thereto under such law; or (2) a failure to comply substantially with any provision specified in subsection (a); the Board shall notify such State agency that further payments will not be made to the State until the Board is satisfied that there is no longer any such denial or failure to comply. Until it is so satisfied it shall make no further certification to the Secretary of the Treasury with respect to such State.

TITLE IV. GRANTS TO STATES FOR AID TO DEPENDENT CHILDREN
[A] Appropriation
SECTION 401. For the purpose of enabling each State to furnish financial assistance, as far as practicable under the conditions in such State, to needy dependent children, there is hereby authorized to be appropriated for the fiscal year ending June 30, 1936, the sum of $24,750,000, and there is hereby authorized to be appropriated for each fiscal year thereafter a sum sufficient to carry out the purposes of this title. The sums made available under this section shall be used for making payments to States which have submitted, and had approved by the Board, State plans for aid to dependent children.....

SEC. 403. (a) From the sums appropriated therefore, the Secretary of the Treasury shall pay to each State which has an approved plan for aid to dependent children, for each quarter, beginning with the quarter commencing July 1, 1935, an amount, which shall be used exclusively for carrying out the State plan, equal to one-third of the total of the sums expended during such quarter under such plan, not counting so much of such expenditure with respect to any dependent child for any month as exceeds $18, or if there is more than one dependent child in the same home, as exceeds $18 for any month with respect to one such dependent child and $12 for such month with respect to each of the other dependent children....

[B] Definitions
SEC. 406. When used in this title—

(a) The term "dependent child" means a child under the age of sixteen who has been deprived of parental support or care by reason of the death, continued absence from the home, or physical or mental incapacity of a parent, and who is living with his father, mother, grandfather, grandmother, brother, sister, stepfather, stepmother, step brother, stepsister, uncle, or aunt, in a place of residence maintained by one or more of such relatives as his or their own home....

TITLE V. GRANTS TO STATES FOR MATERNAL AND CHILD WELFARE
Part 1—Maternal and Child Health Services
[A] Appropriation
SECTION 501. For the purpose of enabling each State to extend and improve, as far as practicable under the conditions in such State, services for promoting the health of mothers and children, especially in rural areas and in areas suffering from severe economic distress, there is hereby authorized to be appropriated for each fiscal year, beginning with the fiscal year ending June 30, 1936, the sum of $3,800,000. The sums made available under this section shall be used for making payments to States which have submitted, and had approved by the Chief of the Children's Bureau, State plans for such services.

[B] Allotments to States
SEC. 502. (a) Out of the sums appropriated pursuant to section 501 for each fiscal year the Secretary of Labor shall allot to each State $20,000, and such part of $1,800,000 as he finds that the number of live births in such State bore to the total number of live births in the United States, in the latest calendar year for which the Bureau of the Census has available statistics.

(b) Out of the sums appropriated pursuant to section 501 for each fiscal year the Secretary of Labor shall allot to the States $980,000 (in addition to the allotments made under subsection (a)), according to the financial need for each

State for assistance in carrying out its State plan, as determined by him after taking into consideration the number of live births in such State....

[C] Approval of State Plans

SEC. 503. (a) A State plan for maternal and child health services must (1) provide for financial participation by the State; (2) provide for the administration of the plan by the State health agency or the supervision of the administration of the plan by the State health agency; (3) provide such methods of administration (other than those relating to selection, tenure of office, and compensation of personnel) as are necessary for the efficient operation of the plan; (4) provide that the State health agency will make such reports, in such form and containing such information, as the Secretary of Labor may from time to time require, and comply with such provisions as he may from time to time find necessary to assure the correctness and verification of such reports; (5) provide for the extension and improvement of local maternal and child health services administered by local child health units; (6) provide for cooperation with medical, nursing, and welfare groups and organizations; and (7) provide for the development of demonstration services in needy areas and among groups in special need....

Part 2—Services for Crippled Children Appropriation

SEC. 511. For the purpose of enabling each State to extend and improve (especially in rural areas and in areas suffering from severe economic distress), as far as practicable under the conditions in such State, services for locating crippled children, and for providing medical, surgical, corrective, and other services and care, and facilities for diagnosis, hospitalization, and aftercare, for children who are crippled or who are suffering from conditions which lead to crippling, there is hereby authorized to be appropriated for each fiscal year, beginning with the fiscal year ending June 30, 1936, the sum of $2,850,000. The sums made available under this section shall be used for making payments to States which have submitted, and had approved by the Chief of the Children's Bureau, State plans for such services.

[A] Allotments to States

SEC. 512. (a) Out of the sums appropriated pursuant to section 511 for each fiscal year the Secretary of Labor shall allot to each State $20,000, and the remainder to the States according to the need of each State as determined by him after taking into consideration the number of crippled children in such State in need of the services referred to in section 511 and the cost of furnishing such services to them.

Part 3—Child Welfare Services

SEC. 521. (a) For the purpose of enabling the United States, through the Children's Bureau, to cooperate with State public-welfare agencies in establishing, extending, and strengthening, especially in predominantly rural areas, public-welfare services (hereinafter in this section referred to as "child welfare services") for the protection and care of homeless, dependent, and neglected children, and children in danger of becoming delinquent, there is hereby authorized to be appropriated for each fiscal year, beginning with the fiscal year ending June 30, 1936, the sum of $1,500,000. Such amount shall be allotted by the Secretary of Labor for use by cooperating State public-welfare agencies on the basis of plans developed jointly by the State agency and the Children's Bureau, to each State, $10,000, and the remainder to each State on the basis of such plans, not to exceed such part of the remainder as the rural population of such State bears to the total rural population of the United States. The amount so allotted shall be expended for payment of part of the cost of district, county or other local child-welfare services in areas predominantly rural, and for developing State services for the encouragement and assistance of adequate methods of community child-welfare organization in areas predominantly rural and other areas of special need....

Part 4—Vocational Rehabilitation

SEC. 531. (a) In order to enable the United States to cooperate with the States and Hawaii in extending and strengthening their programs of vocational rehabilitation of the physically disabled, and to continue to carry out the provisions and purposes of the Act entitled "An Act to provide for the promotion of vocational rehabilitation of persons disabled in industry or otherwise and their return to civil employment," approved June 2, 1920...there is hereby authorized to be appropriated for the fiscal years ending June 30, 1936, and June 30, 1937, the sum of $841,000 for each such fiscal year in addition to the amount of the existing authorization, and for each fiscal year thereafter the sum of $1,938,000.

TITLE VI. PUBLIC HEALTH WORK
[A] Appropriation
SECTION 601. For the purpose of assisting States, counties, health districts, and other political subdivisions of the States in establishing and maintaining adequate public-health services, including the training of personnel for State and local health work, there is hereby authorized to be appropriated for each fiscal year, beginning with the fiscal year ending June 30, 1936, the sum of $8,000,000 to be used as hereinafter provided.

[B] State and Local Public Health Services
SEC. 602. (a) The Surgeon General of the Public Health Service, with the approval of the Secretary of the Treasury, shall, at the beginning of each fiscal year, allot to the States the total of (1) the amount appropriated for such year pursuant to section 601; and (2) the amounts of the allotments under this section for the preceding fiscal year remaining unpaid to the States at the end of such fiscal year. The amounts of such allotments shall be determined on the basis of (1) the population; (2) the special health problems; and (3) the financial needs; of the respective States. Upon making such allotments the Surgeon General of the Public Health Service shall certify the amounts thereof to the Secretary of the Treasury.

(b) The amount of an allotment to any State under subsection (a) for any fiscal year, remaining unpaid at the end of such fiscal year, shall be available for allotment to States under subsection (a) for the succeeding fiscal year, in addition to the amount appropriated for such year.

(c) Prior to the beginning of each quarter of the fiscal year, the Surgeon General of the Public Health Service shall, with the approval of the Secretary of the Treasury, determine in accordance with rules and regulations previously prescribed by such Surgeon General after consultation with a conference of the State and Territorial health authorities, the amount to be paid to each State for such quarter from the allotment to such State, and shall certify the amount so determined to the Secretary of the Treasury. Upon receipt of such certification, the Secretary of the Treasury shall, through the Division of Disbursement of the Treasury Department and prior to audit or settlement by the General Accounting Office, pay in accordance with such certification.

(d) The moneys so paid to any State shall be expended solely in carrying out the purposes specified in section 601, and in accordance with plans presented by the health authority of such State and approved by the Surgeon General of the Public Health Service.

[C] Investigations
SEC. 603. (a) There is hereby authorized to be appropriated for each fiscal year, beginning with the fiscal year ending June 30, 1936, the sum of $2,000,000 for expenditure by the Public Health Service for investigation of disease and problems of sanitation....

TITLE VII. SOCIAL SECURITY BOARD
[A] Establishment
SEC. 701. There is hereby established a Social Security Board to be composed of three members to be appointed by the President, by and with the advice and consent of the Senate. During his term of membership on the Board, no member shall engage in any other business, vocation, or employment. Not more than two of the members of the Board shall be members of the same political party. Each member shall receive a salary at the rate of $10,000 a year and shall hold office for a term of six years....

[B] Duties of the Social Security Board
SEC. 702. The Board shall perform the duties imposed upon it by this Act and shall also have the duty of studying and making recommendations as to the most effective methods of providing economic security through social insurance, and as to legislation and matters of administrative policy concerning old-age pensions, unemployment compensation, accident compensation, and related subjects.

TITLE VIII. TAXES WITH RESPECT TO EMPLOYMENT
[A] Income Tax on Employees
SEC. 801. In addition to other taxes, there shall be levied, collected, and paid upon the income of every individual a tax equal to the following percentages of the wages (as defined in section 811) received by him after December 31, 1936, with respect to employment (as defined in section 811) after such date:
(1) With respect to employment during the calendar years 1937, 1938, and 1939, the rate shall be 1 per centum.
(2) With respect to employment during the calendar years 1940, 1941, and 1942, the rate shall be 1 1/2 per centum.

(3) With respect to employment during the calendar years 1943, 1944, and 1945, the rate shall be 2 per centum.

(4) With respect to employment during the calendar years 1946, 1947, and 1948, the rate shall be 2 1/2 per centum.

(5) With respect to employment after December 31, 1948, the rate shall be 3 per centum.

[B] Deduction of Tax from Wages

SEC. 802. (a) The tax imposed by section 801 shall be collected by the employer of the taxpayer, by deducting the amount of the tax from the wages as and when paid....

[C] Excise Tax on Employers

SEC. 804. In addition to other taxes, every employer shall pay an excise tax, with respect to having individuals in his employ, equal to the following percentages of the wages (as defined in section 811) paid by him after December 31, 1936, with respect to employment (as defined in section 811) after such date:

(1) With respect to employment during the calendar years 1937, 1938, and 1939, the rate shall be 1 per centum.

(2) With respect to employment during the calendar years 1940, 1941, and 1942, the rate shall be 134 per centum.

(3) With respect to employment during the calendar years 1943, 1944, and 1945, the rate shall be 2 per centum.

(4) With respect to employment during the calendar years 1946, 1947, and 1948, the rate shall be 2 per centum.

(5) With respect to employment after December 31, 1948, the rate shall be 3 per centum....

[D] Definitions

SEC. 811. When used in this title—

(b) The term "employment" means any service, of whatever nature, performed within the United States by an employee for his employer, except—

(1) Agricultural labor;

(2) Domestic service in a private home;

(3) Casual labor not in the course of the employer's trade or business;

(4) Service performed by an individual who has attained the age of sixty-five;

(5) Service performed as an officer or member of the crew of a vessel documented under the laws of the United States or of any foreign country;

(6) Service performed in the employ of the United States Government or of an instrumentality of the United States;

(7) Service performed in the employ of a State, a political subdivision thereof, or an instrumentality of one or more States or political subdivisions;

(8) Service performed in the employ of a corporation, community chest, fund, or foundation, organized and operated exclusively for religious, charitable, scientific, literary, or educational purposes, or for the prevention of cruelty to children or animals, no part of the net earnings of which inures to the benefit of any private shareholder or individual.

TITLE IX. TAX ON EMPLOYERS OF EIGHT OR MORE
[A] Imposition of Tax

SECTION 901. On and after January 1, 1936, every employer shall pay for each calendar year an excise tax, with respect to having individuals in his employ, equal to the following percentages of the total wages payable by him with respect to employment during such calendar year:

(1) With respect to employment during the calendar year 1936 the rate shall be 1 per centum;

(2) With respect to employment during the calendar year 1937 the rate shall be 2 per centum;

(3) With respect to employment after December 31, 1937, the rate shall be 3 per centum....

[B] Certification of State Laws

SEC. 903. (a) The Social Security Board shall approve any State law submitted to it, within thirty days of such submission, which it finds provides that—

(1) All compensation is to be paid through public employment offices in the State or such other agencies as the Board may approve;

(2) No compensation shall be payable with respect to any day of unemployment occurring within two years after the first day of the first period with respect to which contributions are required;

(3) All money received in the unemployment fund shall immediately upon such receipt be paid over to the Secretary of the Treasury to the credit of the Unemployment Trust Fund....

(5) Compensation shall not be denied in such State to any otherwise eligible individual for refusing to accept new work under any of the following conditions: (A) If the position offered is vacant due

directly to a strike, lockout, or other labor dispute, (B) if the wages, hours, or other conditions of the work offered are substantially less favorable to the individual than those prevailing for similar work in the locality, (C) if as a condition of being employed the individual would be required to join a company union or to resign from or refrain from joining any bona fide labor organization.

[C] Unemployment Trust Fund

SEC. 904. (a) There is hereby established in the Treasury of the United States a trust fund to be known as the "Unemployment Trust Fund..."

(b) It shall be the duty of the Secretary of the Treasury to invest such portion of the Fund as is not, in his judgment, required to meet current withdrawals. Such investment may be made only in interest bearing obligations of the United States or in obligations guaranteed as to both principal and interest by the United States....

[D] Interstate Commerce

SEC. 906. No person required under a State law to make payments to an unemployment fund shall be relieved from compliance therewith on the ground that he is engaged in interstate commerce, or that the State law does not distinguish between employees engaged in interstate commerce and those engaged in intrastate commerce.

[E] Definitions

SEC. 907. When used in this title—

(a) The term "employer" does not include any person unless on each of some twenty days during the taxable year, each day being in a different calendar week, the total number of individuals who were in his employ for some portion of the day (whether or not at the same moment of time) was eight or more....

XXXII
Herbert Hoover:
Spending, Deficits, Debts, and Their Consequences
California Republican Assembly
Oakland, California, October 5, 1935

You represent the young men and women in American life. Before you is the responsibility of determining the fate of your generation. Three years ago we were warning America against the consequences of the adoption of the ideas and the system which have since been forced upon us. You have now had nearly three years in which these ideas and policies have dominated the nation. They are no longer glowing promises of the more abundant life. They are no longer emotional expressions of high objectives or good intentions. They are practices in government. You now deal with somber realities. Now they can be examined and appraised in the cold light of daily experience.

And we have need to awake from the spell of hypnotic slogans. Phrases can be made to scintillate like the aurora borealis, but such phrases are of as much practical utility in government of a great people as the aurora itself. But the issue of America is not a battle of phrases, but a battle between straight and crooked thinking. We need a return from muddling to sanity and realism. We need to test ideas and actions with the plain hard common sense which the America people possess more greatly than any other nation. We must bring that common sense into use if we are to resume the march of real progress.

The few minutes of this occasion do not afford time for examination or discussion of the enormous range of actions and confusions of public mind in these last three years. I therefore shall confine myself to one hard practical subject—the fiscal policies of this administration. In plain words I will discuss this policy of deliberate spending of public money.

I am taking up this issue because in this gigantic spending and this unbalanced budget is the most subtle and one of the most powerful dangers which has been set in motion by this administration. If it be continued, its result to you, the young men and women of America, is as inexorable as an avalanche.

We must first examine the record as to what is being done and then diagnose the consequences.

As to the records, if you will examine the Reports of the Bureau of the Budget, you will find that the Roosevelt Administration has changed the form of publishing governmental accounts. That raises a barrier against easy comparisons with previous administrations. All administrations since Washington were old-fashioned and simply put expenses down on one side of the ledger and receipts on the other. They did not try to fool the taxpayer or make the taxpayer feel better than he really was. Under the New Deal the expenditures have been divided into "Regular" expenditures and "Emergency" or "Recovery" expenditures. These are new words for an old South American and European device of dividing the budget into "ordinary" and "extraordinary" budgets.

That device is most helpful in abundant spending. By liberalism in what you designate as the "emergency" and "regular" expenditures you can blandly pronounce the ordinary budget as balanced. Then all your deficit is concentrated in the "extraordinary" or "emergency" part of the budget, and having made the deficit a plausible necessity you justify borrowing, and make the spending happier for everybody. The theory is that the next generation should pay for the emergencies of this generation.

The report of the Federal Budget Bureau shows that large items which have been an essential part of the government expenditures for years have now been styled "emergency." The vast area of spending through loans guaranteed by the government is not represented in the budget with any taxpayer's liability. Under this arrangement the losses on that will come to the next generation. And there are large items now excluded from the statements of expenditures which improve the looks of the accounts. These jugglings will no doubt ease the taxpayer's mind, but they will not relieve his pocket.

However, we can with diligence dig the facts out from under these methods, and despite all these obstacles can compute with fair certainty from the present commitments where the nation will be in another fifteen months.

The first conclusion is that all losses counted in the expenditures are now running over $8,000,000,000 a year. The annual deficit is running nearly three and a half billions, and each dollar of deficit is of course added to the national debt.

The second conclusion is that the unpaid government obligations which will fall upon the taxpayer at the end of the Roosevelt administration will exceed $35,000,000,000.

The third conclusion is that this peacetime debt will at the end of 1936 exceed our World War debt by ten billions, and the cost of the New Deal threatens to exceed that of the Great War.

Incidentally, outside of recoverable loans, the Roosevelt Administration spending will exceed the Hoover administration by from $14,000,000,000 to $15,000,000,000. I always have difficulty trying to comprehend what $14,000,000,000 or even $3,500,000,000 really is. But I know that even the mere $3,500,000,000 would buy me 90,000,000 suits of clothes. At least that is about one suit for every mile between the earth and the sun.

It is of course true that during the last years of the last Republican Administration deficits were incurred. Just as advance information on misrepresentation, I may state that the deficits of those years were not as large as are being made to appear by the New Deal publications. They include expenditures which the New Deal now excludes in publishing its own accounts. They also include over two billions of loans to industry, agriculture, and banks, which have since been mostly collected and spent by the New Deal administration. But the important thing is that the Republican administration genuinely endeavored to balance the whole government budget. That was not a pious subterfuge. It was a definite program. The record shows that in the year 1931 the Democratic Congress was urged by the Republican administration to enact additional revenues of $1,200,000,000 and to co-operate in a cut of $600,000,000 of less pressing expenditures. Only a part of this revenue was wrung from the Democratic Congress after nearly six months of fighting, delay, and obstruction, punctuated by vetoes of pork-barrel appropriations. Even then over half of the recommended decreases in expenditures were rejected. Again in 1932, $700,000,000 of additional revenues and $300,000,000 of additional reductions in expenditures were urged, and again, after months of delay, were refused altogether.

It is not overstatement to say that had the Republican principles of balancing the budget been accepted in 1931 and 1932, the final stone in the foundation of permanent recovery would have been laid three years ago instead of deferred for years hence.

I do not need recall the promises so vigorously put forward by the Democratic platform, the Democratic candidate, and the Democratic orators in the campaign of 1932—the promises that they would balance the budget and reduce expenditures by one billion a year. I may suggest that our opponents in 1932 would have received far less votes had they disclosed to the country their intention to increase the expenditures by $14,000,000,000 in four years; or had they disclosed that they would maintain a deficit of three and a half billions per annum; that they would increase the number of government bureaucracy by 160,000 persons and create five thousand paid committees and commissions. They would have lost still more votes had they informed us that they would abandon the gold standard; that they would devalue the dollar by 41 percent; that they would repudiate government obligations; that they would seek to circumvent the Constitution; that they would attempt to socialize and regiment Americans. It is perhaps not an overstatement that on the now demonstrated principles of this administration they could not have won the election of 1932.

But the wreckage of representative governments is strewn with broken promises.

I do not need to tell any one within the sound of my voice of that huge waste in government expenditures that is going on. Every one of you knows instance after instance of waste and folly in your own city and village. It appears day by day in the headlines of your papers. Think it over and multiply it by all the thousands of other towns and communities in the United States and get the appalling total.

I would call your attention to the numbers and potency of the army of spenders which has been created. According to the reports of the Civil Service Commission, there were about 573,000 civilian employees in the Federal Government at the end of the Coolidge administration. There were about 565,000 at the end of the Hoover administration. There are 730,000 today. And this does not include some 100,000 part-time paid members of some 5,000 committees and agencies of one sort or another who all spend money. Nor does it include the people on relief. The whole system of non-political appointments under the Civil Service which had been steadily built up by every administration for years has now been practically ignored. Almost this whole addition of 260,000 new people on the Federal payroll constitutes the most gigantic spoils raid in our history. Even Andrew Jackson appointed less than ten thousand.

Whenever you increase the numbers of political bureaucracy you not only have to pay them but they are veritable research laboratories for new inventions in spending money. Bureaucracy rushes headlong into visions of the millennium and sends the bill to the Treasury. And there are three implacable spirits in bureaucracy—self-perpetuation, expansion, and demand for more power. Moreover, they also serve to help win elections.

The Roosevelt Administration is now clutched in the meshes of the gigantic spending bureaucracy which it has created. Even with expenditures of some eight billions annually, with deficits of about $3,500,000,000, there is to be no "breathing spell" in spending, as witness the ten billions of new appropriations just passed by Congress. One administration writer kindly assures us that the budget will be balanced four years hence in 1939. That happy ending no doubt marks the end of anything to spend.

Incidentally the Congress supinely surrendered one of the hardest-won battles of human liberty—the control of the nation's purse.

When we protest at those expenditures we are met with the sneer, "Would you let the people starve?" No, never! It was, in fact, a Republican Administration that in 1930 announced that no American should go hungry or cold through no fault of his own. It organized the relief so effectively by co-operation of the Federal Government with the state and local authorities that the public health actually improved during that whole period. And here let me pay tribute to the thousands of devoted men and women who gave of their time and energies to conduct that relief over three long years. Theirs was no political objective. Nor was it their object to spend the people's money to prime economic pumps, nor to make social experiments which delayed real jobs. Theirs was a solicitude that those in distress from no fault of their own should be tided over until productive jobs returned.

Real relief is imperative, but its necessary and generous cost unmixed with other objectives would be but a minor part of this eight billions per annum. The presumed purpose of this spending has been to secure recovery. And we may well inquire what has been accomplished toward finding real jobs in productive industry and commerce by this roaring torrent of Federal spending and deficit. The best measure of the depression is the number of employed. Justly, I take the date of the election of November, 1932, for this test. For months prior to that election unemployment had been steadily decreasing, but with the election, industrial orders were canceled; the nation at once slowed down its engine. As the fiscal and currency policies of the New Deal were gradually disclosed, the nation skidded into a bank panic. From the day of that election, the New Deal policies dominated economic and business life. In October, 1932, prior to the election, there were 11,585,000 people out of work, according to the American Federation of Labor. Sixty days ago, two years and eight months after election, after all this gigantic spending, there were still 10,900,000 unemployed, according to the same authority, or a decrease of only 700,000. And if it were not for artificial support of industry by this hugely increased flood of government money, the unemployment would be greater than in 1932.

In any event, all this spending of deficits has not consequently restored genuine jobs in industry and commerce. The reduction of the unemployed was its only conceivable justification. As a matter of fact, until the Supreme Court decisions of last spring, the industrial world had been so scared as to stifle employment. By destroying confidence the administration has retarded recovery.

Since those Supreme Court decisions, the nation is showing some hopeful signs of progress. Every American prays that it may be genuine and come quickly—not alone because it would end infinite misery but because with recovery would come an atmosphere in which the vast problems of the nation can be solved more rationally and more fully. They could be solved in a spirit of Americanism rather than be dominated by the spirit of Europeanism. But whatever recovery we have is constantly endangered by this riotous spending and this unbalanced budget. We cannot spend ourselves into real prosperity. Certainly an artificial prosperity can be created by borrowing to spend, whether by individuals or governments. That is joy-riding to bankruptcy.

These gigantic budget deficits must inevitably be paid for somehow, sometime. There are only three ways to meet the unpaid bills of a government. The first is taxation. The second is repudiation. The third is inflation.

Already our country is highly taxed. Our total taxes today—Federal, state and local—are the highest of any great country in the world except the British, even in proportion to our national income. But the British have a balanced budget and are yearly reducing taxes. We, even with our burden of taxes today, must take on the further load from a budget about fifty percent balanced. We are on the way deeper into the morass of more and more taxes. The British are on their way out of the stifling swamp of taxation.

Who will pay these taxes? We have just seen a tax bill estimated to produce $300,000,000 per annum. That apparently could not have been designed to meet the regular annual deficit of three and a half billions. It was put forward with the slogan "Soak the Rich." But with the passage of that bill the rich are now "soaked." We may therefore conclude that some one else will have to meet the $3,250,000,000 remaining annual deficit if the bill is paid. If it is paid by taxes those taxes must fall on the so-called economic middle class and the poor. There is no one else left. The poor will pay out of indirect taxes, hidden in the rent and everything they buy. And when the price of the necessaries of life to those who have but a living wage is advanced by hidden taxes, those people are not sharing a surplus with the government. They have no surplus. The poor must go without something in order to pay the taxes wrapped up in the package they take from the store. Every butcher knows that today the poor are depriving themselves of bacon and meat. The economic middle class—whether they be farmers or workers at the bench or the desk, professional or businessmen—produce eighty percent of the national income. They, like the poor, will pay by indirect taxes in the cost of living, and in addition, they will pay again and again in direct taxes. No matter where you place taxes, the bulk of them must come from those who work and produce.

The subtle process of issuing government bonds to pay that deficit not only leaves it to be paid from your lifelong earnings, but it daily creates new dangers. No doubt these unpaid bills can be canceled by repudiation. The New Deal form of repudiation is devaluation. We can further devalue the dollar—which is, of course, repudiation on the installment plan. Devaluation is a modern and polite term for clipping the coin. Rome relied upon this method during its decline. If devaluation has the inflationary effect that the New Deal claims, then in the long run it raises the prices of everything we buy and the cost of living goes up to everybody, farmer and worker alike. The loss comes out of the people. But more than that, the returns from your insurance policy, your savings account for old age and for your children, your veteran's allowance, and your old-age pension, are also depleted in purchasing power. Who then pays? It is the same economic middle class and the poor. That would still be true if the rich were taxed to the whole amount of their fortunes.

It is not my purpose to discuss the credit or currency policies of this administration, but you may put it down both economically and historically that every continued government deficit has led to inflation in some form. That is the implacable avenger of profligate spending in government. Our government today is in large degree financing its deficit by credits from banks and financial institutions upon the government promise to pay. By this action a large part of that credit is being manufactured. I will not take your time to describe the process. It is a sort of dervish dance, whirling from budget deficits to government bonds, from bonds to bank credit, from bank credit to more government spending. That is one of the oldest and most dangerous expedients used by spendthrift governments. The new banking laws make it all easy. Governments must, in some emergencies, finance through the banks. But it must be only for the short interval necessary to raise increased revenues and reduce expenses.

This flood of spending is but one of the many realities of the New Deal. It is your duty to examine them all with the torch of common sense and appraise them in the sole light of the future of America. And you should examine them with open mind. You will find some that you should commend. You will find some of right objective and wrong method, such as the acts regulating securities, the old-age pensions, and unemployment insurance. You will find many that are destructive of every ideal and aspiration of American life and will destroy the value of all the acts that are good—and more.

And there is but one test you should apply—will these measures restore the prosperity of America? Will they restore agriculture? Will they give real jobs instead of the dole? Will they maintain personal liberty? Will they make America a happier, a better place in which to live?

In dealing with these great problems you need to remember that the shocks we have received from the War and the depression have created great despair and great discontent with representative government, and individual freedom. Our system has faults but these faults are but marginal. They must be constantly corrected. Special privilege, exploitation of labor, the consumer, or the investor have no right or part in it. But the soil of the American heritage of liberty is still fertile with vast harvest of human security and human betterment.

Alert opposition and incisive criticism and debate are the safeguards of a Republic. But that is not enough. The vast revolution in the powers of science and technology has placed within our grasp a future and a security never hitherto glimpsed by mankind. The people hunger for the comfort, the security, and the freedom of spirit which we know they may bring. But we would have but an empty husk should they come at the sacrifice of liberty. Those securities will come if we do not stifle and handcuff the productive genius which alone thrives in freedom. In the large, our problem is to stimulate and utilize the great productive capacity of our people. Herein is the great constructive program—to find the road by which we may attain the vast enrichments of science and technology within the province of private enterprise and personal liberty. Therein we must add the new upon the structure of the old—for therein lie the foundations of centuries of human effort. It will succeed not through vast generalizations but through human sympathy, detailed policies, hard common sense, and political realism. That is the greatest opportunity of statesmanship in two generations.

In the coming months the Republican Party will meet in convention with the responsibility of determining its policies. It will be the most vital convention since 1860. That convention should comprise the thousand best men of the Republican Party. Theirs is the duty to enunciate great principles. They should be inspired to determine a program of policies to solve great issues. Minor issues, petty opposition, sectional interest, group ideas, and every shred of personal ambition must be dumped, that this great responsibility, this great spiritual purpose may be accomplished. None of these things must count in the fate of the nation. Upon the wisdom and courage of these men will depend the future of America.

XXXIII
Franklin D. Roosevelt:
The Meaning of Progress
Atlanta, Georgia, November 29, 1935

My Friends and Neighbors:

I am happy to be in Georgia. I am proud of Georgia. Happy today especially because of this moving reception which my friends, the Senators and all of the Representatives in the Congress from this State, have tendered me, and to which you, the good people of this State, have responded with such warmth and hospitality. Happy because I meet again so many old friends and neighbors. Proud because I see signs on every hand that the overwhelming majority of the people of this State are keeping pace with the millions of others throughout the nation who believe in progress, are willing to work for progress and are going to get progress. Proud because I see clear signs of a revival of material prosperity in country and in city, and especially because I sense a swelling prosperity of the spirit that spells a greater help and a deeper happiness for our fellow men.

Eleven years ago I came to live at Warm Springs for the first time. That was a period of great so-called prosperity. But I would not go back to the conditions of 1924, and I do not believe that you people would want to go back to those conditions either.

Of that year and of the five years that followed, I have a clear recollection which you can verify for yourselves. In that orgy of "prosperity" a wild speculation was building speculative profits for the speculators and preparing the way for you, the public, to be left "holding the bag." In that orgy of "prosperity," banks, individually and by chains, were closing their doors at the expense of the depositors. In that orgy of "prosperity" the farmers of the South had become involuntary speculators themselves, never certain when they planted their cotton whether it would bring twenty-five cents or fifteen cents or a nickel. In that orgy of "prosperity" the poorest vied with the richest in throwing their earnings and their savings into a cauldron of land and stock speculation. In that orgy of "prosperity" slum conditions went unheeded, better education was neglected, usurious interest charges mounted, child labor continued, starvation wages were too often the rule instead of the exception. Yes, in those days Mammon ruled America. That is why we are not going back to them.

Those are the years for us to remember in the future—those fool's paradise years before the crash came. Too much do we harp on the years that followed, when from 1929 to 1933 this whole nation slipped spirally downward—ever downward—to the inevitable point when the mechanics of civilization came to a dead stop on March 3, 1933.

You and I need not rehearse the four years of disaster and gloom. We know that simple fact that at the end of this four years America acted before it was too late. America turned about, and by a supreme, well-nigh unanimous national effort, started on the upward path again.

You and I have reason to remember the past two and a half years that have gone by so quickly, reason to remember the fine spirit of the average American citizen which made my task vastly lighter. Memory is short, but yours is not too short to recollect those great meetings of the representatives of the farmers, regionally and in Washington, in the spring and summer of 1933, when they agreed overwhelmingly that unfairly low prices for farm crops could never be raised to, and maintained at, a reasonable level until and unless the government of the United States acted to help them reduce the tremendous carryovers and surpluses which threatened us and the whole world.

You and I can well remember the overwhelming demand that the national government come to the rescue of the home owners and farm owners of the nation who were losing the roofs over their heads through inflated valuations and exorbitant rates of interest.

You and I still recollect the need for and the successful attainment of a banking policy which not only opened the closed banks but guaranteed the deposits of the depositors of the nation.

You and I have not forgotten the enthusiastic support that succeeded in ending the labor of children in mills and factories, in seeing a fairer wage level for those on starvation pay, and in giving to the workers hope for the right collectively to bargain with their employers. That success, I am glad to say, in large part still persists.

You and I will not forget the long struggle to put an end to the indiscriminate distribution of "fly-by-night" securities and to provide fair regulation of the stock exchanges and of the great interstate public utility companies of our country.

You and I—yes, every individual and every family in the land—are being brought close to that supreme achievement of this great Congress, the Social Security law which, in days to come, will provide the aged against distressing want, will set up a national system of insurance for the employed, and will expand well-merited care to sick and crippled children.

You and I are enlisted today in a great crusade in every part of the land to cooperate with Nature and not to fight her, to cooperate to stop destructive floods, to prevent dust storms, to prevent the washing away of our precious soils, to grow trees, to give thousands of farm families a chance to live, and to seek to provide more and better food for the city dwellers of the nation.

In this connection it is, I think, of interest to point out that national surveys which have been conducted in the past year or two prove that the average of the citizenship of the United States lives today on what the doctors would call a third-class diet. If the country lived on a second-class diet instead of a third-class diet, do you know what that would mean? It would mean we would need to put many more acres than we use today back into the production of foodstuffs for domestic consumption. If the nation lived—as I wish it did—on a first-class diet, we would have to put more acres than we have ever cultivated into the production of an additional supply of things for Americans to eat.

That raises a question: Why—to speak in broad terms in following up this particular illustration—why are we living on a third-class diet? Well, the best answer I know is this: The masses of American people have not the purchasing power to eat more and better food.

4

"The Confused State of the Union" (1936)

XXXIV
United States v. Butler, et al., 297 U.S. 1
January 6, 1936
(Opinion of the Court)

Mr. Justice ROBERTS delivered the opinion of the Court.

In this case we must determine whether certain provisions of the Agricultural Adjustment Act, 1933, conflict with the Federal Constitution.

Title 1 of the statute is captioned "Agricultural Adjustment." Section 1 recites that an economic emergency has arisen, due to disparity between the prices of agricultural and other commodities, with consequent destruction of farmers' purchasing power and breakdown in orderly exchange, which, in turn, have affected transactions in agricultural commodities with a national public interest and burdened and obstructed the normal currents of commerce, calling for the enactment of legislation.

Section 2 declares it to be the policy of Congress: "To establish and maintain such balance between the production and consumption of agricultural commodities, and such marketing conditions therefore, as will reestablish prices to farmers at a level that will give agricultural commodities a purchasing power with

242

respect to articles that farmers buy, equivalent to the purchasing power of agricultural commodities in the base period."

The base period, in the case of cotton, and all other commodities except tobacco, is designated as that between August, 1909, and July, 1914.

The further policies announced are an approach to the desired equality by gradual correction of present inequalities "at as rapid a rate as is deemed feasible in view of the current consumptive demand in domestic and foreign markets," and the protection of consumers" interest by readjusting farm production at such level as will not increase the percentage of the consumers" retail expenditures for agricultural commodities or products derived therefrom, which is returned to the farmer, above the percentage returned to him in the base period.

Section 8 provides, amongst other things, that, "In order to effectuate the declared policy," the Secretary of Agriculture shall have power

"(1) To provide for reduction in the acreage or reduction in the production for market, or both, of any basic agricultural commodity, through agreements with producers or by other voluntary methods, and to provide for rental or benefit payments in connection therewith or upon that part of the production of any basic agricultural commodity required for domestic consumption, in such amounts as the Secretary deems fair and reasonable, to be paid out of any moneys available for such payments."

"(2) To enter into marketing agreements with processors, associations of producers, and others engaged in the handling, in the current of interstate or foreign commerce of any agricultural commodity or product thereof, after due notice and opportunity for hearing to interested parties."

"(3) To issue licenses permitting processors, associations of producers, and others to engage in the handling, in the current of interstate or foreign commerce, of any agricultural commodity or product thereof, or any competing commodity or product thereof."

It will be observed that the Secretary is not required, but is permitted, if, in his uncontrolled judgment, the policy of the act will so be promoted, to make agreements with individual farmers for a reduction of acreage or production upon such terms as he may think fair and reasonable.

Section 9(a) enacts: "To obtain revenue for extraordinary expenses incurred by reason of the national economic emergency, there shall be levied processing taxes as hereinafter provided. When the Secretary of Agriculture determines that rental or benefit payments are to be made with respect to any basic agricultural commodity, he shall proclaim such determination, and a processing tax shall be in effect with respect to such commodity from the beginning of the marketing year therefor next following the date of such proclamation. The processing tax shall be levied, assessed, and collected upon the first domestic processing of the commodity, whether of domestic production or imported, and shall be paid by the processor."

The Secretary may from time to time, if he finds it necessary for the effectuation of the policy of the act, readjust the amount of the exaction to meet the requirements of subsection (b). The tax is to terminate at the end of any marketing year if the rental or benefit payments are discontinued by the Secretary with the expiration of that year.

Section 9(b) fixes the tax "at such rate as equals the difference between the current average farm price for the commodity and the fair exchange value," with power in the Secretary, after investigation, notice, and hearing, to readjust the tax so as to prevent the accumulation of surplus stocks and depression of farm prices.

Section 9(c) directs that the fair exchange value of a commodity shall be such a price as will give that commodity the same purchasing power with respect to articles farmers buy as it had during the base period, and that the fair exchange value and the current average farm price of a commodity shall be ascertained by the Secretary from available statistics in his department.

Section 12(a) appropriates $100,000,000 "to be available to the Secretary of Agriculture for administrative expenses under this title and for rental and benefit payments;" and Section 12(b), appropriates the proceeds derived from all taxes imposed under the act "to be available to the Secretary of Agriculture for expansion of markets and removal of surplus agricultural products. Administrative expenses, rental and benefit payments, and refunds on taxes."

Section 15(d) permits the Secretary, upon certain conditions, to impose compensating taxes on commodities in competition with those subject to the processing tax.

By section 16, a floor tax is imposed upon the sale or other disposition of any article processed wholly or in chief value from any commodity with respect to which a processing tax is to be levied in amount equivalent to that of the processing tax which would be payable with respect to the commodity from which the article is processed if the processing had occurred on the date when the processing tax becomes effective. On July 14, 1933, the Secretary of Agriculture, with the approval of the President, proclaimed that he had determined rental and benefit payments should be made with respect to cotton; that the marketing year for that commodity was to begin August 1, 1933; and calculated and fixed the rates of processing and floor taxes on cotton in accordance with the terms of the act.

The United States presented a claim to the respondents as receivers of the Hoosac Mills Corporation for processing and floor taxes on cotton levied under sections 9 and 16 of the act. The receivers recommended that the claim be disallowed. The District Court found the taxes valid and ordered them paid. Upon appeal the Circuit Court of Appeals reversed the order. The judgment under review was entered prior to the adoption of the amending act of August 24, 1935, and we are therefore concerned only with the original act.

First. At the outset the United States contends that the respondents have no standing to question the validity of the tax. The position is that the act is merely a revenue measure levying an excise upon the activity of processing cotton—a proper subject for the imposition of such a tax-the proceeds of which go into the federal Treasury and thus become available for appropriation for any purpose. It is said that what the respondents are endeavoring to do is to challenge the intended use of the money pursuant to Congressional appropriation when, by concession, that money will have become the property of the government and the taxpayer will no longer have any interest in it. Massachusetts v. Mellon, 262 U.S. 447, is claimed to foreclose litigation by the respondents or other taxpayers, as such, looking to restraint of the expenditure of government funds. That case might be an authority in the petitioners' favor if we were here concerned merely with a suit by a taxpayer to restrain the expenditure of the public moneys. It was there held that a taxpayer of the United States may not question expenditures from its treasury on the ground that the alleged unlawful diversion will deplete the public funds and thus increase the burden of future taxation. Obviously the asserted interest of a taxpayer in the federal government's funds and the supposed increase of the future burden of taxation is minute and indeterminable. But here the respondents, who are called upon to pay moneys as taxes, resist the exaction as a step in an unauthorized plan. This circumstance clearly distinguishes the case. The government in substance and effect asks us to separate the Agricultural Adjustment Act into two statutes, the one levying an excise on processors of certain commodities; the other appropriating the public moneys independently of the first. Passing the novel suggestion that two statutes enacted as parts of a single scheme should be tested as if they were distinct and unrelated, we think the legislation now before us is not susceptible of such separation and treatment.

The tax can only be sustained by ignoring the avowed purpose and operation of the act, and holding it a measure merely laying an excise upon processors to raise revenue for the support of government. Beyond cavil the sole object of the legislation is to restore the purchasing power of agricultural products to a parity with that prevailing in an earlier day; to take money from the processor and bestow it upon farmers who will reduce their acreage for the accomplishment of the proposed end, and, meanwhile, to aid these farmers during the period required to bring the prices of their crops to the desired level.

The tax plays an indispensable part in the plan of regulation. As stated by the Agricultural Adjustment Administrator, it is "the heart of the law," a means of "accomplishing one or both of two things intended to help farmers attain parity prices and purchasing power." A tax automatically goes into effect for a commodity when the Secretary of Agriculture determines that rental or benefit payments are to be made for reduction of production of that commodity. The tax is to cease when rental or benefit payments cease. The rate is fixed with the purpose of bringing about crop reduction and price raising. It is to equal the difference between the "current average farm price" and "fair exchange value." It may be altered to such amount as will prevent accumulation of surplus stocks. If the Secretary finds the policy of the act will not be promoted by the levy of the tax for a given commodity, he may exempt it. The whole revenue from the levy is appropriated in aid of crop control; none of it is made available for general governmental use. The entire agricultural adjustment program embodied in title 1 of the act is to become inoperative when, in the judgment of the President, the national economic emergency ends;

and as to any commodity he may terminate the provisions of the law, if he finds them no longer requisite to carrying out the declared policy with respect to such commodity.

We conclude that the act is one regulating agricultural production; that the tax is a mere incident of such regulation; and that the respondents have standing to challenge the legality of the exaction.

It does not follow that, as the act is not an exertion of the taxing power and the exaction not a true tax, the statute is void or the exaction uncollectible. For, to paraphrase what was said in the Head Money Cases, if this is an expedient regulation by Congress, of a subject within one of its granted powers, "and the end to be attained powers, within that power, the act is not void because, within a loose and more extended sense than was used in the constitution," the exaction is called a tax.

Second. The government asserts that even if the respondents may question the propriety of the appropriation embodied in their statute, their attack must fail because Article 1, Section 8 of the Constitution, authorizes the contemplated expenditure of the funds raised by the tax. This contention presents the great and the controlling question in the case. We approach its decision with a sense of our grave responsibility to render judgment in accordance with the principles established for the governance of all three branches of the government.

There should be no misunderstanding as to the function of this court in such a case. It is sometimes said that the court assumes a power to overrule or control the action of the people's representatives. This is a misconception. The Constitution is the supreme law of the land ordained and established by the people. All legislation must conform to the principles it lays down. When an act of Congress is appropriately challenged in the courts as not conforming to the constitutional mandate, the judicial branch of the government has only one duty; to lay the article of the Constitution which is invoked beside the statute which is challenged and to decide whether the latter squares with the former. All the court does, or can do, is to announce its considered judgment upon the question. The only power it has, if such it may be called, is the power of judgment. This court neither approves nor condemns any legislative policy. Its delicate and difficult office is to ascertain and declare whether the legislation is in accordance with, or in contravention of, the provisions of the Constitution; and, having

done that, its duty ends.   The question is not what power the
federal government ought to have, but what powers in fact have
been given by the people. It hardly seems necessary to reiterate that
ours is a dual form of government; that in every state there are two
governments; the state and the United States. Each state has all
governmental powers save such as the people, by their
Constitution, have conferred upon the United States, denied to the
states, or reserved to themselves.   The federal union is a
government of delegated powers. It has only such as are expressly
conferred upon it and such as are reasonably to be implied from
those granted.   In this respect we differ radically from nations
where all legislative power, without restriction or limitation, is
vested in a parliament or other legislative body subject to no
restrictions except the discretion of its members.

Article 1, Section 8, of the Constitution, vests sundry powers in
the Congress. But only two of its clauses have any bearing upon
the validity of the statute under review.

The third clause endows the Congress with power "to regulate
Commerce...among the several States." Despite a reference in its
first section to a burden upon, and an obstruction of the normal
currents of, commerce, the act under review does not purport to
regulate transactions in interstate or foreign commerce. Its stated
purpose is the control of agricultural production, a purely local
activity, in an effort to raise the prices paid the farmer. Indeed, the
government does not attempt to uphold the validity of the act on
the basis of the commerce clause, which, for the purpose of the
present case, may be put aside as irrelevant.

The clause thought to authorize the legislation, the first, confers
upon the Congress power "to lay and collect Taxes, Duties,
Imposts and Excises, to pay the Debts and provide for the common
Defense and general Welfare of the United States...."   It is not
contended that this provision grants power to regulate agricultural
production upon the theory that such legislation would promote
the general welfare. The government concedes that the phrase "to
provide for the general welfare" qualifies the power "to lay and
collect taxes." The view that the clause grants power to provide for
the general welfare, independently of the taxing power, has never
been authoritatively accepted. Mr. Justice Story points out that, if it
were adopted, "it is obvious that under color of the generality of
the words, to "provide for the common defense and general
welfare", the government of the United States is, in reality, a

government of general and unlimited powers, notwithstanding the subsequent enumeration of specific powers." The true construction undoubtedly is that the only thing granted is the power to tax for the purpose of providing funds for payment of the nation's debts and making provision for the general welfare.

Nevertheless, the government asserts that warrant is found in this clause for the adoption of the Agricultural Adjustment Act. The argument is that Congress may appropriate and authorize the spending of moneys for the "general welfare"; that the phrase should be liberally construed to cover anything conducive to national welfare; that decision as to what will promote such welfare rests with Congress alone, and the courts may not review its determination; and, finally, that the appropriation under attack was in fact for the general welfare of the United States.

The Congress is expressly empowered to lay taxes to provide for the general welfare. Funds in the Treasury as a result of taxation may be expended only through appropriation. (Article 1, Section 9, Cl. 7) They can never accomplish the objects for which they were collected, unless the power to appropriate is as broad as the power to tax. The necessary implication from the terms of the grant is that the public funds may be appropriated "to provide for the general welfare of the United States." These words cannot be meaningless, else they would not have been used. The conclusion must be that they were intended to limit and define the granted power to raise and to expend money. How shall they be construed to effectuate the intent of the instrument?

Since the foundation of the nation, sharp differences of opinion have persisted as to the true interpretation of the phrase. Madison asserted it amounted to no more than a reference to the other powers enumerated in the subsequent clauses of the same section; that, as the United States is a government of limited and enumerated powers, the grant of power to tax and spend for the general national welfare must be confined to the enumerated legislative fields committed to the Congress. In this view the phrase is mere tautology, for taxation and appropriation are or may be necessary incidents of the exercise of any of the enumerated legislative powers. Hamilton, on the other hand, maintained the clause confers a power separate and distinct from those later enumerated, is not restricted in meaning by the grant of them, and Congress consequently has a substantive power to tax and to appropriate, limited only by the requirement that it shall be exercised to provide for the general welfare of the United States. Each contention has had the support of those whose views are entitled to weight. This court has noticed the question, but has never found it necessary to decide which is the true construction. Mr. Justice Story, in his Commentaries, espouses the Hamiltonian position. We shall not review the writings of public men and commentators or discuss the legislative practice. Study of all these leads us to conclude that the reading advocated by Mr. Justice Story is the correct one. While, therefore, the power to tax is not unlimited, its confines are set in the clause which confers it, and not in those of Section 8 which bestow and define the legislative powers of the Congress. It results that the power of Congress to authorize expenditure of public moneys for public purposes is not limited by the direct grants of legislative power found in the Constitution.

But the adoption of the broader construction leaves the power to spend subject to limitations.

As Story says: "The Constitution was, from its very origin, contemplated to be the frame of a national government, of special and enumerated powers, and not of general and unlimited powers."

Again he says: "A power to lay taxes for the common defense and general welfare of the United States is not in common sense a general power. It is limited to those objects. It cannot constitutionally transcend them."

That the qualifying phrase must be given effect all advocates of broad construction admit. Hamilton, in his well known "Report on Manufactures," states that the purpose must be "general, and not local." Monroe, an advocate of Hamilton's doctrine, wrote: "Have Congress a right to raise and appropriate the money to any and to every purpose according to their will and pleasure? They certainly have not." Story says that if the tax were not proposed for the common defense or general welfare, but for other objects wholly extraneous, it would be wholly indefensible upon constitutional principles. And he makes it clear that the powers of taxation and appropriation extend only to matters of national, as distinguished from local, welfare.

As elsewhere throughout the Constitution the section in question lays down principles, which control the use of the power, and does not attempt meticulous or detailed directions. Every presumption is to be indulged in favor of faithful compliance by Congress with the mandates of the fundamental law. Courts are reluctant to adjudge any statute in contravention of them. But, under our frame of government, no other place is provided where the citizen may be heard to urge that the law fails to conform to the limits set upon the use of a granted power. When such a contention comes here we naturally require a showing that by no reasonable possibility can the challenged legislation fall within the wide range of discretion permitted to the Congress. How great is the extent of that range, when the subject is the promotion of the general welfare of the United States, we need hardly remark. But, despite the breadth of the legislative discretion, our duty to hear and to render judgment remains. If the statute plainly violates the stated principle of the Constitution we must so declare. We are not now required to ascertain the scope of the phrase "general welfare of the United States" or to determine whether an appropriation in aid of agriculture falls within it. Wholly apart from that question, another principle embedded in our Constitution prohibits the enforcement of the Agricultural Adjustment Act. The act invades the reserved rights of the states. It is a statutory plan to regulate and control agricultural production, a matter beyond the powers delegated to the federal government. The tax, the appropriation of the funds raised, and the direction for their disbursement, are but parts of the plan. They are but means to an unconstitutional end.

From the accepted doctrine that the United States is a government of delegated powers, it follows that those not expressly granted, or reasonably to be implied from such as are conferred, are reserved to the states or to the people. To forestall any suggestion to the contrary, the Tenth Amendment was adopted. The same proposition, otherwise stated, is that powers not granted are prohibited. None to regulate agricultural production is given, and therefore legislation by Congress for that purpose is forbidden.

It is an established principle that the attainment of a prohibited end may not be accomplished under the pretext of the exertion of powers which are granted.

"Should Congress, in the execution of its powers, adopt measures which are prohibited by the constitution; or should Congress, under the pretext of executing its powers, pass laws for the accomplishment of objects not intrusted to the government; it would become the painful duty of this tribunal, should a case requiring such a decision come before it, to say, that such an act was not the law of the land." (McCulloch v. Maryland)

"Congress cannot, under the pretext of executing delegated power, pass laws for the accomplishment of objects not intrusted to the federal government. And we accept as established doctrine that any provision of an act of Congress ostensibly enacted under power granted by the Constitution, not naturally and reasonably adapted to the effective exercise of such power, but solely to the achievement of something plainly within power reserved to the states, is invalid and cannot be enforced." (Linder v. United States)

These principles are as applicable to the power to lay taxes as to any other federal power. Said the court, in McCulloch v. Maryland, supra, Wheat. "Let the end be legitimate, let it be within the scope of the constitution, and all means which are appropriate, which are plainly adapted to that end, which are not prohibited, but consist with the letter and spirit of the constitution, are constitutional."

The power of taxation, which is expressly granted, may, of course, be adopted as a means to carry into operation another power also expressly granted. But resort to the taxing power to effectuate an end which is not legitimate, not within the scope of the Constitution, is obviously inadmissible.

"Congress is not empowered to tax for those purposes which are within the exclusive province of the states." (Gibbons v. Ogden)

"There are, indeed, certain virtual limitations, arising from the principles of the Constitution itself. It would undoubtedly be an abuse of the (taxing) power if so exercised as to impair the separate existence and independent self-government of the States, or if exercised for ends inconsistent with the limited grants of power in the Constitution." (Veazie Bank v. Fenno)

Third. If the taxing power may not be used as the instrument to enforce a regulation of matters of state concern with respect to which the Congress has no authority to interfere, may it, as in the present case, be employed to raise the money necessary to purchase a compliance which the Congress is powerless to command? The government asserts that whatever might be said against the validity of the plan, if compulsory, it is constitutionally sound because the end is accomplished by voluntary co-operation. There are two sufficient answers to the contention. The regulation is not in fact voluntary. The farmer, of course, may refuse to comply, but the price of such refusal is the loss of benefits. The amount offered is intended to be sufficient to exert pressure on him to agree to the proposed regulation. The power to confer or withhold unlimited benefits is the power to coerce or destroy. If the cotton grower elects not to accept the benefits, he will receive less for his crops; those who receive payments will be able to undersell him. The result may well to financial ruin. The coercive purpose and intent of the statute is not obscured by the fact that it has not been perfectly successful. It is pointed out that, because there still remained a minority whom the rental and benefit payments were insufficient to induce to surrender their independence of action, the Congress has gone further, and, in the Bankhead Cotton Act, used the taxing power in a more directly minatory fashion to compel submission. This progression only serves more fully to expose the coercive purpose of the so-called tax imposed by the present act. It is clear that the Department of Agriculture has properly described the plan as one to keep a non-cooperating minority in line. This is coercion by economic pressure. The asserted power of choice is illusory.

In Frost & Frost Trucking Company v. R.R. Commission, 271 U.S. 583, a state act was considered which provided for supervision and regulation of transportation for hire by automobile on the public highways. Certificates of convenience and necessity were to be obtained by persons desiring to use the highways for this purpose. The regulatory commission required that a private contract carrier should secure such a certificate as a condition of its operation. The effect of the commission's action was to transmute the private carrier into a public carrier. In other words, the privilege of using the highways as a private carrier for compensation was conditioned upon his dedicating his property to the quasi public use of public transportation. While holding that the private carrier was not obliged to submit himself to the condition, the commission denied him the privilege of using the highways if he did not do so. The argument was, as here, that the carrier had a free choice. This court said, in holding the act as construed unconstitutional: "If so, constitutional guaranties, so carefully safeguarded against direct assault, are open to destruction by the indirect, but no less effective, process of requiring a surrender, which, though in form voluntary, in fact lacks none of the elements of compulsion. Having regard to form alone, the act here is an offer to the private carrier of a privilege, which the state may grant or deny, upon a condition which the carrier is free to accept or reject. In reality, the carrier is given no choice, except a choice between the rock and the whirlpool—an option to forego a privilege which may be vital to his livelihood or submit to a requirement which may constitute an intolerable burden."

But if the plan were one for purely voluntary co-operation it would stand no better so far as federal power is concerned. At best, it is a scheme for purchasing with federal funds submission to federal regulation of a subject reserved to the states.

It is said that Congress has the undoubted right to appropriate money to executive officers for expenditure under contracts between the government and individuals; that much of the total expenditures is so made. But appropriations and expenditures under contracts for proper governmental purposes cannot justify contracts which are not within federal power. And contracts for the reduction of acreage and the control of production are outside the range of that power. An appropriation to be expended by the United States under contracts calling for violation of a state law clearly would offend the Constitution. Is a statute less objectionable which authorizes expenditure of federal moneys to induce action in a field in which the United States has no power to intermeddle? The Congress cannot invade state jurisdiction to compel individual action; no more can it purchase such action.

Congress has no power to enforce its commands on the farmer to the ends sought by the Agricultural Adjustment Act. It must follow that it may not indirectly accomplish those ends by taxing and spending to purchase compliance. The Constitution and the entire plan of our government negative any such use of the power to tax and to spend as the act undertakes to authorize. It does not help to declare that local conditions throughout the nation have created a situation of national concern; for this is but to say that whenever there is a widespread similarity of local conditions, Congress may ignore constitutional limitations upon its own powers and usurp those reserved to the states. If, in lieu of compulsory regulation of subjects within the states" reserved jurisdiction, which is prohibited, the Congress could invoke the taxing and spending power as a means to accomplish the same end, Clause 1 of Section 8 of Article 1 would become the instrument for total subversion of the governmental powers reserved to the individual states.

If the act before us is a proper exercise of the federal taxing power, evidently the regulation of all industry throughout the United States may be accomplished by similar exercises of the same power. It would be possible to exact money from one branch of an industry and pay it to another branch in every field of activity which lies within the province of the states. The mere threat of such a procedure might well induce the surrender of rights and the compliance with federal regulation as the price of continuance in business. A few instances will illustrate the thought.

Let us suppose Congress should determine that the farmer, the miner, or some other producer of raw materials is receiving too much for his products, with consequent depression of the processing industry and idleness of its employees. Though, by confession, there is no power vested in Congress to compel by statute a lowering of the prices of the raw material, the same result might be accomplished, if the questioned act be valid, by taxing the producer upon his output and appropriating the proceeds to the processors, either with or without conditions imposed as the consideration for payment of the subsidy.

We have held in A. L. A. Schechter Poultry Corp. v. United States, that Congress has no power to regulate wages and hours of labor in a local business. If the petitioner is right, this very end may be accomplished by appropriating money to be paid to employers from the federal treasury under contracts whereby they agree to comply with certain standards fixed by federal law or by contract.

Should Congress ascertain that sugar refiners are not receiving a fair profit, and that this is detrimental to the entire industry, and in turn has its repercussions in trade and commerce generally, it might, in analogy to the present law, impose an excise of 2 cents a pound on every sale of the commodity and pass the funds collected to such refiners, and such only, as will agree to maintain a certain price.

Assume that too many shoes are being manufactured throughout the nation; that the market is saturated, the price depressed, the factories running half time, the employees suffering. Upon the principle of the statute in question, Congress might authorize the Secretary of Commerce to enter into contracts with shoe manufacturers providing that each shall reduce his output, and that the United States will pay him a fixed sum proportioned to such reduction, the money to make the payments to be raised by a tax on all retail shoe dealers on their customers.

Suppose that there are too many garment workers in the large cities; that this results in dislocation of the economic balance. Upon the principle contended for, an excise might be laid on the manufacture of all garments manufactured and the proceeds paid to those manufacturers who agree to remove their plants to cities having not more than a hundred thousand population. Thus, through the asserted power of taxation, the federal government, against the will of individual states, might completely redistribute the industrial population.

A possible result of sustaining the claimed federal power would be that every business group which thought itself underprivileged might demand that a tax be laid on its vendors or vendees, the proceeds to be appropriated to the redress of its deficiency of income. These illustrations are given, not to suggest that any of the purposes mentioned are unworthy, but to demonstrate the scope of the principle for which the government contends; to test the principle by its applications; to point out that, by the exercise of the asserted power, Congress would, in effect, under the pretext of exercising the taxing power, in reality accomplish prohibited ends. It cannot be said that they envisage improbable legislation. The supposed cases are no more improbable than would the present act have been deemed a few years ago.

Until recently no suggestion of the existence of any such power in the federal government has been advanced. The expressions of the framers of the Constitution, the decisions of this court interpreting that instrument and the writings of great commentators will be searched in vain for any suggestion that there exists in the clause under discussion or elsewhere in the Constitution, the authority whereby every provision and every fair, implication from that instrument may be subverted, the independence of the individual states obliterated, and the United States converted into a central government exercising uncontrolled police power in every state of the Union, superseding all local control or regulation of the affairs or concerns of the states.

Hamilton himself, the leading advocate of broad interpretation of the power to tax and to appropriate for the general welfare, never suggested that any power granted by the Constitution could be used for the destruction of local self-government in the states. Story countenances no such doctrine. It seems never to have occurred to them, or to those who have agreed with them, that the general welfare of the United States (which has aptly been termed "an indestructible Union, composed of indestructible States,") might be served by obliterating the constituent members of the Union. But to this fatal conclusion the doctrine contended for would inevitably lead. And its sole premise is that, though the makers of the Constitution, in erecting the federal government, intended sedulously to limit and define its powers, so as to reserve to the states and the people sovereign power, to be wielded by the states and their citizens and not to be invaded by the United States, they nevertheless by a single clause gave power to the Congress to tear down the barriers, to invade the states" jurisdiction, and to become a parliament of the whole people, subject to no restrictions save such as are self-imposed. The argument, when seen in its true character and in the light of its inevitable results, must be rejected.

Since, as we have pointed out, there was no power in the Congress to impose the contested exaction, it could not lawfully ratify or confirm what an executive officer had done in that regard. Consequently the Act of 1935, 30, adding section 21(b) to Act of May 12, 1933, does not affect the rights of the parties.

The judgment is affirmed.

XXXV
Franklin D. Roosevelt:
Annual Message to Congress
January 3, 1936

Within democratic Nations the chief concern of the people is to prevent the continuance or the rise of autocratic institutions that beget slavery at home and aggression abroad. Within our borders, as in the world at large, popular opinion is at war with a power-seeking minority.

That is no new thing. It was fought out in the Constitutional Convention of 1787. From time to time since then, the battle has been continued, under Thomas Jefferson, Andrew Jackson, Theodore Roosevelt and Woodrow Wilson

In these latter years we have witnessed the domination of government by financial and industrial groups, numerically small but politically dominant in the twelve years that succeeded the World War. The present group of which I speak is indeed numerically small and, while it exercises a large influence and has much to say in the world of business, it does not, I am confident, speak the true sentiments of the less articulate but more important elements that constitute real American business.

In March, 1933, I appealed to the Congress of the United States and to the people of the United States in a new effort to restore power to those to whom it rightfully belonged. The response to that appeal resulted in the writing of a new chapter in the history of popular government. You, the members of the Legislative branch, and I, the Executive, contended for and established a new relationship between Government and people.

What were the terms of that new relationship? They were an appeal from the clamor of many private and selfish interests, yes, an appeal from the clamor of partisan interest, to the ideal of the public interest. Government became the representative and the trustee of the public interest. Our aim was to build upon essentially democratic institutions, seeking all the while the adjustment of burdens, the help of the needy, the protection of the weak, the liberation of the exploited and the genuine protection of the people's property.

It goes without saying that to create such an economic constitutional order, more than a single legislative enactment was called for. We, you in the Congress and I as the Executive, had to build upon a broad base. Now, after thirty-four months of work, we contemplate a fairly rounded whole. We have returned the control of the Federal Government to the City of Washington.

To be sure, in so doing, we have invited battle. We have earned the hatred of entrenched greed. The very nature of the problem that we faced made it necessary to drive some people from power and strictly to regulate others. I made that plain when I took the oath of office in March, 1933. I spoke of the practices of the unscrupulous money-changers who stood indicted in the court of public opinion. I spoke of the rulers of the exchanges of mankind's goods, who failed through their own stubbornness and their own incompetence. I said that they had admitted their failure and had abdicated.

Abdicated? Yes, in 1933, but now with the passing of danger they forget their damaging admissions and withdraw their abdication.

They seek the restoration of their selfish power. They offer to lead us back round the same old corner into the same old dreary street.

Yes, there are still determined groups that are intent upon that very thing. Rigorously held up to popular examination, their true character presents itself. They steal the livery of great national constitutional ideals to serve discredited special interests. As guardians and trustees for great groups of individual stockholders they wrongfully seek to carry the property and the interests entrusted to them into the arenas of partisan politics. They seek—this minority in business and industry—to control and often do control and use for their own purposes legitimate and highly honored business associations; they engage in vast propaganda to spread fear and discord among the people—they would "gang up" against the people's liberties.

The principle that they would instill into government if they succeed in seizing power is well shown by the principles which many of them have instilled into their own affairs: autocracy toward labor, toward stockholders, toward consumers, toward public sentiment. Autocrats in smaller things, they seek autocracy in bigger things. "By their fruits ye shall know them."

If these gentlemen believe, as they say they believe, that the measures adopted by this Congress and its predecessor, and carried out by this Administration, have hindered rather than promoted recovery, let them be consistent. Let them propose to this Congress the complete repeal of these measures. The way is open to such a proposal.

Let action be positive and not negative. The way is open in the Congress of the United States for an expression of opinion by yeas and nays. Shall we say that values are restored and that the Congress will, therefore, repeal the laws under which we have been bringing them back? Shall we say that because national income has grown with rising prosperity, we shall repeal existing taxes and thereby put off the day of approaching a balanced budget and of starting to reduce the national debt?   Shall we abandon the reasonable support and regulation of banking? Shall we restore the dollar to its former gold content?

Shall we say to the farmer, "The prices for your products are in part restored. Now go and hoe your own row?"

Shall we say to the home owners, "We have reduced your rates of interest. We have no further concern with how you keep your home or what you pay for your money. That is your affair?"

Shall we say to the several millions of unemployed citizens who face the very problem of existence, of getting enough to eat, "We will withdraw from giving you work. We will turn you back to the charity of your communities and those men of selfish power who tell you that perhaps they will employ you if the Government leaves them strictly alone?"

Shall we say to the needy unemployed, "Your problem is a local one except that perhaps the Federal Government, as an act of mere generosity, will be willing to pay to your city or to your county a few grudging dollars to help maintain your soup kitchens?"

Shall we say to the children who have worked all day in the factories, "Child labor is a local issue and so are your starvation wages; something to be solved or left unsolved by the jurisdiction of forty-eight States?"

Shall we say to the laborer, "Your right to organize, your relations with your employer have nothing to do with the public interest; if your employer will not even meet with you to discuss your problems and his, that is none of our affair?"

Shall we say to the unemployed and aged, "Social security lies not within the province of the Federal Government; you must seek relief elsewhere?"

Shall we say to the men and women who live in conditions of squalor in country and in city, "The health and the happiness of you and your children are no concern of ours?"

Shall we expose our population once more by the repeal of laws which protect them against the loss of their honest investments and against the manipulation of dishonest speculators? Shall we abandon the splendid efforts of the Federal Government to raise the health standards of the Nation and to give youth a decent opportunity through such means as the Civilian Conservation Corps?

Members of the Congress, let these challenges be met. If this is what these gentlemen want, let them say so to the Congress of the United States. Let them no longer hide their dissent in a cowardly cloak of generality. Let them define the issue. We have been specific in our affirmative action. Let them be specific in their negative attack.

But the challenge faced by this Congress is more menacing than merely a return to the past—bad as that would be. Our resplendent economic autocracy does not want to return to that individualism of which they prate, even though the advantages under that system went to the ruthless and strong. They realize that in thirty-four months we have built up new instruments of public power. In the hands of a people's Government this power is wholesome and proper. But in the hands of political puppets of an economic autocracy such power would provide shackles for the liberties of the people. Given them their way and they will take the course of every autocracy of the past—power for themselves, enslavement for the public.

Their weapon is the weapon of fear. I have said, "The only thing we have to fear is fear itself." That is as true today as it was in 1933. But such fear as they instill today is not a natural fear, a normal fear; it is a synthetic, manufactured, poisonous fear that is being spread subtly, expensively and cleverly by the same people who cried in those other days, "Save us, save us, lest we perish."

I repeat, with the same faith and the same determination, my words of March 4, 1933: "We face the arduous days that lie before us in the warm courage of national unity; with a clear consciousness of seeking old and precious moral values; with a clean satisfaction that comes from the stern performance of duty by old and young alike. We aim at the assurance of a rounded and permanent national life. We do not distrust the future of essential democracy."

XXXVI
Herbert Hoover:
The Confused State of the Union
Lincoln Birthday Dinner Address
Portland, Oregon, February 12, 1936

In less than a year our country must make a decision no less fateful than that which confronted Abraham Lincoln.

Since the Great War Liberty has fallen in a score of nations. In America where it blazed brightest and by its glow shed light to all others it is today impaired and endangered.

Again "we are...testing whether that nation or any nation so conceived and so dedicated can long endure."

When that test confronted Lincoln, he carried it to the people in national debate. No greater tribute can be paid him than that we shall devote this day of his memory to that high purpose.

If the truth and right decisions are to be found, this discussion must be held to the mold of courtesy, good humor, hard hitting, and above all to the intellectual honesty which Lincoln kept in all his fateful years.

Personalities and mud slinging never clarified a national issue.

There has lately been a new avalanche of oratory on behalf of the "common people," the "average man," the "economic middle class," and the "rank and file." That is right. These are the people for whom America was made. They carry the burdens of America. They make its moral fiber. They are the people whose interest needs defense right now. Mr. Lincoln said the Lord must have loved them because he created so many of them. There are others who love their votes.

The President stated a month ago that the issue before us is "the right of the average man and woman to lead a finer, better, and happier life."

That is an objective to which we all agree. That is the ideal of Americans since it was first mentioned in the Declaration of Independence. That is not at issue. The issue is the New Deal methods and objectives which are destroying this very thing.

The issue is the attempt to fasten upon the American people some sort of a system of personal government for a government of laws; a system of centralization under a political bureaucracy; a system of debt; a system of inflation; a system which would stifle the freedom and liberty of men. And it can be examined in the cold light of three years' experience.

It would seem that since the Supreme Court decisions we have abandoned the issue of the More Abundant Life. That was found to contain many roads to trouble.

It is the actual State of the Union that I propose to discuss this evening.

The outstanding State of this Union at this hour is a state of confusion. Confusion in thought, confusion in government, confusion in economic life, and confusion in ideals. Few national problems have been really solved. I have time for only a few illustrations of this bewildering muddle which jeopardizes the liberty of a great people.

And the test of it all is, whether we are moving to the "finer, better, and happier life for the average man and woman."

Confusion of Fear

The President in his message on the State of the Union seems to fear that fear is prevalent in the Union. He says, "The only thing we have to fear is fear." He finds malevolent forces creating fear. Just so.

The New Deal has been a veritable foundation of fear. The day after the New Deal was given life at the election of 1932 began the Great Fear which created the bank panic of March 4. The stock boom today is not from confidence in the future; it is partly from fear of inflation. The unemployment of millions of men in the capital goods industries is due to fear of New Deal currency policies. It was the Supreme Court decisions crashing through New Deal tyrannies which brought a gleam of confidence from the fears that had retarded recovery. The guiding spirit of the alphabet has not been love. It has been fear.

Confusion as to Greed

The President in reporting on the State of the Union also found it alive with "money-changers," "seekers for selfish power," "dishonest speculators," "economic autocrats," and "entrenched greed."

However, that has points in confusing the public mind. Any judge of debate would admit it. It has merit as a call to class war, a red herring across the trail of failure, an implication that all opponents are defenders of evil, a claim that righteousness now has refuge alone in Washington, and an avoidance of facts and figures. It is not the mold of debate of Abraham Lincoln. It does not heal the wounds of the nation.

In any event, in opposing the New Deal you did not know you were allied with those forces of darkness. You know it now.

No one defends such wickedness. But it happens that after three years of the New Deal the same men direct business today that were there three years ago. But what has become of the new laws designed to reform the wicked? We have seen no indictments except political oratory. That is confusing.

You will recall that three years ago the President gave the comforting assurance that "The money-changers have fled from their high seats in the temple of our civilization." It would appear that after three years of the New Deal they have all come back again with helpers. Also I had the impression that the New Deal had taken over the business of changing the money.

The human animal has many primitive instincts that morals, religion, and the law have not been able wholly to eradicate. He has two forms of greed—the greed for money and the greed for power. The lust for power is infinitely the worse. The greed for money can be curbed by law, but the greed for power seizes the law itself for its ends. At least the greed for money does not afflict us with fine phrases and slogans as to what is good for us.

The abuses of liberty by greed for money are weeds which grow in the garden of productive enterprise. If government is clean it can pull them up. The abuse of liberty by the greed for power is a blight that destroys the garden itself.

Confusion of Dictatorship with Democracy

The President states "In thirty-four months we have built up new instruments of public power. In the hands of the people's government this power is wholesome and proper." The President concedes that in other hands it would "provide shackles for the liberties of the people." That is confusion of dictatorship with democracy. The very origin of this Republic was in order that nobody should possess such power over the people.

These instruments of power march to the "finer, better, and happier life" under a banner of strange device—"Planned Economy." By this time you know this glittering phrase does not mean economy in government spending. It has proved to mean Politically Dictated Economic Life. It is of many battalions. We have seen so far Planned Industry, Planned Farming, Planned Government in Business, Planned Relief, Planned Credit, Planned Currency, and Planned Attack on the Constitution. And I might suggest two more. They are Planned Deficits and Planned Politics.

I need recall only those first two builders of confusion, the NRA and AAA. These two Towers of Babel, which the children of men built, were also to reach to Heaven. The headlines tell us of the character of the bricks and the mortar. Must Legislation. No Debate. Personal government by Proclamation. Ballyhoo. Codes. Factory Production Restricted. Competition Limited. Monopolies Created. Government Price Fixing. Increasing Costs. Increased Prices. Decreased consumption. Increased Cost of Living. Strikes. Lockouts. Boycott. Coercion. Crack Down. Jail. Small Business Men Washed Out. Crops Plowed Under. Animals Slaughtered. Housewife Strikes. Consumption of Food Decreases. Nation Imports Foods. Farmers' Markets Given to Foreigners. Economy of Scarcity. Nation Gets Richer by Producing Less at Higher Costs.

Their language was confounded and they were scattered by the Supreme Court.

But a new confusion arises. The spokesmen of the administration talk of the resurrection of these theories as the basis of our future economic life. The President refuses to say that they are finished. On the contrary in his address of January 3, after asserting the success of New Deal measures, he says: "I recommend to Congress that we advance, that we do not retreat." My impression is that Napoleon used somewhat the expression when he was marching to Moscow.

The American people have a right to have this clarified. Has the President abandoned these theories or not?

Confusion in Fiscal and Monetary Policies

The third battalion of confusion has been the spending, budget deficit debts, currency, and credit. Within a month since the President's budget message it has become more confused by four or five billions more expenditures.

Those who judge progress by the size of figures will agree that great improvements have taken place in the National Debt since the Mechanics of Civilization came to a stop on March 4, 1933. During the Hoover Administration the debt increased about $1,250,000,000 after allowing for recoverable loans. That is only about 10 percent of what the New Mechanics will accomplish. That increase will be about up to $14,000,000,000, less recoverable loans and plus large losses on guaranteed mortgages. The National Debt now bids fair to rise to a minimum of $35,000,000,000.

I note in the budget message President Roosevelt said, "The finances of the government are in better condition than at any time in the past seven years." You may remember the uneasiness of the decimal point which I mentioned some months ago. It has moved steadily to the left.

The New Deal could also report, "As a part of our fiscal policies we have set up 'Managed Credit' under the political seizure of the Federal Reserve System. We have set up 'Managed Currency' under political control of the value of the dollar. We have abandoned the gold standard. We have repudiated government obligations. We have made vast purchases of foreign silver at double the price of 1933. We are glad to say we have now enough foreign silver to plate all the spoons in the world."

Soon after assuming office three years ago President Roosevelt commented upon my partial failure to persuade a Democratic Congress to balance the budget. He said sternly; "Too often in recent history liberal governments have been wrecked on the rocks of loose fiscal policies. We must avoid this danger."

Those rocks are now looming up out of this fog. The nation has been steered into the dangerous channels of borrowing these vast deficits from the banks, by a huge cycle of bank credit inflation. That is printing press credit. The charts of all history show this channel leads to currency inflation. Every democracy which entered these straits has been sunk.

The explosive forces of inflation are already being generated. That is easily proved. The average price of industrial common stocks today are up to the level of 1926. But in 1926 there were no unemployed; today there are 10,000,000 unemployed. In 1926 our foreign trade was flourishing; today it is demoralized. In 1926 our budget was balanced, our currency was stable; today the budget is the worst unbalanced in history, the currency has its foundation in the will of one man.

The average price of industrial stocks has been restored to 1926, but have the real incomes of farmers and labor been restored to 1926?

We may well explore a little further as to what all this confusion of national finances means to the average man or woman. These currency and credit policies have driven men all over the nation into a scramble of buying equities to protect themselves. These policies have made a paradise for the speculator. He lives by shrewd anticipation in a land of confusion. Millions have been made in the stock market. Millions have been made by foreign speculators in silver. At the same time millions of Americans are tramping the streets looking for work. Speculation drains employment, it does not make it. Having opened the channels of greed, rightly the President may be worried over the greedy.

But worse than all that, out of these devaluation and inflation policies the cost of living inevitably and inexorably rises. The average man and his housewife will find these policies in every package they buy. The will find them in the decreased purchasing power of their insurance policy and their savings. Did it ever occur to American wage earners that the devaluation was a cut in wages? Some European statesmen were frank enough to say it when they did it. And on top of that somebody has to pay for this spending. Both we and our children will pay for these follies of our generation even if our liberal government escapes wreck upon the rocks of these loose fiscal policies. Does that point the average man to a "finer, better, happier life?"

The American people have a right to know and to know now what steps the President proposes to clean up this budget and money confusion. Unless this confusion can be quickly dissolved it will lead to one of the great tragedies of all humanity—inflation.

Confusion in Relief

The fourth battalion of confusion is the administration of relief. Under that guise great sociological experiments have been undertaken. The government has gone into private business on a high scale. These enterprises have created a million confusions and fears. Relief run from Washington and not from home has resulted in billions of waste spread over every town and county.

It has impaired self-reliance and morals both in individuals and in local government. The poison of politics is mixed in the bread of the helpless. The New Deal is optimistic that with relief under political control from Washington its dependents can be persuaded in their vote. But the ballot box is secret and the conscience of the average American man and woman may not be confused.

No Confusion in Politics

The New Deal is not confused in politics. National Planning has been a success in that field. But it is a moral confusion of every ideal of American government. For fifty years it has been an aspiration of America that our government officials should be removed from the political spoils system. The selection by merit through the Civil Service Commission was not alone to gain efficiency in government. Its purpose as to raise the morals of public life. It was to make impossible the bribe-taker, the invisible government of the greedy, and the corruption of elections. Since 1880 every President has steadily builded that service.

Let us examine the record. The Coolidge officials under the Civil Service were about 75 percent. The Hoover increase was to over 81 percent. The Roosevelt decrease has been to 57 percent. This is exhibit A of New Deal idealism.

All this sometimes reminds me of the small girl who said, "Mother, you know that beautiful jug that you said had been handed down to us from generation to generation?" Mother replied, "Yes, Ann, what of it?" And Ann answered solemnly, "This generation dropped it."

But we may explore that still further. During the Hoover Administration, despite the many emergency agencies needed to meet the depression, the total number of Federal officials was decreased by 10,000. But under the New Deal, part of full-time political officials have been increased by over 335,000. In his Jackson Day speech the President urged committees of one to support the New Deal in the campaign. He has a good start with 335,000 committees—and their wives.

But the average man who does not get his feet into the trough has to carry these officials on his back.

We have started upon the road of business recovery. That began instantly upon the restoration of some degree of confidence by the Supreme Court. But it is a confused recovery. We have still 10,000,000 people on relief after three years. Our durable goods industries lag behind. That is where the bulk of the 20,000,000 on relief come from. Our construction industries depend upon long-term confidence. But long-term confidence is weak. By a confused currency, men do not have confidence in what $100 may buy five years hence.

Moreover, real and permanent recovery will not take place so long as every businessman must make a blind bet on these confusions in Washington.

A balanced budget and a stable currency, would put more men to work than the whole WPA. They need confidence, not confusion.

Confusion in Administration

These gigantic plans of dictated economy were undertaken without searching inquiry as to fact or experience. They were undertaken without even shaping on the anvil of debate. They were undertaken in disregard of the Constitution. They have been without adequate administrative checks and balances. They have been administered by political appointees of inadequate executive experience. Despite this horde of officials there is not disintegration and confusion in the halls of government.

We are deluged with inconsistencies in action and conflict in purposes. Statements, propaganda, and philosophy collide every day. Many are half-truths and some are murky on that other half.

Confusion in Authorities

President Roosevelt has called upon the shades of his favorite past presidents to enliven the effervescence of righteousness which bubbles through intoxicating waters of the finer life. He has at time recalled Jefferson, Jackson, Lincoln, and Theodore Roosevelt to justify this State of the Union. I have not noticed any call upon the shade of Grover Cleveland.

To clear up some confusion as to their views I may also summon the shades of these favorite presidents upon the same subjects.

First, Thomas Jefferson, who said, "Were we directed from Washington when to sow and when to reap we should soon want bread." Apparently this was forgotten when they created the AAA.

Jefferson also said, "...the principle of spending money to be paid by posterity, under the name of funding, is but swindling futurity on a large scale." That would seem even truer to the children of this generation.

President Jackson said, "All history tells us that a free people should be watchful of delegated power." He did not know what it was to watch perpetual motion in delegated powers.

Jackson also believed in "To the victors belong the spoils." He was contented by appointing 2,000 of his followers to office. After all, he had a moderate spirit.

Theodore Roosevelt said, "If a change in currency were so enacted as to amount to dishonesty, that is repudiation of debts, it would be very bad morally."

The quotation was not sent to Congress with New Deal currency bills.

And may I add one quotation from Daniel Webster, who says: "He who tampers with the currency robs labor of its bread. He panders indeed to greedy capital, which is keen-sighted and may shift for itself, but he beggars labor, which is unsuspecting and too busy with the present to calculate the future. The prosperity of the working people lives, moves, and has its being in established credit and steady medium of payment."

Theodore Roosevelt also made many remarks upon the Civil Service. For instance; "No question of internal administration is so important...as...Civil Service Reform, because the spoils system...has been for seventy years the most potent of all the forces tending to bring about the degradation of our politics." That is not often quoted out loud.

Theodore Roosevelt further said, "A broken promise is bad enough in private life. It is worse in the field of politics. No man is worth his salt in public life who makes on the stump a pledge which he does not keep after election...."

There is more to that quotation, but I omit it lest it would create hard feelings.

The President quotes Josiah Royce. Perhaps he overlooked this remark from that philosopher: "The present tendency to the centralization of power in our national government seems to me, then, a distinct danger. It is a substitution of power for loyalty."

Just a quotation or two from Lincoln. He asked that President Polk answer certain questions, and said, "Let him answer fully, fairly, and candidly. Let him answer with facts and not with arguments. Let him remember that he sits where Washington sat, and so remembering, let him answer as Washington would answer."

That shows they used to treat Presidents less gently than we do.

Confusion of the Constitution

Beyond all this there are more somber confusions. The ideals of liberty have been confused.

Behind all this is the great and fundamental conflict which has brought infinite confusion to the nation. That is the conflict between a philosophy of orderly individual liberty and a philosophy of government dictation.

Ten of the assaults upon liberty have already cracked against the Constitution of the United States. And has there been public outcry at their loss? There has been a lift to the soul of the nation. Millions of average men and women have given thanks to the Almighty that the forethought of great Americans has saved for them freedom itself.

But the Court cannot deal with all the assaults upon the spirit of American liberty. It was the spirit of liberty which made our American civilization. That spirit made the Constitution. If that spirit is gone the Constitution is gone, even though its words remain. The undermining of local government by centralization at Washington, the spoils system, the reduction of Congress to a rubber stamp, these monetary policies—what of these?

The President implies he will not retreat, despite the decisions of the Court. We have heard mutterings that the Constitution must be changed, that it is outmoded, that it was useful only in the horse and buggy days. There was sinister invitation to Congress to "find means to protect its own prerogative."

No progressive mind will feel that the Constitution shall not be changed to meet the needs of changing national life.

But what is the change these men harbor in their minds? The American people have a right to know. They have the right to know it now.

Whatever the change may be, it must be clear of those confusions which impair the great safeguards of human liberty.

There must never be confusion in the Bill of Rights, the balance of powers, local government, and a government of laws, not of men.

Do you not conclude that the State of the Union is one of Confusion? Is this in the interest of the average man and woman?

Does this advance our children toward a "finer, better, and happier life?"

A great American once said in application to another crisis: "We have, as all will agree, a free government, where every man has the right to be equal with every other man. In this great struggle, this form of government and every form of human right is endangered if our enemies succeed. There is more involved in this contest than is realized by everyone. There is involved in this struggle the question whether your children and my children shall enjoy the privileges we have enjoyed." That was Abraham Lincoln.

XXXVII
Herbert Hoover:
Crisis to Free Men
Republican National Convention
June 10, 1936

In this room rests the greatest responsibility that has come to a body of Americans in three generations. In the lesser sense this is a convention of a great political party. But in the larger sense it is a convention of Americans to determine the fate of those ideals for which this nation was founded. That far transcends all partisanship.

There are elemental currents which make or break the fate of nations. There is a moral purpose in the universe. Those forces which affect the vitality and the soul of a people will control their destinies. The sum of years of public service in these currents is the overwhelming conviction of their transcendent importance over the more transitory, even though difficult, issues of national life.

I have given about four years to research into the New Deal, trying to determine what its ultimate objectives were, what sort of a system it is imposing on the country.

To some people it appears to be a strange interlude in American history in that it has no philosophy, that it is sheer opportunism, that it is a muddle of a spoils system, or emotional economics, of reckless adventure, of unctuous claims to a monopoly of human sympathy, of greed for power, of a desire for popular acclaim and an aspiration to make the front pages of the newspapers. That is the most charitable view.

To other people it appears to be a cold-blooded attempt by starry-eyed boys to infect the American people by a mixture of European ideas, flavored with our native predilection to get something for nothing.

You can choose either one you like best. But the first is the road of chaos which leads to the second. Both of these roads lead over the same grim precipice that is the crippling and possibly the destruction of the freedom of men.

Which of these interpretations is accurate is even disputed by alumni of the New Deal who have graduated for conscience's sake or have graduated by request.

In Central Europe the march of Socialist or Fascist dictatorships and their destruction of liberty did not set out with guns and armies. Dictators began their ascent to the seats of power through the elections provided by liberal institutions. Their weapons were promise and hate. They offered the mirage of Utopia to those in distress. They flung the poison of class hatred. They may not have maimed the bodies of men, but they maimed their souls.

The 1932 campaign was a pretty good imitation of this first stage of European tactics. You may recall the promises of the abundant life, the propaganda of hate.

Once seated in office, the first demand of these European despotisms was for power and "actions." Legislatures were told they "must" delegate their authorities. Their free debate was suppressed. The powers demanded are always the same pattern. They all adopt Planned Economy. They regimented industry and agriculture. They put the government into business. They engaged in gigantic government expenditures. They created vast organizations of spoils henchmen and subsidized dependents. They corrupted currency and credit. They drugged the thinking of the people with propaganda at the people's expense.

If there are any items in the stage in the march of European collectivism that the New Deal has not imitated it must have been an oversight.

But at this point this parallel with Europe halts—at least for the present. The American people should thank Almighty God for the Constitution and the Supreme Court. They should be grateful to a courageous press.

You might contemplate what would have happened if Mr. Roosevelt could have appointed enough Supreme Court Justices in the first year of his administration. Suppose these New Deal acts had remained upon the statute books. We would have been a regimented people. Have you any assurance that he will not have the appointments if he is re-elected?

[A] Ministers Whom Roosevelt Retains

The succeeding stages of violence and outrage by which European despotisms have crushed all liberalism and all freedom have filled our headlines for years.

But what comes next in the United States? Have the New Dealers dropped their ideas of centralization of government? Have they abandoned the notion of regimenting the people into a planned economy? Has that greed for power become cooled by the resistance of a people with a heritage of liberty? Will they resume if they are re-elected?

When we examine the speeches of Tugwell, Wallace, Ickes and others, we see little indication of repentance.

[B] New Deal Laws Attack Our Freedom

So much for the evidence that the New Deal is a definite attempt to replace the American system of freedom with some sort of European planned existence. But let us assume that the explanation is simply hit-and-run opportunism, spoils system and muddle.

We can well take a moment to explore the prospects of American ideals of liberty and self-government under that philosophy. We may take only seven short examples.

The Supreme Court has reversed some ten or twelve of the New Deal major enactments. Many of these acts were a violation of the rights of men and of self-government. Despite the sworn duty of the Executive and Congress to defend these rights they have sought to take them into their own hands. That is an attack on the foundations of freedom.

More than this, the independence of the Congress, the Supreme Court and the Executive are pillars at the door of liberty. For three years the word "must" has invaded the independence of Congress. And the Congress has abandoned its responsibility to check even the expenditures of money. They have turned open appropriations into personal power. These are destructions of the very safeguards of free people.

We have seen these gigantic expenditures and this torrent of waste pile up a national debt which two generations cannot repay. One time I told a Democratic Congress that "you cannot spend yourselves into prosperity." You recall that advice did not take then. It hasn't taken yet.

Billions have been spent to prime the economic pump. It did employ a horde of paid officials upon the pump handle. We have seen the frantic attempts to find new taxes on the rich. Yet three-quarters of the bill will be sent to the average man and the poor. He and his wife and his grandchildren will be giving a quarter of all their working days to pay taxes. Freedom to work for himself is changed into a slavery of work for the follies of government.

[C] Explosive Inflation is seen in Borrowing

We have seen an explosive inflation of bank credits by this government borrowing. We have seen varied steps toward currency inflation that have already enriched the speculator and deprived the poor. If this is to continue, the end result is the tears and anguish of universal bankruptcy and distress. No democracy in history has survived the final stages of inflation.

We have seen the building up of a horde of political officials. We have seen the pressures upon the helpless and destitute to trade political support for relief. Both are a pollution of the very fountains of liberty.

We have seen the most elemental violation of economic law and experience. The New Deal forgets it is solely by production of more goods and more varieties of goods and services that we advance the standard of living and security of men. If we constantly decrease costs and prices and keep up earnings, the production of plenty will be more and more widely distributed. These laws may be re-stitched in new phrases but they are the very shoes of human progress.

We had so triumphed in this long climb of mankind toward plenty that we had reached Mount Pisgah, where we looked over the promised land of abolished poverty. Then men began to quarrel over the division of the goods. The depression produced by war destruction temporarily checked our march toward the promised land.

Then came the little prophets of the New Deal. They announce the striking solution that the way out is to produce less and to increase prices so the people can buy less. They have kept on providing some new restriction or burden or fright down to a week ago.

At least it has enabled the New Deal to take a few hundred thousand earnest party workers to the promised land. It takes the rest of us for a ride into the wilderness of unemployment.

[D] Hubbard School of Economics

Can democracy stand the strain of Mother Hubbard economics for long? Will there be anything left in the economic cupboard but a bone?

Any examination of the economic muddle of the past three years shows the constant threat of price fixing, restriction of production and drive against small business. That is the soul of monopoly. That has maintained from the NRA to the last tax bill. These are old tricks in no new disguise which put shackles upon the freedom of men.

In desperate jumping from one muddle to another we have seen repeated violation of morals and honor in government. Do I need to recall the repudiation of obligations, the clipping of the coin, the violation of trust to guard the Constitution, and the coercion of the voter? When the standards of honor and morals fail in government, they will fail in a people.

There are some moral laws written in a Great Book. Over all there is the Gospel of Brotherhood. For the first time in the history of America we have heard the gospel of class hatred preached from the White House. That is human poison far more deadly than fear. Every reader of the history of democracy knows that is the final rock upon which all democracies have been wrecked.

There is the suggestion in the Gospels that it is the meek who will inherit the earth. The New Deal will have little inheritance. There are recommendations as to righteousness for righteousness' sake only. I will not elaborate that.

If all this is the theory and practice of muddle, where has it brought us, even now? We have spent $15,000,000,000 more than the last administration. We have a debt ten billions greater than even the Great War debt. After three years we still have the same number of unemployed that we had at the election of November, 1932. These actions are bringing injury to the well being of people it purports to serve. It has produced gross reactionarism in the guise of liberalism. And above all, the New Deal has brought that which George Washington called "alterations which may impair the energy of the system and thus overthrow that which cannot be directly overthrown."

Republicans! After a hundred and fifty years, we have arrived at that hour.

[E] Americanism Poisoned by New Deal

The New Deal may be a revolutionary design to replace the American system with despotism. It may be the dream stuff of a false liberalism. It may be the valor of muddle. Their relationship to each other, however, is exactly the sistership of the witches who brewed the caldron of powerful trouble for Macbeth. Their product is the poisoning of Americanism.

The President has constantly reiterated that he will not retreat. For months, to be sure, there has been a strange quiet. Just as the last campaign was fought on promises that have been broken, so apparently this campaign is to be slipped through by evasion.

But the American people have the right to know now, while they still have power to act. What is going to be done after election with these measures which the Constitution forbids and the people by their votes have never authorized? What do the New Dealers propose to do with these unstable currencies, unbalanced budgets, debts and taxes? Fifty words would make it clear. Surely the propaganda agencies which emit half a million words a day could find room for these fifty. I noticed they recently spent 300 words on how to choose a hat. It is slightly more important to know the fate of a nation.

You have the duty to determine the principles upon which the Republican party will stand. You make the laws of the party. Whether it is within the party or a government, our system is a government of laws and not of men, and the Republican party holds its promises and its laws.

The immediate task is to set the country on the road of genuine recovery from the paths of instability. We have enough inventions and enough accumulated needs to start the physical rebuilding of America. The day the Republican party can assure right principles we can turn this nation from the demoralization of relief to the contentment of constructive jobs. Herein—and herein alone—is a guarantee of jobs for the 11,000,000 idle based upon realities, and not on political claptrap.

In the meantime, the party which organized efficient relief of the unemployed three years before the New Deal was born will not turn from those in need. That support to distress comes from the conscience and sympathy of a people, not from the New Deal.

[F] Party's First Job is to Put Men to Work

Four years ago I stated that the Republican Party must undertake progressive reforms from evils exposed by the boom and depression. But I stated our first job was to restore men to work. The New Deal has attempted many reforms. They have delayed recovery. Parts of them are good. Some have failed. Some are tainted with collectivist ideas. That task must be undertaken anew by the Republican Party.

A new danger is created to the Republic in that the swing from the foolishness of radicalism may carry us to the selfishness of reaction.

The Republican party must achieve true social betterment. But we must produce measures that will not work confusion and disappointment. We must propose a real approach to social evils, not the prescription for them, by quacks, of poison in place of remedy.

We must achieve freedom in the economic field. We have grave problems in relation of government to agriculture and business. Monopoly is only one of them. The Republican party is against the greed for power of the wanton boys who waste the people's savings. But it must be equally adamant against the greed for power and exploitation in the seekers of special privilege. At one time I said: "We can no more have economic power without checks and balances than we can have political power without checks and balances. Either one leads to tyranny."

The Republican party must be a party that accepts the challenge of each new day. The last word in human accomplishment has not been spoken. The last step in human progress has not been made. We welcome change when it will produce a fairer, more just and satisfying civilization. But change which destroys the safeguards of free men and women are only apples of Sodom.

Great calamities have come to the whole world. These forces have reached into every calling and every cottage. They have brought tragedy and suffering to millions of firesides. I have great sympathy for those who honestly reach for short cuts to the immensity of our problems.

While design of the structure of betterment for the common man must be inspired by the human heart, it can only be achieved by the intellect. It can only be builded by using the mold of justice, by laying brick upon brick from the materials of scientific research; by the painstaking sifting of truth from the collection of fact and experience.   Any other mold is distorted; any other bricks are without straw; any other foundations are sand.   That great structure of human progress can be built only by free men and women.

The gravest task which confronts the party is to regenerate these freedoms.

There are principles which neither tricks of organization nor the rigors of depression, nor the march of time, nor New Dealers, nor Socialists, nor Fascists can change. There are some principles which came into the universe along with the shooting stars of which worlds are made, and they have always been and ever will be true. Such are the laws of mathematics, the law of gravitation, the existence of God and the ceaseless struggle of humankind to be free.

Throughout the centuries of history, man's vigil and his quest have been to be free. For this, the best and bravest of earth have fought and died.   To embody human liberty in workable government, America was born. Shall we keep that faith? Must we condemn the unborn generations to fight again and to die for the right to be free?

There are some principles that cannot be compromised. Either we shall have a society based upon ordered liberty and the initiative of the individual, or we shall have a planned society that means dictation, no matter what you call it or who does it.   There is no half-way ground. They cannot be mixed. Government must either release the powers off the individual for honest achievement or the very forces it creates will drive it inexorably to lay its paralyzing hand more and more heavily upon individual effort.

Less than twenty years ago we accepted those ideals as the air we breathed. We fought a Great War for their protection. We took upon ourselves obligations of billions.   We buried our sons in foreign soil. But in this score of years we have seen the advance of collectivism and its inevitable tyranny in more than half the civilized world.   In this thundering era of world crisis distracted America stands confused and uncertain.

The Whig party temporized, compromised upon the issue of slavery for the black man. That party disappeared. It deserved to disappear. Shall the Republican party deserve or receive any better fate if it compromises upon the issue of freedom for all men, white as well as black?

You of this convention must make the answer.

Let us not blink at the difficulties. Throughout the land there are multitudes of people who have listened to the songs of sirens. Thousands of men, if put to the choice, would willingly exchange liberty for fancied security even under dictatorship. Under their distress they doubt the value of their own rights and liberties. They do not see the Constitution as a fortress for their defense. They have been led to believe that it is an iron cage against which the wings of idealism beat in vain.

They do not realize that their only relief and their hope of economic security can come only from the enterprise and initiative of free men.

Let this convention declare without shrinking that the source of economic prosperity is freedom. Man must be free to use his own powers in his own way. Free to think, to speak, to worship. Free to plan his own life. Free to use his own initiative. Free to dare in his own adventure. It is the essence of true liberalism that these freedoms are limited by the rights of others.

Freedom both requires and makes increased responsibilities. There is no freedom from exploitation of the weak or from the dead hand of bureaucracy.

[G] Today's Issues Bigger than Payrolls

There's something vastly bigger than payrolls, than economics, than materialism at issue in this campaign. The free spirit of men is the source of self-respect, of sturdiness, of moral and spiritual progress. With the inspirations of freedom come fidelity to public trust, honor and morals in government. The social order does not rest upon orderly economic freedom alone. It rests even more upon the ideals and character of a people. Governments must express those ideals in frugality, in justice, in courage, in decency, and in regard for the less fortunate, and, above all, in honor. Nations die when these weaken, no matter what their material prosperity.

Fundamental American liberties are at stake. Is the Republican party ready for the issue? Are you willing to cast your all upon the issue, or would you falter and look back? Will you, for expediency's sake also offer will-o'-the-wisps which beguile the people? Or have you determined to enter in a holy crusade for freedom which shall determine the future and the perpetuity of a nation of free men? That star shell fired today over the no man's land of world despair would illuminate the world with hope.

In another great crisis in American history that great Republican, Abraham Lincoln, said: "Fellow-citizens, we cannot escape history. We...will be remembered in spite of ourselves. No personal significance or insignificance can spare one or another of us. The fiery trial through which we pass will light us down in honor or dishonor to the latest generation...We—even we here—hold the power and bear the responsibility. We shall nobly save or meanly lose the last, best hope of earth. The way is plain. a way which, if followed, the world will forever applaud."

Republicans and fellow-Americans! This is your call. Stop the retreat. In the chaos of doubt, confusion and fear yours is the task to command. Stop the retreat, and turning the eyes of your fellow-Americans to the sunlight of freedom, lead the attack to retake, recapture and remain the citadels of liberty. Thus can America be preserved. Thus can the peace, plenty and security be re-established and expanded. Thus can the opportunity, the inheritance and the spiritual future of your children be guaranteed. And thus you will win the gratitude of posterity and the blessings of Almighty God.

XXXVIII
Republican Party Platform
June 11, 1936

America is in peril. The welfare of American men and women and the future of our youth are at stake. We dedicate ourselves to the preservation of their political liberty, their individual opportunity and their character as free citizens, which today for the first time are threatened by government itself. For three long years the New Deal Administration has dishonored American traditions and flagrantly betrayed the pledges upon which the Democratic Party sought and received public support.

The powers of Congress have been usurped by the President.

The integrity and authority of the Supreme Court have been flouted.

The rights and liberties of American citizens have been violated.

Regulated monopoly has displaced free enterprise.

The New Deal Administration constantly seeks to usurp the rights reserved to the states and the people.

It has insisted on the passage of laws contrary to the Constitution.

It has intimidated witnesses and interfered with the right of petition.

It has dishonored our country by repudiating its most sacred obligations.

It has been guilty of frightful waste and extravagance, using public funds for partisan political purposes.

It has promoted investigations to harass and intimidate American citizens, at the same time denying investigations into its own improper expenditures.

It has created a vast multitude of new offices, filled them with its favorites, set up a centralized bureaucracy, and sent out swarms of inspectors to harass our people.

It had bred fear and hesitation in commerce and industry, thus discouraging new enterprises, preventing employment and prolonging the depression.

It secretly has made tariff agreements with our foreign competitors, flooding our markets with foreign commodities.

It has coerced and intimidated voters by withholding relief from those opposing its tyrannical policies.

It has destroyed the morale of many of our people and made them dependent upon government.

Appeals to passion and class prejudice have replaced reason and tolerance.

To a free people these actions are insufferable.

This campaign cannot be waged on the traditional differences between the Republican and Democratic parties. The responsibility of this election transcends all previous political divisions. We invite all Americans, irrespective of party, to join us in defense of American institutions.

[A] Constitutional Government and Free Enterprise

We Pledge Ourselves: 1) To maintain the American system of constitutional and local self government, and to resist all attempts to impair the authority of the Supreme Court of the United States, the final protector of the rights of our citizens against the arbitrary encroachments of the legislative and executive branches of government. There can be no individual liberty without an independent judiciary; 2) To preserve the American system of free enterprise, private competition, and equality of opportunity, and to seek its constant betterment in the interests of all.

[B] Reemployment

The only permanent solution of the unemployment problem is the absorption of the unemployed by industry and agriculture. To that end, we advocate: Removal of restrictions on production. Abandonment of all New Deal policies that raise production costs, increase the cost of living, and thereby restrict buying, reduce volume and prevent reemployment. Encouragement instead of hindrance to legitimate business.

Withdrawal of government from competition with private payrolls.

Elimination of unnecessary and hampering regulations.

Adoption of such policies as will furnish a chance for individual enterprise, industrial expansion, and the restoration of jobs.

[C] Relief

The necessities of life must be provided for the needy, and hope must be restored pending recovery. The administration of relief is a major failure of the New Deal. It has been faithless to those who most deserve our sympathy. To end confusion, partisanship, waste and incompetence,

We Pledge: 1) The return of responsibility for relief administration to non-political local agencies familiar with community problems; 2) Federal grants-in-aid to the States and Territories while the need exists, upon compliance with these conditions: (a) a fair proportion of the total relief burden to be provided from the revenues of States and local governments; (b) all engaged in relief administration to be selected on the basis of merit and fitness; (c) adequate provision to be made for the encouragement of those persons who are trying to become self-supporting; 3) Undertaking of Federal public works only on their merits and separate from the administration of relief; 4) A prompt determination of the facts concerning relief and unemployment.

[D] Security

Real security will be possible only when our productive capacity is sufficient to furnish a decent standard of living for all American families and to provide a surplus for future needs and contingencies. For the attainment of that ultimate objective, we look to the energy, self-reliance and character of our people, and to our system of free enterprise. Society has an obligation to promote the security of the people, by affording some measure of protection against involuntary unemployment and dependency in old age. The New Deal policies, while purporting to provide social security, have, in fact, endangered it.

We propose a system of old age security.

We propose to encourage adoption by the States and Territories of honest and practical measures for meeting the problems of unemployment insurance.

The unemployment insurance and old age annuity sections of the present Social Security Act are unworkable and deny benefits to about two-thirds of our adult population, including professional men and women and all those engaged in agriculture and domestic service, and the self employed, while imposing heavy tax burdens upon all. The so-called reserve fund estimated at forty-seven billion dollars for old age insurance is no reserve at all, because the fund will contain nothing but the government's promise to pay, while the taxes collected in the guise of premiums will be wasted by the government in reckless and extravagant political schemes.

[E] Labor

The welfare of labor rests upon increased production and the prevention of exploitation.

We pledge ourselves to: 1) Protect the right of labor to organize and to bargain collectively through representatives of its own choosing without interference from any source; 2) Prevent governmental job holders from exercising autocratic powers over labor; 3) Support the adoption of State laws and interstate compacts to abolish sweatshops and child labor, and to protect women and children with respect to maximum hours, minimum wages and working conditions. We believe that this can be done within the Constitution as it now stands.

[F] Agriculture

Our paramount object is to protect and foster the family type of farm, traditional in American life, and to promote policies which will bring about an adjustment of agriculture to meet the needs of domestic and foreign markets. As an emergency measure, during the agricultural depression, Federal benefit payments or grants-in-aid when administered within the means of the Federal Government are consistent with a balanced budget.

We Propose: 1) To facilitate economical production and increased consumption on a basis of abundance instead of scarcity;

2) A national land-use program, including the acquisition of abandoned and nonproductive farm lands by voluntary sale or lease, subject to approval of the legislative and executive branches of the States concerned, and the devotion of such land to appropriate public use, such as watershed protection and flood prevention, reforestation, recreation, and conservation of wild life; 3) That an agricultural policy be pursued for the protection and restoration of the land resources, designed to bring about such a balance between soil-building and soil-depleting crops as will permanently insure productivity, with reasonable benefits to cooperating farmers on family-type farms, but so regulated as to eliminate the New Deal's destructive policy towards the dairy and live-stock industries; 4) To extend experimental aid to farmers developing new crops suited to our soil and climate; 5) To promote the industrial use of farm products by applied science; 6) To protect the American farmer against the importation of all livestock, dairy, and agricultural products, substitutes therefor, and derivatives therefrom, which will depress American farm prices; 7) To provide effective quarantine against imported livestock, dairy and other farm products from countries which do not impose health and sanitary regulations fully equal to those required of our own producers; 8) To provide for ample farm credit at rates as low as those enjoyed by other industries, including commodity and livestock loans, and preference in land loans to the farmer acquiring or refinancing a farm as a home; 9) To provide for decentralized, non-partisan control of the Farm Credit Administration and the election by National Farm Loan Associations of at least one-half of each Board of Directors of the Federal Land Banks, and thereby remove these institutions from politics; 10) To provide, in the case of agricultural products of which there are exportable surpluses, the payment of reasonable benefits upon the domestically consumed portion of such crops in order to make the tariff effective. These payments are to be limited to the production level of the family-type farm; 11) To encourage and further develop cooperative marketing; 12) To furnish government assistance in disposing of surpluses in foreign trade by bargaining for foreign markets selectively by countries both as to exports and imports. We strenuously oppose so-called reciprocal treaties which trade off the American farmer; 13) To give every reasonable assistance to producers in areas suffering from

temporary disaster, so that they may regain and maintain a self-supporting status.

[G] Monopolies

A private monopoly is indefensible and intolerable. It menaces and, if continued, will utterly destroy constitutional government and the liberty of the citizen.

We favor the vigorous enforcement of the criminal laws, as well as the civil laws, against monopolies and trusts and their officials, and we demand the enactment of such additional legislation as is necessary to make it impossible for private monopoly to exist in the United States.

We will employ the full powers of the government to the end that monopoly shall be eliminated and that free enterprise shall be fully restored and maintained.

[H] Regulation of Business

We recognize the existence of a field within which governmental regulation is desirable and salutary. The authority to regulate should be vested in an independent tribunal acting under clear and specific laws establishing definite standards. Their determinations on law and facts should be subject to review by the Courts. We favor Federal regulation, within the Constitution, of the marketing of securities to protect investors. We favor also Federal regulation of the interstate activities of public utilities.

[I] Civil Service

Under the New Deal, official authority has been given to inexperienced and incompetent persons. The Civil Service has been sacrificed to create a national political machine. As a result the Federal Government has never presented such a picture of confusion and inefficiency.

We pledge ourselves to: the merit system, virtually destroyed by New Deal spoilsmen. It should be restored, improved and extended.

[J] Government Finance

The New Deal Administration has been characterized by shameful waste and general financial irresponsibility. It has piled deficit upon deficit. It threatens national bankruptcy and the destruction through inflation of insurance policies and savings bank deposits.

We pledge ourselves to: 1) Stop the folly of uncontrolled spending; 2) Balance the budget—not by increasing taxes but by cutting expenditures, drastically and immediately; 3) Revise the Federal tax system and coordinate it with State and local tax systems; 4) Use the taxing power for raising revenue and not for punitive or political purposes.

[K] Money and Banking

We advocate a sound currency to be preserved at all hazards.

The first requisite to a sound and stable currency is a balanced budget.

We oppose further devaluation of the dollar.

We will restore to the Congress the authority lodged with it by the Constitution to coin money and regulate the value thereof by repealing all the laws delegating this authority to the executive.

We will cooperate with other countries toward stabilization of currencies as soon as we can do so with due regard for our national interests and as soon as other nations have sufficient stability to justify such action.

[L] Bill of Rights

We pledge ourselves to preserve, protect and defend, against all intimidation and threat, freedom of religion, speech, press and radio; and the right of assembly and petition and immunity from unreasonable searches and seizures.

We offer the abiding security of a government of laws as against the autocratic perils of a government of men.

[M] Furthermore

We are opposed to legislation which discriminates against women in Federal and State employment.

[N] Conclusion

We assume the obligations and duties imposed upon government by modern conditions.   We affirm our unalterable conviction that, in the future as in the past, the fate of the nation will depend, not so much on the wisdom and power of government, as on the character and virtue, self-reliance, industry and thrift of the people and on their willingness to meet the responsibilities essential to the preservation of a free society.

Finally, as our party affirmed in its first Platform in 1856: "Believing that the spirit of our institutions as well as the Constitution of our country guarantees liberty of conscience and equality of rights among our citizens, we oppose all legislation tending to impair them," and "we invite the affiliation and cooperation of the men of all parties, however differing from us in other respects, in support of the principles herein declared."

XXXIX
Democratic Party Platform
June 25, 1936

We hold this truth to be self-evident—that the test of a representative government is its ability to promote the safety and happiness of the people.

We hold this truth to be self-evident—that twelve years of Republican leadership left our nation sorely stricken in body, mind and spirit; and that three years of Democratic leadership have put it back on the road to restored health and prosperity.

We hold this truth to be self-evident—that twelve years of Republican surrender to the dictatorship of a privileged few have supplanted by a Democratic leadership which has returned the people themselves to the place of authority, and has revived in them new faith and restored the hope which they had almost lost.

We hold this truth to be self-evident—that this three-year recovery in all the basic values of life and the reestablishment of the American way of living has been brought by humanizing the policies of the Federal Government as they affect the personal, financial, industrial and agricultural well-being of the American people.

We hold this truth to be self-evident—that government in a modern civilization has certain inescapable obligations to its citizens, among which are: (1) Protection of the family and the home; (2) Establishment of a democracy of opportunity for all the people; (3) Aid to those overtaken by disaster.

These obligations, neglected through twelve years of the old leadership, have once more been recognized by American Government. Under the new leadership they will never be neglected.

[A] Savings and Investment
We have safeguarded the thrift of our citizens by restraining those who would gamble with other people's savings, by requiring truth in the sale of securities; by putting the brakes upon the use of credit for speculation; by outlawing the manipulation of prices in

stock and commodity markets; by curbing the overweening power and unholy practices of utility holding companies; by insuring fifty million banks accounts.

[B] Old Age and Social Security

We have built foundations for the security of those who are faced with the hazards of unemployment and old age, for the orphaned, the crippled and the blind. On the foundation of the Social Security Act we are determined to erect a structure of economic security for all our people, making sure that this benefit shall keep step with the ever-increasing capacity of America to provide a high standard of living for all its citizens.

[C] Consumer

We will act to secure to the consumer fair value, honest sales and a decreased spread between the price he pays and the price the producer receives.

[D] Rural Electrification

This administration has fostered power rate yardsticks in the Tennessee Valley and in several other parts of the nation. As a result electricity has been made available to the people at a lower rate. We will continue to promote plans for rural electrification and for cheap power by means of the yardstick method.

[E] Housing

We maintain that our people are entitled to decent, adequate housing at a price which they can afford. In the last three years the Federal Government, having saved more than two million homes from foreclosure, has taken the first steps in our history to provide decent housing for people of meager incomes. We believe every encouragement should be given to the building of new homes by private enterprise, and that the government should steadily extend its housing program toward the goal of adequate housing for those forced through economic necessities to live in unhealthy and slum conditions.

[F] Veterans

We shall continue just treatment of our war veterans and their dependents.

[G] Agriculture

We have taken the farmers off the road to ruin.

We have kept our pledge to agriculture to use all available means to raise farm income towards its pre-war purchasing power.

By Federal legislation we have reduced the farmer's indebtedness and doubled his net income. In cooperation with the States and through the farmers' own committees, we are restoring the fertility of his land and checking the erosion of his soil. We are bringing electricity and good roads to his home.

We shall continue to improve the soil conservation and domestic allotment program with payments to farmers.

We recognize the gravity of the evils of farm tenancy, and we pledge the full cooperation of the government in the refinancing of farm indebtedness at the lowest possible rates of interest and over a long term of years.

We favor the production of all the market will absorb, both at home and abroad, plus a reserve supply sufficient to insure fair prices to consumers; we favor judicious commodity loans on seasonal surpluses; and we favor assistance within Federal authority to enable farmers to adjust and balance production with demand, at a fair profit to the farmers.

We favor encouragement of sound, practical farm cooperatives.

By the purchase and retirement of ten million acres of sub-marginal land, and assistance to those attempting to eke out an existence upon it, we have made a good beginning toward proper land use and rural rehabilitation.

The farmer has been returned to the road to freedom and prosperity. We will keep him on that road.

[H] Labor

We have given the army of America's industrial workers something more substantial than the Republicans' dinner pail full of promises. We have increased the worker's pay and shortened his hours; we have undertaken to put an end to the sweated labor of his wife and children; we have written into the law of the land his right to collective bargaining and self-organization free from the interference of employers; we have provided Federal machinery for the peaceful settlement of labor disputes.

We will continue to protect the worker and we will guard his rights, both as wage earner and consumer, in the production and consumption of all commodities, including coal and water power and other natural resource products.

[I] Business

We have taken the American businessman out of the red. We have saved his bank and given it a sounder foundation; we have extended credit; we have lowered interest rates; we have undertaken to free him from the ravages of cutthroat competition.

[J] Monopoly and Concentration of Economic Power

Monopolies and the concentration of economic power, the creation of Republican rule and privilege, continue to be the master of the producer, the exploiter of the consumer, and the enemy of the independent operator. This is a problem challenging the unceasing effort of untrammeled public officials in every branch of the government. We pledge vigorously and fearlessly to enforce the criminal and civil provisions of the existing anti-trust laws, and to the extent that their effectiveness has been weakened by new corporate devices or judicial construction, we propose by law to restore their efficacy in stamping out monopolistic practices and the concentration of economic power.

[K] Unemployment

We believe that unemployment is a national problem, and that it is an inescapable obligation. Where business fails to supply such employment, we believe that work at prevailing wages should be provided in cooperation with State and local governments on useful public projects, to the end that the national wealth may be increased, the skill and energy of the worker may be utilized, his morale maintained, and the unemployed assured the opportunity to earn the necessities of life.

[L] The Constitution

The Republican platform proposes to meet many pressing national problems solely by action of the separate States. We know that drought, dust storms, floods, minimum wages, maximum hours, child labor and working conditions in industry, monopolistic and unfair business practices cannot be adequately handled exclusively by 48 separate State legislatures, 48 separate State administrations and 48 separate State courts. Transactions and activities which inevitably overflow State boundaries call for both State and Federal treatment.

We have sought and will continue to seek to meet these problems through legislation within the Constitution.

If these problems cannot be effectively solved by legislation within the Constitution, we shall seek such clarifying amendment as will assure to the legislatures of the several States and to the Congress of the United States, each within its proper jurisdiction, the power to enact those laws which the State and Federal legislatures, within their respective spheres, shall find necessary in order adequately to regulate commerce, protect public health and safety and safeguard economic security. Thus we propose to maintain the letter and spirit of the Constitution.

[M] The Merit System in Government

For the protection of government itself and promotion of its efficiency, we pledge the immediate extension of the merit system through the classified civil service—which was first established and fostered under Democratic auspices—to all non-policy-making positions in the Federal service.

We shall subject to the civil service law all continuing positions which, because of the emergency, have been exempt from its operation.

[N] Civil Liberties

We shall continue to guard the freedom of speech, press, radio, religion and assembly which our Constitution guarantees, with equal rights to all and special privileges to none.

The administration has stopped deflation, restored values and enabled business to go ahead with confidence.

[O] The Issue

The issue in this election is plain. The American people are called upon to choose between a Republican Administration that has and would again regiment them in the service of privileged groups and a Democratic Administration dedicated to the establishment of equal economic opportunity for all our people.

We have faith in the destiny of our nation. We are sufficiently endowed with natural resources and with productive capacity to provide for all a quality of life that meets the standards of real Americanism.

Dedicated to a government of liberal American principles, we are determined to oppose equally, the despotism of Communism and the menace of concealed Fascism.

We hold this final truth to be self-evident—that the interests, the security and the happiness of the people of the United States of America can be perpetuated only under the democratic government as conceived by the founders of our nation.

XL
Franklin D. Roosevelt:
Presidential Re-Nomination Address
Democratic National Convention
June 27, 1936

Senator Robinson, Members of the Democratic Convention, my friends:

Here, and in every community throughout the land, we are met at a time of great moment to the future of the nation. It is an occasion to be dedicated to the simple and sincere expression of an attitude toward problems, the determination of which will profoundly affect America.

I come not only as a leader of a party, not only as a candidate for high office, but as one upon whom many critical hours have imposed and still impose a grave responsibility.

For the sympathy, help and confidence with which Americans have sustained me in my task I am grateful. For their loyalty I salute the members of our great party, in and out of political life in every part of the Union. I salute those of other parties, especially those in the Congress of the United States who on so many occasions have put partisanship aside. I thank the Governors of the several States, their Legislatures, their State and local officials who participated unselfishly and regardless of party in our efforts to achieve recovery and destroy abuses. Above all I thank the millions of Americans who have borne disaster bravely and have dared to smile through the storm.

America will not forget these recent years, will not forget that the rescue was not a mere party task. It was the concern of all of us. In our strength we rose together, rallied our energies together, applied the old rules of common sense, and together survived.

In those days we feared fear. That was why we fought fear. And today, my friends, we have won against the most dangerous of our foes. We have conquered fear.

But I cannot, with candor, tell you that all is well with the world. Clouds of suspicion, tides of ill will and intolerance gather darkly in many places. In our own land we enjoy indeed a fullness of life greater than that of most nations. But the rush of modern civilization itself has raised for us new difficulties, new problems which must be solved if we are to preserve to the United States the political and economic freedom for which Washington and Jefferson planned and fought.

Philadelphia is a good city in which to write American history. This is fitting ground on which to reaffirm the faith of our fathers; to pledge ourselves to restore to the people a wider freedom; to give to 1936 as the founders gave to 1776—an American way of life.

That very word freedom, in itself and of necessity, suggests freedom from some restraining power. In 1776 we sought freedom from the tyranny of a political autocracy—from the eighteenth century royalists who held special privileges from the crown. It was to perpetuate their privilege that they governed without the consent of the governed; that they denied the right of free assembly and free speech; that they restricted the worship of God; that they put the average man's property and the average man's life in pawn to the mercenaries of dynastic power; that they regimented the people.

And so it was to win freedom from the tyranny of political autocracy that the American Revolution was fought. That victory gave the business of governing into the hands of the average man, who won the right with his neighbors to make and order his own destiny through his own government. Political tyranny was wiped out at Philadelphia on July 4, 1776.

Since that struggle, however, man's inventive genius released new forces in our land which reordered the lives of our people. The age of machinery, of railroads; of steam and electricity; the telegraph and the radio; mass production, mass distribution—all of these combined to bring forward a new civilization and with it a new problem for those who sought to remain free.

For out of this modern civilization economic royalists carved new dynasties. New kingdoms were built upon concentration of control over material things. Through new uses of corporations, banks and securities, new machinery of industry and agriculture, of labor and capital—all undreamed of by the fathers—the whole structure of modern life was impressed into this royal service.

There was no place among this royalty for our many thousands of small businessmen and merchants who sought to make a worthy use of the American system of initiative and profit. They were no more free than the worker or the farmer. Even honest and progressive minded men of wealth, aware of their obligation to their generation, could never know just where they fitted into this dynastic scheme of things.

It was natural and perhaps human that the privileged princes of these new economic dynasties, thirsting for power, reached out for control over government itself. They created a new despotism and wrapped it in the robes of legal sanction. In its service new mercenaries sought to regiment the people, their labor, and their property. And as a result the average man once more confronts the problem that faced the Minute Man.

The hours men and women worked, the wages they received, the conditions of their labor—these had passed beyond the control of the people, and were imposed by this new industrial dictatorship. The savings of the average family, the capital of the small businessman, the investments set-aside for old age—other people's money—these were tools which the new economic royalty used to dig itself in.

Those who tilled the soil no longer reaped the rewards which were their right. The small measure of their gains was decreed by men in distant cities.

Throughout the nation, opportunity was limited by monopoly. Individual initiative was crushed in the cogs of a great machine. The field open for free business was more and more restricted. Private enterprise, indeed, became too private. It became privileged enterprise, not free enterprise.

An old English judge once said: "Necessitous men are not free men." Liberty requires opportunity to make a living—a living decent according to the standard of the time, a living which gives man not only enough to live by, but something to live for.

For too many of us the political equality we once had won was meaningless in the face of economic inequality. A small group had concentrated into their own hands an almost complete control over other people's property, other people's money, other people's labor —other people's lives. For too many of us life was no longer free; liberty no longer real; men could no longer follow the pursuit of happiness.

Against economic tyranny such as this, the American citizen could appeal only to the organized power of government. The collapse of 1929 showed up the despotism for what it was. The election of 1932 was the people's mandate to end it. Under that mandate it is being ended.

The royalists of the economic order have conceded that political freedom was the business of the government, but they have maintained that economic slavery was nobody's business. They granted that the government could protect the citizen in his right to vote, but they denied that the government could do anything to protect the citizen in his right to work and his right to live.

Today we stand committed to the proposition that freedom is no half-and-half affair. If the average citizen is guaranteed equal opportunity in the polling place, he must have equal opportunity in the market place.

These economic royalists complain that we seek to overthrow the institutions of America. What they really complain of is that we seek to take away their power. Our allegiance to American institutions requires the overthrow of this kind of power. In vain they seek to hide behind the Flag and the Constitution. In their blindness they forget what the Flag and the Constitution stand for. Now, as always, they stand for democracy, not tyranny; for freedom, not subjection; and against a dictatorship by mob rule and the over privileged alike.

The brave and clear platform adopted by this Convention, to which I heartily subscribe, sets forth that the government in a modern civilization has certain inescapable obligations to its citizens, among which are protection of the family and the home, the establishment of a democracy of opportunity, and aid to those over-taken by disaster.

But the resolute enemy within our gates is ever ready to beat down our words unless in greater courage we will fight for them.

For more than three years we have fought for them. This Convention, in every word and deed, has pledged that that fight will go on.

The defeats and victories of these years have given to us as a people a new understanding of our government and of ourselves. Never since the early days of the New England town meeting have the affairs of government been so widely discussed and so clearly appreciated. It has been brought home to us that the only effective guide for the safety of this most worldly of worlds, the greatest guide of all, is moral principle.

We do not see faith, hope and charity as unattainable ideals, but we use them as stout supports of a nation fighting the fight for freedom in a modern civilization.

Faith—in the soundness of democracy in the midst of dictatorships.

Hope—renewed because we know so well the progress we have made.

Charity—in the true spirit of that grand old word. For charity literally translated from the original means love, the love that understands, that does not merely share the wealth of the giver, but in true sympathy and wisdom helps men to help themselves.

We seek not merely to make government a mechanical implement, but to give it the vibrant personal character that is the very embodiment of human charity.

We are poor indeed if this nation cannot afford to lift from every recess of American life the dread fear of the unemployed that they are not needed in the world. We cannot afford to accumulate a deficit in the books of human fortitude.

In the place of the palace of privilege we seek to build a temple out of faith and hope and charity.

It is a sobering thing, my friends, to be a servant of this great cause. We try in our daily work to remember that the cause belongs not to us, but to the people. The standard is not in the hands of you and me alone. It is carried by America. We seek daily to profit from experience, to learn to do better as our task proceeds.

Governments can err, Presidents do make mistakes, but the immortal Dante tells us that divine justice weighs the sins of the cold-blooded and the sins of the warm-hearted in different scales.

Better the occasional faults of a government that lives in a spirit of charity than the consistent omissions of a government frozen in the ice of its own indifference.

There is a mysterious cycle in human events. To some generations much is given. Of other generations much is expected. This generation of Americans has a rendezvous with destiny.

In this world of ours in other lands, there are some people, who, in times past, have lived and fought for freedom, and seem to have grown too weary to carry on the fight. They have sold their heritage of freedom for the illusion of a living. They have yielded their democracy.

I believe in my heart that only our success can stir their ancient hope. They begin to know that here in America we are waging a great and successful war. It is not alone a war against want and destitution and economic democracy. We are fighting to save a great and precious form of government for ourselves and for the world.

I accept the commission you have tendered me. I join with you. I am enlisted for the duration of the war.

XLI
Franklin D. Roosevelt:
Fireside Chat, *The Dignity of Labor*
September 6, 1936

I have been on a journey of husbandry. I went primarily to see at first hand conditions in the drought states; to see how effectively Federal and local authorities are taking care of pressing problems of relief and also how they are to work together to defend the people of this country against the effects of future droughts.

I saw drought devastation in nine states.

I talked with families who had lost their wheat crop, lost their corn crop, lost their livestock, lost the water in their well, lost their garden and come through to the end of the summer without one dollar of cash resources, facing a winter without feed or food— facing a planting season without seed to put in the ground.

That was the extreme case, but there are thousands and thousands of families on western farms who share the same difficulties.

I saw cattlemen who because of lack of grass or lack of winter feed have been compelled to sell all but their breeding stock and will need help to carry even these through the coming winter. I saw livestock kept alive only because water had been brought to them long distances in tank cars. I saw other farm families who have not lost everything but who, because they have made only partial crops, must have some form of help if they are to continue farming next spring.

First let me talk for a minute about this autumn and the coming winter. We have the option, in the case of families who need actual subsistence, of putting them on the dole or putting them to work. They do not want to go on the dole and they are one thousand percent right. We agree, therefore, that we must put them to work for a decent wage, and when we reach that decision we kill two birds with one stone, because these families will earn enough by working, not only to subsist themselves, but to buy food for their stock, and seed for next year's planting. Into this scheme of things there fit of course the government lending agencies which next year, as in the past, will help with production loans.

Every Governor with whom I have talked is in full accord with this program of doing work for these farm families, just as every

Governor agrees that the individual states will take care of their unemployables but that the cost of employing those who are entirely able and willing to work must be borne by the Federal Government.

If then we know, as we do today, the approximate number of farm families who will require some form of work relief from now on through the winter, we face the question of what kind of work they should do. Let me make it clear that this is not a new question because it has already been answered to a greater or less extent in every one of the drought communities. Beginning in 1934, when we also had serious drought conditions, the state and Federal governments cooperated in planning a large number of projects—many of them directly aimed at the alleviation of future drought conditions. In accordance with that program literally thousands of ponds or small reservoirs have been built in order to supply water for stock and to lift the level of the underground water to protect wells from going dry. Thousands of wells have been drilled or deepened; community lakes have been created and irrigation projects are being pushed.

Water conservation by means such as these is being expanded as a result of this new drought all through the Great Plains area, the western corn belt and in the states that lie further south. In the Middle West water conservation is not so pressing a problem. Here the work projects run more to soil erosion control and the building of farm-to-market roads.

Spending like this is not waste. It would spell future waste if we did not spend for such things now. These emergency work projects provide money to buy food and clothing for the winter; they keep the livestock on the farm; they provide seed for a new crop, and, best of all, they will conserve soil and water in the future in those areas most frequently hit by drought.

If, for example, in some local area the water table continues to drop and the topsoil to blow away, the land values will disappear with the water and the soil. People on the farms will drift into the nearby cities; the cities will have no farm trade and the workers in the city factories and stores will have no jobs. Property values in the cities will decline. If, on the other hand, the farms within that area remain as farms with better water supply and no erosion, the farm population will stay on the land and prosper and the nearby cities will prosper too. Property values will increase instead of disappearing. That is why it is worth our while as a nation to spend money in order to save money.

I have, however, used the argument in relation only to a small area [but] it holds good in its effect on the nation as a whole. Every state in the drought area is now doing and always will do business with every state outside it. The very existence of the men and women working in the clothing factories of New York, making clothes worn by farmers and their families; of the workers in the steel mills in Pittsburgh, in the automobile factories of Detroit, and in the harvester factories of Illinois, depend upon the farmers' ability to purchase the commodities they produce. In the same way it is the purchasing power of the workers in these factories in the cities that enables them and their wives and children to eat more beef, more pork, more wheat, more corn, more fruit and more dairy products, and to buy more clothing made from cotton, wool and leather. In a physical and a property sense, as well as in a spiritual sense, we are members one of another.

I want to make it clear that no simple panacea can be applied to the drought problem in the whole of the drought area. Plans must depend on local conditions, for these vary with annual rainfall, soil characteristics, altitude and topography. Water and soil conservation methods may differ in one county from those in an adjoining county. Work to be done in the cattle and sheep country differs in type from work in the wheat country or work in the corn belt.

The farmers of America want a sound national agricultural policy in which a permanent land use program will have an important place. They want assurance against another year like 1932 when they made good crops but had to sell them for prices that meant ruin just as surely as did the drought. Sound policy must maintain farm prices in good crop years as well as in bad crop years. It must function when we have drought; it must also function when we have bumper crops.

The maintenance of a fair equilibrium between farm prices and the prices of industrial products is an aim which we must keep ever before us, just as we must give constant thought to the sufficiency of the food supply of the nation even in bad years. Our modern civilization can and should devise a more successful means by which the excess supplies of bumper years can be conserved for use in lean years.

On my trip I have been deeply impressed with the general efficiency of those agencies of the Federal, state and local governments which have moved in on the immediate task created by the drought. In 1934 none of us had preparation; we worked without blueprints and made the mistakes of inexperience. Hindsight shows us this. But as time has gone on we have been making fewer and fewer mistakes. Remember that the Federal and state governments have done only broad planning. Actual work on a given project originates in the local community. Local needs are listed from local information. Local projects are decided on only after obtaining the recommendations and help of those in the local community who are best able to give it. And it is worthy of note that on my entire trip, though I asked the question dozens of times, I heard no complaint against the character of a single works relief project.

The elected heads of the states concerned, together with their state officials and their experts from agricultural colleges and state planning boards, have shown cooperation with and approval of the work which the Federal Government has headed up. I am grateful also to the men and women in all these states who have accepted leadership in the work in their locality.

In the drought area people are not afraid to use new methods to meet changes in Nature, and to correct mistakes of the past. If overgrazing has injured range lands, they are willing to reduce the grazing. If certain wheat lands should be returned to pasture they are willing to cooperate. If trees should be planted as windbreaks or to stop erosion they will work with us. If terracing or summer fallowing or crop rotation is called for, they will carry them out. They stand ready to fit, and not to fight, the ways of Nature.

We are helping, and shall continue to help the farmer to do those things, through local soil conservation committees and other cooperative local, state and federal agencies of government.

I have not the time tonight to deal with other and more comprehensive agricultural policies.

With this fine help we are tiding over the present emergency. We are going to conserve soil, conserve water and conserve life. We are going to have long-time defenses against both low prices and drought. We are going to have a farm policy that will serve the national welfare. That is our hope for the future.

There are two reasons why I want to end by talking about reemployment. Tomorrow is Labor Day. The brave spirit with which so many millions of working people are winning their way out of depression deserves respect and admiration. It is like the courage of the farmers in the drought areas.

That is my first reason. The second is that healthy employment conditions stand equally with healthy agricultural conditions as a buttress of national prosperity. Dependable employment at fair wages is just as important to the people in the towns and cities as good farm income is to agriculture. Our people must have the ability to buy the goods they manufacture and the crops they produce. Thus city wages and farm buying power are the two strong legs that carry the nation forward.

Re-employment in industry is proceeding rapidly. Government spending was in large part responsible for keeping industry going and putting it in a position to make this reemployment possible. Government orders were the backlog of heavy industry; government wages turned over and over again to make consumer purchasing power and to sustain every merchant in the community. Businessmen with their businesses, small and large, had to be saved. Private enterprise is necessary to any nation which seeks to maintain the democratic form of government. In their case, just as certainly as in the case of drought-stricken farmers, government spending has saved.

Government having spent wisely to save it, private industry begins to take workers off the rolls of the government relief program. Until this administration we had no free employment service, except in a few states and cities. Because there was no unified employment service, the worker, forced to move as industry moved, often traveled over the country, wandering after jobs which seemed always to travel just a little faster than he did. He was often victimized by fraudulent practices of employment clearing houses, and the facts of employment opportunities were at the disposal neither of himself nor of the employer.

In 1933, the United States Employment Service was created—a cooperative state and Federal enterprise, through which the Federal Government matches dollar for dollar the funds provided by the states for registering the occupations and skills of workers and for actually finding jobs for these registered workers in private industry. The Federal-State cooperation has been splendid. Already employment services are operating in 32 states, and the areas not covered by them are served by the Federal Government.

We have developed a nationwide service with seven hundred District offices, and one thousand branch offices, thus providing facilities through which labor can learn of jobs available and employers can find workers.

Last Spring I expressed the hope that employers would realize their deep responsibility to take men off the relief rolls and give them jobs in private enterprise. Subsequently I was told by many employers that they were not satisfied with the information available concerning the skill and experience of the workers on the relief rolls. On August 25th I allocated a relatively small sum to the employment service for the purpose of getting better and more recent information in regard to those now actively at work on WPA Projects—information to their skills and previous occupations—and to keep the records of such men and women up-to-date for maximum service in making them available to industry. Tonight I am announcing the allocation of two and a half million dollars more to enable the Employment Service to make an even more intensive search then it has yet been equipped to make, to find opportunities in private employment for workers registered with it.

Tonight I urge the workers to cooperate with and take full advantage of this intensification of the work of the Employment Service. This does not mean that there will be any lessening of our efforts under our WPA and PWA and other work relief programs until all workers have decent jobs in private employment at decent wages. We do not surrender our responsibility to the unemployed. We have had ample proof that it is the will of the American people that those who represent them in national, state and local government should continue as long as necessary to discharge that responsibility. But it does mean that the government wants to use resource to get private work for those now employed on government work, and thus to curtail to a minimum the government expenditures for direct employment.

Tonight I ask employers, large and small, throughout the nation, to use the help of the state and Federal Employment Service whenever in the general pick-up of business they require more workers.

Tomorrow is Labor Day. Labor Day in this country has never been a class holiday. It has always been a national holiday. It has never had more significance as a national holiday than it has now. In other countries the relationship of employer and employee has more or less been accepted as a class relationship not readily to be broken through. In this country we insist, as an essential of the American way of life, that the employer-employee relationship should be one between free men and equals. We refuse to regard those who work with hand or brain as different from or inferior to those who live from their property. We insist that labor is entitled to as much respect as property. But our workers with hand and brain deserve more than respect for their labor. They deserve practical protection in the opportunity to use their labor at a return adequate to support them at a decent and constantly rising standard of living, and to accumulate a margin of security against the inevitable vicissitudes of life.

The average man must have that twofold opportunity if we are to avoid the growth of a class conscious society in this country.

Tomorrow, Labor Day, belongs to all of us. Tomorrow, Labor Day, symbolizes the hope of all Americans. Anyone who calls it a class holiday challenges the whole concept of American democracy.

The Fourth of July commemorates our political freedom—a freedom which without economic freedom is meaningless indeed. Labor Day symbolizes our determination to achieve an economic freedom for the average man which will give his political freedom reality.

XLII
Franklin D. Roosevelt:
Address on the Survival of Private Enterprise
October 23, 1936

When these dinners of businessmen throughout the country were first organized, I was asked to talk specifically for the businessmen of the nation. But I said that it was impossible to make a speech for businessmen as members of a separate and distinct occupation from the rest of the people in America. There cannot be one type of speech for businessmen and another type of speech for industrial workers and for farmers.

We have no separate interests in America. There is nothing to say to one group that ought not to be said to all groups. What is good for one ought to be good for all. We can make our machinery of private enterprise work only so long as it does not benefit one group at the expense of another.

No one in the United States believes more firmly than I in the system of private business, private property and private profit. No administration in the history of our country has done more for it. It was this administration which dragged it back out of the pit into which it had fallen in 1933.

If the administration had had the slightest inclination to change that system, all that it would have had to do was to fold its hands and wait—let the system continue to default to itself and to the public.

Instead we did what the previous administration had declined to do through all the years of the depression—we acted quickly and drastically to save it. It was because of our belief in private enterprise that we acted, because of our faith in the essential and fundamental virtue of democracy and our conviction that individual initiative and private profit served it best.

You who read the business sections of the newspapers, the financial and commercial reports, know what we did and what its results have been.

But as your profits return and the values of your securities and investments come back, do not forget the lessons of the past. We must hold constantly to the resolve never again to become committed to the philosophy of the boom era, to individualism run wild, to the false promise that American business was great because it had built up financial control of industrial production and distribution in the hands of a few individuals and corporations by the use of other people's money; that government should be ever ready to purr against the legs of high finance; that the benefits of the free competitive system should trickle down by gravity from the top to the bottom; and above all, that government had no right, in any way, to interfere with those who were using the system of private profit to the damage of the rest of the American citizens.

Collapse of business was the price we paid for not facing intelligently the problems of private enterprise in a modern world.

There were those who advised extreme courses in the days of the crisis in 1933. Many said that deflation should take its course, wiping out in bankruptcy all but a handful of the strongest.

Some, including many businessmen, urged that the only solution was for government to take everything over and run things itself.

We took the middle road. We used the facilities and resources available only to government, to permit individual enterprise to resume its normal functions in a socially sound competitive order. We provided credit at one end of the business mechanism and purchasing power at the other. The broken pipes of the circulatory system of business have been welded together again.

An overwhelming majority of independent individual businessmen approve in their hearts what we did to save American business. I am equally sure that a handful of monopolistic businessmen hate what we did for American business. Business had become regimented. Free enterprise was being gobbled up piece by piece. Economic control of business in these few persons had developed into political control of government itself. They did not want us to take American business out of their grip.

But we not only have freed government from their domination; we are now freeing business also from their domination.

We have loosened the grip of monopoly by taking from monopolists their chief tools—the devices of high finance.

We are resolved to keep politics out of business. But at the same time we ask that business refrain from coercion in politics. Not only wage earners but nearly all businessmen resent the present attempts by a few employers to frighten their employees by misrepresentation. For example, a few employers are spreading half-truths about the Social Security Law, half-truths that tell the workers only of the workers' contribution, and fail to mention the employers' contribution. They conceal from the workers the fact that for every dollar which the employee contributes, the employer also contributes a dollar, and that both dollars are held in a government trust fund solely for the social security of the workers.

Things like this bring certain types of employers into disrepute with other employers and with the great mass of our citizens. The real objective of this minority is the repeal of any form of social security to which they themselves have to contribute. For many years the record shows that this minority has been willing to take only a plan of unemployment insurance and old-age pensions to which the workers would be the sole contributors and which would cost the employers nothing at all.

All we ask of business and for business is the greater good of the greater number—fair treatment by it and fair treatment for it. We are reaching for the security which comes from an intelligent and honorable system of interdependent economics which every businessman as well as everyone else can trust and into which he can venture with confidence.

We seek to guarantee the survival of private enterprise by guaranteeing conditions under which it can work.

We seek to insure the material well being of America, and to make more firm the real foundations of a lasting democracy.

5

"Layman's Document or Lawyer's Contract?" (1937)

XLIII
Franklin D. Roosevelt:
The Second Inaugural Address
January 20, 1937

When four years ago we met to inaugurate a President, the Republic, single-minded in anxiety, stood in spirit here. We dedicated ourselves to the fulfillment of a vision—to speed the time when there would be for all the people that security and peace essential to the pursuit of happiness. We of the Republic pledged ourselves to drive from the temple of our ancient faith those who had profaned it, to end by action, tireless and unafraid, the stagnation and despair of that day. We did those first things first.

Our covenant with ourselves did not stop there. Instinctively we recognized a deeper need—the need to find through government the instrument of our united purpose to solve for the individual the ever-rising problems of a complex civilization. Repeated attempts at their solution without the aid of government had left us baffled and bewildered. For, without that aid, we had been unable to create those moral controls over the services of science, which are necessary to make science a useful servant instead of a ruthless master of mankind. To do this we knew that we must find practical controls over blind economic forces and blindly selfish men.

We of the Republic sensed the truth that democratic government has innate capacity to protect its people against disasters once considered inevitable, to solve problems once considered unsolvable. We would not admit that we could not find a way to master economic epidemics just as, after centuries of fatalistic suffering, we had found a way to master epidemics of disease. We refused to leave the problems of our common welfare to be solved by the winds of chance and the hurricanes of disaster.

In this we Americans were discovering no wholly new truth; we were writing a new chapter in our book of self-government.

This year marks the one hundred and fiftieth anniversary of the Constitutional Convention, which made us a nation. At that Convention our forefathers found the way out of the chaos which followed the Revolutionary War; they created a strong government with powers of united action sufficient then and now to solve problems utterly beyond individual or local solution. A century and a half ago they established the Federal Government in order to promote the general welfare and secure the blessings of liberty to the American people.

Today we invoke those same powers of government to achieve the same objectives.

Four years of new experience have not belied our historic instinct. They hold out the clear hope that government within communities, government within the separate States, and government of the United States can do the things the times require, without yielding its democracy. Our tasks in the last four years did not force democracy to take a holiday.

Nearly all of us recognize that as intricacies of human relationships increase, so power to govern them also must increase—power to stop evil; power to do good. The essential democracy of our Nation and the safety of our people depend not upon the absence of power, but upon lodging it with those whom the people can change or continue at stated intervals through an honest and free system of elections. The Constitution of 1787 did not make our democracy impotent.

In fact, in these last four years, we have made the exercise of all power more democratic. For we have begun to bring private autocratic powers into their proper subordination to the public's government. The legend that they were invincible—above and beyond the processes of a democracy—has been shattered. They have been challenged and beaten.

Our progress out of the depression is obvious. But that is not all that you and I mean by the new order of things. Our pledge was not merely to do a patchwork job with second-hand materials. By using the new materials of social justice we have undertaken to erect on the old foundations a more enduring structure for the better use of future generations.

In that purpose we have been helped by achievements of mind and spirit. Old truths have been relearned; untruths have been unlearned. We have always known that heedless self-interest was bad morals; we know now that it is bad economics. Out of the collapse of a prosperity whose builders boasted their practicality has come the conviction that in the long run economic morality pays. We are beginning to wipe out the line that divides the practical from the ideal; and in so doing we are fashioning an instrument of unimagined power for the establishment of a morally better world.

This new understanding undermines the old admiration of worldly success as such. We are beginning to abandon our tolerance of the abuse of power by those who betray for profit the elementary decencies of life.

In this process evil things formerly accepted will not be so easily condoned. Hard-headedness will not so easily excuse hard-heartedness. We are moving toward an era of good feeling. But we realize that there can be no era of good feeling save among men of good will.

For these reasons I am justified in believing that the greatest change we have witnessed has been the change in the moral climate of America.

Among men of good will, science and democracy together offer an ever-richer life and ever-larger satisfaction to the individual. With this change in our moral climate and our rediscovered ability to improve our economic order, we have set our feet upon the road of enduring progress.

Shall we pause now and turn our back upon the road that lies ahead? Shall we call this the Promised Land? Or, shall we continue on our way? For "each age is a dream that is dying, or one that is coming to birth."

Many voices are heard as we face a great decision. Comfort says, "Tarry a while." Opportunism says, "This is a good spot." Timidity asks, "How difficult is the road ahead?"

True, we have come far from the days of stagnation and despair. Vitality has been preserved. Courage and confidence have been restored. Mental and moral horizons have been extended.

But our present gains were won under the pressure of more than ordinary circumstance. Advance became imperative under the goad of fear and suffering. The times were on the side of progress.

To hold to progress today, however, is more difficult. Dulled conscience, irresponsibility, and ruthless self-interest already reappear. Such symptoms of prosperity may become portents of disaster! Prosperity already tests the persistence of our progressive purpose.

Let us ask again: Have we reached the goal of our vision of that fourth day of March 1933? Have we found our happy valley?

I see a great nation, upon a great continent, blessed with a great wealth of natural resources. Its hundred and thirty million people are at peace among themselves; they are making their country a good neighbor among the nations. I see a United States which can demonstrate that, under democratic methods of government, national wealth can be translated into a spreading volume of human comforts hitherto unknown, and the lowest standard of living can be raised far above the level of mere subsistence.

But here is the challenge to our democracy: In this nation I see tens of millions of its citizens—a substantial part of its whole population—who at this very moment are denied the greater part of what the very lowest standards of today call the necessities of life.

I see millions of families trying to live on incomes so meager that the pall of family disaster hangs over them day by day.

I see millions whose daily lives in city and on farm continue under conditions labeled indecent by a so-called polite society half a century ago.

I see millions denied education, recreation, and the opportunity to better their lot and the lot of their children

I see millions lacking the means to buy the products of farm and factory and by their poverty denying work and productiveness to many other millions.

I see one-third of a nation ill housed, ill clad, and ill nourished.

It is not in despair that I paint you that picture. I paint it for you in hope—because the Nation, seeing and understanding the injustice in it, proposes to paint it out. We are determined to make every American citizen the subject of his country's interest and concern; and we will never regard any faithful, law-abiding group within our borders as superfluous. The test of our progress is not whether we add more to the abundance of those who have much; it is whether we provide enough for those who have too little.

If I know aught of the spirit and purpose of our Nation, we will not listen to Comfort, Opportunism, and Timidity. We will carry on.

Overwhelmingly, we of the Republic are men and women of good will; men and women who have more than warm hearts of dedication; men and women who have cool heads and willing hands of practical purpose as well. They will insist that every agency of popular government use effective instruments to carry out their will.

Government is competent when all who compose it work as trustees for the whole people. It can make constant progress when it keeps abreast of all the facts. It can obtain justified support and legitimate criticism when the people receive true information of all that government does.

If I know aught of the will of our people, they will demand that these conditions of effective government shall be created and maintained. They will demand a nation uncorrupted by cancers of injustice and, therefore, strong among the nations in is example of the will to peace.

Today we re-consecrate our country to long-cherished ideals in a suddenly changed civilization. In every land there are always at work forces that drive men apart and forces that draw men together. In our personal ambitions we are individualists. But in our seeking for economic and political progress as a nation, we all go up; or else we all go down, as one people.

To maintain a democracy of effort requires a vast amount of patience in dealing with differing methods, a vast amount of humility. But out of the confusion of many voices rises an understanding of dominant public need. Then political leadership can voice common ideals, and aid in their realization.

In taking again the oath of office as President of the United States, I assume the solemn obligation of leading the American

people forward along the road over which they have chosen to
advance.

While this duty rests upon me, I shall do my utmost to speak
their purpose and to do their will, seeking Divine guidance to help
us each and every one to give light to them that sit in darkness and
to guide our feet into the way of peace.

XLIV
Herbert Hoover:
Hands Off the Supreme Court
Union League Club, Chicago, Illinois
February 20, 1937

I have been glad to meet a long-standing invitation of this
Society. The Union League Club of Chicago was originally formed
in the time of a great Constitutional crisis. Its great purpose was to
fight for human liberty under the banner of Abraham Lincoln. It is
now and has long been a nonpartisan body. But it is no less
devoted to Constitutional government. And today from President
Roosevelt's proposals as to the Supreme Court we are faced with
the greatest Constitutional question in these seventy years.

It is a magnificent thing for the nation that the debate upon this
question has risen far above partisanship. The proposal is too
grave to be dealt with on such terms. It is an inspiring thing that
the leadership to maintain the integrity of the American form of
government has been begun by eminent Senators belonging to the
President's own party. This leadership, which we all gladly follow,
places this issue on the highest plane of citizenship without regard
to party, to partisan politics, to personal ambition.

Neither is the country divided upon group or class lines. Some
people seem to think that all Americans can be pigeonholed into
Radicals, Tories, Liberals, Conservatives, Progressives,
Reactionaries, "right wing" or "left wing." These imported terms
do not fit very well in America. They are used often as epithets to
express our bad opinions of somebody else. But whatever they do
mean, we find outstanding leaders of each of these supposed
classifications carrying the banner of opposition to the President's
proposals. At least our opponents who look for pigeonholes cannot
place me either with the Liberty League, whose leading members so
bitterly opposed my election, nor among those radicals with whose
ideas of a collectivist America I have so often been collision.

Some months ago I made an address at Cleveland in which I directed attention to the problems of human liberty. Nation-wide the press, even those who had long been my opponents, were extraordinarily eulogistic of that speech. As a method of spreading flowers over the termination of my party career the opposition press insisted on electing me to the office of elder statesman. I have not assumed that high office. But at least it marks their acceptance of the fact that the era in my life has gone by when party aspects of such an issue concern me.

I am speaking tonight not as a Republican; I am speaking as an American who has witnessed the decay and destruction of human liberty in many lands, who as President has witnessed the movement of these great floods which are testing the American levees built to protect free men.

Seldom has debate so quickly flamed up across the nation. It is not alone public men and journalists who are engaged in this discussion. It is alive today between farmers in the field, workers at the bench, women in their homes, and men in their offices. The very spread of the debate illuminates the gravity of the issue.

By this debate the issue has already been greatly clarified. That real issue is whether the President by the appointment of additional judges upon the Supreme Court shall revise the Constitution—or whether change in the Constitution shall be submitted to the people as the Constitution itself provides.

This is not lawyers' dispute over legalisms. This is the people's problem. And it is the duty of every citizen to concern himself with this question. It reaches to the very center of his liberties.

I

We may quickly dismiss the secondary parts of the President's proposals. We can accept the view that justice would be expedited if we had more Federal District Courts. There may not be enough Circuit Courts of Appeal. But there can be only one Supreme Court.

Here Mr. Roosevelt demands the power to appoint a new justice parallel with every existing justice who is over seventy years of age. This means that two-thirds of the Court, or six of them, are to be given a sort of intellectual nurse, having half of the vote of each patient. It is the implications of this proposal which have thrust us with startling suddenness into an issue greater and deeper than any in our generation.

We may also deal quickly with the reasons for this proposal to which Mr. Roosevelt has given the most emphasis.

It has been shown by the reports of the Department of Justice that the Supreme Court is not behind with its work. Moreover, more members of the Supreme Court would not speed action. The fact is each justice must in every case individually give his own opinion. Certainly each individual of fifteen justices is likely to take as long in making up his individual mind as each individual among nine justices.

One of the reasons given for the President's proposal is old age. Mr. Walter Lippmann has said, "By an act of lawless legality he would force two-thirds of the Court to choose between resignation and being publicly branded as senile." I do not for a moment believe that was the purpose of this proposal, but it might be the consequence. I wonder if those noble interpreters of human liberty, John Marshall and Oliver Wendell Holmes, would have served America as well in the last years of their lives had they possessed an intellectually nurse who also divided their vote.

II

But the President's proposal is far deeper and more far-reaching in purpose than these details. The people must probe it in the light of its background, of the incidents that have led up to it. They must probe it in the light of its real effect upon their own security. They must probe it in the light of the forces moving in the world today.

Mr. Roosevelt has sought many Acts of Congress which lead to increase in the personal power of the Executive. He has sought greatly to centralize the government. I am not for the moment debating the merits of these measures, for some of them are of good purpose. The Supreme Court has found in fourteen of these laws which profoundly affect the public welfare that Mr. Roosevelt was within the Constitution in six cases and violated the Constitution in eight cases. In many of those decisions justices supposed to be of Mr. Roosevelt's realm of thought have concurred. Of eight important decisions adverse to Mr. Roosevelt's wishes four have been decided unanimously and of the six cases where the decisions were favorable three were unanimous. There can therefore be no real charge that the Court has not decided in accord with what the Constitution means. The Court was not engaged in vetoing Mr. Roosevelt's proposals, as his Attorney General alleges.

It was finding according to the law as established by the people of the United States.

And what was the effect of these decisions which are now criticized? The unanimous decision on the NRA relieved the American people of a gigantic system of monopolies conducted by big business—a monopoly that even reached down to a jail sentence for pressing pants for less than the presidential approved price. Another of these acts was thrown out because it was based upon coercion of men to surrender their rights of freedom. And coercion is the antithesis of liberty.

III

Mr. Roosevelt has felt it necessary repeatedly to criticize the decisions, even those which were unanimous. To complain of the umpire is real human. However, nobody in this country can believe that if these decisions had been in accord with his wishes he would have made these proposals to add six new justices. Most of the supporters of the President's proposal have ceased to defend it on the grounds of either expedition of justice or old age. Their support is now boldly that it means quick and revolutionary change in the Constitution. And that without reference to the people and we are not even told where the Constitution is at fault or what changes they would make. They are asking for a blank check upon which they can write future undisclosed purposes.

In the light of this background no one can conclude other than the President seeks not to secure a Supreme Court that will find in accordance with the Constitution as it stands. He wants one that will revise the Constitution so it will mean what he wishes it to mean.

And this is not a loose assertion. Mr. Roosevelt himself specifically confirms this purpose. In his message to Congress he says that if these proposals be accepted then "we may be relieved of the necessity of considering any fundamental changes in the powers of the Courts or the Constitution of our government."

Thus we are plainly told that Constitutional change is sought not by open and frank amendment of the Constitution but by judicial decision.

If this is to be accomplished the new judges must necessarily be men who will ratify Mr. Roosevelt's projects. Unless they are pledged to Mr. Roosevelt's way of thinking he would not be, to use his own words, relieved of the necessity of considering fundamental

changes in the Constitution. I am wondering what esteem these
pledged judges would hold with the people.

IV

If Mr. Roosevelt can change the Constitution to suit his purposes
by adding to the members of the Court, any succeeding President
can do it to suit his purposes. If a troop of "President's judges"
can be sent into the halls of justice to capture political power, then
his successor with the same device can also send a troop of new
"President's judges" to capture some other power. That is not
judicial process. That is force.

V

The Court and the Constitution thus become the tool of the
Executive and not the sword of the people. A leading newspaper
which usually supports the President sums it up: "It proposes to
sanction a precedent which would make any President the master
of the Supreme Court by the mere process of enlarging it." Thus
we are face to face with the proposition that the Supreme Court
shall be made subjective to the Executive. Stripped to its bare
bones that is the heart of this proposal. And that reaches to the
very center of human liberty. The ultimate safeguard of liberty is
the independence of the courts.

VI

In all the centuries of struggle for human freedom the
independence of the judiciary from political domination has been
the first battle against autocratic power.

In America we have builded over these two centuries certain
sacred rights which are the very fibers of human freedom. Upon
them depends freedom of speech. Upon them depends security
from individual oppression. Upon the protection of these rights
depends religious freedom.

Our Constitution was not alone a statement of these rights. It
was a framework of government for the safeguarding of these
rights. Every school boy and girl knows that the very pillars of that
temple are the independence of the Supreme Court, the Legislative
branch, the Executive, and the division of powers with the states.

But these securities and these rights are no stronger than their
safeguards. And of these safeguards none is so final and so
imperative as the independence of the courts. It is here alone where
the humblest citizen and the weakest minority have their only
sanctuary.

Governor Lowden has recently emphasized that the farmers of this country are less than 25 percent of the whole people; that labor is only 25 percent of the whole people; that the Executive and the Congress are elected by a majority. That when the day comes that the majority are displeased with farm prices or the majority displeased with wages, then protection of the rights of the minority rests upon the Constitution and the Supreme Court.

VII

Self-government never dies from direct attack. No matter what his real intentions may be, no man will arise and say that he intends to suspend one atom of the rights guaranteed by the Constitution. Liberty dies from the encroachments and disregard of the safeguards of those rights. And unfortunately it is those whose purposes have often been good who have broken the levees of liberty to find a short cut to their ends.

These are serious times. Liberty is crumbling over two-thirds of the world. In less than a score of years the courts in a dozen nations have been made subjective to political power, and with this subjection the people's securities in these countries have gone out of the window. And, mark you this—in every instance the persuaders have professed to be acting for the people and in the name of progress. As we watch the parade of nations down that suicide road every American has cause to be anxious for our republic.

I have said this is the people's problem. It is the Supreme Court defending the people's rights and securities guaranteed by the Constitution which time and again has protected the people from those who seek for economic power or political power or to suppress free worship and free thought. It is the people's rights that are endangered. Once political power makes use of the Court, its strength and its moral prestige are irretrievably weakened.

This meeting is the annual occasion in memory of George Washington. In his farewell address to the American people he said: "One method of assault may be to effect in the form of the Constitution alterations which may impair the energy of the system and thus undermine that which cannot be directly overthrown."

VIII

It is not that our Constitution is a shackle on progress. It is a commonplace to repeat that the growth of social ideas and mechanical invention and the ingenuity of wickedness force new problems in our national life. So far as they relate to government the vast majority of them are solvable within the Constitution. When specific problems arise which do require constitutional amendment then the people have ever been willing to grant it. Such changes are not lightly to be undertaken. But the Constitution provides an open and aboveboard method by which they may be quickly accomplished.

What is the hurry in all this? The nation is recovering from depression. There is no emergency. Surely a year or two is no waste in the life of a great nation when its liberties are the stake of haste.

If historic liberalism cannot be maintained under the present provisions of the Constitution, I shall be the first to support the President in amendment of it.

But there are certain things that must not change. These things are the fundamental safeguards of human rights. We have already gone far on the road of personal government. The American people must halt when it is proposed to lay hands on the independence of the Supreme Court. That is the ultimate security of every cottage. It is the last safeguard of free men.

Ladies and gentlemen, I offer you a watchword—Hands off the Supreme Court.

XLV
Franklin D. Roosevelt:
Fireside Chat, *The Judicial Reorganization Plan*
March 9, 1937

Last Thursday I described in detail certain economic problems which everyone admits now face the nation. For the many messages which have come to me after that speech, and which it is physically impossible to answer individually, I take this means of saying "thank you."

Tonight, sitting at my desk in the White House, I make my first radio report to the people in my second term of office.

I am reminded of that evening in March, four years ago, when I made my first radio report to you. We were then in the midst of the great banking crisis.

Soon after, with the authority of the Congress, we asked the nation to turn over all of its privately held gold, dollar for dollar, to the government of the United States.

Today's recovery proves how right that policy was.

But when, almost two years later, it came before the Supreme Court its constitutionality was upheld only by a five-to-four vote. The change of one vote would have thrown all the affairs of this great nation back into hopeless chaos. In effect, four Justices ruled that the right under a private contract to exact a pound of flesh was more sacred than the main objectives of the Constitution to establish an enduring nation.

In 1933 you and I knew that we must never let our economic system get completely out of joint again—that we could not afford to take the risk of another great depression.

We also became convinced that the only way to avoid a repetition of those dark days was to have a government with power to prevent and to cure the abuses and the inequalities, which had thrown that system out of joint.

We then began a program of remedying those abuses and inequalities—to give balance and stability to our economic system—to make it bombproof against the causes of 1929.

Today we are only part-way through that program—and recovery is speeding up to a point where the dangers of 1929 are again becoming possible, not this week or month perhaps, but within a year or two.

National laws are needed to complete that program. Individual or local or state effort alone cannot protect us in 1937 any better than ten years ago.

It will take time—and plenty of time—to work out our remedies administratively even after legislation is passed. To complete our program of protection in time, therefore, we cannot delay one moment in making certain that our national government has power to carry through.

Four years ago action did not come until the eleventh hour. It was almost too late.

If we learned anything from the depression we will not allow ourselves to run around in new circles of futile discussion and debate, always postponing the day of decision.

The American people have learned from the depression. For in the last three national elections an overwhelming majority of them voted a mandate that the Congress and the President begin the task of providing that protection—not after long years of debate, but now.

The Courts, however, have cast doubts on the ability of the elected Congress to protect us against catastrophe by meeting squarely our modern social and economic conditions.

We are at a crisis in our ability to proceed with that protection. It is a quiet crisis. There are no lines of depositors outside closed banks. But to the far-sighted it is far-reaching in its possibilities of injury to America.

I want to talk with you very simply about the need for present action in this crisis—the need to meet the unanswered challenge of one-third of a nation ill nourished, ill-clad, ill-housed.

Last Thursday I described the American form of government as a three-horse team provided by the Constitution to the American people so that their field might be plowed. The three horses are, of course, the three branches of government—the Congress, the Executive and the Courts. Two of the horses are pulling in unison today; the third is not. Those who have intimated that the President of the United States is trying to drive that team, overlook the simple fact that the President, as Chief Executive, is himself one of the three horses.

It is the American people themselves who are in the driver's seat.

It is the American people themselves who want the furrow plowed.

It is the American people themselves who expect the third horse to pull in unison with the other two.

I hope that you have re-read the Constitution of the United States in these past few weeks. Like the Bible, it ought to be read again and again.

It is an easy document to understand when you remember that it was called into being because the Articles of Confederation under which the original thirteen States tried to operate after the Revolution showed the need of a national government with power enough to handle national problems. In its Preamble, the Constitution states that it was intended to form a more perfect Union and promote the general welfare; and the powers given to the Congress to carry out those purposes can be best described by saying that they were all the powers needed to meet each and every problem which then had a national character and which could not be met by merely local action.

But the framers went further. Having in mind that in succeeding generations many other problems then undreamed of would become national problems, they gave to the Congress the ample broad powers "to levy taxes...and provide for the common defense and general welfare of the United States."

That, my friends, is what I honestly believe to have been the clear and underlying purpose of the patriots who wrote a Federal Constitution to create a national government with national power, intended as they said, "to form a more perfect union for ourselves and our posterity."

For nearly twenty years there was no conflict between the Congress and the Court. Then Congress passed a statute which, in 1803, the Court said violated an express provision of the Constitution. The Court claimed the power to declare it unconstitutional and did so declare it. But a little later the Court itself admitted that it was an extraordinary power to exercise and through Mr. Justice Washington laid down this limitation upon it: "It is but a decent respect due to the wisdom, the integrity and the patriotism of the legislative body, by which any law is passed, to presume in favor of its validity until its violation of the Constitution is proved beyond all reasonable doubt."

But since the rise of the modern movement for social and economic progress through legislation, the Court has more and more often and more and more boldly asserted a power to veto laws passed by the Congress and State Legislatures in complete disregard of this original limitation.

In the last four years the sound rule of giving statutes the benefit of all reasonable doubt has been cast aside. The Court has been acting not as a judicial body, but as a policy-making body.

When the Congress has sought to stabilize national agriculture, to improve the conditions of labor, to safeguard business against unfair competition, to protect our national resources, and in many other ways, to serve our clearly national needs, the majority of the Court has been assuming the power to pass on the wisdom of these Acts of the Congress and to approve or disapprove the public policy written into these laws.

How then could we proceed to perform the mandate given us? It was said in last year's Democratic platform, "If these problems cannot be effectively solved within the Constitution, we shall seek such clarifying amendment as will assure the power to enact those laws, adequately to regulate commerce, protect public health and safety, and safeguard economic security." In other words, we said we would seek an amendment only if every other possible means by legislation were to fail.

When I commenced to review the situation with the problem squarely before me, I came by a process of elimination to the conclusion that, short of amendments, the only method which was clearly constitutional, and would at the same time carry out other much needed reforms, was to infuse new blood into all our Courts. We must have men worthy and equipped to carry out impartial justice. But, at the same time, we must have Judges who will bring to the Courts a present-day sense of the Constitution—Judges who will retain in the Courts the judicial functions of a court, and reject the legislative powers which the courts have today assumed.

In forty-five out of the forty-eight States of the Union, Judges are chosen not for life but for a period of years. In many States Judges must retire at the age of seventy. Congress has provided financial security by offering life pensions at full pay for Federal Judges on all Courts who are willing to retire at seventy. In the case of Supreme Court Justices, that pension is $20,000 a year. But all Federal Judges, once appointed, can, if they choose, hold office for life, no matter how old they may get to be.

What is my proposal? It is simply this: whenever a Judge or Justice of any Federal Court has reached the age of seventy and does not avail himself of the opportunity to retire on a pension, a new member shall be appointed by the President then in office, with the approval, as required by the Constituion, of the Senate of the United States.

That plan has two chief purposes. By bringing into the judicial system a steady and continuing stream of new and younger blood, I hope, first, to make the administration of all Federal justice speedier and, therefore, less costly; secondly, to bring to the decision of social and economic problems younger men who have had personal experience and contact with modern facts and circumstances under which average men have to live and work is a plan that will save our national Constitution from hardening of the judicial arteries. The number of Judges to be appointed would depend wholly on the decision of present Judges now over seventy, or those who would subsequently reach the age of seventy.

If, for instance, any one of the six Justices of the Supreme Court now over the age of seventy should retire as provided under the plan, no additional place would be created. Consequently, although there never can be more than fifteen, there may be only fourteen, or thirteen, or twelve. And there may be only nine.

There is nothing novel or radical about this idea. It seeks to maintain the Federal bench in full vigor. It has been discussed and approved by many persons of high authority ever since a similar proposal passed the House of Representatives in 1869.

Why was the age fixed at seventy? Because the laws of many States, the practice of the Civil Service, the regulations of the Army and Navy, and the rules of many of our Universities and of almost every great private business enterprise, commonly fix the retirement age at seventy years or less.

The statute would apply to all the courts in the Federal system. There is general approval so far as the lower Federal courts are concerned. The plan has met opposition only so far as the Supreme Court of the United States itself is concerned. If such a plan is good for the lower courts it certainly ought to be equally good for the highest Court from which there is no appeal.

Those opposing this plan have sought to arouse prejudice and fear by crying that I am seeking to "pack" the Supreme Court and that a baneful precedent will be established.

What do they mean by the words "packing the Court"?

Let me answer this question with a bluntness that will end all honest misunderstanding of my purposes.

If by that phrase "packing the Court" it is charged that I wish to place on the bench spineless puppets who would disregard the law and would decide specific cases as I wished them to be decided, I make this answer: that no President fit for his office would appoint, and no Senate of honorable men fit for their office would confirm, that kind of appointees to the Supreme Court.

But if by that phrase the charge is made that I would appoint and the Senate would confirm Justices worthy to sit beside present members of the Court who understand those modern conditions, that I will appoint Justices who will not undertake to override the judgment of the Congress on legislative policy, that I will appoint Justices who will act as Justices and not as legislators—if the appointment of such Justices can be called "packing the Courts," then I say that I and with me the vast majority of the American people favor doing just that thing—now.

Is it a dangerous precedent for the Congress to change the number of the Justices? The Congress has always had, and will have, that power. The number of justices has been changed several times before, in the administration of John Adams and Thomas

Jefferson—both signers of the Declaration of Independence—
Andrew Jackson, Abraham Lincoln and Ulysses S. Grant.

I suggest only the addition of Justices to the bench in accordance
with a clearly defined principle relating to a clearly defined age
limit. Fundamentally, if in the future, America cannot trust the
Congress it elects to refrain from abuse of our Constitutional
usages, democracy will have failed far beyond the importance to it
of any kind of precedent concerning the judiciary.

We think it so much in the public interest to maintain a vigorous
judiciary that we encourage the retirement of elderly Judges by
offering them a life pension at full salary. Why then should we
leave the fulfillment of this public policy to chance or make it
dependent upon the desire or prejudice of any individual Justice?

It is the clear intention of our public policy to provide for a
constant flow of new and younger blood into the judiciary.
Normally every President appoints a large number of District and
Circuit Court Judges and a few members of the Supreme Court.
Until my first term practically every President of the United States
has appointed at least one member of the Supreme Court.
President Taft appointed five members and named a Chief Justice;
President Wilson, three; President Harding, four, including a Chief
Justice; President Coolidge, one; President Hoover, three, including
a Chief Justice.

Such a succession of appointments should have provided a
Court well balanced as to age. But chance and the disinclination of
individuals to leave the Supreme bench have now given us a Court
in which five Justices will be over seventy-five years of age before
next June and one over seventy. Thus a sound public policy has
been defeated.

I now propose that we establish by law an assurance against
any such ill-balanced Court in the future. I propose hereafter, when
a Judge reaches the age of seventy, a new and younger Judge shall
be added to the Court automatically. In this way I propose to
enforce a sound public policy by law instead of leaving the
composition of our Federal Courts, including the highest, to be
determined by chance or the personal indecision of individuals.

If such a law as I propose is regarded as establishing a new
precedent, is it not a most desirable precedent?

Like all lawyers, like all Americans, I regret the necessity of this
controversy. But the welfare of the United States, and indeed of the
Constitution itself, is what we all must think about first. Our

difficulty with the Court today rises not from the Court as an institution but from human beings within it. But we cannot yield our constitutional destiny to the personal judgment of a few men who, being fearful of the future, would deny us the necessary means of dealing with the present.

This plan of mine is no attack on the Court; it seeks to restore the Court to its rightful and historic place in our Constitutional Government and to have it resume its high task of building anew on the Constitution "a system of living law." The Court itself can best undo what the Court has done.

I have thus explained to you the reasons that lie behind our efforts to secure results by legislation within the Constitution. I hope that thereby the difficult process of constitutional amendment may be rendered unnecessary. But let us examine the process.

There are many types of amendment proposed. Each one is radically different from the other. There is no substantial group within the Congress or outside it who are agreed on any single amendment.

It would take months or years to get substantial agreement upon the type and language of the amendment. It would take months and years thereafter to get a two-thirds majority in favor of that amendment in both Houses of the Congress.

Then would come the long course of ratification by three-fourths of all the States. No amendment which any powerful economic interests or the leaders of any powerful political party have had reason to oppose has ever been ratified within anything like a reasonable time. And thirteen states which contain only five percent of the voting population can block ratification even though the thirty-five States with ninety-five percent of the population are in favor of it.

A very large percentage of newspaper publishers, Chambers of Commerce, Bar Associations, Manufacturers' Associations, who are trying to give the impression that they really do want a constitutional amendment would be the first to exclaim as soon as an amendment was proposed, "Oh! I was for an amendment all right, but this amendment you proposed is not the kind of amendment that I was thinking about. I am therefore, going to spend my time, my efforts and my money to block the amendment, although I would be awfully glad to help get some other kind of amendment ratified."

Two groups oppose my plan on the ground that they favor a constitutional amendment. The first includes those who fundamentally object to social and economic legislation along modern lines. This is the same group who during the campaign last fall tried to block the mandate of the people.

Now they are making a last stand. And the strategy of that last stand is to suggest the time-consuming process of amendment in order to kill off by delay the legislation demanded by the mandate.

To them I say: I do not think you will be able long to fool the American people as to your purposes.

The other group is composed of those who honestly believe the amendment process is the best and who would be willing to support a reasonable amendment if they could agree on one.

To them I say: we cannot rely on an amendment as the immediate or only answer to our present difficulties. When the time comes for action, you will find that many of those who pretend to support you will sabotage any constructive amendment, which is proposed. Look at these strange bedfellows of yours. When before have you found them really at your side in your fights for progress?

And remember one thing more. Even if an amendment were passed, and even if in the years to come it were to be ratified, its meaning would depend upon the kind of Justices who would be sitting on the Supreme Court Bench. An amendment, like the rest of the Constitution, is what the Justices say it is rather than what its framers or you might hope it is.

This proposal of mine will not infringe in the slightest upon the civil or religious liberties so dear to every American.

My record as Governor and President proves my devotion to those liberties. You who know me can have no fear that I would tolerate the destruction by any branch of government of any part of our heritage of freedom.

The present attempt by those opposed to progress to play upon the fears of danger to personal liberty brings again to mind that crude and cruel strategy tried by the same opposition to frighten the workers of America in a pay-envelope propaganda against the Social Security Law. The workers were not fooled by that propaganda then. The people of America will not be fooled by such propaganda now.

I am in favor of action through legislation:

First, because I believe that it can be passed at this session of the Congress.

Second, because it will provide a reinvigorated, liberal-minded judiciary necessary to furnish quicker and cheaper justice from bottom to top.

Third, because it will provide a series of Federal Courts willing to enforce the Constitution as written, and unwilling to assert legislative powers by writing into it their own political and economic policies.

During the past half century the balance of power between the three great branches of the Federal Government, has been tipped out of balance by the Courts in direct contradiction of the high purposes of the framers of the Constitution. It is my purpose to restore that balance. You, who know me will accept my solemn assurance that in a world in which democracy is under attack, I seek to make American democracy succeed. You and I will do our part.

XLVI
West Coast Hotel Co. v. Parrish, 300 U.S. 379
March 29, 1937
(Opinion of the Court)

Mr. Chief Justice HUGHES delivered the opinion of the Court.

This case presents the question of the constitutional validity of the minimum wage law of the state of Washington.

By a later act the Industrial Welfare Commission was abolished and its duties were assigned to the Industrial Welfare Committee consisting of the Director of Labor and Industries, the Supervisor of Industrial Insurance (300 U.S. 379), the Supervisor of Industrial Relations, the Industrial Statistician, and the Supervisor of Women in Industry. (Laws 1921 (Washington) c. 7, p. 12, Remington's Rev. Stat. (1932) 10840, 10893)

The appellant conducts a hotel. The appellee Elsie Parrish was employed as a chambermaid and (with her husband) brought this suit to recover the difference between the wages paid her and the minimum wage fixed pursuant to the state law. The minimum wage was $14.50 per week of 48 hours. The appellant challeged the act as repugnant to the due process clause of the Fourteenth Amendment of the Constitution of the United States. The Supreme Court of the state, reversing the trial court, sustained the statute and directed judgment for the plaintiffs. (Parrish v. West Coast Hotel Co., 185 Wash. 581, 55 P.(2d) 1083) The case is here on appeal.

The appellant relies upon the decision of this Court in Adkins v. Children's Hospital, 261 U.S. 525, which held invalid the District of Columbia Minimum Wage Act (40 Stat. 960) which was attacked under the due process clause of the Fifth Amendment. On the argument at bar, counsel for the appellees attempted to distinguish the Adkins Case upon the ground that the appellee was employed in a hotel and that the business of an innkeeper was affected with a public interest. That effort at distinction is obviously futile, as it appears that in one of the cases ruled by the Adkins opinion the employee was a woman employed as an elevator operator in a hotel. (Adkins v. Lyons, 261 U.S. 525)

The recent case of Morehead v. New York ex rel. Tipaldo, 298 U.S. 587, came here on certiorari to the New York court which had held the New York minimum wage act for women to be invalid. A minority of this Court thought that the New York statute was distinguishable in a material feature from that involved in the Adkins Case and that for that and other reasons the New York statute should be sustained. But the Court of Appeals of New York had said that it found no material difference between the two statutes and this Court held that the "meaning of the statute" as fixed by the decision of the state court "must be accepted here as if the meaning had been specifically expressed in the enactment." (298 U.S. 587) That view led to the affirmance by this Court of the judgment in the Morehead Case, as the Court considered that the only question before it was whether the Adkins Case was distinguishable and that reconsideration of that decision had not been sought. Upon that point the Court said: "The petition for the writ sought review upon the ground that this case (Morehead) is distinguishable from that one (Adkins). No application has been made for reconsideration of the constitutional question there decided. The validity of the principles upon which that decision rests is not challenged. This court confines itself to the ground upon which the writ was asked or granted...Here the review granted was no broader than sought by the petitioner...He is not entitled and does not ask to be heard upon the question whether the Adkins Case should be overruled. He maintains that it may be distinguished on the ground that the statutes are vitally dissimilar." (298 U.S. 587)

We think that the question which was not deemed to be open in the Morehead Case is open and is necessarily presented here. The Supreme Court of Washington has upheld the minimum wage statute of that state. It has decided that the statute is a reasonable exercise of the police power of the state. In reaching that conclusion, the state court has invoked principles long established by this Court in the application of the Fourteenth Amendment. The state court has refused to regard the decision in the Adkins Case as determinative and has pointed to our decisions both before and since that case as justifying its position. We are of the opinion that this ruling of (300 U.S. 379) the state court demands on our part a re-examination of the Adkins Case. The importance of the question, in which many states having similar laws are concerned, the close division by which the decision in the Adkins Case was reached, and the economic conditions which have supervened, and in the light of which the reasonableness of the exercise of the protective power of the state must be considered, make it not only appropriate, but we think imperative, that in deciding the present case the subject should receive fresh consideration.

Throughout this entire period the Washington statute now under consideration has been in force. The principle which must control our decision is not in doubt. The constitutional provision invoked is the due process clause of the Fourteenth Amendment governing the states, as the due process clause invoked in the Adkins Case governed Congress. In each case the violation alleged by those attacking minimum wage regulation for women is deprivation of freedom of contract. What is this freedom? The Constitution does not speak of freedom of contract. It speaks of liberty and prohibits the deprivation of liberty without due process of law. In prohibiting that deprivation, the Constitution does not recognize an absolute and uncontrollable liberty. Liberty in each of its phases has its history and connotation. But the liberty safeguarded is liberty in a social organization, which requires the protection of law against the evils, which menace the health, safety, morals, and welfare of the people. Liberty under the Constitution is thus necessarily subject to the restraints of due process, and regulation, which is reasonable in relation to its subject and is adopted in the interests of the community, is due process. (300 U.S. 379) This essential limitation of liberty in general governs freedom of contract in particular. More than twenty-five years ago we set forth the applicable principle in these words, after referring to the cases

where the liberty guaranteed by the Fourteenth Amendment had
been broadly described.

"But it was recognized in the cases cited, as in many others,
that freedom of contract is a qualified, and not an absolute, right.
There is no absolute freedom to do as one wills or to contract as one
chooses.   The guaranty of liberty does not withdraw from
legislative supervision that wide department of activity, which
consists of the making of contracts, or deny to government the
power to provide restrictive safeguards.   Liberty implies the
absence of arbitrary restraint, not immunity from reasonable
regulations and prohibitions imposed in the interests of the
community." (Chicago, Burlington & Quincy R. Co. v. McGuire,
219 U.S.)

This power under the Constitution to restrict freedom of
contract has had many illustrations. That it may be exercised in the
public interest with respect to contracts (300 U.S. 379) between
employer and employee is undeniable.   Thus statutes have been
sustained limiting employment in underground mines and smelters
to eight hours a day (Holden v. Hardy, 169 U.S. 366); in requiring
redemption in cash of store orders or other evidences of
indebtedness issued in the payment of wages (Knoxville Iron Co. v.
Harbison, 183 U.S. 13); in forbidding the payment of seamen's
wages in advance (Patterson v. The Bark Eudora, 190 U.S. 169); in
making it unlawful to contract to pay miners employed at quantity
rates upon the basis of screened coal instead of the weight of the
coal as originally produced in the mine (McLean v. Arkansas, 211
U.S. 539); in prohibiting contracts limiting liability for injuries to
employees (Chicago, Burlington & Quincy R. Co. v. McGuire,
supra); in limiting hours of work of employees in manufacturing
establishments (Bunting v. Oregon, 243 U.S. 426; and in
maintaining workmen's compensation laws (New York Central R.
Co. v. White, 243 U.S. 188, Mountain Timber Co. v. Washington,
243 U.S. 219).   In dealing with the relation of employer and
employed, the Legislature has necessarily a wide field of discretion
in order that there may be suitable protection of health and safety,
and that peace and good order may be promoted through
regulations designed to insure wholesome conditions of work and
freedom from oppression. (Chicago, Burlington & Quincy R. Co. v.
McGuire, supra, 219 U.S. 549)

The point that has been strongly stressed that adult employees
should be deemed competent to make their own contracts was

decisively met nearly forty years ago in <u>Holden v. Hardy</u>, supra, where we pointed out the inequality in the footing of the parties. We said (Id., 169 U.S. 366, 397, 390):

"The legislature has also recognized the fact, which the experience of legislators in many states has corroborated, that the proprietors of these establishments and their operatives do not stand upon an equality, and that (300 U.S. 379) their interests are, to a certain extent, conflicting. The former naturally desire to obtain as much labor as possible from their employees, while the latter are often induced by the fear of discharge to conform to regulations which their judgment, fairly exercised, would pronounce to be detrimental to their health or strength. In other words, the proprietors lay down the rules, and the laborers are practically constrained to obey them. In such cases self-interest is often an unsafe guide, and the legislature may properly interpose its authority."

And we added that the fact "that both parties are of full age, and competent to contract, does not necessarily deprive the state of the power to interfere, where the parties do not stand upon an equality, or where the public heath demands that one party to the contract shall be protected against himself." "The state still retains an interest in his welfare, however reckless he may be. The whole is no greater than the sum of all the parts, and when the individual health, safety, and welfare are sacrificed or neglected, the state must suffer."

With full recognition of the earnestness and vigor which characterize the prevailing opinion in the Adkins Case, we find it impossible to reconcile that ruling with these well-considered declarations. What can be closer to the public interest than the health of women and their protection from unscrupulous and overreaching employers? And if the protection of women is a legitimate end of the exercise of state power, how can it be said that the requirement of the payment of a minimum wage fairly fixed in order to meet the very necessities of existence is not an admissible means to that end? The Legislature of the state was clearly entitled to consider the situation of women in employment, the fact that they are in the class receiving the least pay, that their bargaining power is relatively weak, and that they are the ready victims of those who would take advantage of their necessitous circumstances. The Legislature was entitled to adopt measures to reduce the evils of the "sweating system," the exploiting of workers at wages so low as to be insufficient to meet the bare cost of living, thus making their very helplessness the occasion of a most injurious competition. The Legislature had the right to consider that its minimum wage requirements would be an important aid in carrying out its policy of protection. The adoption of similar requirements by many states evidences a deep-seated conviction both as to the presence of the evil and as to the means adapted to check it. Legislative response to that conviction cannot be regarded as arbitrary or capricious and that is all we have to decide. Even if the wisdom of the policy be regarded as debatable and its effects uncertain, still the Legislature is entitled to its judgment.

Our conclusion is that the case of <u>Adkins v. Children's Hospital</u>, supra, should be, and it is, overruled. The judgment of the Supreme Court of the state of Washington is affirmed.

Affirmed.

XLVII
N.L.R.B. v. Jones & Laughlin Steel Corp., 301 U.S. 1
April 12, 1937
(Opinion of the Court)

HUGHES, C. J. In a proceeding under the National Labor Relations Act of 1935, the National Labor Relations Board found that the petitioner, Jones & Laughlin Steel Corporation, had violated the Act by engaging in unfair labor practices affecting commerce. The proceeding was instituted by the Beaver Valley Lodge No. 200, affiliated with the Amalgamated Association of Iron, Steel and Tin Workers of America, a labor organization. The unfair labor practices charged were that the corporation was discriminating against members of the union with regard to hire and tenure of employment, and was coercing and intimidating its employees in order to interfere with their self-organization. The discriminatory and coercive action alleged was the discharge of certain employees.

The National Labor Relations Board, sustaining the charge, ordered the corporation to cease and desist from such discrimination and coercion, to offer reinstatement to ten of the employees named, to make good their losses in pay, and to post for thirty days notices that the corporation would not discharge or discriminate against members, or those desiring to become members, of the labor union. As the corporation failed to comply, the Board petitioned the Circuit Court of Appeals to enforce the order. The court denied the petition, holding that the order lay beyond the range of federal power. (83 F. (2d) 998) We granted certiorari.

The scheme of the National Labor Relations Act may be briefly stated. Respondent, appearing specially for the purpose of objecting to the jurisdiction of the Board, filed its answer. Respondent admitted the discharges, but alleged that they were made because of inefficiency or violation of rules or for other good reasons and were not ascribable to union membership or activities. As an affirmative defense respondent challenged the constitutional validity of the statute and its applicability in the instant case.

Contesting the ruling of the Board, the respondent argues (1) that the Act is in reality a regulation of labor relations and not of interstate commerce; (2) that the Act can have no application to the respondent's relations with its production employees because they are not subject to regulation by the federal government; and (3) that the provisions of the Act violate Section 2 of Article III and the Fifth and Seventh Amendments of the Constitution of the United States.

The facts as to the nature and scope of the business of the Jones & Laughlin Steel Corporation have been found by the Labor Board and, so far as they are essential to the determination of this controversy, they are not in dispute. The Labor Board has found: The corporation is organized under the laws of Pennsylvania and has its principal office at Pittsburgh. It is engaged in the business of manufacturing iron and steel in plants situated in Pittsburgh and nearby Aliquippa, Pennsylvania. It manufactures and distributes a widely diversified line of steel and pig iron, being the fourth largest producer of steel in the United States. With its subsidiaries—nineteen in number—it is a completely integrated enterprise, owning and operating ore, coal and limestone properties, lake and river transportation facilities and terminal railroads located at its manufacturing plants. It owns or controls mines in Michigan and Minnesota. It operates four ore steamships on the Great Lakes, used in the transportation of ore to its factories. It owns coal mines in Pennsylvania. It operates towboats and steam barges used in carrying coal to its factories. It owns limestone properties in various places in Pennsylvania and West Virginia. It owns the Monongahela connecting railroad which connects the plants of the Pittsburgh works and forms an interconnection with the Pennsylvania, New York Central and Baltimore and Ohio

Railroad systems. It owns the Aliquippa and Southern Railroad Company which connects the Aliquippa works with the Pittsburgh and Lake Erie, part of the New York Central system. Much of its product is shipped to its warehouses in Chicago, Detroit, Cincinnati and Memphis, to the last two places by means of its own barges and transportation equipment. In Long Island City, New York, and in New Orleans it operates structural steel fabricating shops in connection with the warehousing of semi-finished materials sent from its works. Through one of its wholly-owned subsidiaries it owns, leases and operates stores, warehouses and yards for the distribution of equipment and supplies for drilling and operating oil and gas mills and for pipe lines, refineries and pumping stations. It has sales offices in twenty cities in the United States and a wholly-owned subsidiary which is devoted exclusively to distributing its product in Canada. Approximately 75 percent of its product is shipped out of Pennsylvania.

Summarizing these operations, the Labor Board concluded that the works in Pittsburgh and Aliquippa "might be likened to the heart of a self-contained, highly integrated body. They draw in the raw materials from Michigan, Minnesota, West Virginia, Pennsylvania in part through arteries and by means controlled by the respondent, they transform the materials and then pump them out to all parts of the nation through the vast mechanism which the respondent has elaborated."

To carry on the activities of the entire steel industry, 33,000 men mine ore, 44,000 men mine coal, 4,000 men quarry limestone 16,000 men manufacture coke, 343,000 men manufacture steel, and 83,000 men transport its product. Respondent has about 10,000 employees in its Aliquippa plant, which is located in a community of about 30,000 persons.

Practically all the factual evidence in the case, except that which dealt with the nature of respondent's business, concerned its relations with the employees in the Aliquippa plant whose discharge was the subject of the complaint. These employees were active leaders in the labor union.

While respondent criticizes the evidence and the attitude of the Board, which is described as being hostile toward employers and particularly toward those who insisted upon their constitutional rights, respondent did not take advantage of its opportunity to present evidence to refute that which was offered to show discrimination and coercion. In this situation, the record presents no ground for setting aside the order of the Board so far as the facts pertaining to the circumstances and purpose of the discharge of the employees are concerned. Upon that point it is sufficient to say that the evidence supports the findings of the Board that respondent discharged these men "because of their union activity and for the purpose of discouraging membership in the union." We turn to the questions of law which respondent urges in contesting the validity and application of the Act.

First: The Scope of the Act

The Act is challenged in its entirety as an attempt to regulate all industry, thus invading the reserved powers of the States over their local concerns. It is asserted that the references in the Act to interstate and foreign commerce are colorable at best; that the Act is not a true regulation of such commerce or of matters which directly affect it but on the contrary has the fundamental object of placing under the compulsory supervision of the federal government all industrial labor relations within the nation. The argument seeks support in the broad words of the preamble and in the sweep of the provisions of the Act, and it is further insisted that its legislative history shows an essential universal purpose in the light of which its scope cannot be limited by either construction or by the application of the separability clause.

   If this conception of terms, intent and consequent inseparability were sound, the Act would necessarily fall by reason of the limitation upon the federal power which inheres in the constitutional grant, as well as because of the explicit reservation of the Tenth Amendment. (Schechter Corporation v. United States, 295 U.S. 495) The authority of the federal government may not be pushed to such an extreme as to destroy the distinction, which the commerce clause itself establishes, between commerce "among the several States" and the internal concerns of a State. That distinction between what is national and what is local in the activities of commerce is vital to the maintenance of our federal system.

   But we are not at liberty to deny effect to specific provisions, which Congress has constitutional power to enact, by superimposing upon them inferences from general legislative declarations of an ambiguous character, even if found in the same statute. The cardinal principle of statutory construction is to save and not to destroy. We have repeatedly held that as between two possible interpretations of a statute, by one of which it would be unconstitutional and by the other valid, our plain duty is to adopt that which will save the act. Even to avoid a serious doubt the rule is the same.

We think it clear that the National Labor Relations Act may be construed so as to operate within the sphere of constitutional authority. The jurisdiction conferred upon the Board, and invoked in this instance, is found in Section 10 (a), which provides:

Sec. 1 (a). The Board is empowered, as hereinafter provided, to prevent any person from engaging in any unfair labor practice (listed in Section 8) affecting commerce.

The critical words of this provision, prescribing the limits of the Board's authority in dealing with the labor practices, are "affecting commerce." The Act specifically defines the "commerce" to which it refers (Sec. 2 (6)).

There can be no question that the commerce thus contemplated by the Act (aside from that within a Territory or the District of Columbia) is interstate and foreign commerce in the constitutional sense. The Act also defines the term "affecting commerce" (Sec. 2 (7)).

This definition is one of exclusion as well as inclusion. The grant of authority to the Board does not purport to extend to the relationship between all industrial employees and employers. Its terms do not impose collective bargaining upon all industry regardless of effects upon interstate or foreign commerce. It purports to reach only what may be deemed to burden or obstruct that commerce and, thus qualified, it must be construed as contemplating the exercise of control within constitutional bounds. It is a familiar principle that acts which directly burden or obstruct interstate or foreign commerce, or its free flow, are within the reach of the congressional power. Acts having that effect are not rendered immune because they grow out of labor disputes. It is the effect upon commerce, not the source of the injury, which is the criterion. Whether or not particular action does affect commerce in such a close and intimate fashion as to be subject to federal control, and hence to lie within the authority conferred upon the Board, is left by the statute to be determined as individual cases arise. We are thus to inquire whether in the instant case the constitutional boundary has been passed.

Second: The Unfair Labor Practices in Question

The unfair labor practices found by the Board are those defined in Section 8 subdivisions (1) and (3). These provide:

Sec. 8. It shall be an unfair labor practice for an employer—

(1) To interfere with, restrain, or coerce employees in the exercise of the rights guaranteed in section 7.

(3) By discrimination in regard to hire or tenure of employment or any term or condition of employment to encourage or discourage membership in any labor organization.

Section 8, subdivision (1), refers to Section 7, which is as follows:

Sec. 7. Employees shall have the right to self-organization, to form, join, or assist labor organizations, to bargain collectively through representatives of their own choosing, and to engage in concerted activities, for the purpose of collective bargaining or other mutual aid or protection.

Thus, in its present application, the statute goes no further than to safeguard the right of employees to self-organization and to select representatives of their own choosing for collective bargaining or other mutual protection without restraint or coercion by their employer.

Third: The Application of the Act to Employees Engaged in Production—The Principle Involved

Respondent says that whatever may be said of employees engaged in interstate commerce, the industrial relations and activities in the manufacturing department of respondent's enterprise are not subject to federal regulation. The argument rests upon the proposition that manufacturing in itself is not commerce.

The government distinguishes these cases. The various parts of respondent's enterprise are described as interdependent and as thus involving "a great movement of iron ore, coal and limestone along well-defined paths to the steel mills, thence through them, and thence in the form of steel products into the consuming centers of the country—a definite and well-understood course of business." It is urged that these activities constitute a "stream" or "flow" of commerce, of which the Aliquippa manufacturing plant is the focal point, and that industrial strife at that point would cripple the entire movement. Reference is made to our decision sustaining the Packers and Stockyards Act. The Court found that the stockyards were but a "throat" through which the current of commerce flowed and the transactions which there occurred could not be separated from that movement.

Respondent contends that the instant case presents material distinctions.

We do not find it necessary to determine whether these features of defendant's business dispose of the asserted analogy to the "stream of commerce" cases. The congressional authority to protect interstate commerce from burdens and obstructions is not limited to transactions which can be deemed to be an essential part of a "flow" of interstate or foreign commerce. Burdens and obstructions may be due to injurious action springing from other sources. The fundamental principle is that the power to regulate commerce is the power to enact "all appropriate legislation" for "its protection and advancement," to adopt measures "to promote its growth and insure its safety"; "to foster, protect, control and restrain." That power is plenary and may be exerted to protect interstate commerce "no matter what the source of the dangers which threaten it." Although activities may be intrastate in character when separately considered, if they have such a close and substantial relation to interstate commerce that their control is essential or appropriate to protect that commerce from burdens and obstructions, Congress cannot be denied the power to exercise that control. Undoubtedly the scope of this power must be considered in the light of our dual system of government and may not be extended so as to embrace effects upon interstate commerce so indirect and remote that to embrace them, in view of our complex society, would effectually obliterate the distinction between what is national and what is local and create a completely centralized government. The question is necessarily one of degree.

It is thus apparent that the fact that the employees here concerned were engaged in production is not determinative. The question remains as to the effect upon interstate commerce of the labor practice involved.

Fourth: Effects of the Unfair Labor Practice in Respondent's Enterprise

Giving full weight to respondent's contention with respect to a break in the complete continuity of the "stream of commerce" by reason of respondent's manufacturing operations, the fact remains that the stoppage of those operations by industrial strife would have a most serious effect upon interstate commerce. In view of respondent's far-flung activities, it is idle to say that the effect would be indirect or remote. It is obvious that it would be immediate and might be catastrophic. We are asked to shut our eyes to the plainest facts of our national life and to deal with the question of direct and indirect effects in an intellectual vacuum. Because there may be but indirect and remote effects upon interstate commerce in connection with a host of local enterprises throughout the country, it does not follow that other industrial activities do not have such a close and intimate relation to interstate commerce as to make the presence of industrial strife a matter of the most urgent national concern.   When industries organize themselves on a national scale, making their relation to interstate commerce the dominant factor in their activities, how can it be maintained that their industrial labor relations constitute a forbidden field into which Congress may not enter when it is necessary to protect interstate commerce from the paralyzing consequences of industrial war? We have often said that interstate commerce itself is a practical conception. It is equally true that interferences with that commerce must be appraised by a judgment that does not ignore actual experience.

Experience has abundantly demonstrated that the recognition of the right of employees to self-organization and to have representatives of their own choosing for the purpose of collective bargaining is often an essential condition of industrial peace. Refusal to confer and negotiate has been one of the most prolific causes of strife. This is such an outstanding fact in the history of labor disturbances that it is a proper subject of judicial notice and requires no citation of instances.   But with respect to the appropriateness of the recognition of self-organization and representation in the promotion of peace, the question is not essentially different in the case of employees in industries of such a character that interstate commerce is put in jeopardy from the case of employees of transportation companies. And of what avail is it to protect the facility of transportation, if interstate commerce is throttled with respect to the commodities to be transported!

These questions have frequently engaged the attention of Congress and have been the subject of many inquiries. The steel industry is one of the great basic industries of the United States, with ramifying activities affecting interstate commerce at every point. The government aptly refers to the steel strike of 1919-1920 with its far-reaching consequences. The fact that there appears to have been no major disturbance in that industry in the more recent period did not dispose of the possibilities of future and like dangers to interstate commerce which Congress was entitled to foresee and to exercise its protective power to forestall. It is not necessary again to detail the facts as to respondent's enterprise. Instead of being beyond the pale, we think that it presents in a most striking way the close and intimate relation which a manufacturing industry may have to interstate commerce and we have no doubt that Congress had constitutional authority to safeguard the right of respondent's employees to self-organization and freedom in the choice of representatives for collective bargaining.

Fifth: The Means which the Act Employs—
Questions Under the Due Process Clause and Other
Constitutional Restrictions

Respondent asserts its right to conduct its business in an orderly manner without being subjected to arbitrary restraints. What we have said points to the fallacy in the argument. Employees have their correlative right to organize for the purpose of securing the redress of grievances and to promote agreements with employers relating to rates of pay and conditions of work. Restraint for the purpose of preventing an unjust interference with that right cannot be considered arbitrary or capricious.

Our conclusion is that the order of the Board was within its competency and that the Act is valid as here applied. The judgment of the Circuit Court of Appeals is reversed and the cause is remanded for further proceedings in conformity with this opinion.

XLVIII
Franklin D. Roosevelt:
A Fair Day's Pay for a Fair Day's Work
May 24, 1937

The time has arrived for us to take further action to extend the frontiers of social progress. Such further action initiated by the legislative branch of the government, administered by the executive, and sustained by the judicial, is within the common sense framework and purpose of our Constitution and receives beyond doubt the approval of our electorate.

The overwhelming majority of our population earns its daily bread either in agriculture or in industry. One third of our population, the overwhelming majority of which is in agriculture or industry, is ill-nourished, ill-clad, and ill-housed.

The overwhelming majority of this nation has little patience with that small minority which vociferates today that prosperity has returned, that wages are good, that crop prices are high, and that government should take a holiday.

Today, you and I are pledged to take further steps to reduce the lag in the purchasing power of industrial workers and to strengthen and stabilize the markets for the farmers' products. The two go hand in hand. Each depends for its effectiveness upon the other. Both working simultaneously will open new outlets for productive capital. Our nation so richly endowed with natural resources and with a capable and industrious population should be able to devise ways and means of insuring to all our able-bodied working men and women a fair day's pay for a fair day's work. A self-supporting and self-respecting democracy can plead no justification for the existence of child labor, no economic reason for chiseling workers' wages or stretching workers' hours.

Enlightened business is learning that competition ought not to cause bad social consequences, which inevitably react upon the profits of business itself. All but the hopelessly reactionary will agree that to conserve our primary resources of man power, government must have some control over maximum hours, minimum wages, the evil of child labor and the exploitation of unorganized labor.

Nearly twenty years ago in his dissenting opinion in <u>Hammer v. Dagenhart</u>, Mr. Justice Holmes expressed his views as to the power of the Congress to prohibit the shipment in interstate or foreign commerce of the product of the labor of children in factories below what Congress then deemed to be civilized social standards. Surely the experience of the last twenty years has only served to reinforce the wisdom and the rightness of his views. And, surely if he was right about the power of the Congress over the work of children in factories, it is equally right that the Congress has the power over decent wages and hours in those same factories.

"I had thought that the propriety of the exercise of a power admitted to exist in some cases was for the consideration of Congress alone and that this Court has always disavowed the right to intrude its judgment upon questions of policy or morals. It is not for this Court to pronounce when prohibition is necessary to regulation if it ever may be necessary—to say that it is permissible as against strong drink but not as against the product of ruined lives."

But although Mr. Justice Holmes spoke for a minority of the Supreme Court he spoke for a majority of the American people.

One of the primary purposes of the formation of our federal union was to do away with the trade barriers between the states. To the Congress and not to the states was given the power to regulate commerce among the several states. Congress cannot interfere in local affairs but when goods pass through the channels of commerce from one state to another they become subject to the power of the Congress, and the Congress may exercise that power to recognize and protect the fundamental interests of free labor.

And so to protect the fundamental interests of free labor and a free people we propose that only goods, which have been produced under conditions, which meet the minimum standards of free labor, shall be admitted to interstate commerce. Goods produced under conditions which do not meet rudimentary standards of decency should be regarded as contraband and ought not to be allowed to pollute the channels of interstate trade.

Our problem is to workout in practice those labor standards which will permit the maximum but prudent employment of our human resources to bring within the reach of the average man and woman a maximum of goods and of services conducive to the fulfillment of the promise of American life.

Legislation can, I hope, be passed at this session of the Congress further to help those who toil in factory and on farm. We have promised it. We cannot stand still.

XLIX
Steward Machine Co. v. Davis, 301 U.S. 548
May 24, 1937
(Opinion of the Court)

CARDOZO, J. The validity of the tax imposed by the Social Security Act on employers of eight or more is here to be determined.

Petitioner, an Alabama corporation, paid a tax in accordance with the statute, filed a claim for refund with the Commissioner of Internal Revenue, and sued to recover the payment asserting a conflict between the statute and the Constitution of the United States. Upon demurrer the District Court gave judgment for the defendant dismissing the complaint, and the Circuit Court of Appeals for the Fifth Circuit affirmed.... An important question of constitutional law being involved, we granted certiorari.

The Social Security Act is divided into eleven separate titles, of which only Titles IX and III are so related to this case as to stand in need of summary.

The assault on the statute proceeds on an extended front. Its assailants take the ground that the tax is not an excise; that it is not uniform throughout the United States as excises are required to be; that its exceptions are so many and arbitrary as to violate the Fifth Amendment; that its purpose was not revenue, but an unlawful invasion of the reserved powers of the states; and that the states in submitting to it have yielded to coercion and have abandoned governmental functions which they are not permitted to surrender.

The objections will be considered seriatim with such further explanation as may be necessary to make their meaning clear.

First: The tax, which is described in the statute as an excise, is laid with uniformity throughout the United States as a duty, an impost or an excise upon the relation of employment.

1. We are told that the relation of employment is one so essential to the pursuit of happiness that it may not be burdened with a tax. Appeal is made to history. From the precedents of colonial days we are supplied with illustrations of excises common in the colonies. They are said to have been bound up with the enjoyment of particular commodities. Appeal is also made to principle or the analysis of concepts. An excise, we are told, imports a tax upon a privilege; employment, it is said, is a right, not a privilege, from which it follows that employment is not subject to an excise. Neither the one appeal nor the other leads to the desired goal....

The historical prop failing, the prop or fancied prop of principle remains. We learn that employment for lawful gain is a "natural" or "inherent" or "inalienable" right, and not a "privilege" at all. But natural rights, so called, are as much subject to taxation as rights of less importance. An excise is not limited to vocations or activities that may be prohibited altogether. It is not limited to those that are the outcome of a franchise. It extends to vocations or activities pursued as of common right. What the individual does in the operation of a business is amenable to taxation just as much as what he owns, at all events if the classification is not tyrannical or arbitrary. "Business is as legitimate an object of the taxing powers as property." (City of Newton v. Atchison, 31 Kan. 151, 154, per Brewer, J.) Indeed, ownership itself, as we had occasion to point out the other day, is only a bundle of rights and privileges invested with a single name. (Henneford v. Silas Mason Co., Inc., March 29,

1937, 300 U.S. 577)   Employment is a business relation, if not itself a business.   It is a relation without which business could seldom be carried on effectively.   The power to tax the activities and relations that constitute a calling considered as a unit is the power to tax any of them.   The whole includes the parts.

The subject matter of taxation open to the power of the Congress is as comprehensive as that open to the power of the states, though the method of apportionment may at times be different.   "The Congress shall have power to lay and collect taxes, duties, imposts and excises."   (Art. 1, § 8)   If the tax is a direct one, it shall be apportioned according to the census or enumeration.   If it is a duty, impost, or excise, it shall be uniform throughout the United States. Together, these classes include every form of tax appropriate to sovereignty.   Whether the tax is to be classified as an "excise" is in truth not of critical importance.   If not that, it is an "impost" or a "duty."   A capitation or other "direct" tax it certainly is not....

Second: The excise is not invalid under the provisions of the Fifth Amendment by force of its exemptions.

The statute does not apply, as we have seen, to employers of less than eight.   It does not apply to agricultural labor, or domestic service in a private home or to some other classes of less importance.   Petitioner contends that the effect of these restrictions is an arbitrary discrimination vitiating the tax.

The Fifth Amendment unlike the Fourteenth has no equal protection clause.   But even the states, though subject to such a clause, are not confined to a formula of rigid uniformity in framing measures of taxation.   They may tax some kinds of property at one rate, and others at another, and exempt others altogether.   They may lay an excise on the operations of a particular kind of business and exempt some other kind of business closely akin thereto.   If this latitude of judgment is lawful for the states, it is lawful, a fortiori, in legislation by the Congress, which is subject to restraints less narrow and confining.

Third: The excise is not void as involving the coercion of the States in contravention of the Tenth Amendment or of restrictions implicit in our federal form of government.

The proceeds of the excise when collected are paid into the Treasury at Washington, and therefore are subject to appropriation like public moneys generally.   No presumption can be indulged that they will be misapplied or wasted.   Even if they were collected in the hope or expectation that some other and collateral good would be furthered as an incident, that without more would not make the act invalid. This indeed is hardly questioned. The case for the petitioner is built on the contention that here an ulterior aim is wrought into the very structure of the act, and what is even more important that the aim is not only ulterior, but essentially unlawful. In particular, the 90 percent credit is relied upon as supporting that conclusion. But before the statute succumbs to an assault upon these lines, two propositions must be made out by the assailant. There must be a showing in the first place that separated from the credit the revenue provisions are incapable of standing by themselves. There must be a showing in the second place that the tax and the credit in combination are weapons of coercion, destroying or impairing the autonomy of the states. The truth of each proposition being essential to the success of the assault, we pass for convenience to a consideration of the second, without pausing to inquire whether there has been a demonstration of the first.

To draw the line intelligently between duress and inducement there is need to remind ourselves of facts as to the problem of unemployment that are now matters of common knowledge.... The fact developed quickly that the states were unable to give the requisite relief. The problem had become national in area and dimensions. There was need of help from the nation if the people were not to starve. It is too late today for the argument to be heard with tolerance that in a crisis so extreme the use of the moneys of the nation to relieve the unemployed and their dependents is a use for any purpose narrower than the promotion of the general welfare. The nation responded to the call of the distressed. Between January 1, 1933 and July 1, 1936, the states (according to statistics submitted by the Government) incurred obligations of $689,291,802 for emergency relief; local subdivisions an additional $775,675,366. In the same period the obligations for emergency relief incurred by the national government were $2,929,307,125, or twice the obligations of states and local agencies combined. According to the President's budget message for the fiscal year 1938, the national government expended for public works and unemployment relief for the three fiscal years 1934, 1935, and 1936, the stupendous total of $8,681,000,000. The *parens patriae* has many reasons—fiscal and economic as well as social and moral—for planning to mitigate disasters that bring these burdens in their train.

In the presence of this urgent need for some remedial expedient, the question is to be answered whether the expedient adopted has overstepped the bounds of power. The assailants of the statute say that its dominant end and aim is to drive the state legislatures under the whip of economic pressure into the enactment of unemployment compensation laws at the bidding of the central government. Supporters of the statute say that its operation is not constraint, but the creation of a larger freedom, the states and the nation joining in a cooperative endeavor to avert a common evil.

The Social Security Act is an attempt to find a method by which all these public agencies may work together to a common end. Every dollar of the new taxes will continue in all likelihood to be used and needed by the nation as long as states are unwilling, whether through timidity or for other motives, to do what can be done at home. At least the inference is permissible that Congress so believed, though retaining undiminished freedom to spend the money as it pleased. On the other hand fulfillment of the home duty will be lightened and encouraged by crediting the taxpayer upon his account with the Treasury of the nation to the extent that his contributions under the laws of the locality have simplified or diminished the problem of relief and the probable demand upon the resources of the fisc. Duplicated taxes, or burdens that approach them, are recognized hardships that government, state or national, may properly avoid. If Congress believed that the general welfare would better be promoted by relief through local units than by the system then in vogue, the cooperating localities ought not in all fairness to pay a second time.

Who then is coerced through the operation of this statute? Not the taxpayer. He pays in fulfillment of the mandate of the local legislature. Not the state. Even now she does not offer a suggestion that in passing the unemployment law she was affected by duress. For all that appears she is satisfied with her choice, and would be sorely disappointed if it were now to be annulled. The difficulty with the petitioner's contention is that it confuses motive with coercion. "Every tax is in some measure regulatory. To some extent it interposes an economic impediment to the activity taxed as compared with others not taxed." (Sonzinsky v. United States, supra, March 29, 1937) In like manner every rebate from a tax when conditioned upon conduct is in some measure a temptation. But to hold that motive or temptation is equivalent to coercion is to plunge the law in endless difficulties. The outcome of such a doctrine is the acceptance of a philosophical determinism by which choice becomes impossible. Till now the law has been guided by a robust common sense which assumes the freedom of the will as a working hypothesis in the solution of its problems. The wisdom of the hypothesis has illustration in this case. Nothing in the case suggests the exertion of a power akin to undue influence, if we assume that such a concept can ever be applied with fitness to the relations between state and nation. Even on that assumption the location of the point at which pressure turns into compulsion, and ceases to be inducement, would be a question of degree, at times, perhaps, of fact. The point had not been reached when Alabama made her choice. We cannot say that she was acting, not of her unfettered will, but under the strain of a persuasion equivalent to undue influence, when she chose to have relief administered under laws of her own making, by agents of her own selection, instead of under federal laws, administered by federal officers, with all the ensuing evils, at least to many minds, of federal patronage and power. There would be a strange irony, indeed, if her choice were now to be annulled on the basis of an assumed duress in the enactment of a statute which her courts have accepted as a true expression of her will. We think the choice must stand....

The judgment is affirmed.

L
Helvering, et. al. v. Davis, 301 U.S. 619
May 24, 1937

CARDOZO, J. The Social Security Act is challenged once again....

In this case Titles VIII and II are the subject of attack. Title VIII...lays a special income tax upon employees to be deducted from their wages and paid by the employers. Title II provides for the payment of Old Age benefits, and supplies the motive and occasion, in the view of the assailants of the statute, for the levy of the taxes imposed by Title VIII....

Congress may spend money in aid of the, "general welfare." (Constitution, Art. I, Section 8; United States v. Butler, 297 U.S. 1; Steward Machine Co. v. Davis) There have been great statesmen in our history who have stood for other views. We will not resurrect the contest. It is now settled by the decision in United States v. Butler. The conception of the spending power advocated by

Hamilton prevailed over that of Madison, which has not been lacking in adherents. Yet difficulties are left when the power is conceded. The line must still be drawn between one welfare and another, between particular and general. Where this shall be placed cannot be known through a formula in advance of the event. There is a middle ground or certainly a penumbra in which discretion is at large. The discretion, however, is not confided to the courts. The discretion belongs to Congress unless the choice is clearly wrong, a display of arbitrary power, not an exercise of judgment. This is now familiar law. "When such a contention comes here we naturally require a showing that by no reasonable possibility can the challenged legislation fall within the wide range of discretion permitted to the Congress." (United States v. Butler, supra, p. 67) Nor is the concept of the general welfare static. Needs that were narrow or parochial a century ago may be interwoven in our day with the well-being of the nation. What is critical or urgent changes with the times.

The purge of nation-wide calamity that began in 1929 has taught us many lessons. Not the least is the solidarity of interests that may once have seemed to be divided. Unemployment spreads from state to state, the hinterland now settled that in pioneer days gave an avenue of escape. Spreading from state to state, unemployment is an ill not particular but general, which may be checked, if Congress so determines, by the resources of the nation. If this can have been doubtful until now, our ruling today in the case of the Steward Machine Co. has set the doubt at greatly different whether men are thrown out of work because there is no longer work to do or because the disabilities of age make them incapable of doing it. Rescue becomes necessary irrespective of the cause. The hope behind this statute is to save men and women from the rigors of the poor house as well as from the haunting fear that such a lot awaits them when journey's end is near.

Congress did not improvise a judgment when it found that the award of old age benefits would be conducive to the general welfare. The President's Committee on Economic Security made an investigation and report, aided by a research staff of Government officers and employees, and by an Advisory Council and seven other advisory groups. Extensive hearings followed before the House Committee on Ways and Means, and the Senate Committee on Finance. A great mass of evidence was brought together supporting the policy which finds expression in the act. Among the relevant facts are these: The number of persons in the United States 65 years of age or over is increasing proportionately as well as absolutely. What is even more important the number of such persons unable to take care of themselves is growing at a threatening pace. More and more our population is becoming urban and industrial instead of rural and agricultural. The evidence is impressive that among industrial workers the younger men and women are preferred over the older. In time of retrenchment the older are commonly the first to go, and even if retained, their wages are likely to be lowered. The plight of men and women at so low an age as 40 is hard, almost hopeless, when they are driven to seek for reemployment. Statistics are in the brief. A few illustrations will be chosen from many there collected. In 1930, out of 224 American factories investigated, 71, or almost one third, had fixed maximum hiring age limits; in 4 plants the limit was under 40; in 41 it was under 46. In the other 153 plants there were no fixed limits, but in practice few were hired if they were over 50 years of age. With the loss of savings inevitable in periods of idleness, the fate of workers over 65, when thrown out of work, is little less than desperate. A recent study of the Social Security Board informs us that "one-fifth of the aged in the United States were receiving old-age assistance, emergency relief, institutional care, employment under the works program, or some other form of aid from public or private funds; two-fifths to one-half were dependent on friends and relatives, one-eighth had some income from earnings; and possibly one-sixth had some savings or property. Approximately three out of four persons 65 or over were probably dependent wholly or partially on others for support." We summarize in the margin the results of other studies by state and national commissions. They point the same way.

The problem is plainly national in area and dimensions. Moreover, laws of the separate states cannot deal with it effectively. Congress, at least, had a basis for that belief. States and local governments are often lacking in the resources that are necessary to finance an adequate program of security for the aged. This is brought out with a wealth of illustration in recent studies of the problem. Apart from the failure of resources, states and local governments are at times reluctant to increase so heavily the burden of taxation to be borne by their residents for fear of placing themselves in a position of economic disadvantage as compared with neighbors or competitors. We have seen this in our study of the problem of unemployment compensation. (<u>Steward Machine Co. v. Davis</u>) A system of old age pensions has special dangers of its own, if put in force in one state and rejected in another. The existence of such a system is a bait to the needy and dependent elsewhere, encouraging them to migrate and seek a haven of repose. Only a power that is national can serve the interests of all.

Whether wisdom or unwisdom resides in the scheme of benefits set forth in Title II, it is not for us to say. The answer to such inquiries must come from Congress, not the courts. Our concern here as often is with power, not with wisdom. Counsel for respondent has recalled to us the virtues of self-reliance and frugality. There is a possibility he says, that aid from a paternal government may sap those sturdy virtues and breed a race of weaklings. If Massachusetts so believes and shapes her laws in that conviction, must her breed of sons be changed, he asks because some other philosophy of government finds favor in the halls of Congress? But the answer is not doubtful. One might ask with equal reason whether the system of protective tariffs is to be set aside at will in one state or another whenever local policy prefers the rule of *laissez faire*. The issue is a closed one. It was fought out long ago. When money is spent to promote the general welfare, the concept of welfare or the opposite is shaped by Congress, not the states. So the concept be not arbitrary, the locality must yield. (Constitution, Art. VI, Par. 2)

LI
Senate Judiciary Committee
Adverse Report on Judicial Reorganization Plan
June 7, 1937

The Committee on the Judiciary, to whom was referred the bill to reorganize the judicial branch of the government, after full consideration, having unanimously amended the measure, hereby report the bill adversely with the recommendation that it do not pass....

The Argument
The committee recommends that the measure be rejected for the following primary reasons:

I. The bill does not accomplish any one of the objectives for which it was originally offered.

II. It applies force to the judiciary and in its initial and ultimate effect would undermine the independence of the courts.

III. It violates all precedents in the history of our government and would in itself be a dangerous precedent for the future.

IV. The theory of the bill is in direct violation of the spirit of the American Constitution and its employment would permit alteration of the Constitution without the people's consent or approval; it undermines the protection our constitution system gives to minorities and is subversive of the rights of individuals.

V. It tends to centralize the Federal district judiciary by the power of assigning judges from one district to another at will.

VI. It tends to expand political control over the judicial department by adding judges from one district to another at will.

Objectives As Originally Stated

As offered to the Congress, this bill was designed to effectuate only three objectives, described as follows in the President's message: 1. To increase the personnel of the Federal courts "so that cases may be promptly decided in the first instance, and may be given adequate and prompt hearing on all appeals"; 2. To "invigorate all the courts by the permanent infusion of new blood"; 3. To "grant to the Supreme Court further power and responsibility in maintaining the efficiency of the entire Federal judiciary."

The third of these purposes was to be accomplished by the provisions creating the office of the Proctor and dealing with the assignment of judges to courts other than those to which commissioned.

The first two objectives were to be attained by the provisions authorizing the appointment of not to exceed 50 additional judges when sitting judges of retirement age, as defined in the bill, failed to retire or resign. How totally inadequate the measure is to achieve either of the named objectives, the most cursory examination of the facts reveals.

Question of Age Not Solved

The next question is to determine to what extent "the persistent infusion of new blood" may be expected from this bill.

It will be observed that the bill before us does not and cannot compel the retirement of any judge, whether on the Supreme Court or any other court, when he becomes 70 years of age. It will be remembered that the mere attainment of three score and ten by a particular judge does not, under this bill require the appointment of another. The man on the bench may be 80 years of age, but this bill will not authorize the President to appoint a new judge to sit beside him unless he has served as a judge for 10 years. In other words, age itself is not penalized; the penalty falls only when age is attended with experience.

No one should overlook the fact that under this bill the President, whoever he may be and whether or not he believes in the constant infusion of young blood in the courts, may nominate a man 69 years and 11 months of age to the Supreme Court, or to any court, and if confirmed, such nominee, if he never had served as a judge, would continue to sit upon the bench unmolested by this law until he had attained the ripe age of 79 years and 11 months.

We are told that "modern complexities call also for a constant infusion of new blood in the courts, just as it is needed in executive functions of the government and in private business." Does this bill provide for such? The answer is obviously no. As has been just demonstrated, the introduction of old and inexperienced blood into the courts is not prevented by this bill.

More than that, the measure, by its own terms, makes impossible the "constant" or "persistent" infusion of new blood. It is to be observed that the word is "new," not "young."

The Supreme Court may not be expanded to more than 15 members. No more than two additional members may be appointed to any circuit court of appeals, to the Court of Claims, to the Court of Customs and Patent Appeals, or to the Customs Court, and the number of judges now serving in any district or group of districts may not be more than doubled. There is, therefore, a specific limitation of appointment regardless of age. That is to say, this bill, ostensibly designed to provide for the infusion of new blood, sets up insuperable obstacles to the "constant" or "persistent" operation of that principle.

It thus appears that the bill before us does not with certainty provide for increasing the personnel of the Federal judiciary, does not remedy the law's delay, does not serve the interest of the "poorer litigant" and does not provide for the "constant" or "persistent infusion of new blood" into the judiciary. What, then, does it do?

The Bill Applies Force to the Judiciary

The answer is clear. It applies force to the judiciary. It is an attempt to impose upon the courts a course of action, a line of decision which, without that force, without that imposition, the judiciary might not adopt.

Those of us, who hold office in this government, however humble or exalted it may be, are creatures of the Constitution. To it we owe all the power and authority we possess. Outside of it we have none. We are bound by it in every official act.

By this bill another and wholly different cause is proposed for the intervention of executive influence, namely, age. Age and behavior have no connection; they are unrelated subjects. By this bill, judges who have reached 70 years of age may remain on the bench and have their judgment augmented if they agree with the new appointee, or vetoed if they disagree. This is far from the independence intended for the courts by the framers of the Constitution. This is an unwarranted influence accorded the appointing agency, contrary to the spirit of the Constitution. The bill sets up a plan which has as its stability the changing will or inclination of an agency not a part of the judicial system. Constitutionally, the bill can have no sanction. The effect of the bill, as stated by the Attorney General to the committee, and indeed by the President in both his message and speech, is in violation of the organic law.

Object of Plan Acknowledged

No amount of sophistry can cover up this fact. The effect of this bill is not to provide for an increase in the number of Justices composing the Supreme Court. The effect is to provide a forced retirement, or, failing in this, to take from the Justices affected a free exercise of their independent judgment.

Let us, for the purpose of the argument, grant that the Court has been wrong, wrong not only in that it has rendered mistaken opinions, but wrong in the far more serious sense that it has substituted its will for the congressional will in the matter of legislation. May we nevertheless safely punish the Court?

Today it may be the Court which is charged with forgetting its constitutional duties. Tomorrow it may be the Congress. The next day it may be the executive. If we yield to temptation now to lay the lash upon the Court, we are only teaching others how to apply it to ourselves and to the people when the occasion seems to

warrant.   Manifestly, if we may force the hand of the Court to
secure our interpretation of the Constitution, then some succeeding
Congress may repeat the process to secure another and a different
interpretation and one which may not sound so pleasant in our ears
as that for which we now contend.

There is a remedy for usurpation or other judicial wrongdoing.
If this bill be supported by the toilers of this country upon the
ground that they want a Court which will sustain legislation
limiting hours and providing minimum wages, they must
remember that the procedure employed in the bill could be used in
another administration to lengthen hours and to decrease wages.   If
farmers want agricultural relief and favor this bill upon the ground
that it gives them a Court which will sustain legislation in their
favor, they must remember that the procedure employed might
some day be used to derive them of every vestige of a farm relief.

When members of the Court usurp legislative powers or attempt
to exercise political power, they lay themselves open to the charge
of having lapsed from that "good behavior" which determines the
period of their official life.   But, if you say, the process of
impeachment is difficult and uncertain, the answer is, the people
made it so when they framed the Constitution.   It is not for us, the
servants of the people, the instruments of the Constitution, to find
a more easy way to do that which our masters made difficult.

But, if the fault of the judges is not so grievous as to warrant
impeachment, if their offense is merely that they have grown old,
and we feel, therefore, that there should be a "constant infusion of
new blood," then obviously the way to achieve that result is by
constitutional amendment fixing definite terms for the members of
the judiciary or making mandatory their retirement at a given age.
Such a provision would indeed provide for the constant infusion of
new blood, not only now but at all times in the future.   The plan
before us is but a temporary expedient which operates once and
then never again, leaving the Court as permanently expanded to
become once more a court of old men, gradually year by year
falling behind the times.

A Measure Without Precedent

This bill is an invasion of judicial power such as has never before
been attempted in this country.   It is true that in the closing days of
the administration of John Adams, a bill was passed creating 16
new circuit judges while reducing by one the number of places on

the Supreme Court. It was charged that this was a bill to use the judiciary for a political purpose by providing official positions for members of a defeated party. The repeal of that law was the first task of the Jefferson Administration.

Neither the original act nor the repealer was an attempt to change the course of judicial decision. And never in the history of the country has there been such an act. The present bill comes to us, therefore, wholly without precedent.

It is true that the size of the Supreme Court has been changed from time to time, but in every instance after the Adams Administration, save one, the changes were made for purely administrative purposes in aid of the Court, not to control it.

A Precedent of Loyalty to the Constitution

Shall we now, after 150 years of loyalty to the constitutional ideal of an untrammeled judiciary, duty bound to protect the constitutional rights of the humblest citizen even against the government itself, create the vicious precedent which must necessarily undermine our system? The only argument for the increase, which survives analysis, is that Congress should enlarge the Court so as to make the policies of this administration effective.

We are told that a reactionary oligarchy defies the will of the majority, that this is a bill to "unpack" the Court and give effect to the desires of the majority; that is to say, a bill to increase the number of Justices for the express purpose of neutralizing the views of some of the present members. In justification we are told, but without authority, by those who would rationalize this program, that Congress was given the power to determine the size of the Court so that the legislative branch would be able to impose its will upon the judiciary. This amounts to nothing more than the declaration that when the Court stands in the way of a legislative enactment, the Congress may reverse the ruling by enlarging the Court. When such a principle is adopted, our constitutional system is overthrown!

This, then, is the dangerous precedent we are asked to establish. When proponents of the bill assert, as they have done, that Congress in the past has altered the number of Justices upon the Supreme Court and that this is reason enough for our doing it now, they show how important precedents are and prove that we should now refrain from any action that would seem to establish one which could be followed hereafter whenever a Congress and an executive should become dissatisfied with the decisions of the Supreme Court.

This is the first time in the history of our country that a proposal to alter the decisions of the court by enlarging its personnel has been so boldly made. Let us meet it. Let us now set a salutary precedent that will never be violated. Let us, of the Seventy-fifth Congress, in words that will never be disregarded by any succeeding Congress, declare that we would rather have an independent Court, a fearless Court, a Court that will dare to announce its honest opinions in what it believes to be the defense of the liberties of the people, than a Court that, out of fear or sense of obligation to the appointing power, or factional passion, approves any measure we may enact. We are not the judges of the judges. We are not above the Constitution.

Even if every charge brought against the so-called "reactionary" members of this Court be true, it is far better that we await orderly but inevitable change of personnel than that we impatiently overwhelm them with new members. Exhibiting this restraint, thus demonstrating our faith in the American system, we shall set an example that will protect the independent American judiciary from attack as long as this government stands...True it is, that courts like Congresses, should take account of the advancing strides of civilization. True it is that the law, being a progressive science, must be pronounced progressively and liberally; but the milestones of liberal progress are made to be noted and counted with caution rather than merely to be encountered and passed. Progress is not a mad mob march; rather, it is a steady, invincible stride.

Summary
We recommend the rejection of this bill as a needless, futile, and utterly dangerous abandonment of constitutional principle.

It was presented to the Congress in a most intricate form and for reasons that obscured its real purpose.

It would not banish age from the bench nor abolish divided decisions.

It would not affect the power of any court to hold laws unconstitutional nor withdraw from any judge the authority to issue injunctions.

It would not reduce the expense of litigation nor speed the decision of cases.

It is a proposal without precedent and without justification.

It would subjugate the courts to the will of Congress and the President and thereby destroy the independence of the judiciary, the only certain shield of individual rights.

It contains the germ of a system of centralized administration of law that would enable an executive so minded to send his judges into every judicial district in the land to sit in judgment on controversies between the government and the citizen.

It points the way to the evasion of the Constitution and established the method whereby the people may be deprived of their right to pass upon all amendments of the fundamental law.

It stands now before the country, acknowledged by its proponents as a plan to force judicial interpretation of the Constitution, a proposal that violates every sacred tradition of American democracy.

Under the form of the Constitution it seeks to do that which is unconstitutional.

Its ultimate operation would be to make this government one of men rather than one of law, and its practical operation would be to make the Constitution what the executive or legislative branches of the government choose to say it is—an interpretation to be changed with each change of administration.

It is a measure, which should be so emphatically rejected that its parallel will never again be presented to the free representatives of the free people of America.

LII
Franklin D. Roosevelt:
Address on Constitution Day
September 17, 1937

One hundred fifty years ago tonight, thirty-eight weary delegates to a Convention in Philadelphia signed the Constitution. Four handwritten sheets of parchment were enough to state the terms on which thirteen independent weak little republics agreed to try to survive together as one strong nation.

A third of the original delegates had given up and gone home. The moral force of Washington and Franklin had kept the rest together. Those remained who cared the most; and caring most, dared most.

The world of 1787 provided a perfect opportunity for the organization of a new form of government thousands of miles removed from influences hostile to it. How we then governed ourselves did not greatly concern Europe. And what occurred in Europe did not immediately affect us.

Today the picture is different.

Now what we do has enormous immediate effect not only among the nations of Europe but also among those of the Americas and the Far East, and what in any part of the world they do as surely and quickly affects us.

In such an atmosphere our generation has watched democracies replace monarchies which had failed their people, and dictatorships displace democracies which had failed to function. And of late we have heard a clear challenge to the democratic idea of representative government.

We do not deny that the methods of the challengers—whether they be called "communistic" or "dictatorial" or "military"—have obtained for many who live under them material things they did not obtain under democracies which they had failed to make function. Unemployment has been lessened, even though the cause is a mad manufacturing of armaments. Order prevails, even though maintained by fear, at the expense of liberty and individual rights.

So their leaders laugh at all constitutions, predict the copying of their own methods and prophesy the early end of democracy throughout the world.

Both that attitude and the prediction are denied by those of us who still believe in democracy—that is, by the overwhelming majority of the nations of the world and by the overwhelming majority of the people of the world.

And the denial is based on two reasons eternally right.

The first reason is that modern men and women will not tamely commit to one man or one group the permanent conduct of their governments. Eventually they will insist not only on the right to choose who shall govern them, but also upon the periodic reconsideration of that choice by the free exercise of the ballot.

And the second reason is that the state of world affairs brought about by those new forms of government threatens civilization. Armaments and deficits pile up together. Trade barriers multiply and merchant ships are threatened on the high seas. Fear spreads throughout the world, fear of aggression, fear of invasion, fear of revolution, fear of death.

The people of America are rightly determined to keep that growing menace from our shores.

The known and measurable danger of becoming involved in war we face confidently. As to that, your government knows your mind.

But it takes even more foresight, intelligence and patience to meet the subtle attack which spreading dictatorship makes upon the morale of a democracy.

In our generation, a new idea has come to dominate thought about government, the idea that the resources of the nation can be made to produce a far higher standard of living for the masses of the people if only government is intelligent and energetic in giving the right direction to economic life.

That idea—or more properly that ideal—is wholly justified by the facts. It cannot be thrust aside by those who want to go back to the conditions of ten years ago or even preserve the conditions of today. It puts all forms of government to their proof.

That ideal makes understandable the demands of labor for shorter hours and higher wages, the demands of farmers for a more stable income, the demands of the great majority of business men for relief from disruptive trade practices, the demands of all for the end of that kind of license, often mistermed "Liberty," which permits a handful of the population to take far more than its tolerable share from the rest of the people.

And as other forms of government in other lands parade their pseudo-science of economic organization, even some of our own people may wonder whether democracy can match dictatorship in giving this generation the things it wants from government.

We have those who really fear the majority rule of democracy, who want old forms of economic and social control to remain in a few hands. They say in their hearts: "If constitutional democracy continues to threaten our control why should we be against a *plutocratic* dictatorship if that would perpetuate our control?"

And we have those who are in too much of a hurry, who are impatient at the processes of constitutional democracies, who want Utopia overnight and are not sure that some vague form of *proletarian* dictatorship is not the quickest road to it.

Both types are equally dangerous. One represents cold-blooded resolve to hold power. We have so far engaged in a definite, and so far successful, contest against that. The other represents a reckless resolve to seize power. Equally, we are against that.

And the overwhelming majority of the American people fully understand and completely approve that course as the course of the present government of the United States.

To hold to that course our constitutional democratic form of government must meet the insistence of the great mass of our people that economic and social security and the standard of American living be raised from what they are to levels which the people know our resources justify.

Only by succeeding in *that* can we ensure against internal doubt as to the worthwhileness of our democracy and dissipate the illusion that the necessary price of efficiency is dictatorship with its attendant spirit of aggression.

That is why I have been saying for months that there is a crisis in American affairs which demands action now, a crisis particularly dangerous because its external and internal difficulties re-enforce each other.

Purposely I paint a broad picture. For only if the problem is seen in perspective can we see its solution in perspective.

I am not a pessimist. I believe that democratic government in this country can do all the things which common-sense people, seeing that picture as a whole, have the right to expect. I believe that these things can be done under the Constitution, without the surrender of a single one of the civil and religious liberties it was intended to safeguard.

And I am determined that under the Constitution these things *shall* be done.

The men who wrote the Constitution were the men who fought the Revolution. They had watched a weak emergency government almost lose the war, and continue economic distress among thirteen little republics, at peace but without effective national government.

So when these men planned a new government, they drew the kind of agreement which men make when they really want to work together under it for a very long time.

For the youngest of nations they drew what is today the oldest written instrument under which men have continuously lived together as a nation.

The Constitution of the United States was a layman's document, not a lawyer's contract. *That* cannot be stressed too often. Madison, most responsible for it, was not a lawyer; nor was Washington or Franklin, whose sense of the give-and-take of life had kept the Convention together.

This great layman's document was a charter of general principles, completely different from the "whereases" and the "parties of the first part" and the fine print which lawyers put into leases and insurance policies and installment agreements.

When the Framers were dealing with what they rightly considered eternal verities, unchangeable by time and circumstance, they used specific language. In no uncertain terms, for instance, they forbade titles of nobility, the suspension of habeas corpus and the withdrawal of money from the Treasury except after appropriation by law. With almost equal definiteness they detailed the Bill of Rights.

But when they considered the fundamental powers of the new national government they used generality, implication and statement of mere objectives, as intentional phrases which flexible statesmanship of the future, within the Constitution, could adapt to time and circumstance. For instance, the framers used broad and general language capable of meeting evolution and change when they referred to commerce between the States, the taxing power and the general welfare.

Even the Supreme Court was treated with that purposeful lack of specification. Contrary to the belief of many Americans, the Constitution says nothing about any power of the Court to declare legislation unconstitutional; nor does it mention the number of judges for the Court. Again and again the Convention voted down proposals to give Justices of the Court a veto over legislation. Clearly a majority of the delegates believed that the relation of the Court to the Congress and the Executive, like the other subjects treated in general terms, would work itself out by evolution and change over the years.

But for one hundred and fifty years we have had an unending struggle between those who would preserve this original broad concept of the Constitution as a layman's instrument of government and those who would shrivel the Constitution into a lawyer's contract.

Those of us who really believe in the enduring wisdom of the Constitution hold no rancor against those who professionally or politically talk and think in purely legalistic phrases. We cannot seriously be alarmed when they cry "unconstitutional" at every effort to better the condition of our people.

Such cries have always been with us; and, ultimately, they have always been overruled.

Lawyers distinguished in 1787 insisted that the Constitution itself was unconstitutional under the Articles of Confederation. But the ratifying conventions overruled them.

Lawyers distinguished in their day warned Washington and Hamilton that the protective tariff was unconstitutional, warned Jefferson that the Louisiana Purchase was unconstitutional, warned Monroe that to open up roads across the Alleghenies was unconstitutional. But the Executive and the Congress overruled them.

Lawyers distinguished in their day persuaded a divided Supreme Court that the Congress had no power to govern slavery in the territories, that the long-standing Missouri Compromise was unconstitutional. But a war between the states overruled them.

Lawyers distinguished in their day persuaded the Odd Man on the Supreme Court that the methods of financing the Civil War were unconstitutional. But a new Odd Man overruled them.

That great Senatorial constitutional authority of his day, Senator Evarts, issued a solemn warning that the proposed Interstate Commerce Act and the Federal regulation of railway rates which the farmers demanded would be unconstitutional. But both the Senate and the Supreme Court overruled him.

Less than two years ago fifty-eight of the highest priced lawyers in the land gave the nation (without cost to the nation) a solemn and formal opinion that the Wagner Labor Relations Act was unconstitutional. And in a few months, first a national election and later the Supreme Court overruled them.

For twenty years the Odd Man on the Supreme Court refused to admit that State minimum wage laws for women were constitutional. A few months ago, after my message to the Congress on the rejuvenation of the judiciary, the Odd Man admitted that the Court had been wrong—for all those twenty years—and overruled himself.

In this constant struggle the lawyers of no political party, mine or any other, have had a consistent or unblemished record. But the lay rank and file of political parties *has* had a consistent record.

Unlike some lawyers, they have respected as sacred *all* branches of their government. They have seen nothing *more* sacred about one branch than about either of the others. They have considered as most sacred the concrete welfare of the generation of the day. And with laymen's common sense of what government is for, they have demanded that all three branches be efficient, that all three be interdependent as well as independent, and that all three work together to meet the living generation's expectations of government.

That lay rank and file can take cheer from the historic fact that every effort to construe the constitution as a lawyer's contract rather than a layman's charter has ultimately failed. When ever legalistic interpretation has clashed with contemporary sense on great questions of broad national policy, ultimately the people and the Congress have had their way.

But that word "ultimately" covers a terrible cost.

It cost a Civil War to gain recognition of the constitutional power of the Congress to legislate for the territories.

It cost twenty years of exploitation of women's labor to recognize the constitutional power of the States to pass minimum wage laws for their protection.

It has cost twenty years already—and no one knows how many more are to come—to obtain a constitutional interpretation that will let the nation regulate the shipment in national commerce of goods sweated from the labor of little children.

We know it takes time to adjust government to the needs of society. But modern history proves that reforms too long delayed or denied have jeopardized peace, undermined democracy and swept away civil and religious liberties.

Yes, time more than ever before is vital in statesmanship and government, in all three branches of it.

We will no longer be permitted to sacrifice each generation in turn while the law catches up with life.

We can no longer afford the luxury of twenty-year lags.

You will find no justification in any of the language of the Constitution for delay in the reforms which the mass of the American people now demand.

Yet nearly every attempt to meet those demands for social and economic betterment has been jeopardized or actually forbidden by those who have sought to *read* into the Constitution language which the framers refused to *write* into the Constitution.

No one cherishes more deeply than I the civil and religious liberties achieved by so much blood and anguish through the many centuries of Anglo-American history. But the Constitution guarantees liberty, not license masquerading as liberty.

Let me put the real situation in the simplest terms. The present government of the United States has never taken away and never will take away any liberty from any minority, unless it be a minority which so abuses its liberty as to do positive and definite harm to its neighbors constituting the majority. But the government of the United States refuses to forget that the Bill of Rights was put into the Constitution not only to protect minorities against intolerance of majorities, but to protect majorities against the enthronement of minorities.

Nothing would so surely destroy the substance of what the Bill of Rights protects than its perversion to prevent social progress. The surest protection of the individual and of minorities is that fundamental tolerance and feeling for fair play which the Bill of Rights assumes. But tolerance and fair play would disappear here as it has in some other lands if the great mass of people were denied confidence in their justice, their security and their self-respect. Desperate people in other lands surrendered their liberties when freedom came merely to mean humiliation and starvation. The crisis of 1933 should make us understand that.

On this solemn anniversary I ask that the American people rejoice in the wisdom of their Constitution.

I ask that they guarantee the effectiveness of each of its parts by living by the Constitution as a *whole*.

I ask that they have faith in its ultimate capacity to work out the problems of democracy, but that they justify that faith by making it work now rather than twenty years from now.

I ask that they give their fealty to the Constitution *itself* and not to its misinterpreters.

I ask that they exalt the glorious simplicity of its purposes rather than a century of complicated legalism.

I ask that majorities and minorities subordinate intolerance and power alike to the common good of all.

For us the Constitution is a common bond, without bitterness, for those who see America as Lincoln saw it, "the last, best hope of earth."

So we revere it, not because it is old but because it is ever new, not in the worship of its past alone but in the faith of the living who keep it young, now and in the years to come.

LIII
Herbert Hoover:
Economic Security and the Present Situation
Economic Club of Chicago, December 16, 1937

PART I
No Anxieties from Abroad

If we look over the national scene we will find every city, village and hamlet torn with dissension and a feeling of insecurity and even fear.

This anxiety does not come from outside our borders. America almost alone of all the countries in the world is secure from the dangers of war. There is not the remotest fear that our national independence will be challenged from abroad.

We possess the resources and the equipment to produce more than mere food, shelter, and clothing for the whole of our population.

We are still able to contend for the right to govern ourselves. Ours has been a great adventure in free men and free ideas and free enterprise. That experiment has not failed. At present it has become muddled.

PART II
The Present Recession

These anxieties, distractions and fears swell up from something far deeper in our national life than this immediate business recession.

I like this new word "recession." It is no doubt easier to bear than those old English words "slump" or "depression." It no doubt softens the pain from falling off the roof if you call it a "recession." I can be wholly objective on this depression because certainly I did not create it.

This recession need not be serious. The reason I believe this is that we are not today dragged by two of the terrible horsemen of the world-wide crisis beginning in 1929.

No major depression comes without a large element of credit collapse. There is today no inflated bubble of speculative private credit as in 1929. There is no bubble of European inflation and unliquidated war finance, the collapse of which pulled down the whole world. The world economic movement is still upward.

The grim recollections of the Great World Depression naturally contribute to fears of the present situation which reason does not confirm.

What is imperative for the moment is relief from pressures which stagnate billions of industrial and home construction and millions of jobs for men.   But it is currents deeper than this recession that we are discussing tonight, although this recession is one of the indications of profound currents.

PART III
Past Movements in Economic and Social Forces

Perhaps we could get under the surface of these deeper distractions by a short analysis of the shift in economic and social forces in recent years.

We had for nearly a century industrial pioneers who mainly devoted themselves to building up the great industrial tools provided by scientific discovery. Those generations did a good job. They won for America the greatest economic triumph in all history. That is the unique ability to produce a plenty for a wholesome standard of living and comfort to all the people. Private initiative and enterprise proved to be the very mother of plenty.

It has social weaknesses. That generation gave too little heed to equitable diffusion among all the people of the output of their triumph in production.

Some thousands of a marginal group out of 120,000,000 got too much of the productive pie for the service they gave. Some millions of another marginal group got too little. But we had so triumphed in the long journey of mankind away from scarcity and want that we began to see the promised land of abolished poverty.

Our greatest economic weakness was the organization and shocking abuses in finance and banking. Our segment of the war depression was deepened by our credit inflations and failures. Our people were amply warned. But democracies seldom act until the shock comes. Then they get impatient.

From the miseries of the depression the whole economic system was condemned without discrimination as to its strengths or its faults.

Before recovery had been attained came a set of ideas under the euphonious title of "Planned Economy." They brought a conflict between two fundamentally opposite philosophies of government and economics in operation at the same time.

Whether Planned Economy is an infection from Europe of creeping collectivism or whether it is a native American product is less important than its actual results upon us. I shall analyze it solely from its practical aspects.

PART IV
Confusion in the Present Direction of Economic and Social Forces

We must not confuse true liberal reforms with Planned Economy, which has other purposes. Constant reform is a necessity of growth. The objectives of this administration in reforms directed to cure business abuses, to remedy social ills, old age needs, housing, sweated labor, etc., are right. Nor is "Planned Economy" necessary to bring them about.

The central idea of Planned Economy which concerns me is the gigantic shift of government from the function of umpire to the function of directing, dictating and competing in our economic life. No one will deny that the government is today increasingly controlling prices, wages, volume of production and investment.

Its weapons include politically managed currency, managed credit, managed interest rates, huge expenditure in pump priming and inflation of bank deposits. Further weapons are to use relief funds to build the government into competitive business. It has stretched the taxing powers deep into the control of business conduct. Regulation to prevent abuse has been stretched into instruments of dictation. The policeman on the streets of commerce to expedite the traffic, to keep order and stop robbery, now orders our destination and tells us what to do when we get there. It will be a depressing day for America when the farmer can be put in jail for failure to obey the dictates of Washington as to what he may sow and what he may reap.

I do not agree with these New Deal objectives, for there are here fundamental conflicts with free men in which there is no compromise, no middle ground.

PART V
Its Results

We have now had nearly five years' experience with these ideas. They were put forward as only for an emergency. And yet every session of Congress faces demands for more and more.

The very forces of Planned Economy involve constantly increasing delegation of discretionary power to officials. They involve constantly greater centralization of government. They involve conflicts with the Constitution. They involve minimizing the independence of the Congress and the Judiciary. They involve huge deficits, great increase in debt and taxes and dangers of inflation.

Somehow I do not believe these things make for either economic or social security or enlarge the opportunities of the people.

The results are obvious violations of common sense. Transient political officials cannot plan the evolution of 120,000,000 people. We cannot assume that Americans are incapable of conducting their own lives and their daily affairs for their own good. We cannot increase standards of living by restricting production. We cannot spend ourselves into prosperity. We cannot hate ourselves into it either. We cannot constantly increase costs of production without increasing prices and therefore decreasing consumption and employment. We cannot place punitive taxes on industry without stifling new enterprise and jobs.

However, the consumer is the nemesis of all Planned Economy. It may control production. It cannot control the consumer. He is on strike in residential building today because he does not like the distorted building costs.

Today in a system part free the citizen confronts a new and unpredictable factor in conducting his affairs. That is political action. The people move hourly upon their own judgments as to supply and demand, as to prices and outlook. But today every plan in life is a bet on Washington. Every investment of savings is a gamble on the currency. Every future price is another bet on Washington.

Do these things make for increase in either the economic security or enlarged opportunity of the people? Do they not lead to confusion?

When the government expands into business then in order to protect itself it is driven irresistibly toward control of men's thoughts and the press. We see it daily in propaganda. We have seen the Labor Board doing it in the last week.

Group conflicts in the country have been magnified. We have become a sadly divided America. In the words these groups use and the reprisals they undertake they have brought us fear, confusion, worry, and distraction. If every group gets all it asks for, nobody will get anything.

Do these things make for economic security or equal opportunity?

There are considerations of government far higher than money or comfort. That is its relations to moral and spiritual values. Part of these Planned Economy measures are a surrender of the spiritual for the material. Part of them proceed by unmoral steps. No government can reform the social order unless it set higher standards of morals and rectitude than those whom it governs.

I ask you: Is there economic security without moral security?

All these things affect the mind and spirit of a people. For lack of a better term we call it public psychology. And "psychology is the twin brother of economics." Politicians may be psychologists but they are a poor twin for economists.

I leave it to you to inventory the instabilities of optimism and discouragement during the past year.

In your invitation to me you asked the cause of the confusion, harassment and uncertainties of the day. Perhaps this is enough of an accounting. I could give you more.

PART VI
The Alternative System

You asked for the alternative economic and social system.

What sort of an America do we want? What should be our foundations? What should be our ideals?

American young men and women should have the right to plan, to live their own lives with the limitation that they shall not injure their neighbors. What they want of government is to keep the channels of opportunity open and equal, not to block them and then send them a tax bill for doing it. They want rewards to the winners in the race. They do not want to be planed down to a pattern. To red-blooded men and women there is a joy of work and there is joy in the battle of competition. There is the daily joy of doing something worth while, of proving one's own worth, of telling every evil person where he can go. There is the joy of championing justice to the weak and downtrodden. These are the battles which create the national fiber of self-reliance and self-respect. That is what made America. If you concentrate all adventure in the government it does not leave much constructive joy for the governed.

Let me shortly sketch what I conceive to be a philosophy of government and economics which would promote this sort of living and would preserve free men and women in our modern world. It is no magic formula. It does not lend itself to oratory.

Economic Phases

First: The main anchor of our civilization must be intellectual and spiritual liberty. Ideas, invention, initiative, enterprise and leadership spring best from free men and women. The only economic system which will not limit or destroy these forces of progress is private enterprise.

Second: In the operation of the economic system there is but one hope of increased security, of increased standards of living, and of greater opportunity. That is to drive every new invention, every machine, every improvement, every elimination of waste unceasingly for the reduction of costs and the maximum production that can be consumed. We must work our machines heartlessly, but not our men and women.

By these means we sell goods cheaper. More people can buy. And thereby we have higher wages, more jobs and more new enterprise. New industries and new articles add again to the standards of living. That is the road to more jobs; it is the cure of temporary machine displacement. That is no robbery, it is progress.

Governmental Phases

Third: To preserve freedom and equal opportunity we must regulate business. But true regulation is as far from government-dictated business as the two poles.

The vast tools of technology and power can be used for oppression. They can be used to limit production and to stifle competition. There can no more be economic power without checks and balances than there can be political power without checks and balances. We must compel competition in a large area of business. It is a restless pillow for managers, but it is the motive power of progress. Where we decide as in utilities that special privilege shall be given we must directly or indirectly regulate profits. We must regulate banking and finance to prevent abuse of trust.   But Democracy can be master in its own house without shackling the family.

Fourth: A system of free men implies a vast amount of competence, of self-imposed discipline, and of responsibility. It implies co-operation between groups and sections outside of government and with government. The more co-operation the less government.

Social Phases

Fifth: No system can stand on pure economics. The economic and social gears must be enmeshed. The primary objective of our system must be to eliminate poverty and the fear of it.

Men cannot be free until the minds of men are free from insecurity and want. But security and plenty can be builded only upon a release of the productive energies of men. Moreover, economic security and even social security can be had in jail but it lacks some of the attractions of freedom.

Such an economic system as I have mentioned would constantly diminish the marginal group who do not get a just share of the production pie. And the pie would be far bigger.

Through income and estate taxes, we can take care of the marginal group who get too much.

The economically successful must carry the burdens of social improvement for the less fortunate by taxes or otherwise. Child labor, health, sweated labor, old age, and housing are but part of our social responsibilities. The nation must protect its people in catastrophes beyond their control.

These are indeed but highlights of a system free from so-called Planned Economy. This is no philosophy of *laissez faire* or dog eat dog. It is a philosophy of free men with the responsibilities of freedom. It requires no tampering with the Constitution or the independence of the Judiciary. It is system of faith in the competence, the self-discipline and the moral stamina of the American people and the divine inspiration of free men. It is a system of forward movement to far greater attainment.

Our transcendent need at this moment in America is a change in direction toward this system.

A confident, alert, alive and free people, enthused with incentive and enterprise, can quickly repair losses, repay debts, and bury mistakes. It can build new opportunity and new achievement.

PART VII

All this is but the underlying basis upon which to work. And we need to work out a host of problems. We need their re-examination within these principles that we may find new and forward solutions. Time permits me to outline but a few as illustrations.

Reform in Regulatory Methods

We need for instance an unbiased examination of the whole experience with administrative law in regulation against business abuse. As I have said, it has been stretched over into personal government and punitive action. But the border lands are not easy to determine.

Many of these measures, old and new, should be reformed into definite statutory standards of business conduct and morals. That would restore the people to government by law instead of government by whim of men.

Labor Problems

We need fresh and unbiased consideration of many fields in employer and employee relationships.

There are areas of conflict of interest, but there are greater areas of common interest. If these groups could themselves build on these common interests they might save great tragedies to our country. Certainly the Labor Board has not been a solution.

We can well start with acceptance of the fact that collective bargaining by representatives of their own choosing makes greatly for economic security of the workers.

I have long believed that we cannot secure full economic security in the wage group until we face the question of assured annual income. The greatest insecurity in the world is fear of losing the job. I believe there are large wage groups where employers could extend this greatest of assurances of security in increasing degree to the mutual advantage of both sides. It would be a great demonstration of co-operation in industry to accomplish it.

Again I believe methods could be worked out in industry itself by which so-called technological unemployment could be cared for and thus the mistaken opposition to new improvements and individual hardships could be solved. There are a host of other constructive fields.

Sweated Labor

We need a much more exhaustive consideration of the problem of sweated labor than it has received. The present Wages and Hours Bill runs into Planned Economy fixing of wages. It will reduce productivity at a time when the productive machines because of many shocks is already hesitating. One phase of its consequences has not been ventilated. Any general minimum wage will become a sort of moral wage and will inexorably tend to reduce wages in that vast majority of unorganized labor which today supports much higher minimums.

On re-examination we should envisage this question as solely one of sweated labor. A sweated industry is an industry sick from destructive competition or devoid of effective collective bargaining. The better remedy would be to apply minimums only to those industries which have been found sick after proper diagnosis. The minimum should be applied only while they are sick. Certainly employers would be quickened to collective bargaining as a relief from the restrictions. Such a program should be administered by restraining movement of goods into states where the minimums are maintained and not by centralizing more power in Washington.

Booms and Slumps

We need a new and exhaustive examination into the causes of booms and slumps. And this involves an unbiased and searching consideration into our whole financial, credit, currency and banking regulations and their effects. Certainly the remedy of Planned Economy has not worked.

Corporations

The question of corporation life in its entirety needs study for deeper reforms than prevention of monopoly.

We need a searching inquiry by unbiased minds into our corporate structure and theory, not for purposes of destruction of this necessary engine of civilization but for simplification of the whole tangle of practice and of state and federal regulation. But more important, we need seek for a way by which we may establish, without political control, a more general institutional sense and responsibility in large public corporations. And at the same time we should search for a method in our smaller corporations by which we can restore the sense of personal relationships and the responsibility of partnerships.

Taxes

We need an exhaustive examination of our whole tax system. In old days taxes had little economic or social effect. Now when they are 20 percent or 25 percent of the national income they have the most profound effect. Having this effect we should devise them not to destroy initiative and enterprise. And we could devise the method of levying them to produce most substantial effects. I could imagine a taxing program that would improve our housing far more than any government loans.

Conclusion

My time is ending. It would require several addresses to even partly traverse our multiple problems of agriculture, of currency, of foreign trade, of child labor, of old-age pensions, and a score of others. May I say in conclusion, much of our problem of security and enlarged opportunity is more intellectual and moral than material.

Let us remember the standards of human conduct must be erected upon a far higher base than government regulations and government controls. They spring from the Sermon on the Mount.

The season from Thanksgiving to Christmas and New Years is the time that Americans give life to the highest individual qualities of good-will, and resolve to do a better job. Today as never before if we could lift these qualities into national action, it would set American on a new road of hope and happiness.

Many have rightly urged an era of co-operation. We need it. We need co-operation to place America upon the right road to progress. And we need co-operation between organized groups, outside of government.

It is difficult for timid minds to believe that free men can work out their own salvation. Arrogant minds seeking for power live upon this timidity. In the firm places of your minds you must take some new resolves.

Nations are built around important and stimulating enterprises which demand sacrifice, discipline and mutual consideration. We gave all that in war. But today the nation must have it in peace.

For we have a great enterprise. That is to build our mechanisms so as to hold the greatest possession any nation has ever had. That is human liberty.

These may be times of confusion and uncertainty. But there are lights upon the horizon, for the eternal fires of freedom still burn.

6

The Fate of "Our American System" (1938 – 1941)

LIV
Herbert Hoover:
Challenge to Liberty
San Francisco, California, April 8, 1938

The real, the immediate, the pressing problem of this country is unemployment. When I went abroad we had 10 million or 11 million unemployed. I return to find they have increased by another million or two. Meantime Washington has employed most of its time debating a subject of no aid to these of our countrymen.

That 12,000,000 unemployed is obviously the indication of something terribly wrong in our own economic machine. Let me say something perhaps elementary on this American economic machine and the way it starts and stops. It moves forward and employs people only when there is confidence and hope. A large part of its movement forward depends on confidence and hope. A large part of its stoppage comes from fear. When confidence breaks down fear seizes control and unemployment becomes rampant. Prosperity and depression are greatly influenced by these two emotions. There are other factors but of later years these emotions have become immensely more potent than ever before.

In the United States today everybody has lost some confidence and everybody has some fear. It is nonsense to say that either big or little business is on a strike. It is not so. Business is yearning to sell automobiles and new suits of clothes. It is the people who are

scared. Big business or little business is not scared to take on men
if anybody will give them an order for goods.

With 12,000,000 people out of a job it is our business to explore
the cause of these fears. I was especially interested to find if any of
them were coming from abroad. One of the causes which sucked
us into the whirlpool of worldwide depression in 1931 came from
Europe.

There has been general recovery in Europe from that depression.
There is no financial panic brewing over there to pull down our
credit structure as in 1931. Their regained economic strength is
even helping us now by purchasing our goods, whereas in 1931
they stopped their purchases abruptly.

In the democracies there is no unemployment at all comparable
to ours. They are indeed prosperous. France is of course having
trouble because she adopted the New Deal two years ago. Even in
the authoritarian states and the dictatorships there is less
unemployment than we have per million of people even if we
deduct those employed manufacturing arms. It is true their
standard of living is less than the democracies but the people are
largely employed.

Nor is there immediate danger of general war in Europe.
Certainly we have no fear of war against us. There is no threat of
any one pouring fire or explosives on our cities out of the sky.
There is not the remotest chance that our national independence will
be challenged from abroad. Certainly this great fear among the
American people does not come from outside our borders.

We ought to explore for the sources of fear at home. Today we
have no inflated bubble of gambling credit or a weak banking
system that we must be afraid of as there was in 1929. The banks
are full of surplus credit. There is no over-expansion in industry in
America.   In fact we are short of equipment.   There is no
consequential over-stocking of goods. In fact there are not enough
good homes. There is no crop failure or threatened shortage of food
or clothes. Every one of the factors and forces within our borders
that ordinarily produce fear and its consequence in unemployment
is absent.

Yet we are stark facing the fact of 12,000,000 people out of jobs.
Every one of those families is suffering some privation and worry.
And there is no anxiety on earth like that of not knowing where the
next week's living for your family is to come from.   Some

newspaper said the other day that I must get satisfaction out of human misery.

I do have a recollection of a bitter slogan used against us in the 1932 campaign. They said often and harshly that it could not be worse. But some one said that was about forty billion dollars ago. And we must live in the present.

It is the first job of America to restore genuine self-respecting jobs in productive enterprises. It transcends all other questions. It transcends all party politics. It must be met without flinching, whether it be government theories, taxes, waste, corruption, unmoral acts of men in high places.

And let me say that a confident, alert, alive and free people, enthused with incentive and enterprise, can quickly repair losses, repay debts, and bury mistakes. It can build new opportunity and new achievement. That can be restored in America.

And whence do these forces of destroying fear arise?

This country should sit down and think out every force, governmental, moral, and economic, that is causing this fear, and uproot that cause. We should apply one test to the whole gamut of government action. Does this action stifle initiative and enterprise? Does it cost men their jobs? I am well aware of the importance of reforms. I am still more aware of the misery of 12,000,000 unemployed. And there are dangers to the very institutions of free men from an economic machine dislocated in this fashion.

There is one phase of all this disturbance which we got from Europe. That is the New Deal so-called Planned Economy. At least we invented both the phrase and the methods subsequent to their discovery in Europe. I have been interested to explore that idea in its European scene. I wanted to see their experience and where it led in the end.

We must not confuse true liberal reforms with Planned Economy. Constant reform is a necessity of growth. Reforms directed to cure business abuses, to remedy social ills, to provide old age needs, housing, to end sweated labor, etc., are right. Nor is Planned Economy necessary to bring them about.

First let us examine the central ideas of New Deal Planned Economy.

No one will deny that our government is today increasingly controlling prices, wages, volume of production and investment. Its methods include politically managed currency, managed credit, huge expenditure, deficits, debts, pump priming, and inflation of bank deposits. Further weapons are relief funds to build the government into competitive business. They are used to influence the electorate. The taxing powers have been stretched deep into the control of business conduct. Regulation to prevent abuse has been stretched into instruments of dictation. The policeman on the streets of commerce to expedite the traffic, to keep order and stop robbery, now orders our destination and tells us what to do when we get there. It was a depressing day for America when the farmer could be put in jail for failure to obey the dictates of Washington.

The very forces of Planned Economy involve constantly increasing delegation of discretionary power to officials. They involve constantly greater centralization of government. They involve conflicts with the Constitution. They involve minimizing the independence of the Congress and the Judiciary.

Certainly there is a gigantic shift of government from the function of umpire to the function of directing, dictating, and competing in our economic life.

We have now had nearly five years' experience with these ideas. They were put forward as only for an emergency. And yet every session of Congress faces demands for more and more.

No more heartening news ever came to the American people than today when the House of Representatives regardless of party again halted these methods. To these men we owe a debt of gratitude.

Whether our Planned Economy is an infection from Europe of creeping collectivism or whether it is a Native American product is less important than its actual results upon us and where it leads to. And where have we arrived? At a discouraged and fearful people, with 12,000,000 unemployed. Is not the very system itself making the one-third ill fed and ill clothed?

The primary objective of our system must be to eliminate poverty and the fear of it.

Men cannot be free until the minds of men are free from insecurity and want. But security and plenty can be builded only upon a release of the productive energies of men from fear and handicap. That America must have.

May I say a word in conclusion? Despite the fears and gravity of our home problems I stepped on to the shores of our country with a great release of spirit. I found release from the subconscious dread that haunts all Europe. I found again that greater freedom of human mind, a wider spread of kindliness, a more general sense of individual responsibility, a stronger assertion of personal liberty than anywhere abroad.

One long-held conviction has been greatly hardened. That is that we have grown a long way from Europe in our century and a half of national life. A new race with its own soul has grown on this continent. The life-stream of this nation is the generations of millions of human particles acting under impulses of freedom and advancing ideas gathered from a thousand native springs. These springs and rills have gathered into streams which have nurtured and fertilized the spirit of this great people over centuries.

These streams are the imponderables which differentiate the races of men. Of one thing we may be sure. When a great race has been refreshed over centuries with the waters of liberty, those living waters will not be denied it.

LV
Franklin D. Roosevelt:
Message to Congress on the Concentration of
Economic Power
April 29, 1938

To the Congress of the United States:

Unhappy events abroad have retaught us two simple truths about the liberty of a democratic people.

The first truth is that the liberty of a democracy is not safe if the people tolerate the growth of private power to a point where it becomes stronger than their democratic state itself. That, in its essence, is fascism—ownership of government by an individual, by a group, or by any other controlling private power.

The second truth is that the liberty of a democracy is not safe, if its business system does not provide employment and produce and distribute goods in such a way as to sustain an acceptable standard of living.

Both lessons hit home.

Among us today a concentration of private power without equal in history is growing. This concentration is seriously impairing the economic effectiveness of private enterprise as a way of providing employment for labor and capital and as a way of assuring a more equitable distribution of income and earnings among the people of the nation as a whole.

[I] The Growing Concentration of Economic Power

Statistics of the Bureau of Internal Revenue reveal the following amazing figures for 1935:

Ownership of corporate assets: Of all corporations reporting from every part of the nation, one-tenth of 1 percent of them owned 52 percent of the assets of all of them.

And to clinch the point: Of all corporations reporting, less than 5 percent of them owned 87 percent of all assets of all of them.

Income and profits of corporations: Of all the corporations reporting from every part of the country, one-tenth of 1 percent of them earned 50 percent of the net income of all of them.

And to clinch the point: Of all the manufacturing corporations reporting, less than 4 percent of them earned 84 percent of all the net profits of all of them.

The statistical history of modern times proves that in times of depression concentration of business speeds up. Bigger business then has larger opportunity to grow still bigger at the expense of smaller competitors who are weakened by financial adversity.

The danger of this centralization in a handful of huge corporations is not reduced or eliminated, as is sometimes urged, by the wide public distribution of their securities. The mere number of security holders gives little clue to the size of their individual holdings or to their actual ability to have a voice in the management. In fact, the concentration of stock ownership of corporations in the hands of a tiny minority of the population matches the concentration of corporate assets.

The year 1929 was a banner year for distribution of stock ownership.

But in that year three-tenths of 1 percent of our population received 78 percent of the dividends reported by individuals. This has roughly the same effect as if, out of every 300 persons in our population, one person received 78 cents out of every dollar of corporate dividends, while the other 299 persons divided up the other 22 cents between them.

The effect of this concentration is reflected in the distribution of national income.

A recent study by the National Resources Committee shows that in 1935-36:

Forty-seven percent of all American families and single individuals living alone had incomes of less than $1,000 for the year; and at the other end of the ladder a little less than 1 percent of the nation's families received incomes which in dollars and cents reached the same total as the incomes of the 47 percent at the bottom.

Furthermore, to drive the point home, the Bureau of Internal Revenue reports that estate-tax returns in 1936 show that thirty-three percent of the property which was passed by inheritance was found in only 4 percent of all the reporting estates. (And the figures of concentration would be far more impressive, if we included all the smaller estates which, under the law, do not have to report.)

We believe in a way of living in which political democracy and free private enterprise for profit should serve and protect each other—to insure a maximum of human liberty, not for a few, but for all.

It has been well said that, "The freest government, if it could exist, would not be long acceptable if the tendency of the laws were to create a rapid accumulation of property in few hands and to render the great mass of the population dependent and penniless."

Today many Americans ask the uneasy question: Is the vociferation that our liberties are in danger justified by the facts?

Today's answer on the part of average men and women in every part of the country is far more accurate than it would have been in 1929 for the very simple reason that during the past nine years we have been doing a lot of common-sense thinking. Their answer is that if there is that danger, it comes from that concentrated private economic power which is struggling so hard to master our democratic government. It will not come, as some (by no means all) of the possessors of that private power would make the people believe—from our democratic government itself.

[II] Financial Control Over Industry

Even these statistics I have cited do not measure the actual degree of concentration of control over American industry.

Close financial control, through interlocking spheres of influence over channels of investment and through the use of financial devices like holding companies and strategic minority interests, creates close control of the business policies of enterprises which masquerade as independent units.

That heavy hand of integrated financial and management control lies upon large and strategic areas of American industry. The small businessman is unfortunately being driven into a less and less independent position in American life. You and I must admit that.

Private enterprise is ceasing to be free enterprise and is becoming a cluster of private collectivisms; masking itself as a system of free enterprise after the American model, it is in fact becoming a concealed cartel system after the European model.

We all want efficient industrial growth and the advantages of mass production. No one suggests that we return to the hand loom or hand forge. A series of processes involved in turning out a given manufactured product may well require one or more huge mass-production plants. Modern efficiency may call for this. But modern efficient mass production is not furthered by a central control, which destroys competition between industrial plants each capable of efficient mass production while operating as separate units. Industrial efficiency does not have to mean industrial empire building.

And industrial empire building, unfortunately, has evolved into banker control of industry. We oppose that.

Such control does not offer safety for the investing public. Investment judgment requires the disinterested appraisal of other people's management. It becomes blurred and distorted if it is combined with the conflicting duty of controlling the management it is supposed to judge.

Interlocking financial controls have taken from American business much of its traditional virility, independence, adaptability, and daring—without compensating advantages. They have not given the stability they promised.

Business enterprise needs new vitality and the flexibility that comes from the diversified efforts, independent judgments, and vibrant energies of thousands upon thousands of independent businessmen.

The individual must be encouraged to exercise his own judgment and to venture his own small savings, not in stock gambling but in new enterprise investment.

[III] The Decline of Competition and Its Effects on Employment

In output per man or machine we are the most efficient industrial nation on earth.

In the matter of complete mutual employment of capital and labor we are among the least efficient.

One of the primary causes of our present difficulties lies in the disappearance of price competition in many industrial fields, particularly in basic manufacture where concentrated economic power is most evident—and where rigid prices and fluctuating pay rolls are general.

[IV] Competition Does Not Mean Exploitation

Competition, of course, like all other good things, can be carried to excess. Competition should not extend to fields where it has demonstrably bad social and economic consequences. The exploitation of child labor, the chiseling of workers' wages, the stretching of workers' hours, are not necessary, fair, or proper methods of competition. I have consistently urged a Federal wages-and-hours bill to take the minimum decencies of life for the working man and woman out of the field of competition.

It is, of course, necessary to operate the competitive system of free enterprise intelligently. In gaging the market for their wares, businessmen, like farmers, should be given all possible information by government and by their own associations so that they may act with knowledge, and not on impulse. Serious problems of temporary over-production can and should be avoided by disseminating information that will discourage the production of more goods than the current markets can possibly absorb or the accumulation of dangerously large inventories for which there is obvious need.

It is, of course, necessary to encourage rises in the level of those competitive prices, such as agricultural prices, which must rise to put our price structure into more workable balance and make the debt burden more tolerable. Many such competitive prices are now too low.

It may at times be necessary to give special treatment to chronically sick industries which have deteriorated too far for natural revival, especially those which have a public or quasi-public character.

But generally over the field of industry and finance we must revive and strengthen competition if we wish to preserve and make workable our traditional system of free private enterprise.

The justification of private profit is private risk. We cannot safely make America safe for the businessman who does not want to take the burdens and risks of being a businessman.

[V] The Choice Before Us

Examination of methods of conducting and controlling private enterprise which keep it from furnishing jobs or income or opportunity for one-third of the population is long overdue on the part of those who sincerely want to preserve the system of private enterprise for profit.

No people, least of all a democratic people, will be content to go without work or to accept some standard of living which obviously and woefully falls short of their capacity to produce. No people, least of all a people with our traditions of personal liberty, will endure the slow erosion of opportunity for the common man, the oppressive sense of helplessness under the domination of a few, which are overshadowing our whole economic life.

A discerning magazine of business has editorially pointed out that big-business collectivism in industry compels an ultimate collectivism in government.

The power of a few to manage the economic life of the nation must be diffused among the many or be transferred to the public and its democratically responsible government. If prices are to be managed and administered, if the nation's business is to be allotted by plan and not by competition, that power should not be vested in any private group or cartel, however benevolent its professions profess to be.

Those people, in and out of the halls of government, who encourage the growing restriction of competition either by active efforts or by passive resistance to sincere attempts to change the trend, are shouldering a terrific responsibility. Consciously or unconsciously they are working for centralized business and financial control. Consciously or unconsciously they are therefore either working for control of the government itself by business and finance or the other alternative—a growing concentration of public power in the government to cope with such concentration of private power.

[VI] Program

The traditional approach to the problems I have discussed has been through the antitrust laws. That approach we do not propose to abandon. On the contrary, although we must recognize the inadequacies of the existing laws, we seek to enforce them so that the public shall not be deprived of such protection as they afford.

To enforce them properly requires thorough investigation not only to discover such violations as may exist but to avoid hit-and-miss prosecutions harmful to business and government alike. To provide for the proper and fair enforcement of the existing antitrust laws I shall submit, through the Budget, recommendations for a deficiency appropriation of $200,000 for the Department of Justice.

But the existing antitrust laws are inadequate—most importantly because of new financial economic conditions with which they are powerless to cope.

The Sherman Act was passed nearly 40 years ago. The Clayton and Federal Trade Commission Acts were passed over 20 years ago. We have had considerable experience under those acts. In the meantime we have had a chance to observe the practical operation of large-scale industry and to learn many things about the competitive system which we did not know in those days.

We have witnessed the merging-out of effective competition in many fields of enterprise. We have learned that the so-called competitive system works differently in an industry where there are many independent units, from the way it works in an industry where a few large producers dominate the market.

We have also learned that a realistic system of business regulation has to reach more than consciously immoral acts. The community is interested in economic results. It must be protected from economic as well as moral wrongs. We must find practical controls over blind economic forces as well as over blindly selfish men.

Government can deal and should deal with blindly selfish men. But that is a comparatively small part—the easier part—of our problem. The larger, more important and more difficult part of our problem is to deal with men who are not selfish and who are good citizens, but who cannot see the social and economic consequences of their actions in a modern economically interdependent community. They fail to grasp the significance of some of our most vital social and economic problems because they see them only in the light of their own personal experience and not in perspective with the experience of other men and other industries. They therefore fail to see these problems for the nation as a whole.

To meet the situation I have described, there should be a thorough study of the concentration of economic power in American industry and the effect of that concentration upon the decline of competition. There should be an examination of the existing price system and the price policies of industry, to determine their effect upon the general level of trade, upon employment, upon long-term profits, and upon consumption. The study should not be confined to the traditional antitrust field. The effects of tax, patent, and other government policies cannot be ignored.

No man of good faith will misinterpret these proposals. They derive from the oldest American traditions. Concentration of economic power in the few and the resulting unemployment of labor and capital are inescapable problems for a modern "private enterprise" democracy. I do not believe that we are so lacking in stability that we will lose faith in our own way of living just because we seek to find out how to make that way of living work more effectively.

This program should appeal to the honest common sense of every independent businessman interested primarily in running his own business at a profit rather than in controlling the business of other men.

It is not intended as the beginning of any ill-considered "trust-busting" activity which lacks proper consideration for economic results. It is a program to preserve private enterprise for profit by keeping it free enough to be able to utilize all our resources of capital and labor at a profit.

It is a program whose basic purpose is to stop the progress of collectivism in business and turn business back to the democratic competitive order.

It is a program whose basic thesis is not that the system of free private enterprise for profit has failed in this generation, but that it has not yet been tried.

Once it is realized that business monopoly in America paralyzes the system of free enterprise on which it is grafted, and is as fatal to those who manipulate it as to the people who suffer beneath its impositions, action by the government to eliminate these artificial restraints will be welcomed by industry throughout the nation.

For idle factories and idle workers profit no man.

LVI
Herbert Hoover:
The Dangerous Road for Democracy
Oklahoma City, Oklahoma, May 5, 1938

In a recent speech I frequently used the terms "democracy" or "democratic government." I have received many protests. No. I did not mean the Democratic Party. I meant the system of representative government where the people have personal liberty under constitutional protection.

And before I go further, let me define the economic system which is inseparable from free men.

That is private enterprise regulated to prevent monopoly and exploitation. For that the government must be a vigorous umpire and not a Simon Legree. Nor is a free system a frozen system which resists reform to meet new abuses, new inventions or responsibility for the less fortunate. And our system cannot be free unless it protects the people from exploitation and calamity and unless it strives for equal opportunity among men.

We Americans are traveling a road dangerous not only to such a system but to liberty itself. We are faced with 12,000,000 of our own countrymen unemployed and in want. These things are not unrelated.

I have spent some time in Europe exploring the staggering rise of dictatorships or authoritarian governments on the ashes of democracies. By the simple test of free speech, free press, constitutional guarantees, and representative government, the light of liberty has gone out among 370,000,000 people out of the 500,000,000 in Europe alone. Among 130,000,000 in Russia the short flash of liberty in 1917 was snuffed out by Communism. And even more alarming to free men, in so short a period as nineteen years, the torch of liberty has been dashed out by some sort of Fascism in 14 more nations of over 240,000,000 people.

Tonight I propose to discuss what economic causes contributed to these miseries which ended in the suicide of liberty. And I am not interested in this as an academic student of government. I am interested because it concerns the future of liberty in our country. And I am interested because the experiences of these nations point to the causes of 12,000,000 lost jobs in our country today.

Not one of those 14 nations started with the intention to surrender liberty. They started by adopting panaceas to cure slumps or overcome economic difficulties. They all undertook New Deals under some title, usually Planned Economy. In variable doses they undertook credit and currency manipulation, price fixing, pump priming, and spending with huge deficits and huge taxes. Step by step they sapped the vitality of free enterprise by government experiments in dictation and socialistic competition. They had the illusion that true liberalism was a middle road between Fascism on the right and Socialism on the left. They sacrificed free enterprise to pursue the Utopias of both of them.

Every succeeding step was egged on by politicians fanning class hate, exaggerating every abuse and besmirching every protesting voice. Every step was accompanied by greater corruption of the electorate, increasing intellectual and moral dishonesty in government. They did produce periods of artificial prosperity, only to collapse again.

These forces finally jammed the mainspring by which private enterprise is moved to production. That is confidence. Fear and unemployment paralyzed the consumption of goods.

It was at the end of this dangerous road that hunger came to their cities with violent labor conflict and final despair. Those desperate people willingly surrendered every liberty to some man or group of men who promised economic security, moral regeneration, discipline, and hope.

Now what road have we been traveling in the United States? We followed a sign marked Planned Economy, the way to end all depressions. The subtitle was To Abundant Life. We at least know now where we have got to. It can be said in two sentences.

The New Deal started with a Government debt of $21,000,000,000 and today finds itself with a debt either direct or guaranteed of $42,000,000,000. It started with 12,000,000 unemployed; it finds itself after five years with 12,000,000 unemployed.

And it is not alone the townspeople who suffer. These 12,000,000 men and their families are compelled to skimp, save, and suffer in order to keep life together. Their reduced consumption of farm products represents more acres than Secretary Wallace's already idle fields. The farmer gets no subsidy on these.

What caused this depression? Despite all the alibis, I can show you in a minute or two. Depressions arise from many causes. And the first step in diagnosis is to eliminate those which are not present. Certainly I did not create this depression, so you can eliminate that.

And seriously we can also eliminate the two major causes of the depression of 1929-32. The first of these was our crazy boom stimulated by Federal Reserve policies begun in 1927 and which cracked up in 1929. We were beginning to recover from those sins when the second and far more deadly cause intervened. That was the 1931 collapse of Europe. That European financial panic drained our credit and our gold. For months there was hardly a single new European order for a bale of our cotton or a bushel of our wheat.

I recently explored Europe to discover if they were doing anything to us again. They are not.

This is solely our own depression. Its cause must be searched for right here at home. And we can also eliminate the usual causes of our homemade depressions.

President Roosevelt in his message to the Congress on November 15, 1937, confirmed that fact. He said:

"The fundamental situation is not to be compared with the far different conditions of 1929. The banking system is not over-extended. Interest rates are lower. Inventories are not dangerously large. We are no longer over-extended in new construction or in capital equipment. Speculation requiring liquidation does not overhang our markets."

But if the 12,000,000 unemployed are not due to these causes, to what are they due? Why have a recession in the face of low interest rates, no over-extension of credit, no over-sized inventories, no over-extension of capital equipment, no overstock of goods, no speculation? If there are none of these sins or forces in the financial and business world, such as did exist in previous depressions, obviously the origins cannot be blamed upon finance and business.

And I may add why have a recession when we have abundant capital and are short of power equipment, railway equipment, good houses and a thousand other things that need to be done?

It is nonsense to say that either big or little business is on a strike. It is not so. We have had no such strike. We have been struck. Business is yearning to sell automobiles and new suits of clothes. It is yearning to extend power plants and build houses. Big businessmen or little businessmen are not scared to take on men if anybody will give them an order for goods. But who has the confidence to give the orders?

There is only one place left to search for the causes of this depression. Despite every alibi, this depression is the direct result of governmental actions.

This country was definitely on the way to recovery in 1932 with all the rest of the world. These manipulations beginning in 1933 at first retarded us. Then they produced an artificial and distorted appearance of recovery claimed in 1936-37. Like all shots in the arm, a lovely time was had by all. Except for some 5,000,000 men who never got jobs. Then the President and sub managers concluded the dose of stimulants must have been too big. They gave us antidotes. They reduced bank reserves to curtail credit. They sterilized gold to reduce credit. They publicly denounced prices. They denounced and threatened business. They proposed more measures in control of wages, hours, and farmers. But if this were not sufficient to confuse and scare the people they prepared for more powers by attempting to manipulate the Supreme Court. And out of it all, we have got this depression.

And now let us analyze this whole New Deal philosophy a little more deeply in its practical aspects. We can at least discover why attempts of government to manage a system of private enterprise must have a Nemesis—or several of them—so long as there is any freedom left in it.

The first is that free private enterprise will not mix with either the dictation or the government-competition, for one stymies the other. Germany and Italy have demonstrated that complete Fascism will work for a while. Russia has demonstrated that Socialism will not work. America has demonstrated for over 160 years that a free system will work. Just as did the 14 fallen democracies of Europe, now America is demonstrating all over again that a mixture will never work.

All along the line it weakens the judgment of men. It sickens initiative and enterprise. It knocks the confidence out of men. It substitutes fear. It destroys millions of jobs.

[Another] Nemesis is fear. Half of what people consume can be postponed at least for a time. When our Washington managers say prices are too high, buyers hold off and postpone purchases and a million men lose their jobs.

It was all with good intentions. The objectives as you have heard were magnificent. But the road to a hot spot has again been proved to be paved with good objectives.

But what does the New Deal propose to do about this depression of theirs?

They propose that we travel further down this dangerous road. More bureaucratic dictation to business, more inflation, more pump priming, more Planned Economy. We are to have more budget deficits, new inflations, more increase in national debts, more taxes for the future. We put the pea of $1,400,000,000 of gold under the other shell. These new actions may produce another shot in the arm.

There is in these proposals a hopeless confusion of cause and effect. You do not get employment out of an economic scarcity. You do not prime the pump to any purpose by taking money out of the pockets of the taxpayer and giving it to the consumer. They are the person. Men borrow to expand their businesses, not because money is cheap but because they have confidence in the future. The Nation gets no richer by increasing its debts. Truly you can mortgage your house and go on a spree. It does not add to your productivity and you may lose your house.

The constructive action today is to change the national direction and get off this dangerous road. That would allay fear and re-establish confidence in the future. That would release the enormous reserves of private enterprise in place of a trickle of government money. That would take men back to their jobs tomorrow and permanently.

In order that the government may give real proof that it has abandoned this road dangerous to democracy, we need to get down out of cloudy objectives. We need to take some practical steps. This cannot be done by encouraging words. It must be proved by definite acts that re-establish faith. Faith that ours is going to continue as a system of free men and private enterprise.

For a start we need to:

First, re-establish confidence that there will be no more attacks upon the safeguards of free men. That is the independence of the Congress and of the Courts.

Second, restore common morals and intellectual morals in government. In a democracy or in a Christian country the ends do not justify any means.

Third, abandon this economy of scarcity and go in for production, work, and thrift.

Fourth, stop this spending and inflation and pump priming.

Fifth, revise the taxes so as to free the initiative and enterprise of men. The original Senate proposals were a step in that direction.

Sixth, reduce relief expenditure by one-third through decentralizing its administration. Take it out of the hands of wasters and politicians and put it back into non-political committees in each community and require the states and local communities to fund 5 or 10 percent of the cost. That will provide greater and more sympathetic care for those in distress. It will restore confidence that the Republic is not being destroyed by the purchase of elections.

Seventh, by the savings on relief, and reduction of other expenses and the end of pump priming, drive to really balance this budget.

Eighth, stop credit inflation juggling. Make the currency convertible into bullion at the irreparable 59-cent dollar and repeal all authority for currency inflation.

Ninth, set up a court of 25 responsible non-political men representing business, labor, and agriculture to direct Federal Reserve policies and thus take that control of credit out of the hands of politicians.

Tenth, give the employer and all branches of labor the same rights before the Labor Board and appoint judicially minded men to the board.

Eleventh, stop indiscriminate defamations of business and the creation of class hate. Use the courts for purposes of prosecution.

This would at least be a start on a saner and more cheerful road. Then would begin the emancipation from this fog of ideologies. Morals in government would return again. The energies of our people would be liberated. And above all the farmer's market and the worker's job will be restored.

LVII
Franklin D. Roosevelt:
Annual Message to Congress
January 4, 1939

Mr. Vice President, Mr. Speaker, Members of the Senate and the Congress:

In reporting on the state of the nation, I have felt it necessary on previous occasions to advise the Congress of disturbance abroad and of the need of putting our own house in order in the face of storm signals from across the seas. As this Seventy-sixth Congress opens there is need for further warning.

A war which threatened to envelop the world in flames has been averted; but it has become increasingly clear that world peace is not assured.

All about us rage undeclared wars—military and economic. All about us grow more deadly armaments—military and economic. All about us are threats of new aggression—military and economic.

Storms from abroad directly challenge three institutions indispensable to Americans, now as always. The first is religion. It is the source of the other two—democracy and international good faith.

Religion, by teaching man his relationship to God, gives the individual a sense of his own dignity and teaches him to respect himself by respecting his neighbors.

Democracy, the practice of self-government, is a covenant among free men to respect the rights and liberties of their fellows.

International good faith, a sister of democracy, springs from the will of civilized nations of men to respect the rights and liberties of other nations of men.

In a modern civilization, all three—religion, democracy and international good faith—complement and support each other.

Where freedom of religion has been attacked, the attack has come from sources opposed to democracy. Where democracy has been overthrown, the spirit of free worship has disappeared. And where religion and democracy have vanished, good faith and reason in international affairs have given way to strident ambition and brute force.

An ordering of society which relegates religion, democracy and good faith among nations to the background can find no place within it for the ideals of the Prince of Peace. The United States rejects such an ordering, and retains its ancient faith.

There comes a time in the affairs of men when they must prepare to defend, not their homes alone, but the tenets of faith and humanity on which their churches, their governments and their very civilization are founded. The defense of religion, of democracy and of good faith among nations is all the same fight. To save one we must now make up our minds to save all.

We know what might happen to us of the United States if the new philosophies of force were to encompass the other continents and invade our own. We, no more than other nations, can afford to be surrounded by the enemies of our faith and our humanity. Fortunate it is, therefore, that in this Western Hemisphere we have, under a common ideal of democratic government, a rich diversity of resources and of peoples functioning together in mutual respect and peace.

That hemisphere, that peace, and that ideal we propose to do our share in protecting against storms from any quarter. Our people and our resources are pledged to secure that protection. From that determination no American flinches.

This by no means implies that the American Republics disassociate themselves from the nations of other continents. It does not mean the Americas against the rest of the world. We as one of the Republics reiterate our willingness to help the cause of world peace. We stand on our historic offer to take counsel with all other nations of the world to the end that aggression among them be terminated, that the race of armaments cease and that commerce be renewed.

But the world has grown so small and weapons of attack so swift that no nation can be safe in its will to peace so long as any other powerful nation refuses to settle its grievances at the council table.

For if any government bristling with implements of war insists on policies of force, weapons of defense give the only safety.

In our foreign relations we have learned from the past what not to do. From new wars we have learned what we must do.

We have learned that effective timing of defense, and the distant points from which attacks may be launched are completely different from what they were twenty years ago.

We have learned that survival cannot be guaranteed by arming after the attack begins—for there is new range and speed to offense.

We have learned that long before any overt military act, aggression begins with preliminaries of propaganda, subsidized penetration, the loosening of ties of good will, the stirring of prejudice and the incitement to disunion.

We have learned that God-fearing democracies of the world which observe the sanctity of treaties and good faith in their dealings with other nations cannot safely be indifferent to international lawlessness anywhere. They cannot forever let pass, without effective protest, acts of aggression against sister nations— acts which automatically undermine all of us.

Obviously they must proceed along practical, peaceful lines. But the mere fact that we rightly decline to intervene with arms to prevent acts of aggression does not mean that we must act as if there were no aggression at all. Words may be futile, but war is not the only means of commanding a decent respect for the opinions of mankind. There are many methods short of war, but stronger and more effective than mere words, of bringing home to aggressor governments the aggregate sentiments of our own people.

At the very least, we can and should avoid any action, or any lack of action, which will encourage, assist or build up an aggressor.

We have learned that when we deliberately try to legislate neutrality our neutrality laws may operate unevenly and unfairly-may actually give aid to an aggressor and deny it to the victim. The instinct of self-preservation should warn us that we ought not to let that happen any more.

And we have learned something else—the old, old lesson that probability of attack is mightily decreased by the assurance of an ever ready defense. Since 1931, nearly eight years ago, world events of thunderous import have moved with lightning speed. During these eight years many of our people clung to the hope that the innate decency of mankind would protect the unprepared who showed their innate trust in mankind. Today we are all wiser—and sadder.

Under modern conditions what we mean by "adequate defense"—a policy subscribed to by all of us—must be divided into three elements. First, we must have armed forces and defenses strong enough to ward off sudden attack against strategic positions and key facilities essential to ensure sustained resistance and ultimate victory. Secondly, we must have the organization and location of those key facilities so that they may be immediately utilized and rapidly expanded to meet all needs without danger of serious interruption by enemy attack.

In the course of a few days I shall send you a special message making recommendations for those two essentials of defense against danger which we cannot safely assume will not come.

If these first two essentials are reasonably provided for, we must be able confidently to invoke the third element, the underlying strength of citizenship—the self-confidence, the ability, the imagination and the devotion that give the staying power to see things through.

A strong and united nation may be destroyed if it is unprepared against sudden attack. But even a nation well armed and well organized from a strictly military standpoint may, after a period of time, meet defeat if it is unnerved by self-distrust, endangered by class prejudice, by dissension between capital and labor, by false economy and by other unsolved social problems at home.

In meeting the troubles of the world we must meet them as one people—with a unity born of the fact that for generations those who have come to our shores, representing many kindreds and tongues, have been welded by common opportunity into a united patriotism. If another form of government can present a united front in its attack on a democracy, the attack must and will be met by a united democracy. Such a democracy can and must exist in the United States.

A dictatorship may command the full strength of a regimented nation. But the united strength of a democratic nation can be mustered only when its people, educated by modern standards to know what is going on and where they are going, have conviction that they are receiving as large a share of opportunity for development, as large a share of material success and of human dignity, as they have a right to receive.

Our nation's program of social and economic reform is therefore a part of defense, as basic as armaments themselves.

Against the background of events in Europe, in Africa and in Asia during these recent years, the pattern of what we have accomplished since 1933 appears in even clearer focus.

For the first time we have moved upon deep-seated problems affecting our national strength and have forged national instruments adequate to meet them.

Consider what the seemingly piecemeal struggles of these six years add up to in terms of realistic national preparedness.

We are conserving and developing natural resources—land, water power, forests.

We are trying to provide necessary food, shelter and medical care for the health of our population.

We are putting agriculture—our system of food and fibre supply—on a sounder basis.

We are strengthening the weakest spot in our system of industrial supply—its long smoldering labor difficulties.

We have cleaned up our credit system so that depositor and investor alike may more readily and willingly make their capital available for peace or war.

We are giving to our youth new opportunities for work and education.

We have sustained the morale of all the population by the dignified recognition of our obligations to the aged, the helpless and the needy.

Above all, we have made the American people conscious of their interrelationship and their interdependence. They sense a common destiny and a common need of each other. Differences of occupation, geography, race and religion no longer obscure the nation's fundamental unity in thought and in action.

We have our difficulties, true—but we are a wiser and a tougher nation than we were in 1929, or in 1932.

Never have there been six years of such far-flung internal preparedness in our history. And this has been done without any dictator's power to command, without conscription of labor or confiscation of capital, without concentration camps and without a scratch on freedom of speech, freedom of the press or the rest of the Bill of Rights.

We see things now that we could not see along the way. The tools of government which we had in 1933 are outmoded. We have had to forge new tools for a new role of government operating in a democracy—a role of new responsibility for new needs and increased responsibility for old needs, long neglected.

Some of these tools had to be roughly shaped and still need some machining down. Many of those who fought bitterly against the forging of these new tools welcome their use today. The American people, as a whole, have accepted them. The Nation looks to the Congress to improve the new machinery which we have permanently installed, provided that in the process the social usefulness of the machinery is not destroyed or impaired.

All of us agree that we should simplify and improve laws if experience and operation clearly demonstrate the need. For instance, all of us want better provision for our older people under our social security legislation. For the medically needy we must provide better care.

Most of us agree that for the sake of employer and employee alike we must find ways to end factional labor strife and employer-employee disputes.

Most of us recognize that none of these tools can be put to maximum effectiveness unless the executive processes of government are revamped—reorganized, if you will—into more effective combination. And even after such reorganization it will take time to develop administrative personnel and experience in order to use our new tools with a minimum of mistakes. The Congress, of course, needs no further information on this.

With this exception of legislation to provide greater government efficiency, and with the exception of legislation to ameliorate our railroad and other transportation problems, the past three Congresses have met in part or in whole the pressing needs of the new order of things.

We have now passed the period of internal conflict in the launching of our program of social reform. Our full energies may now be released to invigorate the processes of recovery in order to preserve our reforms, and to give every man and woman who wants to work a real job at a living wage.

But time is of paramount importance. The deadline of danger from within and from without is not within our control. The hourglass may be in the hands of other nations. Our own hourglass tells us that we are off on a race to make democracy work, so that we may be efficient in peace and therefore secure in national defense.

This time element forces us to still greater efforts to attain the full employment of our labor and our capital.

The first duty of our statesmanship is to bring capital and manpower together.

Dictatorships do this by main force. By using main force they apparently succeed at it—for the moment. However we abhor their methods, we are compelled to admit that they have obtained substantial utilization of all their material and human resources. Like it or not, they have solved, for a time at least, the problem of idle men and idle capital. Can we compete with them by boldly seeking methods of putting idle men and idle capital together and, at the same time, remain within our American way of life, within the Bill of Rights, and within the bounds of what is, from our point of view, civilization itself?

We suffer from a great unemployment of capital. Many people have the idea that as a nation we are overburdened with debt and are spending more than we can afford. That is not so. Despite our Federal Government expenditures the entire debt of our national economic system, public and private together, is no larger today than it was in 1929, and the interest thereon is far less than it was in 1929.

The object is to put capital—private as well as public—to work.

We want to get enough capital and labor at work to give us a total turnover of business, a total national income, of at least eighty billion dollars a year. At that figure we shall have a substantial reduction of unemployment; and the Federal Revenues will be sufficient to balance the current level of cash expenditures on the basis of the existing tax structure. That figure can be attained, working within the framework of our traditional profit system.

The factors in attaining and maintaining that amount of national income are many and complicated.

They include more widespread understanding among businessmen of many changes which world conditions and technological improvements have brought to our economy over the last twenty years—changes in the interrelationship of price and volume and employment, for example—changes of the kind in which businessmen are now educating themselves through excellent opportunities like the so-called "monopoly investigation."

They include a perfecting of our farm program to protect farmers' income and consumers' purchasing power from alternate risks of crop gluts and crop shortages.

They include wholehearted acceptance of new standards of honesty in our financial markets.

They include reconcilement of enormous, antagonistic interests—some of them long in litigation—in the railroad and general transportation field.

They include the working out of new techniques—private, state and federal—to protect the public interest in and to develop wider markets for electric power.

They include a revamping of the tax relationships between federal, state and local units of government, and consideration of relatively small tax increases to adjust inequalities without interfering with the aggregate income of the American people.

They include the perfecting of labor organization and a universal ungrudging attitude by employers toward the labor movement, until there is a minimum of interruption of production and employment because of disputes, and acceptance by labor of the truth that the welfare of labor itself depends on increased balanced out-put of goods.

To be immediately practical, while proceeding with a steady evolution in the solving of these and like problems, we must wisely use instrumentalities, like Federal investment, which are immediately available to us.

Here, as elsewhere, time is the deciding factor in our choice of remedies.

Therefore, it does not seem logical to me, at the moment we seek to increase production and consumption, for the Federal Government to consider a drastic curtailment of its own investments.

The whole subject of government investing and government income is one which may be approached in two different ways.

The first calls for the elimination of enough activities of government to bring the expenses of government immediately into balance with income of government. This school of thought maintains that because our national income this year is only sixty billion dollars, ours is only a sixty billion dollar country; that government must treat it as such; and that without the help of government, it may some day, somehow, happen to become an eighty billion dollar country.

If the Congress decides to accept this point of view, it will logically have to reduce the present functions or activities of government by one-third. Not only will the Congress have to accept the responsibility for such reduction; but the Congress will have to determine which activities are to be reduced.

Certain expenditures we cannot possibly reduce at this session, such as the interest on the public debt. A few million dollars saved here or there in the normal or in curtailed work of the old departments and commissions will make no great saving in the Federal budget. Therefore, the Congress would have to reduce drastically some of certain large items, very large items, such as aids to agriculture and soil conservation, veterans' pensions, flood control, highways, waterways and other public works, grants for social and health security, Civilian Conservation Corps activities, relief for the unemployed or national defense itself.

The Congress alone has the power to do all this, as it is the appropriating branch of the government.

The other approach to the question of government spending takes the position that this Nation ought not to be and need not be only a sixty billion dollar nation; that at this moment it has the men and the resources sufficient to make it at least an eighty billion dollar nation. This school of thought does not believe that it can become an eighty billion dollar nation in the near future if government cuts its operations by one-third. It is convinced that if we were to try it, we would invite disaster—and that we would not long remain even a sixty billion dollar nation. There are many complicated factors with which we have to deal, but we have learned that it is unsafe to make abrupt reductions at any time in our net expenditure program.

By our common sense action of resuming government activities last spring, we have reversed a recession and started the new rising tide of prosperity and national income which we are now just beginning to enjoy.

If government activities are fully maintained, there is a good prospect of our becoming an eighty billion dollar country in a very short time. With such a national income, present tax laws will yield enough each year to balance each year's expenses.

It is my conviction that down in their hearts the American public—industry, agriculture, finance—want this Congress to do whatever needs to be done to raise our national income to eighty billion dollars a year.

Investing soundly must preclude spending wastefully. To guard against opportunist appropriations, I have on several occasions addressed the Congress on the importance of permanent long-range planning. I hope, therefore, that following my recommendation of last year, a permanent agency will be set up and authorized to report on the urgency and desirability of the various types of government investment.

Investment for prosperity can be made in a democracy.

I hear some people say, "This is all so complicated. There are certain advantages in a dictatorship. It gets rid of labor trouble, of unemployment, of wasted motion and of having to do your own thinking."

My answer is, "Yes, but it also gets rid of some other things which we Americans intend very definitely to keep—and we still intend to do our own thinking."

It will cost us taxes and the voluntary risk of capital to attain some of the practical advantages which other forms of government have acquired.

Dictatorship, however, involves costs which the American people will never pay: The cost of our spiritual values. The cost of the blessed right of being able to say what we please. The cost of freedom of religion. The cost of seeing our capital confiscated. The cost of being cast into a concentration camp. The cost of being afraid to walk down the street with the wrong neighbor. The cost of having our children brought up, not as free and dignified human beings, but as pawns molded and enslaved by a machine.

If the avoidance of these costs means taxes on my income; if avoiding these costs means taxes on my estate at death, I would bear those taxes willingly as the price of my breathing and my children breathing the free air of a free country, as the price of a living and not a dead world.

Events abroad have made it increasingly clear to the American people that dangers within are less to be feared than dangers from without. If, therefore, a solution of this problem of idle men and idle capital is the price of preserving our liberty, no formless selfish fears can stand in the way.

Once I prophesied that this generation of Americans had a rendezvous with destiny. That prophecy comes true. To us much is given, more is expected.

This generation will "nobly save or meanly lose the last best hope of earth.... The way is plain, peaceful, generous, just-a way which if followed the world will forever applaud and God must forever bless."

LVIII
Herbert Hoover:
Address delivered to Fifty-Third Annual Lincoln Day Dinner of the National Republican Club, *The Real State of the Union* New York City, February 13, 1939

Every year at this time Americans express gratitude for the birth of Abraham Lincoln. Recently both Mr. Roosevelt and Mr. Browder have claimed him as a founder of their faiths. I was under the impression he was a Republican.

But Abraham Lincoln towered far above political partisanship. He rests in the hearts of the American people not as a politician but as a great American who died fighting for the most precious of American possessions—the liberty of men.

During the past month those temporarily in control of the government have expressed their views upon the state of the Union.

Tonight in many assemblies over the nation you will hear views on it from the Party of Lincoln.

Eighty years ago if an observer could have looked down on this Republic from the high stratosphere he would have seen a nation sadly divided and confused. It was a nation professing liberty yet holding millions of slaves. It was furiously debating property rights, states' rights, decisions of the Courts, and secession.

But high above all this din and confusion Lincoln heard the supreme chord of all human emotions—the liberty of men. In the triumph of that deepest of all moral and spiritual issues the old discords sank away. With that renewed inspiration from Abraham Lincoln this nation marched on to a glorious progress unparalleled in the history of mankind.

The Confused State of the Nation

Today if the observer in the high stratosphere were to look down on this Republic he would find a people more sadly divided and confused than at any time since Lincoln's time. He would see the torch of human liberty dimming on every continent.

He would find the richest and most powerful nation in the world confused by its own inventions; disordered in its economic life; hurt by the weakening of private and public morals; arming from fear of foreign violence; discouraged by vast destitution in a land of plenty; frustrated by failure of age-old panaceas. He would find strange doctrines of class struggle, of personal power, of extravagance, of debt, and of hate. He would see our nation still professing liberty yet pursuing ideas which limit and endanger the liberty of men.

Yet nonetheless again today above all this din and discouragement rises that same supreme chord of all human emotions—the liberty of men.

The Start at Clarifying Confusion

Three months ago this observer might have despaired of us. But today he would see flashes of light. He would find that Americans have by the ballot again spoken their demand that the safeguards of liberty be maintained. The people have restored much independence to the Congress. They have returned to office men who fought staunchly for the independence of the Courts. They have lifted to leadership many young, vigorous governors and backed them with high-minded legislatures. The people have proved that elections cannot be controlled by government subsidies.

Today this observer would see another ray of light through all this confusion.   He would see the people steadily forcing a clarification of national thought.   Those who adhere to the traditional liberalism upon which the Republic was founded and which Lincoln sustained are crowding away from the pseudo-liberalism of the New Deal.

That philosophy of conscious or unconscious left-wingers is steadily and openly unfolding itself.   It becomes visible as a mixture of coercion, collectivism and lust for personal power poured into the American system of free men.   And it mortgages the next generation to pay for it.   Anyway their new system is satisfying enough to receive the illuminating support of the Communist Front and their fellow travelers.

Here indeed is a paradox. The Republican Party has become the conservative party in the sense of preserving true liberalism.

The spirit of true liberalism is to create free men; it is not the coercion of men.   True liberalism is found not in striving to spread bureaucracy and personal power but in striving to set bounds to it. And it is equally certain that we can no more have private economic power without checks and balances than we can have political power without checks and balances.   Either one leads to coercion. True liberalism seeks freedom from both bureaucracy and private privilege in the confident belief that without such freedom the pursuit of other blessings is in vain.

Whatever this New Deal system is, it is certain that it did not come from Abraham Lincoln.

The Road to Disunity in a People
The President in his last message on the State of the Union made a moving appeal for unity in the people. But the acerbities of the times were not much allayed when a few days later at the Jackson Day Dinner he smote the to-be-purged Democrats with hints to get out of his party.   That was more of a mustard plaster than an ointment of unity.

Then Mr. Roosevelt took in still more ground of combat when he observed: "Does anyone maintain that the Republican Party from 1868 to 1938 was the party of Abraham Lincoln?"   He excepts possibly his own fifth cousin.   He ought to read the views of Theodore Roosevelt on such policies as his.   He seems to wish to purge the Republican Party also. But the President of all the people did not add to the happy chemistry of national unity with this smear on the political faith of half the people. Certainly Mr. Roosevelt's formula of appeasement does not follow Mr. Lincoln's method of "with malice toward none; with charity for all."

When the great spirit of Abraham Lincoln looks through the long corridor of time upon the party he founded he sees that from the day of his passing on the torch, until the last day of the Republican party in office, it held aloft the light of inalienable liberties of men. And he knows that party never deviated from the Constitution, which he fought to preserve, either in letter or in spirit. And he sees the Union he preserved under adherence to these principles grow to the greatest nation on the earth.

He would witness a people constantly confronted with new human problems, which were the very product of their own freedom and progress.

Mr. Lincoln would not be fooled by the notion that economic righteousness and social good burst upon the world with the New Deal.

He would see that a generation after his time, when big corporations and mass production entered national life, it was the Republican Party that first established the concept that business must be regulated by government if the freedom of men was to be preserved. Indeed, it was the Republican Party that first initiated regulation against monopoly and business abuse in the states. Over the last fifty years it created seven out of the ten great Federal regulating agencies of today. It was Republicans who created the income and estate taxes that fortunes might not accumulate so as to oppress the nation and that there might be relief of tax burdens upon the poor.

Abraham Lincoln would have watched anxiously when the growth of humanitarianism began to press upon the government. And he would have seen it was Republican state administrations that first created the limitation of hours for women that started the abolition of child labor that initiated workmen's compensation acts, state old-age pensions, mothers' pensions public health, and a score of other social reforms. It was Republican national administrations that first brought these problems into national scope. It was they who first proposed the Federal amendment to abolish child labor, which first restricted immigration, which first declared the right of collective bargaining through the creation of the Mediation Board, who first established national public health service. It was

Republicans fighting for morals in government who established and in every administration strengthened Civil Service.

Mr. Lincoln would not be fooled that the New Deal first discovered conservation and public works to benefit the people. It was Republicans who first built up every single one of the great Federal policies dealing with these problems. All over this nation are parks, forests, mineral reservations, irrigation districts, navigable rivers, harbors, great bridges, and canals, all the initiative of Republican administrations. The New Deal has added a few percent to the area or totals. And they have charged them to the next generation.

It was Republicans, following Mr. Lincoln's own platform pledge, which held protection to workers from foreign standards of living by tariffs and sought to hold the home market for farmers against peasant labor abroad.

Lincoln would have seen it was a Republican administration, which first announced the responsibility of government aid in time of great depression. When the Federal Reserve System, admirably added by Democrats, failed to meet the storm of 1929, it was a Republican administration, which again proposed drastic banking reform. It was Republicans who, pending such reforms, created the Reconstruction Finance Corporation, the Home Loan Banks, the Agricultural Credit Banks, and brought the strength of the government to protect savings and homes and insurance policies of all the people.

Mr. Lincoln would have witnessed a Republican administration in 1930 the first to announce the national obligation that no American through no fault of his own should go hungry or cold, and first to organize nation-wide relief for the unemployed. And it organized relief in a fashion which excluded corruption, waste, and demoralization of community responsibility. It is high time to return to a system that does not play politics with human misery.

And Republicans discovered one thing eighty years ago which the New Deal has not rediscovered yet. That is, the greatest gift of government to the ill fed, ill housed and ill clothed is fidelity to government obligation, less taxes. a balanced budget, and a convertible gold currency.

And Mr. Lincoln would observe that all these years it was Republicans who held to the system of free enterprise which, while it had weaknesses, yet produced the highest standard of living known in any nation in the history of the world. And it is the New

Deal destruction of that energy, enterprise, and productivity which today imperils all the humanitarian work of these eighty years.

We followers of Lincoln lay no claim that the Republican Party or any other party has always been perfect. It has at times sorrowed many of us by its lag in prompt action and its faulty action. And we likewise credit the Democratic Party with great service in years gone by.

One thing is sure. With the millions of Americans with faith in this party and with the task now laid upon it to restore liberty in this land, it is certain that the spirit of Abraham Lincoln has not joined the New Deal.

Republican Unity and Purpose

But the high points of achievement of a political party have two values. They are proof of its fidelity to principles of this Republic. They are proof of its ability to find methods within these principles which meet the scene which changes with the progress of invention and new ideas. After all a party is only an instrumentality for future service. The first chore of a political party out of power is corrective opposition. The oxygen of representative government is exposure of the witchery of half-truth and the curb of arrogant and extreme action. Its other great duty is to present to the country a program of reform and forward action.

With our reinforced leadership in new governors and in Congress we are strengthened to these purposes. New vigor and courage have come to us by the rise of youth in our party.

The points of opposition and programs for the future are rising daily from county and state organizations, from our youth and women's organizations, from our Republican leaders and Program Committee. I have made it my business to study these expressions diligently. And I can say at once there has never been a time in the history of the party when in major questions there is such unity as there is today. We may differ among ourselves as to details. We may differ in expression. But we stick together in principle. We are engaged in no purges of honest men.

These many statements of Republican purpose unswervingly demand that moral standards in public and private life be regenerated; that humanitarian action be sanely advanced; that economic productivity be restored; that thrift be re-enthroned as a national virtue; that private enterprise be sustained and regulated to prevent abuse; that personal liberty be safe-guarded; that representative government be purified; that peace be maintained.

And the methods they propose are based on sanity, common sense, and constructive action.

What the everyday people of America want is not labels or slogans, either imported or domestic. They demand emancipation from coercion and taxes and a restoration of their jobs.

Now that you have for once heard a few words favorable to the Republican Party, let me add a few words about the New Deal. The President has introduced us to the seventh New Deal since 1932. It is also the most expensive one. The new gamble with the fate of a people presents some startling features. We have need of bold debate today as never before. I wish here to applaud the President's grasp of one hint from the election. That is the demand that the Congress be independent. The spirit of his acceptance, however, reminds me of the small boy who took the clock to pieces. When reprimanded he suddenly turned on his Dad and said: "If that is the way you feel, then you put the thing together. I want to play with my soldiers."

We also are grateful for the President's assurance that we have passed the period of experiments and should now be free to invigorate the processes of recovery. This is comforting. And it confirms our belief that millions of our people have had to stand aside for six years in unemployment and destitution to make way for ill-fated experiments.

The Financial State of the Union

The country may therefore now take up its greatest humanitarian task. That is to restore 10,000,000 to jobs, revive a paralyzed agriculture and thereby really relieve 20,000,000 destitute. And that task must not be obscured by proposals of entanglement abroad.

The President's solution of this problem is that the government spends on a still larger scale. These 9 billion expenditures and a promise of 50 billion debt are the most startling budget proposals ever laid before the American people in peacetime.

I have felt some anxiety for the punctuation points. They are living a sad and hectic life wandering around among regimented ciphers trying to find some of the old places they used to know. I fear that like the Administration they are moving steadily to the left.

An ancient statesman advised that the art of politics was to find new names for policies that had become unpopular. Mr. Lincoln would probably have phrased this as the art of fooling part of the people a little longer. So today I suppose we ought to be more cheerful when we know that national spending and deficits have become "investing in prosperity." Extravagance with other people's money is shifted from a sin to a virtue. The President in this last message described some new schools of thought. In fact, several of them. In them all, songs of economic hallucination substitute for the brutal clang of the cash register.

The first grade of this high school of economic romances teaches that we should get back 80 billions of yearly national income which we once enjoyed under Republican administrations. We are grateful that the New Deal adopts Republican attainments as the ideal. But the President says that inasmuch as our present income is only 60 billions, we only have to spend as if we had 80 billions in order to lift ourselves up to the Republican level. As the ancient prospector said: "There ain't no gold in them rainbows." That 80 billion national income under Republican administration was due to the people spending their own money, not in taxes but on reproductive enterprises, creating new jobs for men.

The next higher grade of this new school of budgetary magic seeks to hide these gigantic expenditures by claiming government loans and public works are investments. On the basis of this hallucination my administration would have shown a surplus of 2 billion. In fact the budgets of all administrations for seventy years, except the war years, would have shown a surplus. We should have had such an accumulated surplus today that we should have to build a vacuum to hold it.

The recoverable loans are a relief to the taxpayer but public works are not a monetary asset to the government. They are the clothes the nation wears. And they wear out. They only in small degree increase the earning power of the people. Public works and public buildings have social value. But as assets with which to relieve taxpayers they are about as useful as liabilities on a balance sheet. And I trust the time off for precinct work by the SPA is not included as an offset to the national debt.

The New Deal's third grade of economic make-believe teaches that the entire debt of our national economic system, public and private together, is not larger today than it was in 1929. But that is not all the truth. Public debt is paying for a dead horse. Private debt is buying a live one.

They finally graduate from this school of high finance with the valedictory that expenses cannot be reduced. And this in the face of the fact that yearly for ten years prior to the New Deal, on their basis of accounts and excepting loans since recovered, the expenditures were 3.5 billions instead of 9 billions. But that was Republicans.

I should like to see a new school established with some home truths for its curriculum. That school would say that to restore jobs and agriculture the fear of men of their government and the shackles and taxes upon their energies must be removed in order that free men may have hope and confidence in the future.

That school would say that most of the New Deal measurers can be lived down, improved, cured or reformed but that these monetary and financial polities may defeat the nation.

That school would say that some day all this will have to be paid for. If it be through taxes, men and women will be handing their wages to the government instead of buying things for their own betterment.

Nor is that the most important consequence it should teach. That school would say one of the deadly causes of destruction to twenty democracies in twenty years has been government spending and inflation. Mr. Roosevelt says "this generation has a rendezvous with destiny." The most probable spot for this rendezvous today is inflation. When this generation has gone up that alley it will find freedom has gone, and our rendezvous will be with a full-sized dictator.

In Conclusion

In conclusion let me again say that this Republic is founded on inalienable liberties. It is dedicated to the dignity and personality of individual men and women. It is consecrated to truth, justice, tolerance and mercy. These liberties and obligations are inseparable. If political freedom, intellectual freedom, or economic freedom or any one of them undermined all the others will fall.

These high purposes of this nation are being undermined by the policies now pursued at home and by alien theories from abroad. The first great mission of the Republican Party is the preservation of these principles.

Today economic progress is being paralyzed. That destruction is the destruction of social progress. The imperious necessity of America is to restore economic productivity and thereby jobs for men. That alone can support our humanitarian aspirations. For social progress in care of the aged, the young, the ill fed, the ill clad, the ill housed there must be parallel economic strength. Economic restoration is the second great mission of the Republican Party.

We do not want to become entangled in another World War abroad. The third great mission of the Republican Party is peace for America.

We are the living custodians of the torch which fell from the hand of Abraham Lincoln. We may again rekindle the heart and mind of America with the glow of hope and promise for the future. Never since Lincoln has a political party faced such an opportunity for a service to a great people.

LVIX
Herbert Hoover:
Radio Address
Columbus, Ohio, October 24, 1940

I do not suggest that Mr. Roosevelt aspires to be a dictator. It is however understatement to say that he builded personal power to a dangerous point in the Republic. Moreover, there are forces and men around him who are implacably pushing further and further in that direction. The exact reason that this tradition has been a living force over all these years is to meet just such a situation as this. The reasons why that rampart of freedom should be maintained are far higher than partisanship. They reach to the foundations of free men and women.

It is not only a tradition against a third term about which we are concerned. We are concerned with a vital check upon the rise of personal power in the Republic. There has been a gigantic and insidious building up of personal power of the President during these two terms. The President himself admits these powers provide shackles upon liberty which may be dangerous. Many of these extraordinary powers have been obtained under claims of emergencies which proved not to exist or to have expired. Despite many promises, there has been no return of these dangerous powers or the unused powers, or those which proved futile or for which emergencies have passed.

Under assumptions of personal power we are steadily drifting toward war. And one result of the use of these powers has been to stifle the restoration of productive employment, and a prosperous agriculture, and to involve the peace of the American people.

LX
Franklin D. Roosevelt:
Third Inaugural Address
January 20, 1941

On each national day of inauguration since 1789, the people have renewed their sense of dedication to the United States.

In Washington's day the task of the people was to create and weld together a nation.

In Lincoln's day the task of the people was to preserve that nation from disruption from within.

In this day the task of the people is to save that nation and its institutions from disruption from without.

To us there has come a time, in the midst of swift happenings, to pause for a moment and take stock—to recall what our place in history has been, and to rediscover what we are and what we may be. If we do not, we risk the real peril of inaction.

Lives of nations are determined not by the count of years, but by the lifetime of the human spirit. The life of a man is three-score years and ten: a little more, a little less. The life of a nation is the fullness of the measure of its will to live.

There are men who doubt this. There are men who believe that democracy, as a form of government and a frame of life, is limited or measured by a kind of mystical and artificial fate that, for some unexplained reason, tyranny and slavery have become the surging wave of the future—and that freedom is an ebbing tide.

But we Americans know that this is not true.

Eight years ago, when the life of this Republic seemed frozen by a fatalistic terror, we proved that this is not true. We were in the midst of shock—but we acted. We acted quickly, boldly, decisively.

These later years have been living years—fruitful years for the people of this democracy. For they have brought to us greater security and, I hope, a better understanding that life's ideals are to be measured in other than material things.

Most vital to our present and our future is this experience of a democracy which successfully survived crisis at home; put away many evil things; built new structures on enduring lines; and, through it all, maintained the fact of its democracy.

For action has been taken within the three-way framework of the Constitution of the United States. The coordinate branches of the government continue freely to function. The Bill of Rights remains inviolate. The freedom of elections is wholly maintained. Prophets of the downfall of American democracy have seen their dire predictions come to naught.

Democracy is not dying.

We know it because we have seen it revive—and grow.

We know it cannot die—because it is built on the unhampered initiative of individual men and women joined together in a common enterprise—an enterprise undertaken and carried through by the free expression of a free majority.

We know it because democracy alone, of all forms of government, enlists the full force of men's enlightened will.

We know it because democracy alone has constructed an unlimited civilization capable of infinite progress in the improvement of human life.

We know it because, if we look below the surface, we sense it still spreading on every continent—for it is the most humane, the most advanced, and in the end the most unconquerable of all forms of human society.

A nation, like a person, has a body—a body that must be fed and clothed and housed, invigorated and rested, in a manner that measures up to the objectives of our time.

A nation, like a person, has a mind—a mind that must be kept informed and alert, that must know itself, that understands the hopes and the needs of its neighbors—all the other nations that live within the narrowing circle of the world.

And a nation, like a person, has something deeper, something more permanent, something larger than the sum of all its parts. It is that something which matters most to its future—which calls forth the most sacred guarding of its present.

It is a thing for which we find it difficult—even impossible—to hit upon a single, simple word.

And yet we all understand what it is—the spirit—the faith of America. It is the product of centuries. It was born in the multitudes of those who came from many lands—some of high degree, but mostly plain people, who sought here, early and late, to find freedom more freely.

The democratic aspiration is no mere recent phase in human history. It is human history. It permeated the ancient life of early peoples. It blazed anew in the middle ages. It was written in the Magna Charta.

In the Americas its impact has been irresistible. America has been the New World in all tongues, to all peoples, not because this continent was a new-found land, but because all those who came here believed they could create upon this continent a new life—a life that should be new in freedom.

Its vitality was written into our own Mayflower Compact, into the Declaration of Independence, into the Constitution of the United States, into the Gettysburg Address.

Those who first came here to carry out the longings of their spirit, and the millions who followed, and the stock that sprang from them—all have moved forward constantly and consistently toward an ideal which in itself has gained stature and clarity with each generation.

The hopes of the Republic cannot forever tolerate either undeserved poverty or self-serving wealth.

We know that we still have far to go; that we must more greatly build the security and the opportunity and the knowledge of every citizen, in the measure justified by the resources and the capacity of the land.

But it is not enough to achieve these purposes alone. It is not enough to clothe and feed the body of this nation, and instruct and inform its mind. For there is also the spirit. And of the three, the greatest is the spirit.

Without the body and the mind, as all men know, the nation could not live.

But if the spirit of America were killed, even though the nation's body and mind, constricted in an alien world, lived on, the America we know would have perished.

That spirit—that faith—speaks to us in our daily lives in ways often unnoticed, because they seem so obvious. It speaks to us here in the Capital of the nation. It speaks to us through the processes of governing in the sovereignties of 48 States. It speaks to us in our counties, in our cities, in our towns, and in our villages. It speaks to us from the other nations of the hemisphere, and from those across the seas—the enslaved, as well as the free. Sometimes we fail to hear or heed these voices of freedom because to us the privilege of our freedom is such an old, old story.

The destiny of America was proclaimed in words of prophecy spoken by our first President in his first inaugural in 1789—words almost directed, it would seem, to this year of 1941:　"The preservation of the sacred fire of liberty and the destiny of the republican model of government are justly considered...finally staked on the experiment entrusted to the hands of the American people."

If we lose that sacred fire—if we let it be smothered with doubt and fear—then we shall reject the destiny which Washington strove so valiantly and so triumphantly to establish.　The preservation of the spirit and faith of the nation does, and will, furnish the highest justification for every sacrifice that we may make in the cause of national defense.

In the face of great perils never before encountered, our strong purpose is to protect and to perpetuate the integrity of democracy.

For this we muster the spirit of America, and the faith of America.

We do not retreat.　We are not content to stand still.　As Americans, we go forward, in the service of our country, by the will of God.

Index

Acts, 47, 51, 57, 59, 63, 65, 69, 83, 89, 90,
  94, 96, 116, 131, 136, 154, 157, 180,
  181, 183, 187, 188, 189, 190, 191, 192,
  193, 194, 195, 196, 197, 203, 206, 208,
  209, 211, 212, 214, 216, 217, 218, 219,
  220, 221, 222, 230, 232, 247, 248, 249,
  250, 251, 252, 253, 254, 256, 258, 259,
  262, 288, 293, 319, 326, 332, 333, 337,
  338, 340, 341, 342, 345, 347, 348, 350,
  351, 352, 354, 360, 367, 390
Agriculture, 33, 35, 41, 46, 47, 49, 52,
  57, 63, 66, 68, 82, 89, 90, 91, 92, 95, 99,
  103, 104, 105, 106, 116, 117, 118, 133,
  136, 140, 148, 150, 151, 153, 155, 156,
  171, 178, 181, 206, 238, 243, 247, 256,
  277, 282, 287, 288, 294, 298, 305, 306,
  326, 379, 402, 405, 413, 415, 417
American System, 40, 41, 43, 44, 45, 46,
  49, 92, 113, 118, 129, 130, 131, 132,
  133, 134, 135, 136, 138, 139, 140, 142,
  143, 157, 278, 281, 286, 299, 361, 409
Antitrust, 66, 115, 156, 183, 190, 214,
  390, 391

Banking, 60, 65, 81, 83, 86, 88, 115, 135,
  136, 154, 155, 156, 163, 168, 171, 172,
  173, 174, 175, 242, 245, 323, 371, 375,
  378, 381, 394, 411
Budgets, 60, 63, 88, 154, 180, 236, 237,
  270, 281, 390, 414

Campaigns, 40, 41, 52, 83, 100, 101, 102,
  109, 113, 119, 128, 129, 133, 135, 137,
  138, 141, 143, 144, 145, 238, 273, 277,
  281, 286, 331, 382
Centralization, 41, 132, 136, 267, 275,
  278, 373, 383, 385
Challenge, 41, 77, 85, 101, 210, 250, 252,
  256, 308, 314, 315, 325, 338, 352, 353,
  363, 370, 381, 398
Child Labor, 206, 245, 288, 295, 346,
  368, 376, 379, 388, 410
Class, 39, 45, 113, 122, 130, 241, 242,
  266, 268, 277, 280, 286, 308, 317, 336,
  393, 397, 401, 408
Commerce, 31, 32, 35, 38, 46, 48, 49, 55,
  61, 63, 66, 67, 83, 94, 95, 103, 110, 120,
  141, 151, 155, 175, 181, 182, 183, 185,
  186, 187, 189, 194, 195, 208, 213, 214,
  215, 216, 217, 218, 220, 221, 235, 240,
  247, 248, 253, 260, 286, 296, 326, 337,
  338, 340, 341, 342, 343, 344, 346, 347,
  366, 367, 368, 372, 399
Communism, 296, 393
Confidence, 31, 39, 41, 51, 53, 60, 61, 62,
  63, 64, 86, 100, 111, 115, 130, 132, 139,
  154, 162, 163, 164, 167, 168, 171, 174,
  175, 176, 180, 200, 240, 267, 273, 296,
  297, 311, 315, 369, 380, 381, 393, 395,
  396, 397, 401, 415
Confusion, 121, 201, 266, 267, 269, 270,
  271, 272, 273, 274, 275, 276, 287, 290,
  316, 373, 374, 379, 396, 408, 409
Congress, 36, 46, 50, 52, 54, 55, 56, 57,
  59, 61, 62, 63, 64, 65, 66, 67, 69, 73, 83,
  84, 86, 89, 92, 93, 94, 96, 97, 98, 99,
  102, 111, 114, 115, 129, 135, 136, 137,
  139, 144, 149, 151, 152, 154, 155, 156,
  157, 163, 169, 170, 172, 176, 177, 180,
  183, 187, 188, 192, 195, 196, 197, 198,
  199, 200, 201, 204, 207, 210, 211, 213,
  214, 238, 239, 244, 246, 248, 252, 253,
  254, 255, 256, 257, 259, 260, 261, 262,
  275, 278, 279, 291, 296, 297, 319, 320,
  322, 324, 325, 326, 327, 328, 329, 330,
  331, 334, 340, 343, 344, 346, 347, 349,
  351, 352, 353, 354, 355, 356, 359, 360,
  361, 362, 366, 367, 368, 373, 383, 397,
  398, 402, 403, 405, 406, 409, 412, 413
Constitution, 83, 97, 98, 170, 199, 210,
  216, 238, 247, 252, 253, 255, 256, 257,
  259, 261, 269, 273, 275, 277, 280, 281,

284, 285, 288, 290, 291, 295, 296, 300,
313, 318, 319, 320, 321, 322, 323, 324,
325, 326, 327, 330, 331, 332, 334, 335,
338, 345, 347, 352, 355, 356, 358, 359,
360, 361, 362, 365, 366, 367, 368, 369,
373, 376, 383, 410, 418, 419
Cooperation, 31, 35, 37, 46, 48, 49, 50,
52, 53, 54, 55, 59, 60, 90, 94, 99, 111,
117, 131, 136, 137, 149, 150, 151, 153,
154, 158, 171, 173, 199, 210, 229, 240,
257, 259, 292, 294, 295, 305, 307, 376,
377, 379
Crash, 103, 245
Credit, 34, 60, 62, 64, 65, 66, 78, 80, 81,
82, 86, 88, 89, 90, 91, 94, 95, 99, 103,
104, 111, 112, 115, 125, 132, 148, 153,
154, 155, 163, 164, 167, 171, 175, 179,
181, 185, 187, 206, 242, 269, 270, 271,
277, 289, 292, 295, 310, 370, 371, 372,
378, 381, 383, 393, 394, 395, 397, 402,
411
Crisis, 98, 106, 108, 132, 133, 145, 156,
163, 170, 175, 210, 276, 283, 285, 309,
317, 323, 325, 350, 365, 369, 370, 418

Danger, 86, 87, 101, 104, 113, 122, 126,
139, 148, 156, 270, 275, 282, 331, 364,
386, 400, 403
Debt, 60, 63, 86, 93, 110, 147, 177, 186,
235, 237, 253, 267, 270, 274, 279, 280,
281, 373, 376, 382, 383, 388, 393, 396,
404, 405, 408, 413, 414, 415
Declaration of Independence, 122, 267,
329, 419
Deficits, 63, 235, 237, 239, 240, 241, 242,
269, 270, 364, 373, 383, 393, 396, 414
Democracy, 31, 33, 107, 113, 118, 120,
132, 142, 170, 269, 271, 279, 280, 292,
300, 301, 302, 308, 309, 311, 313, 314,
315, 316, 329, 332, 346, 362, 363, 364,
365, 368, 369, 375, 384, 386, 391, 392,
396, 397, 398, 401, 402, 403, 406, 417,
418, 420
Democratic Party, 80, 81, 101, 102, 105,
106, 111, 130, 133, 135, 146, 285, 292,
392, 412

Depression, 52, 53, 54, 55, 57, 58, 59, 60,
62, 63, 69, 76, 85, 91, 101, 102, 110,
115, 117, 120, 123, 135, 139, 144, 147,
150, 153, 157, 180, 204, 240, 243, 249,
272, 279, 282, 283, 286, 306, 309, 314,
323, 324, 370, 371, 380, 381, 385, 394,
395, 396, 411
Dictatorship, 111, 163, 269, 277, 284,
299, 300, 301, 363, 364, 365, 381, 392,
401, 406, 407

Economics, 78, 102, 103, 120, 276, 280,
311, 314, 372, 374, 375, 376
Education, 37, 39, 46, 51, 59, 76, 98, 117,
131, 152, 245, 315, 402
Elections, 99, 122, 143, 152, 163, 195,
196, 198, 238, 239, 240, 267, 272, 274,
277, 280, 281, 286, 289, 296, 300, 313,
318, 324, 367, 397, 409, 413, 418
Emergency, 56, 60, 61, 63, 64, 66, 67, 71,
72, 74, 85, 90, 104, 106, 110, 112, 113,
114, 115, 116, 117, 132, 134, 136, 137,
147, 148, 149, 153, 155, 156, 157, 168,
169, 170, 172, 176, 180, 183, 185, 187,
188, 192, 194, 202, 204, 205, 206, 236,
237, 247, 249, 252, 303, 305, 373, 383
Equality, 38, 39, 40, 42, 43, 44, 48, 49,
51, 69, 95, 101, 112, 125, 130, 137, 141,
142, 157, 218, 248, 286, 291, 299, 336
Europe, 36, 41, 67, 86, 110, 121, 123,
125, 130, 132, 163, 277, 363, 372, 381,
382, 383, 384, 392, 394, 395, 401
Executive, 53, 67, 69, 81, 91, 100, 132,
138, 139, 152, 154, 170, 194, 195, 196,
197, 198, 199, 211, 262, 263, 273, 278,
286, 289, 291, 319, 321, 322, 325, 345,
357, 358, 359, 361, 362, 366, 367, 403

Farms, 33, 34, 35, 37, 41, 47, 48, 49, 57,
64, 67, 72, 73, 82, 84, 87, 89, 90, 91, 92,
95, 104, 105, 106, 109, 110, 116, 117,
125, 131, 135, 136, 150, 151, 153, 156,
168, 176, 177, 178, 181, 183, 190, 245,
246, 248, 249, 251, 288, 289, 294, 302,
303, 304, 306, 315, 322, 359, 404
Fascism, 296, 384, 393, 395

Fear, 31, 32, 44, 53, 54, 87, 102, 110, 111,
    117, 122, 129, 143, 144, 145, 146, 163,
    166, 173, 174, 180, 266, 267, 280, 286,
    297, 315, 328, 331, 363, 364, 370, 371,
    374, 377, 380, 381, 382, 393, 396, 408,
    415, 420
Federal Reserve System, 60, 65, 86, 131,
    153, 155, 173, 270, 411
Free Enterprise, 285, 286, 287, 290, 299,
    310, 370, 386, 387, 388, 391, 393, 395,
    412
Freedom, 35, 36, 38, 40, 41, 42, 44, 45,
    46, 54, 69, 112, 113, 122, 125, 130, 131,
    139, 141, 142, 152, 217, 218, 243, 267,
    275, 277, 278, 280, 283, 284, 291, 296,
    298, 300, 301, 308, 320, 321, 331, 334,
    335, 345, 351, 369, 375, 376, 379, 384,
    395, 402, 409, 410, 415, 416, 417, 419

Hamilton, Alexander, 122, 255, 261,
    353, 367
Happiness, 31, 52, 81, 97, 117, 118, 119,
    120, 128, 167, 177, 201, 244, 292, 296,
    379
Hardship, 38, 66, 109, 110, 111, 117, 129,
    152, 155, 175, 351, 377
Health, 46, 51, 57, 59, 62, 69, 87, 97, 117,
    143, 152, 156, 228, 229, 230, 231, 232,
    240, 289, 292, 296, 326, 334, 335, 336,
    376, 402, 405, 410
Homeowners, 74, 106, 111
Hope, 39, 41, 48, 51, 81, 101, 104, 109,
    110, 113, 117, 128, 133, 140, 143, 147,
    151, 178, 207, 241, 246, 284, 285, 287,
    292, 301, 306, 307, 308, 313, 369, 375,
    379, 380, 400, 407, 415, 416

Immigration, 52, 61, 115, 123, 125, 151,
    411
Individualism, 35, 39, 41, 43, 46, 49, 98,
    113, 122, 127, 130, 157, 309
Instability, 58, 60, 110, 156, 281
Institutions, 35, 38, 47, 53, 62, 64, 65, 70,
    75, 85, 95, 100, 101, 111, 112, 117, 122,
    125, 128, 131, 132, 133, 136, 138, 142,
    152, 157, 175, 176, 242, 277, 286, 289,

    291, 300, 330, 378, 398, 417

Jefferson, Thomas, 122, 128, 273, 274,
    298, 329, 360, 367
Justice, 43, 83, 101, 138, 142, 198, 283,
    284, 301, 318, 320, 327, 332, 369, 374,
    415

Labor, 32, 35, 36, 45, 48, 49, 51, 54, 56,
    82, 85, 92, 94, 95, 102, 107, 122, 123,
    127, 135, 138, 151, 178, 187, 189, 190,
    191, 193, 194, 196, 197, 198, 199, 205,
    206, 208, 209, 216, 218, 219, 221, 233,
    234, 243, 245, 260, 271, 288, 294, 295,
    298, 299, 307, 308, 326, 337, 338, 340,
    341, 342, 343, 344, 346, 347, 364, 368,
    376, 377, 378, 385, 388, 391, 397, 401,
    402, 403, 405, 411
Laissez Faire, 43, 142, 355, 376
Leadership, 31, 37, 38, 43, 45, 46, 49, 50,
    51, 58, 70, 71, 81, 85, 86, 87, 98, 100,
    101, 107, 108, 113, 117, 130, 132, 135,
    142, 145, 147, 148, 150, 152, 157, 166,
    167, 169, 170, 292, 305, 316, 317, 375,
    412
Liberalism, 42, 141
Liberty, 30, 40, 42, 43, 44, 45, 69, 84, 97,
    112, 113, 127, 130, 141, 142, 143, 157,
    212, 217, 239, 243, 267, 268, 275, 277,
    278, 279, 283, 284, 285, 286, 290, 291,
    299, 313, 317, 318, 319, 320, 321, 322,
    331, 334, 335, 363, 369, 379, 384, 386,
    389, 392, 393, 407, 408, 409, 412, 413,
    416

Mandates, 256
Monopoly, 66, 82, 142, 276, 280, 282,
    285, 290, 295, 299, 310, 320, 378, 391,
    392, 404, 410
Moral, 108, 268, 272, 280, 314, 334, 346,
    374, 377, 397, 408, 411
Morals, 284

Opportunity, 32, 33, 35, 37, 38, 39, 40,
    42, 43, 44, 45, 46, 48, 49, 51, 56, 66, 69,
    72, 77, 81, 96, 97, 109, 112, 113, 118,

123, 124, 125, 130, 131, 133, 135, 137, 138, 140, 141, 142, 143, 146, 157, 176, 190, 243, 285, 286, 292, 295, 296, 299, 300, 308, 315, 373, 374, 375, 376, 379, 382, 385, 389, 392, 401, 416, 419
Orders, 154, 196, 240, 306, 395

Panic, 60, 61, 107, 111, 116, 144, 179, 240, 267, 394
Planned Economy, 269, 277, 278, 372, 373, 374, 376, 377, 378, 382, 383, 393, 396
Planning, 58, 76, 77, 78, 82, 105, 108, 144, 148, 149, 150, 168, 178, 205, 272, 303, 305, 351, 406
Platform, 31, 34, 36, 40, 81, 101, 107, 114, 116, 129, 141, 149, 238, 295, 300, 326, 411
Pledge, 34, 36, 84, 85, 89, 92, 96, 97, 99, 101, 109, 119, 149, 152, 169, 274, 286, 287, 288, 290, 291, 294, 295, 298, 314
President, 56, 61, 68, 73, 85, 86, 87, 91, 92, 94, 96, 97, 98, 99, 100, 102, 144, 145, 146, 149, 151, 152, 176, 185, 188, 189, 191, 192, 193, 194, 196, 197, 198, 199, 208, 211, 212, 213, 219, 252, 272, 312, 316, 320, 321, 324, 325, 328, 362, 395, 413, 416
Principles, 30, 31, 40, 42, 44, 46, 69, 81, 84, 85, 87, 92, 94, 99, 111, 112, 113, 114, 119, 128, 134, 136, 141, 142, 145, 148, 157, 205, 211, 238, 244, 252, 255, 256, 257, 281, 283, 292, 296, 333, 334, 366, 377, 410, 412, 416
Program, 34, 36, 41, 46, 47, 54, 55, 56, 61, 66, 72, 73, 82, 85, 86, 87, 98, 100, 101, 104, 105, 107, 111, 112, 116, 129, 133, 141, 144, 147, 150, 151, 169, 172, 173, 175, 176, 192, 193, 200, 201, 202, 203, 205, 230, 238, 243, 244, 252, 289, 293, 294, 303, 304, 306, 307, 324, 354, 360, 378, 379, 391, 401, 403, 404, 406, 412
Programs, 411
Progress, 30, 31, 32, 33, 35, 36, 37, 38, 39, 40, 41, 42, 43, 44, 45, 46, 50, 51, 52,

57, 58, 66, 68, 77, 79, 92, 94, 96, 97, 101, 110, 119, 120, 129, 130, 133, 138, 140, 142, 143, 155, 157, 168, 169, 199, 207, 236, 241, 244, 270, 279, 282, 283, 284, 301, 314, 315, 316, 322, 326, 331, 345, 361, 369, 375, 379, 408, 410, 412, 416, 418
Public Works, 36, 43, 46, 47, 54, 72, 82, 104, 138, 147, 149, 177, 192, 203, 204, 227, 287, 350, 405, 411, 414
Purchasing Power, 32, 72, 73, 79, 103, 106, 147, 150, 180, 181, 184, 188, 217, 242, 246, 247, 248, 249, 251, 271, 294, 304, 306, 310, 346, 404
Pursuit of Happiness, 97, 127, 299, 312, 348

Race, 39, 51, 113, 130, 142, 158, 384, 402
Radicalism, 101, 118, 282
Recession, 370, 371, 394, 395, 406
Regimentation, 113, 131, 141
Regulations, 171, 172, 182, 183, 189, 196, 209, 214, 219, 231, 287, 289, 328, 335, 378, 379
Relief, 33, 34, 35, 41, 52, 54, 55, 61, 74, 81, 82, 83, 85, 87, 88, 90, 91, 93, 99, 104, 106, 108, 115, 116, 123, 131, 135, 148, 149, 153, 168, 177, 193, 194, 203, 204, 205, 239, 240, 269, 272, 273, 279, 281, 286, 287, 302, 303, 305, 306, 307, 350, 351, 352, 354, 359, 371, 372, 383, 397, 405, 410, 411
Republican Party, 31, 40, 41, 47, 84, 88, 89, 90, 91, 92, 93, 94, 95, 96, 97, 99, 100, 101, 119, 132, 136, 138, 243, 282, 285, 409, 410, 412, 413, 416
Responsibility, 36, 37, 40, 41, 42, 47, 48, 54, 59, 61, 62, 67, 69, 84, 87, 99, 102, 108, 112, 114, 119, 121, 127, 128, 131, 132, 133, 138, 141, 146, 148, 149, 153, 157, 163, 191, 204, 235, 243, 252, 276, 278, 284, 285, 286, 287, 291, 297, 307, 356, 376, 378, 384, 392, 402, 405, 411
Royalists, 298, 300

Self-Reliance, 54, 145, 203, 272, 287,

291, 355, 374
Social Justice, 43, 142, 200, 314
Social Security, 222, 232, 234, 246, 288,
   293, 310, 331, 347, 348, 351, 352, 354,
   365, 373, 376, 403, 405
Socialism, 39, 41, 131, 393, 395
Speculators, 84, 127, 244, 268, 271, 279
Spending, 34, 235, 236, 237, 239, 240,
   241, 242, 254, 259, 269, 270, 271, 274,
   290, 303, 306, 353, 393, 397, 404, 406,
   414, 415
Spiritual, 31, 33, 43, 52, 59, 70, 107, 117,
   118, 142, 158, 176, 203, 207, 244, 284,
   304, 374, 407, 408
States, 54, 55, 56, 61, 64, 67, 72, 76, 82,
   83, 84, 85, 88, 89, 91, 94, 96, 97, 99,
   103, 104, 105, 107, 108, 111, 112, 113,
   121, 131, 132, 134, 136, 137, 138, 149,
   150, 152, 153, 168, 177, 191, 192, 194,
   195, 198, 213, 214, 216, 222, 226, 227,
   228, 231, 233, 234, 235, 253, 256, 257,
   259, 261, 285, 295, 296, 297, 303, 305,
   306, 321, 326, 330, 334, 336, 337, 340,
   347, 348, 349, 350, 351, 354, 355, 367,
   397, 408, 413
Stock Market, 271
Supreme Court, 138, 139, 240, 241, 267,
   268, 269, 273, 277, 278, 285, 286, 317,
   318, 319, 320, 321, 322, 323, 324, 327,
   328, 329, 331, 332, 333, 347, 356, 357,
   358, 360, 361, 366, 367, 395

Tariffs, 33, 34, 38, 47, 52, 68, 73, 74, 81,
   84, 89, 90, 91, 92, 105, 107, 114, 116,
   124, 125, 136, 150, 286, 289, 355, 367,
   411
Taxes, 33, 56, 60, 63, 91, 104, 110, 167,
   183, 232, 233, 241, 249, 250, 251, 253,
   254, 255, 257, 279, 281, 288, 290, 326,
   349, 351, 373, 376, 378, 382, 393, 396,
   397, 407, 410, 413, 415
Tenth Amendment, 210, 256, 340, 349
Tyranny, 111, 113, 138, 140, 157, 282,
   283, 298, 299, 300, 417

Unemployment, 32, 36, 38, 47, 49, 55,

60, 61, 63, 66, 67, 72, 82, 85, 87, 99,
   103, 104, 115, 117, 138, 147, 148, 149,
   151, 163, 176, 187, 202, 205, 206, 225,
   226, 227, 232, 234, 235, 240, 243, 267,
   280, 287, 288, 293, 295, 310, 350, 351,
   353, 355, 363, 377, 380, 381, 391, 393,
   404, 413
Unions, 35, 48, 54, 190, 209, 218, 219,
   234, 337, 338, 339, 342

Voluntary, 49, 54, 55, 66, 106, 131, 140,
   153, 158, 177, 182, 189, 191, 196, 210,
   248, 257, 258, 259, 289

Wages, 32, 36, 49, 54, 61, 79, 85, 93, 103,
   141, 176, 191, 194, 208, 213, 215, 216,
   217, 218, 220, 224, 225, 232, 233, 234,
   245, 260, 271, 288, 295, 299, 306, 307,
   322, 332, 335, 336, 346, 354, 359, 364,
   372, 375, 377, 383, 388, 395, 415
Wall Street, 103
War, 30, 31, 33, 40, 41, 43, 60, 64, 67, 71,
   74, 78, 80, 81, 83, 85, 89, 93, 94, 102,
   109, 110, 121, 132, 134, 135, 157, 168,
   210, 237, 243, 262, 266, 279, 280, 283,
   302, 313, 364, 365, 367, 368, 370, 379,
   398, 399, 400, 402, 416, 417
Welfare, 44, 48, 50, 55, 56, 77, 78, 84, 91,
   92, 97, 99, 107, 108, 121, 127, 150, 153,
   172, 187, 188, 204, 229, 230, 253, 256,
   288, 334, 355
Welfare, General, 187, 253, 254, 255,
   256, 261, 285, 306, 313, 319, 325, 326,
   350, 351, 352, 353, 355, 366, 403
Women, 31, 32, 35, 44, 77, 80, 107, 120,
   133, 149, 201, 228, 235, 288, 291, 333,
   334, 336, 367, 368, 410, 415
Work, 32, 35, 37, 50, 54, 55, 56, 58, 60,
   61, 62, 68, 72, 76, 77, 79, 81, 85, 87, 93,
   94, 97, 105, 107, 117, 125, 126, 127,
   134, 135, 143, 149, 150, 151, 167, 168,
   191, 194, 201, 202, 203, 204, 205, 218,
   233, 234, 240, 271, 279, 282, 295, 300,
   302, 303, 307, 315, 335, 345, 346, 353,
   354, 374, 389, 397, 402, 403